THE ILLUSTRATED GUIDE TO TECHNICAL ANALYSIS SIGNALS AND PHRASES

Other Titles by Constance Brown from McGraw-Hill

All About Technical Analysis
Technical Analysis for the Trading Professional

THE ILLUSTRATED GUIDE TO TECHNICAL ANALYSIS SIGNALS AND PHRASES

A Visual Dictionary of the Most Useful Charts in Technical Analysis

CONSTANCE BROWN

McGraw-Hill

New York   Chicago   San Francisco   Lisbon   London
Madrid   Mexico City   Milan   New Delhi
San Juan   Seoul   Singapore
Sydney   Toronto

*The **McGraw·Hill** Companies*

1 2 3 4 5 6 7 8 9 0   DOC/DOC   0 9 8 7 6 5 4

ISBN 0-07-144207-3

This publication is designed to provide accurate and authoritative information in regard to the subject matter covered. It is sold with the understanding that the publisher is not engaged in rendering legal, accounting, or other professional service. If legal advice or other expert assistance is required, the services of a competent professional person should be sought.
> —*From a declaration of principles jointly adopted by a committee of the American Bar Association and a committee of publishers.*

McGraw-Hill books are available at special quantity discounts to use as premiums and sales promotions, or for use in corporate training programs. For more information, please write to the Director of Special Sales, Professional Publishing, McGraw-Hill, Two Penn Plaza, New York, NY 10121-2298. Or contact your local bookstore.

This book is printed on recycled, acid-free paper containing a minimum of 50% recycled, de-inked fiber.

Library of Congress Cataloging-in-Publication Data
Brown, Constance M.
    The illustrated guide to technical analysis signals and phrases : a
visual dictionary of the most useful charts in technical analysis / by
Constance Brown.
        p.   cm.
    ISBN 0-07-144207-3 (hardcover : alk. paper)
    1. Investment analysis—Charts, diagrams, etc. 2. Stocks—Charts,
diagrams, etc. I. Title.
HG4529.B763 2004
332.63'2042—dc22   2004012345

DEDICATION

When I was six, I was a horse.
Soon after life became complex and difficult.

In my sixth life, I became a Horse Whisperer.
Soon after life became less difficult, but I still made it too complex.

Then my friend and mentor Fouzi Al-Sabeeh, a People Whisperer,
taught me to simplify, and that helped put focus back on the most
important goals along life's path.

Soon after, everything in this Horse Whisperer's life became less
complex, and my spirit
  rediscovered
    the simple joy
     of running
      with horses.

CONTENTS

CHART INDEX

ACKNOWLEDGMENTS

Some of the best charting ideas began as manual calculations, but some of those ideas were lost due to practicality issues involved in producing the charts. Today, however, nearly all of the concepts that underlie the practice of technical analysis can be illustrated by the computer-generated charts that are available within various software packages. This book demonstrates some of the best charting tools available to technical analysts. Most of the charts are from Omega Research *TradeStation,* but some are also from Bloomberg, Commodity Quote Graphics (CQG), and Reuters Athena.

Until now, Gann charting software has been labor intensive, misrepresented, or incorrect, and the charts were displayed in such a manner that aspect cycles were hard to read and verify. However, that has changed, as readers will see in the Gann charts in this book. These Gann charts are in many respects revolutionary. A special thank you to Mathew Verdouw, whose company, Premier Software Group in Australia, has been proactive and enthusiastic to incorporate the methods of W.D. Gann into a package that is, for the first time in my opinion, accessible and productive in an institutional environment. The software can activate our custom indicators for you called the *Composite Index* and the *Derivative Oscillator.* The Composite Index is displayed on page 8 in this book, and you can find further discussion in my book *Technical Analysis for the Trading Professional,* which was published by McGraw-Hill in 1998. To learn more about the Gann software used to create the charts in this book please visit www.aeroinvest.com and explore the sections called *Software* and the *Chart Gallery.*

There are so many people involved with publishing a book that there isn't enough space to mention more than just a few of them here. The process began for this book with the sponsoring editor, Stephen Isaacs, who assumed the largest part of the risk when he agreed to publish the book. I explained to Stephen that I was writing it because I could not find something like it on my shelves with which to communicate the concepts. Stephen is the smarts behind the team that designed and named the book and wrote the copy for the cover jacket. Then he ensures that the distributors know all about the book's arrival. This is our third project together, and with each one, I have learned something new about how to effectively communicate visual concepts to you, the reader. Then the manuscript goes to Pattie Amoroso, a senior editing supervisor, who coordinates a host of graphic designers, layout artists, and wordsmiths—all of whom have far more formal titles than these but are known to me by the skills they bring to make me appear to be an author. I'm not. I am just a hard-working trader like you. So without the McGraw-Hill team and what they bring to the book, well, it just would not have happened! My deep appreciation goes to them for their contribution and hard work.

Introduction

The pendulum swing from boom to bust will not change unless human nature itself should change. But the tools we use to chase these excesses will continue to evolve as the manias themselves play out in repeatable patterns.

When 24 men signed the Buttonwood Agreement May 17, 1792, to meet daily near a particular buttonwood tree on Wall Street, to "Broker for the Purchase and Sale of Public Stock" as they termed it, life was slower *but it was not less complex in the context of their times*. The events that brought about the formation of this stockbrokers' group in 1792 were possible only because of the new government-funding loan of $80 million, the chartering of the First Bank of the United States in 1791, and the incorporation of the Bank of New York in 1784. No doubt these brokers respected the house of Alexander Hamilton, who lived nearby the buttonwood tree and was the person behind these events that had created the opportunity for these brokers.

By June 21, 1788, the necessary nine states had ratified the U.S. Constitution, and that allowed the country to hold its first election of the new government's officers. Upon his election, President Washington selected Thomas Jefferson to be his secretary of state and Alexander Hamilton to be his secretary of the new Treasury Department. Both Jefferson and Hamilton had been instrumental in the framing of the articles of the Constitution. As treasury secretary, Hamilton insisted on establishing the government's credit, which he persuaded the Congress and President Washington could be accomplished by means of a funding loan of approximately $80 million. That loan became a significant impetus to business growth because it was used for redeeming the worthless paper currency of the day. This in turn planted the seeds of what would become the first market mania bubble in government notes and land speculation.

New York had been a thriving place, but in the early 1790s it was somewhat subdued socially because the seat of the federal government had been removed to Philadelphia. It was said this removal from New York was the "trade" Hamilton had made to procure Jefferson's unwilling support to Hamilton's funding loan plan. Although Jefferson had strongly opposed banking and the transactions of ownership through paper shares, he supported Hamilton's plan in exchange for Hamilton's support for relocating the nation's capital first to Philadelphia and finally to the shores of the Potomac in Virginia. In consequence, New York concentrated on business and has done so ever since.

In modern times in addition to being fixed on the actions, phrases, and expressions of the Federal Reserve Board chairman Alan Greenspan, a trader on the front lines must also watch the developments in Iraq, the current terrorism threat level in the country, and a constant stream of news items from which one's nerves can be rattled at any moment. But how does this differ from the circumstances of Andrew J. Barclay, the first known speculator within the original group of 24 brokers that traded under the buttonwood tree? He had to follow very closely the actions of Hamilton and Jefferson because Jefferson might have squelched the business opportunities Hamilton had just planted.

We think the events that occurred before our century moved relatively slowly, but that is not an accurate perception. In a book first published in 1936 and now long out of print called *The Stock Exchange* by Humphrey Neill, we learn the circulation of bank notes jumped from $11 million to $45 million in 14 years. Land speculation had run so out of control some people bought land located 30 feet under the Hudson River!

The first recorded bubble burst was the implosion of land prices in 1798 in the North. Meanwhile in the South in a single year in 1792 the plantations produced a total of 6000 bales of cotton (500 pounds to a bale). Then in 1793 the South recorded the production of 16,000 bales of cotton, an increase made possible by Eli Whitney's invention of the cotton gin the year before. If you traded cotton in 1793, you would have thought the world was turning incredibly fast!

So the difference is the speed, volume, and global breadth of information that we have to contend with these days. But human nature has not changed. Market volatility increases as the public reacts to the latest terrorism threat, policy change, war event, or market excess, and we traders find ourselves confronted with information overload. *The solution is to simplify.* Filter out the media stream of verbal and one-line news stories and trade through technical aids alone. The spread between cause and reaction has narrowed to such an extent that we can focus on the market setup alone without full awareness of the trigger itself. Shutting the media stream off is in fact an act of self-preservation!

One day I was looking for a book in my library to help my business partner who was evolving more toward technicals from his strong fundamental background. To my surprise the book I needed had not yet been written. No book existed to visually clarify what was a weak divergence signal versus a strong one. No book existed to offer a simple illustration of an outside day, a key reversal, and railway tracks under one jacket cover. Such technical patterns cannot be described easily in an e-mail. I could have created the charts and sent them as attachments, but if the attachments were not saved, the information would be lost. Learning about technical analysis phrases and terms is difficult when a trader is using only the dictionary help pages written by the software vendors who do not trade for their living. So I called McGraw-Hill and explained that I needed a book. When we could not find one, I soon found a contract in my e-mail folder to create this visual chart library.

As the collection of charts grew, it became clear that it would be useful to people with various skill levels. This is a book full of ideas for the experienced technician. For the newer trader and technician, it provides clarification and quick references. And for the novice it provides motivation to explore further a method or technique that looks promising but requires further knowledge not in these pages to actually implement or set up. This book is without words for good reason; it is not meant to teach the methods but only to demonstrate them and to show how they have been applied in real market conditions. While this book is intended to supplement your own studies, you can learn a great deal from studying a simple illustration alone.

This book solves a problem you might have when you first set up a technical analysis software service if you are very unfamiliar with the methods used or if the software is new to you. For example, vendors such as CQG and TradeStation set up point-and-figure parameters differently to produce the same chart results. This book will introduce you to point-and-figure charting, and if the patterns illustrated tell you a clear story, then you may be more motivated to invest in a book specializing in this area.

As another example, suppose you hear a colleague on the phone referring to "Kagi charts." You can find out what a Kagi chart looks like in this book. The goal is not to teach you Kagi charting. However, if you see that Kagi and Gann swing charts are very similar, you may find you have more in common with the trader you overheard on the phone than you first realized.

The most frequent comment I hear when I teach is, "I've never seen that done before." Use of trendlines from pivots less academic but more meaningful in a geometric sense can be taught through simple illustration. This book is packed full with market geometry applications. Another benefit of an all visual book is in the indicator comparisons that use the same symbols, which offers the new technician a fast way to absorb a lot of technical experience by discovering his or her own indicator preferences.

This book offers you a gold mine of trading directional signals that took years of experience to collect. We traders are just a growing logic tree of signals, and it is hard to put words around them all. Your observation skills will be put to the test by this book. Here are a few guidelines on what to study. Focus closely on such things as price closes versus opens when arrows are added to the chart. Study charts from right to left, and see if the signal or level or pattern has been significant for the market in the past. Any area highlighted in gray is significant. Market geometry is huge in my view. When making a careful evaluation between methods, study the reactions on both market tops and bottoms. Does an indicator make complex tops and simple V bottoms? Study the source of a trendline and the minor anchor points selected. When I teach, I find most people look for patterns that are far too wide or large. It is the attention to detail that makes a great technician, but keep in mind *the goal is to answer what will happen in the next bar*, not to detail the squiggles through a chart for historic prosperity.

Some charts are included simply to set the record straight. As a contributor and grader for the Market Technician Association's Chartered Market Technician (CMT III) certification exam, I am annually discouraged by the number of American candidates who cannot read a currency chart. Once I submitted a question, which was accepted and used in the exam, showing a monthly Swiss franc, weekly euro, and daily yen chart. The exam question asked candidates for a market opinion on the U.S. dollar and asked for the reasons behind their conclusion. The number of people who believed this to be a trick question because it did not display the Dollar Index was disheartening. Clearly this is not an overseas issue but a problem in North America where candidates believe a stock analyst has no need to understand the global financial food chain. Wake up, America! Keep in mind the job application pool for market analysts is global. New analysts expecting to enter the industry as professionals better do the homework needed because the Forex market dictates all the other financial markets. Equities are simply a money flow game, and one must understand the flow behind the buying and selling pressures. A spot currency chart with a label $/yen is read as the U.S. dollar rising and falling in the direction of the price action against the currency cross. If the chart is labeled yen/$, the price rising and falling in correlation with the chart's price action reflects yen. The dollar would be read as the inverse correlation. If you cannot read a currency chart and take the CMT III exam, you will likely be hard pressed to pass this certification.

There are several Gann charts in this book because this method offers accurate time and price analysis. But few people in the industry know very much about this method. The charts can be difficult to set up if you have no knowledge about Gann analysis, but they are easy to read and interpret. So the charts are offered as an introduction so that some may become more curious to explore this methodology further. I will write a comprehensive Gann book some day because most books on the subject at present follow the work of Gann's son, John, and not that of William Delbert ("W.D.") Gann. In terms of returns and probability, there is a huge difference as Gann's son reduced much of his father's methods to percentages, which are less accurate.

For readers learning the Elliott Wave Principle, all 13 Elliott wave patterns are illustrated as a simple reference guide. Robert Prechter believes he has found a 14th, which will be called an *expanding diagonal triangle*. I display the most common diagonal triangle; the termination wedge, and I did not go into detailing the expanding wedge or the difference between a type 1 versus a type 2 diagonal triangle. The termination wedge is the more common, and it is clearly the market reversal pattern of greater importance. You will be fairly advanced if you want to begin to differentiate between type 1 and 2 wedges, and you would likely have books on the topic in your own library.

There are 18 market entry signals in the book. These are given in addition to the numerous reversal and continuation signals demonstrated. *They include buy signals in stochastic oscillators at the 80 level and sell signals at 20.* In the words of George Lane, who first created the stochastic study, "Don't learn to trade from your quote vendor; you'll become a computer programmer." So many quick guides claim that traders should sell at 80 and buy at 20 when using stochastic signals that I felt compelled to show you how this is incredibly wrong as a carte blanche statement.

To add fuel for thought, there are a few examples in various sections of the book of applying technical analysis on fundamental data. But as background, it is becoming more important to see long historical periods of data to help us gain a sense of where we stand now in context with the larger picture of history. It is becoming harder to acquire these data because quote vendors are reducing their historical data services to less than 20 years. This is insufficient for our purposes. Therefore, a few historical charts are offered that include short and long horizon interest rates in the United States and Japan, which will become key in the months ahead.

A comment I often hear is that there needs to be a comparison between major oscillators. So care was taken to keep the same market and time horizon so that a comparison could be made that allows the different oscillator signal formations to be evaluated.

This brings us to the treasury bills to eurodollars (TED) spread chart. This is the one chart a reader can learn how to create from the chart in this book but then run into difficulties finding material that can explain how the spread is used because most books on technical analysis omit this discussion. So let me take a moment to fill this void for readers who have a need to understand it further.

Some financial spreads are so commonly traded that they have their own acronym shorthand name, like the TED spread. The TED spread is simply a two-legged position with a leg in T-Bill futures and an opposite leg in eurodollar futures.

Both T-Bill futures and eurodollar futures are based on the interest rate paid on 90-day deposits. This interest rate can be calculated by subtracting the futures price from 100. (For example, if T-Bills are trading at 95.00, the yield is 100 minus 95.00, or 5.00 percent. Eurodollars work the exact same way.) T-Bills are 90-day deposits with the U.S. government, while eurodollars are 90-day deposits of U.S. dollars in foreign banks. T-Bills are U.S. government debt, so they are backed by the "full faith and credit" of the U.S. government. Because a government can tax its citizens, the deposits backed by the government are deemed to be low risk. (Always an interesting heated debate.) On the other hand, eurodollars are not guaranteed by any government. They therefore have historically demanded a higher yield to attract funds. *The TED spread is said to be narrowing when eurodollars gain in value relative to T-Bills. When T-Bills gain in value relative to eurodollars, the TED spread is said to be widening.*

Because T-Bills are government guaranteed and eurodollars are not, the TED spread represents the yield premium associated with eurodollars. For example, when T-Bills are trading at 96.94 and the same month eurodollars are trading at 96.40, foreign banks have to pay 0.54 percent over the T-Bill rate to attract American dollars overseas.

The fiscal policy in the United States is a major factor affecting the TED spread. When interest rates in the United States are rising, the TED spread has historically widened, as the more risky eurodollars tend to fall in value more than the safer T-Bills. When interest rates are declining, or steady, the TED spread has historically narrowed as the more volatile eurodollars appreciate in value faster relative to T-Bills.

Other factors affecting the TED spread would be world political stability and the balance of trade. But, you may ask, is this not a fundamental topic? A market technician does not live in a vacuum. We understand why a stock should be placed in a certain sector group because its principal business and generated revenue is derived from a common characteristic market service or product for that group. But once this is understood, we technicians do not care what the company's' earnings report may be in the future as our charts will warn us well in advance of the risks or opportunities. Likewise with the TED spread because we need to have an understanding of what it measures. Then we rely upon our charts and technicals to forecast the risk premium measure between T-Bills and eurodollars.

The TED spread is a risk premium between the U.S. government's guaranteed assets and nonguaranteed assets. The political stability of the United States and foreign nations has historically played a key role in the direction of the TED spread. When the world political situation is stable, the TED spread has historically narrowed, meaning that eurodollars have gained in value relative to T-Bills. When political uncertainty is high, T-Bills have historically gained in value relative to eurodollars as people seek safer assets. If you did not recognize this relationship, it would be easy to overlook that the current political instability and terrorism should be widening the TED spread. Something is seriously amiss as the normal relationships are not present. It makes us far more careful as we study our charts knowing it is an election year and Greenspan has fallen seriously behind the yield curve. That means an artificial situation is being created and when the Federal Reserve is finally forced to catch up or establish normalcy in the interest rate environment, it will dramatically impact stocks.

But how does a changing interest rate environment impact stock prices? Not all sectors react in a similar way. A technician will spend countless hours to determine the sectors that will be impacted, but the research will determine only that stocks have a cyclical reaction to a changing interest rate environment.

Six months before the Fed tightening cycle begins, sectors like Aerospace/Defense, Autos and Parts, Chemicals, Construction and Building Materials, Oil, Engines and Machinery, Transport, and Electrical Equipment outperform the general market. On the other hand, Insurance, Leisure, General Retail, and Pharmaceuticals may lag.

But early in the tightening cycle after the first and second rate hike, a change occurs. General Retail, Software and Computer Services as well as Gold Mining stocks begin to outperform sectors negatively impacted by rising rates such as Aerospace/Defense, Banks, Construction and Building Materials, Diversified Industries, Oil, Household Goods, and Real Estate.

Late in the tightening cycle interest rate changes often produce a stronger dollar as higher rates offer higher returns for overseas investors holding U.S. deposits. So sectors with strong overseas sales such as Diversified Industries, Engines and Machinery, and U.S. Autos and Parts underperform further. That is why analysts with responsibilities in stocks alone must have a broader awareness of the financial world about them.

We live in times of increasing market volatility, and you will find numerous charts showing volatility bands, volatility measurements, and several examples of the Volatility Index (VIX). There is not a lot written on this index, and several charting vendors do not even offer VIX data. I have six different data vendors because no one vendor can offer all the markets, indexes, or historical data files I need to do a decent job in a global arena. Frustrating, but it is reality so be prepared to shop for the symbols your principal vendor may not have.

The VIX is a sentiment gauge of fear in the U.S. stock market. As the VIX simply quantifies implied options volatility on the S&P 100 Index, a low value generally means complacency and a high value means violent markets plagued with breathtaking and chaotic volatility. When studying the attributes of any market sentiment measurement like the VIX charts, it is important to view the historical range in which the VIX has traded. Since 1997 the VIX has generally bounced between 20 on the low side and 50 on the high side. Each time in 1998, 2001, and 2002 that an extreme was recorded near 50, the market formed a definable low.

Such sentiment gauges by themselves are difficult to read, and the raw data can be *detrended* to make them more useful. Data are detrended simply by adding a moving average and plotting the difference of the index from the average as an oscillator. You will find examples of this in the VIX charts. Another way to increase the value of a sentiment index is to chart a ratio. The S&P 500 divided by the VIX will give cleaner signals to work from than will the raw data alone.

When the VIX pierced the 20 level, it marked a period in the markets of extreme greed and indifference. A short of the S&P 500 at the VIX trough lows would have been correct directional strategy, but it would also have been poor market timing without a price projection method in place to use for risk management purposes. Price projection methods are without question the weakest component for most new analysts. You will find in this book several different price projection techniques that you can use as a starting point to obtain additional information.

Most of the charts in this book are actual charts used in a trading environment. I hope as you page through the charts, it leads you to new research or clarifies a concept misunderstood. We always have something new to learn. Markets are evolving and so too should we be learning new skills. Never stay in one place as there is always a bigger fish out there looking for its next meal in the financial food chain. Personally I would rather be predator than prey.

Bearish Divergence between Momentum Indicators

Bearish Divergence Strong

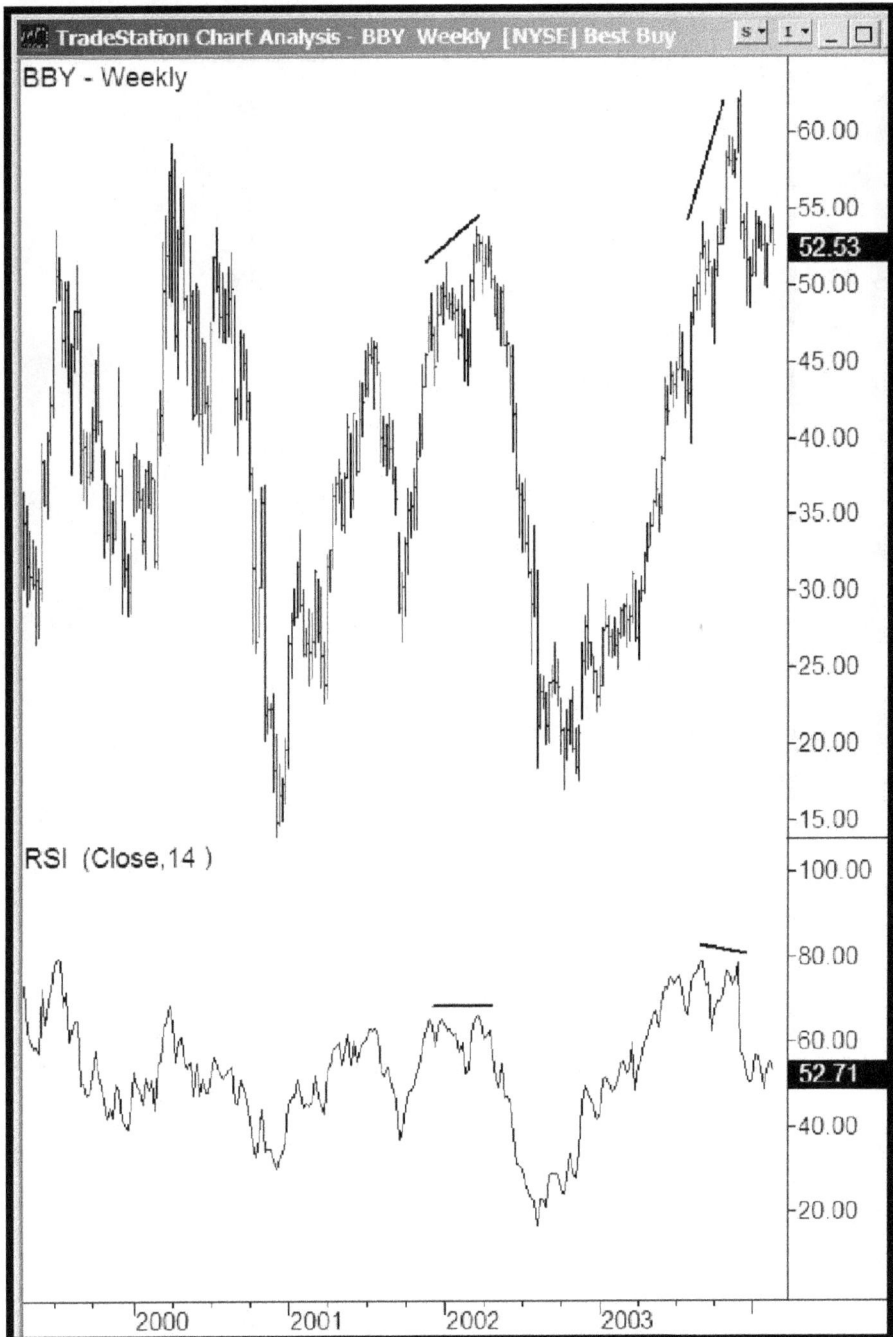

Bearish Divergence Very Strong

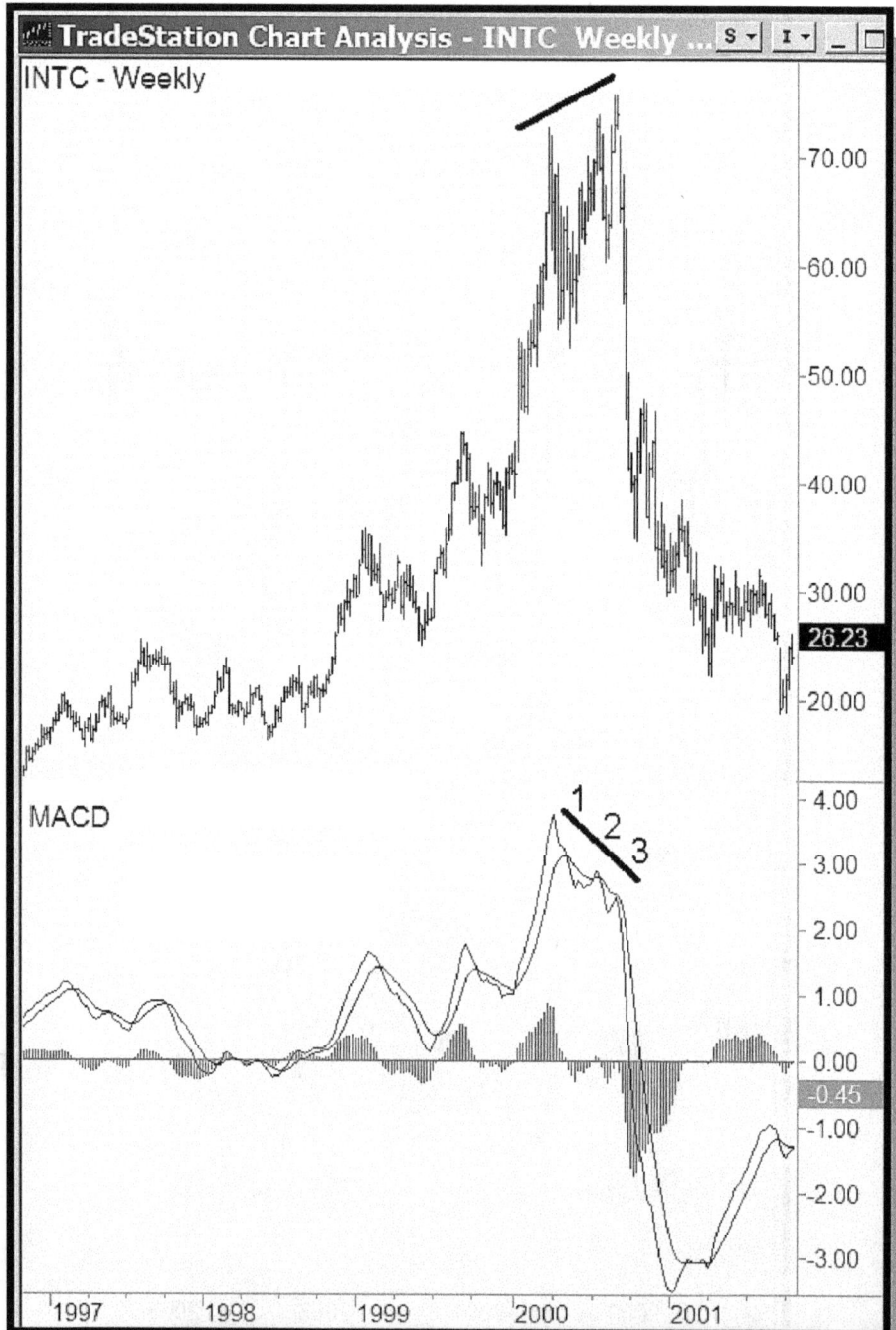

Bearish Divergence Very Strong with Lower Volume Confirmation

Bearish Divergence Very Weak (Too Wide)

Bullish Divergence on Internal Momentum Support

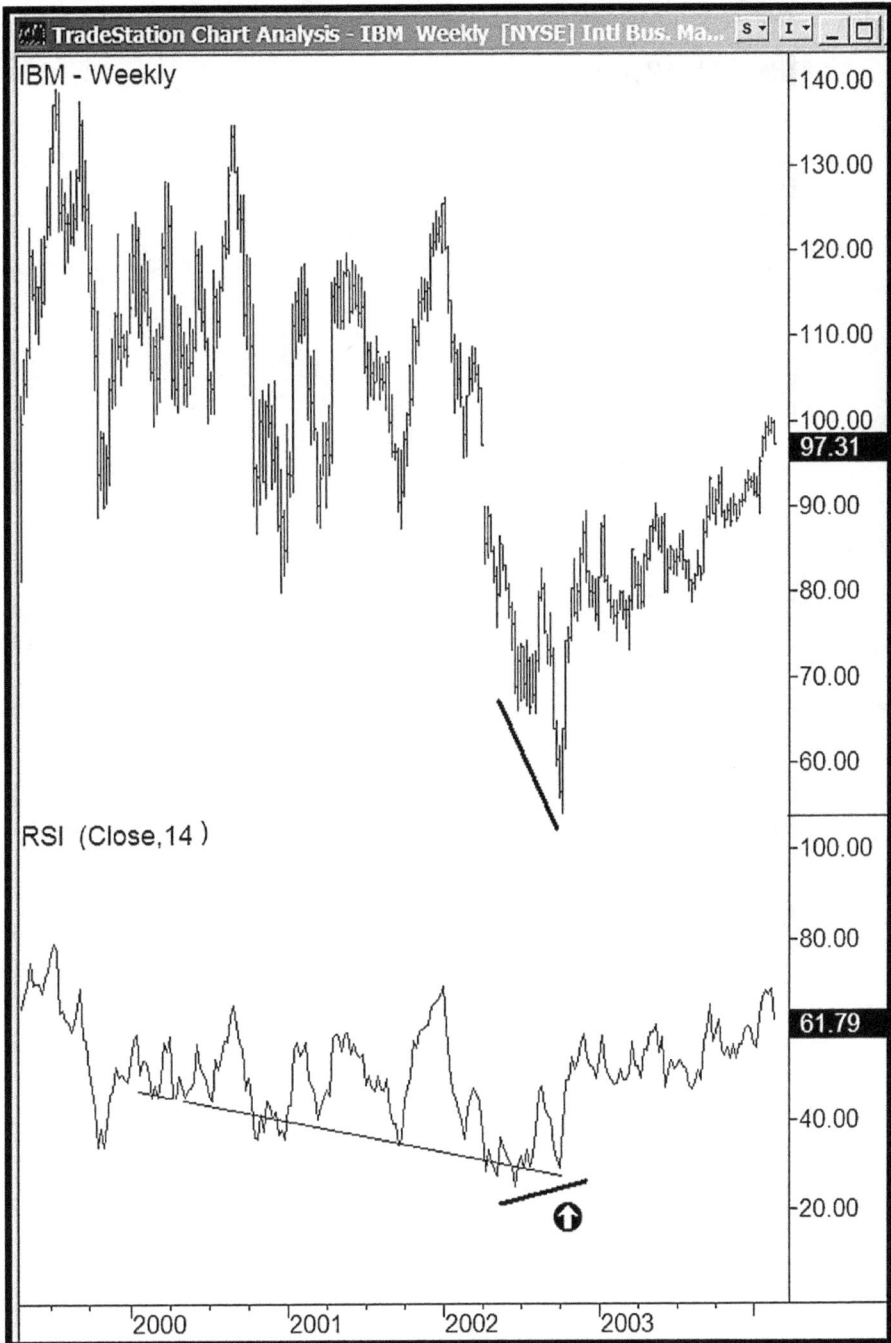

Bullish Divergence Very Strong on Momentum Support

Bullish Divergence Very Strong with Volume Confirmation

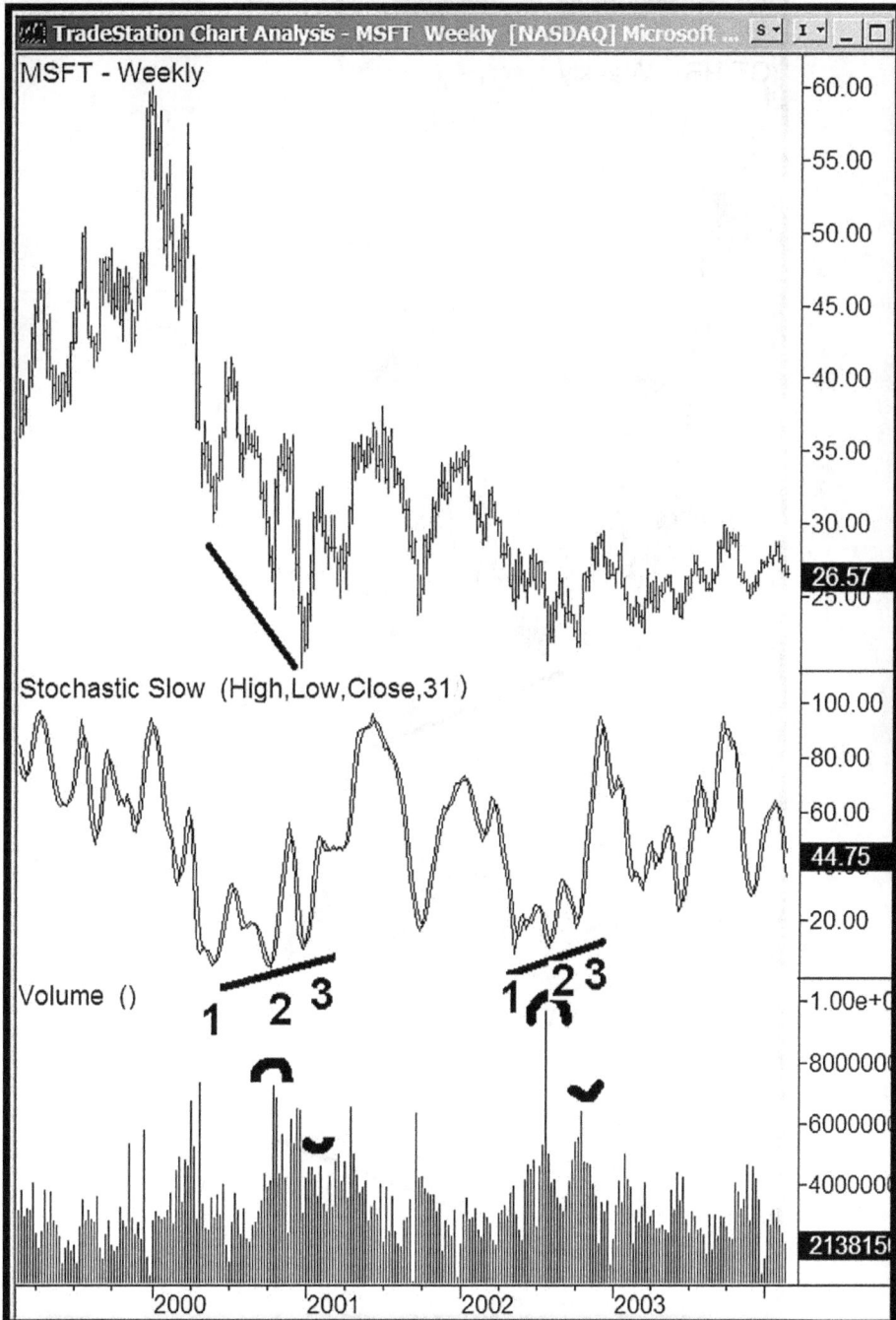

Bullish Divergence Very Weak (Too Wide)

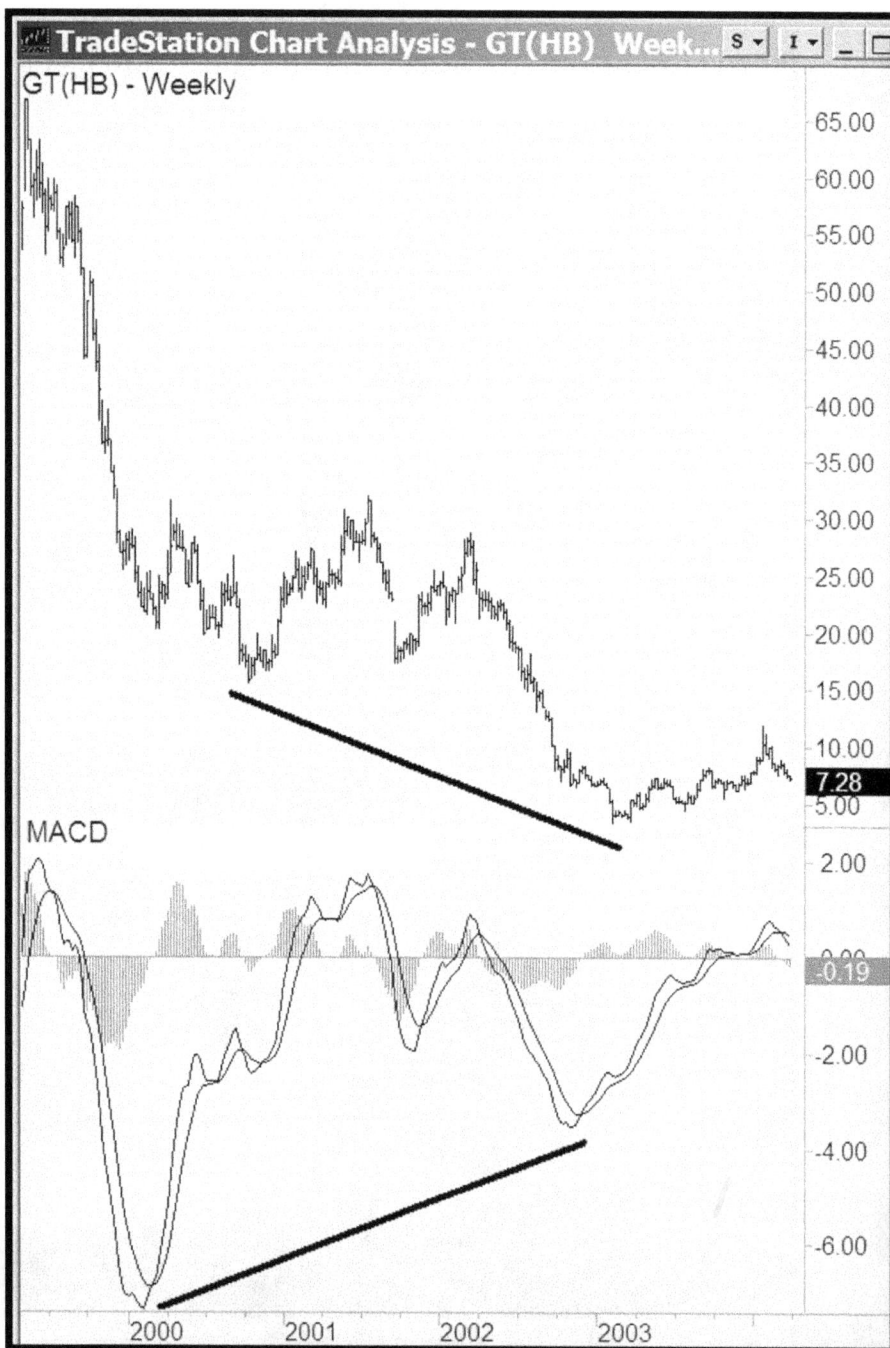

Bullish Divergence with Confirming Lower Volume

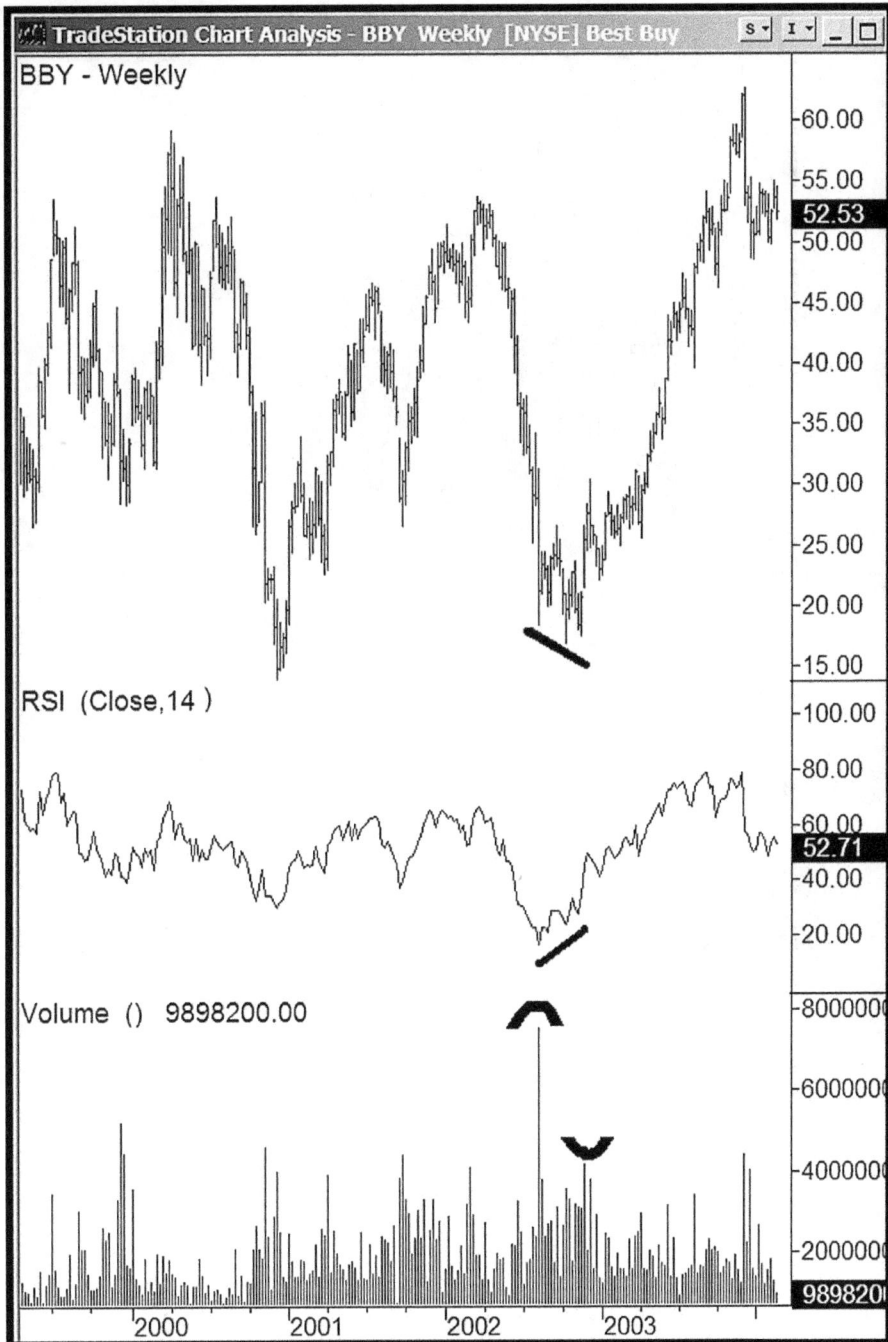

Bullish Divergence with V-Reversal Bottom

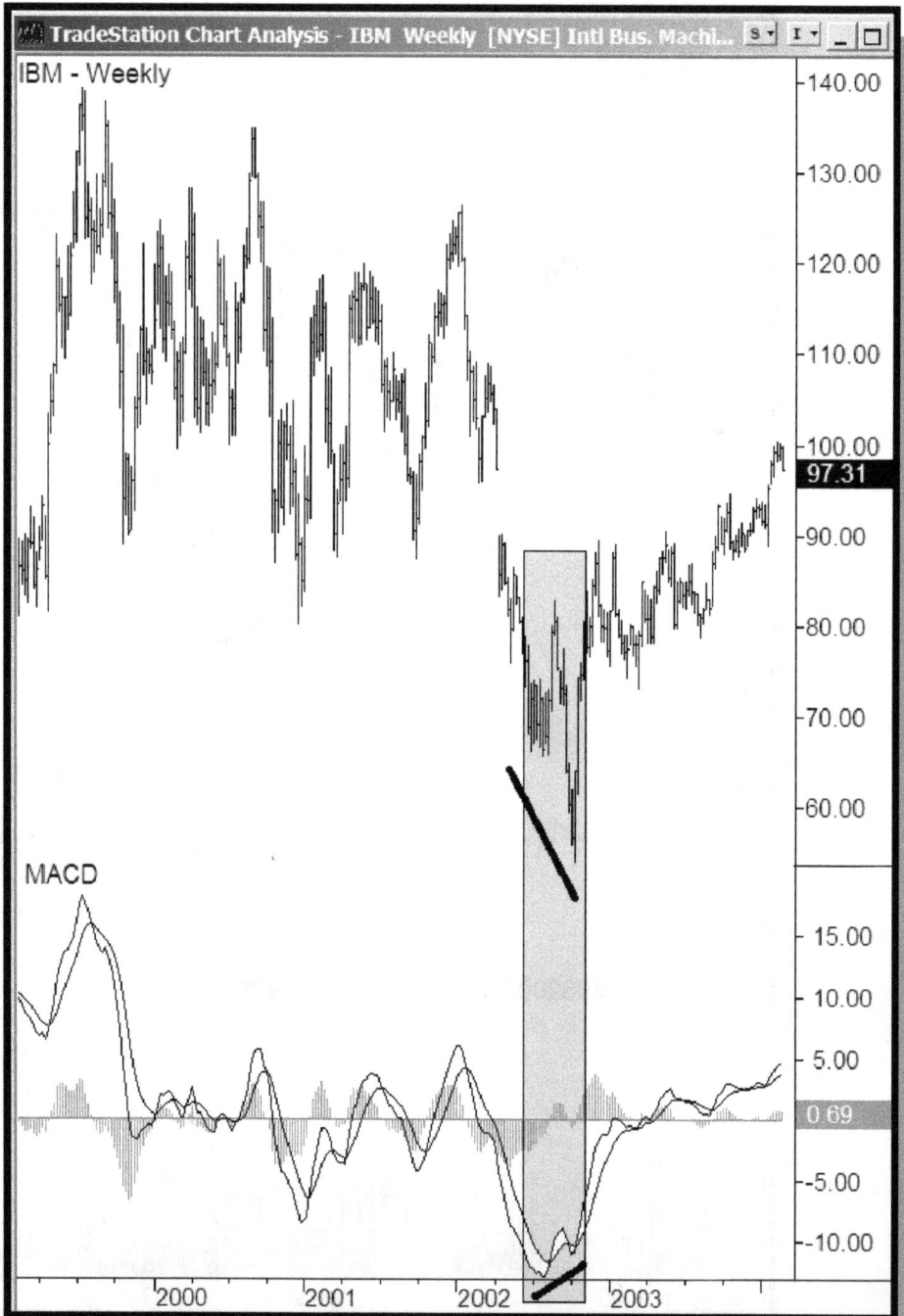

Bullish Divergence without Confirming Lower Volume

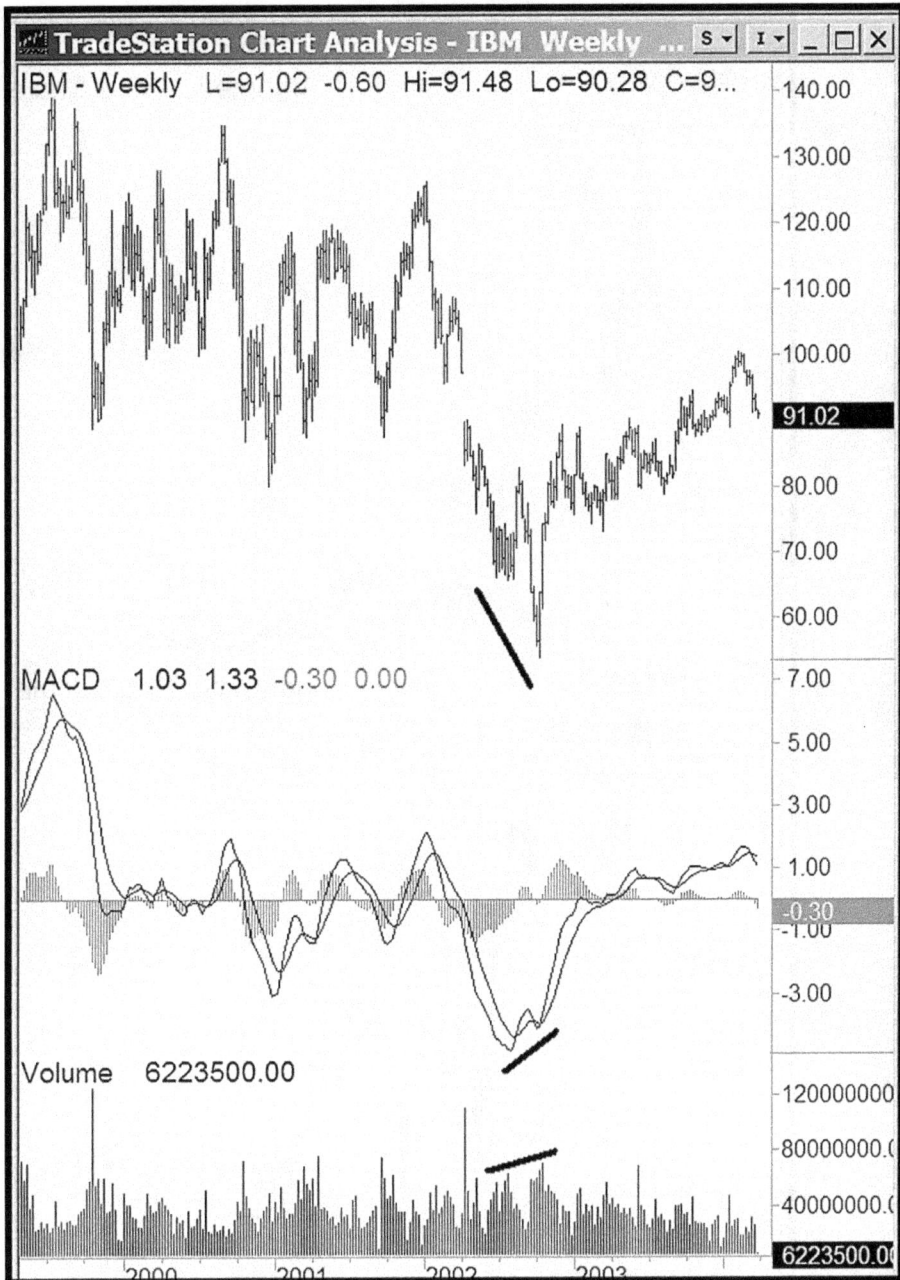

Chart Scales: Arithmetic and Semilogarithmic

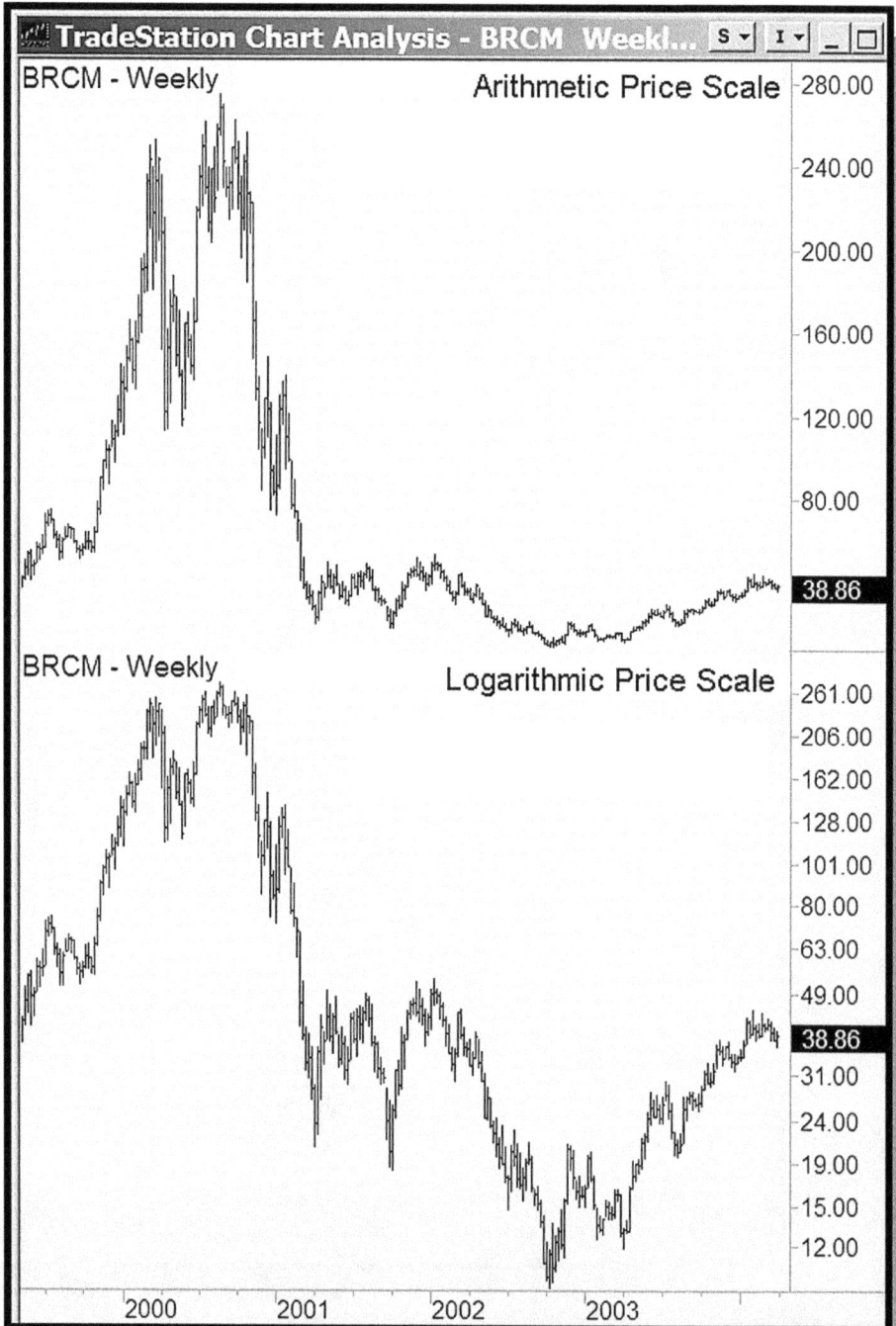

Chart Styles: 3rd-Dimension Harmonic

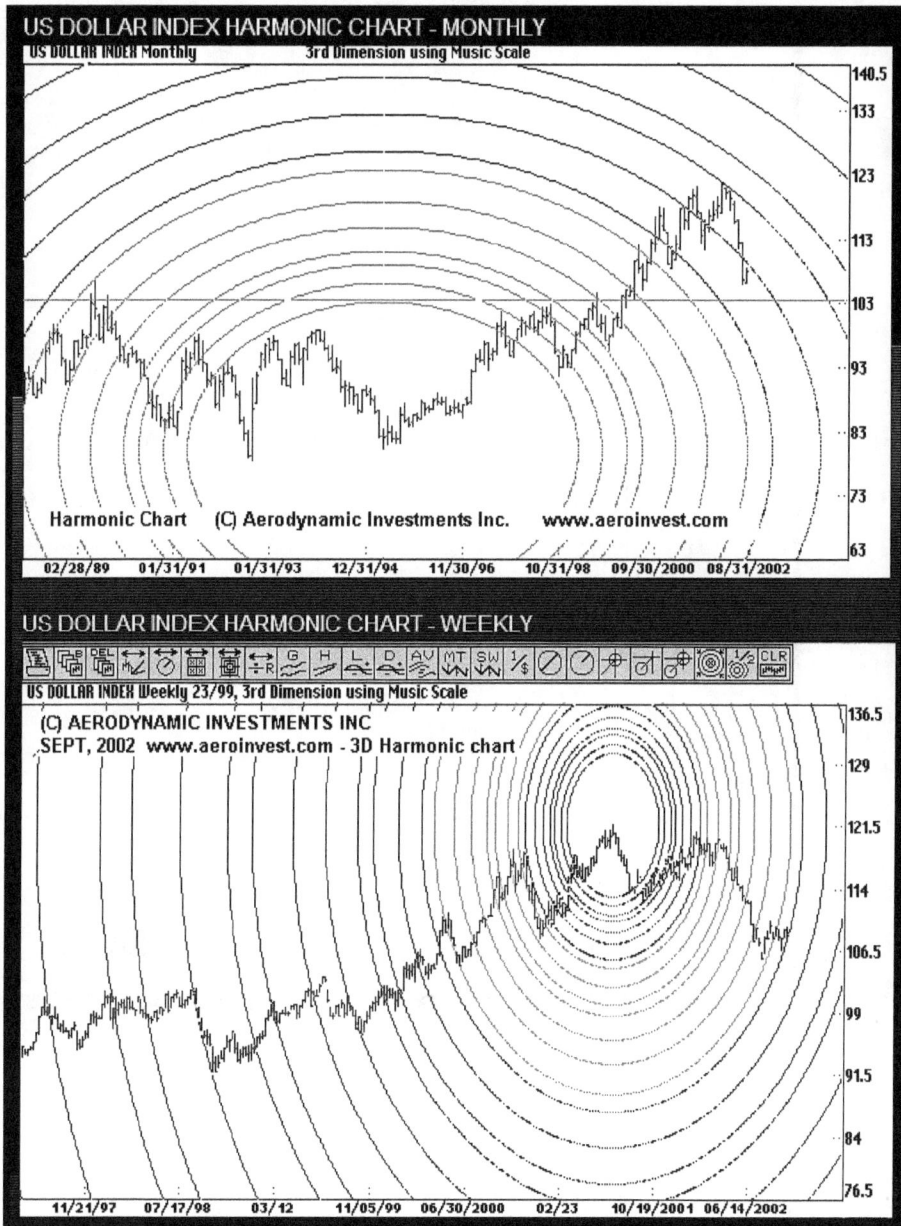

US DOLLAR INDEX HARMONIC CHART - MONTHLY

US DOLLAR INDEX Monthly　　　　3rd Dimension using Music Scale

Harmonic Chart　　　(C) Aerodynamic Investments Inc.　　　www.aeroinvest.com

140.5
133
123
113
103
93
83
73
63

02/28/89　01/31/91　01/31/93　12/31/94　11/30/96　10/31/98　09/30/2000　08/31/2002

US DOLLAR INDEX HARMONIC CHART - WEEKLY

US DOLLAR INDEX Weekly 23/99, 3rd Dimension using Music Scale

(C) AERODYNAMIC INVESTMENTS INC
SEPT, 2002 www.aeroinvest.com - 3D Harmonic chart

136.5
129
121.5
114
106.5
99
91.5
84
76.5

11/21/97　07/17/98　03/12　11/05/99　06/30/2000　02/23　10/19/2001　06/14/2002

Chart Styles: Bar Chart

Chart Styles: Candlestick Chart

Pfizer Inc NYSE (PFE) - 1 Day Candlestick Chart

Chart Styles: Gann Swing Chart

Pfizer Inc.NYSE (PFE) – 1 Day Gann Swing Chart

Chart Styles: Kagi Chart

Pfizer Inc.NYSE (PFE) - 1 Day Kagi Chart

Chart Styles: Line on Close Chart

Chart Styles: Percentage Swing Chart

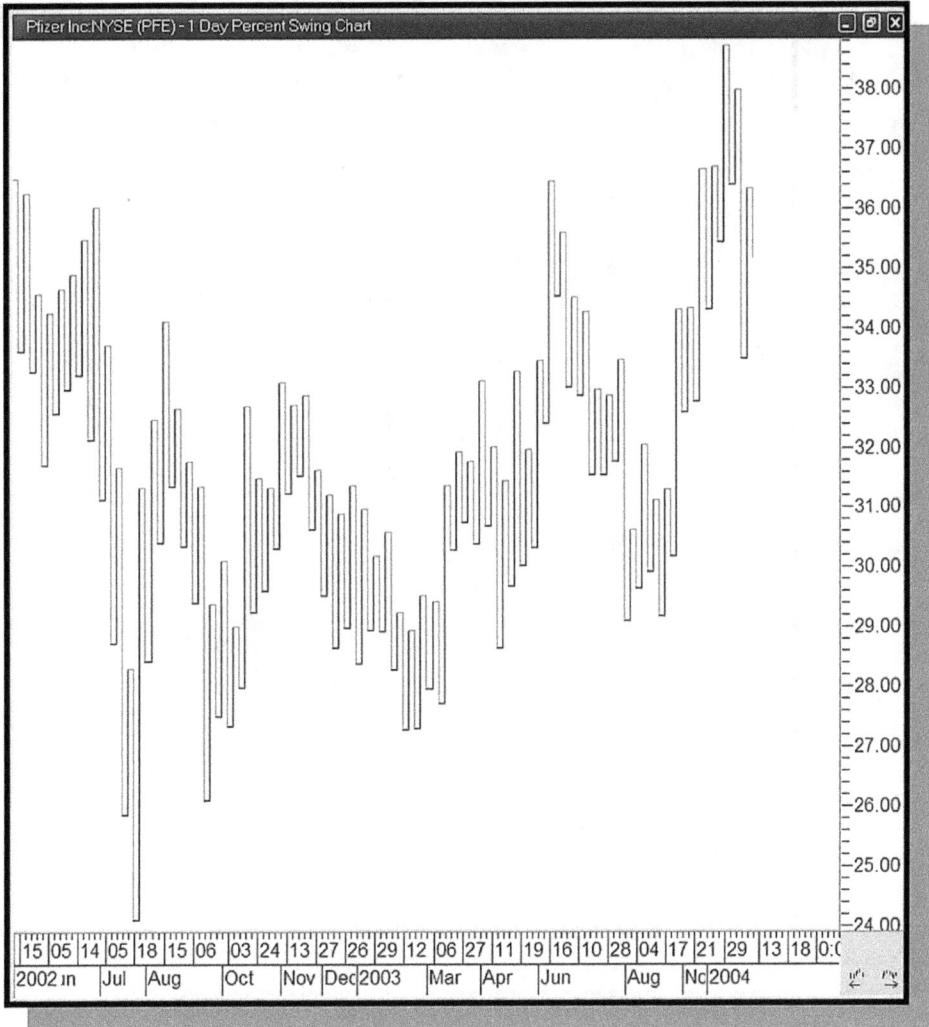

Pfizer Inc.NYSE (PFE) - 1 Day Percent Swing Chart

Chart Styles: Point-and-Figure Chart

Pfizer Inc.NYSE (PFE) - 1 Day Point and Figure Chart

Chart Styles: Point Swing Chart

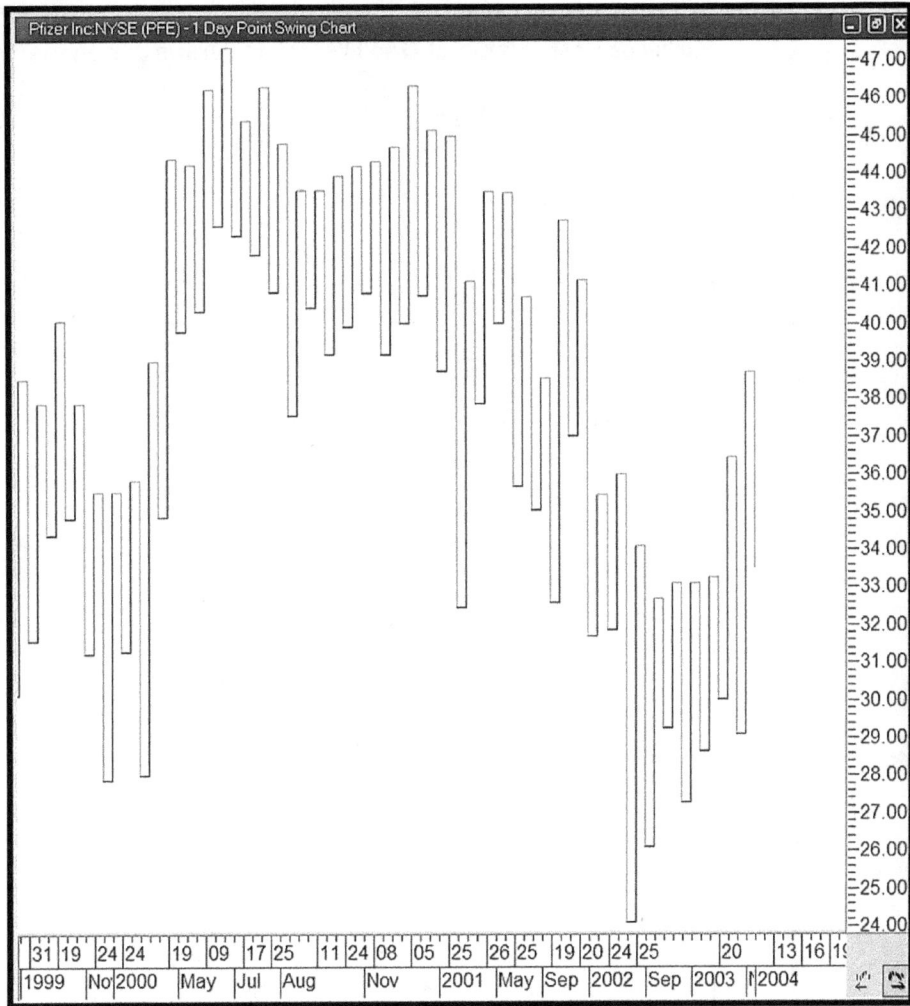

Pfizer Inc.NYSE (PFE) - 1 Day Point Swing Chart

Currency Exchange Rate

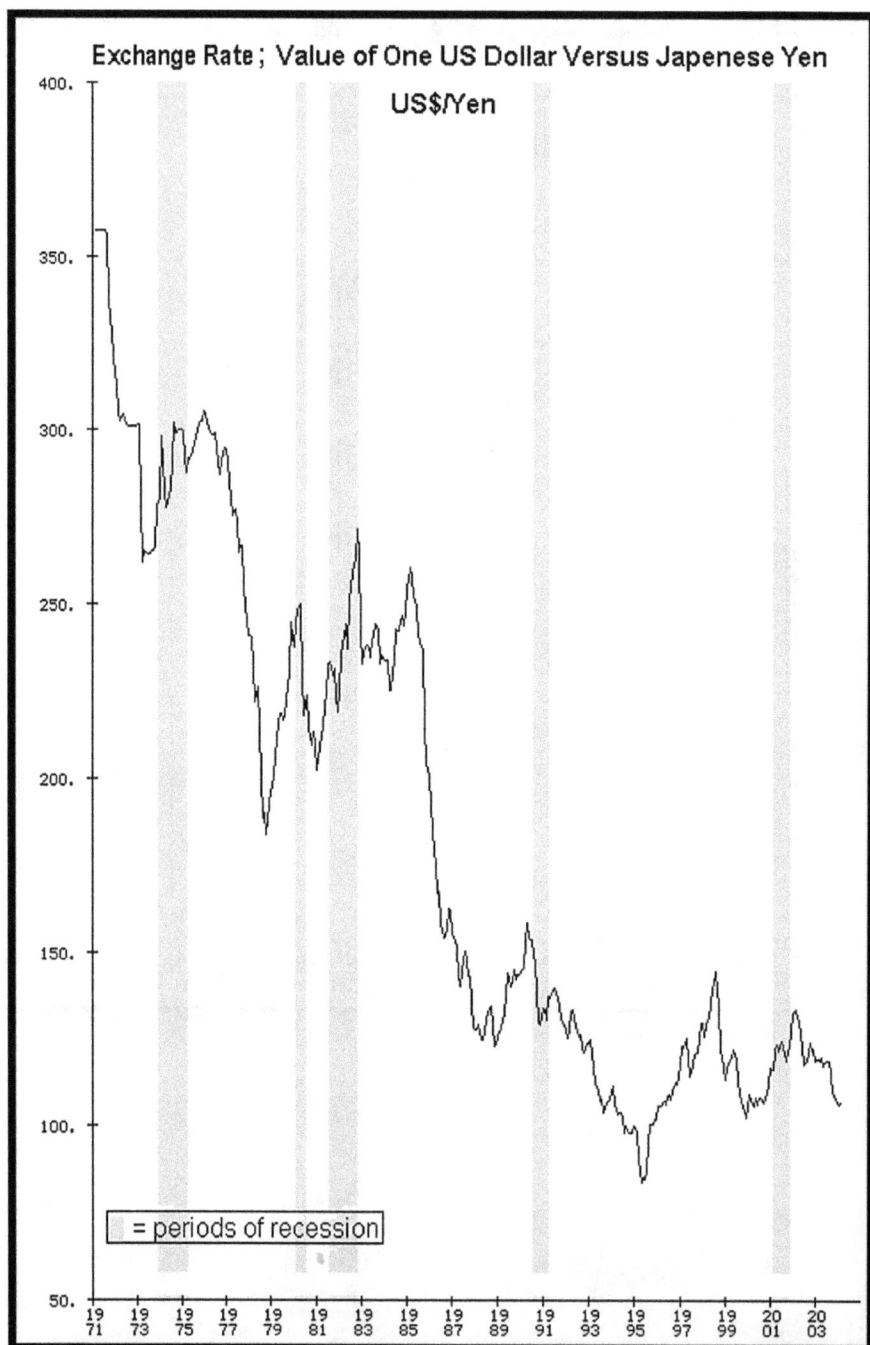

Exchange Rate ; Value of One US Dollar Versus Japenese Yen
US$/Yen

= periods of recession

Cycles: Fibonacci Time Intervals

Cycles: Fixed Period

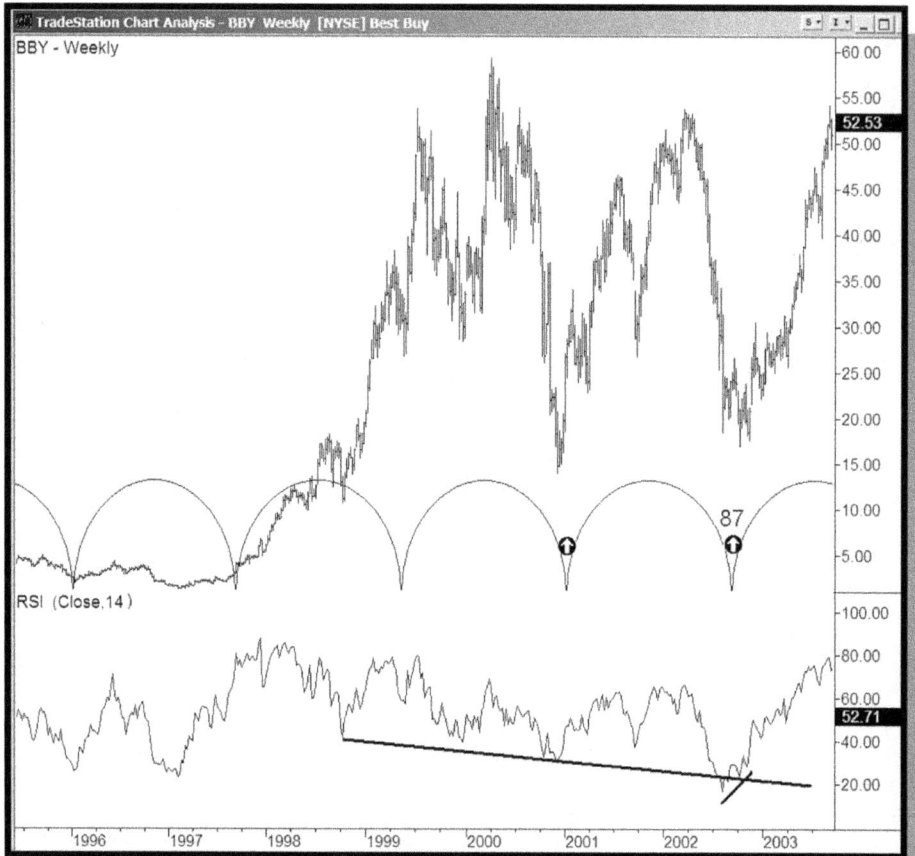

Cycles: Gann Aspect Conjunction (0)

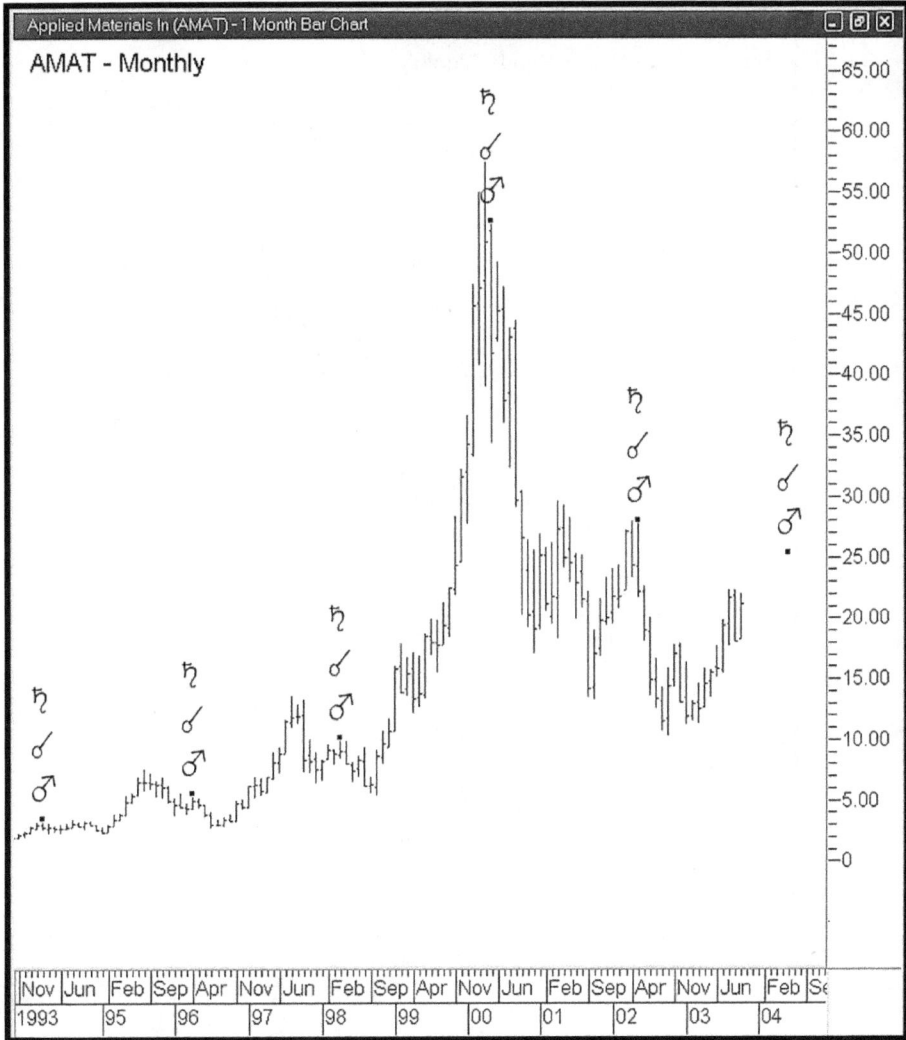

Cycles: Gann Aspect Opposition (180)

Govt Bond-Japanese10 (JGB) - 1 Month Bar Chart

Japanese Govt 10Yr Bond - Monthly

Cycles: Gann Aspect Sextile (60)

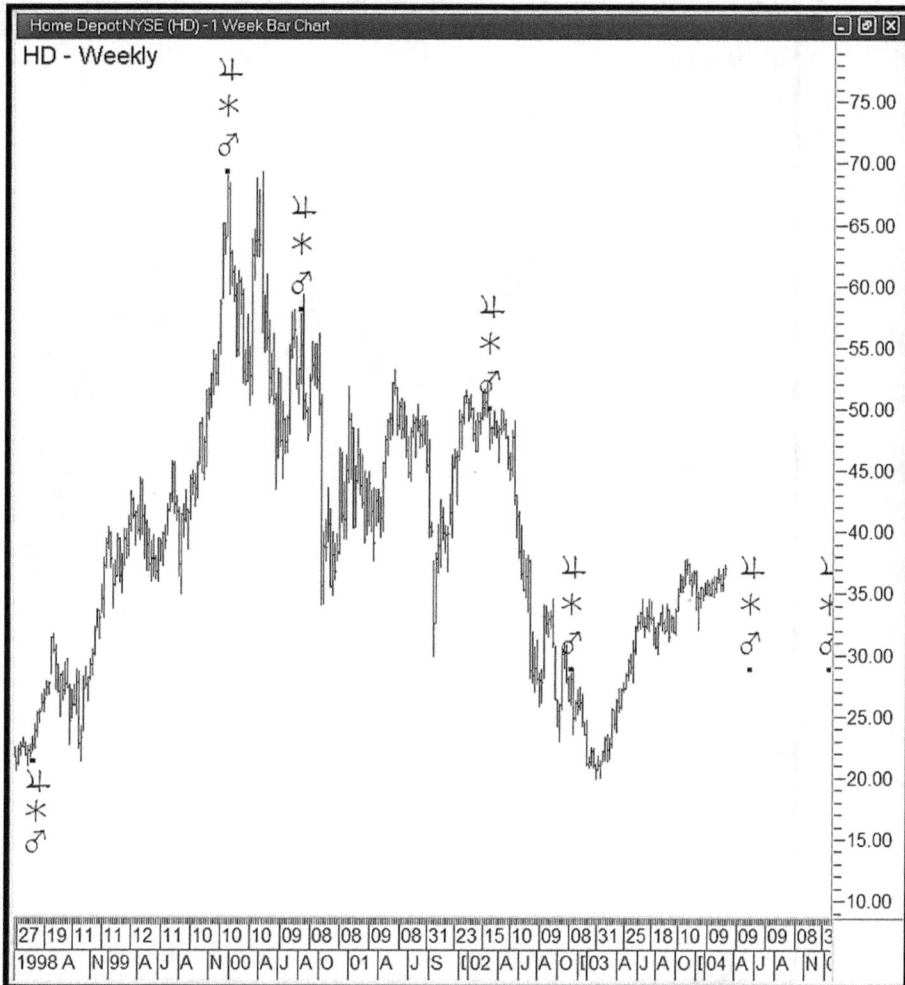

Home Depot NYSE (HD) - 1 Week Bar Chart

HD - Weekly

Cycles: Gann Aspect Square (90)

Cycles: Gann Aspect Trine (120)

Cycles: Gann Declination Overlay

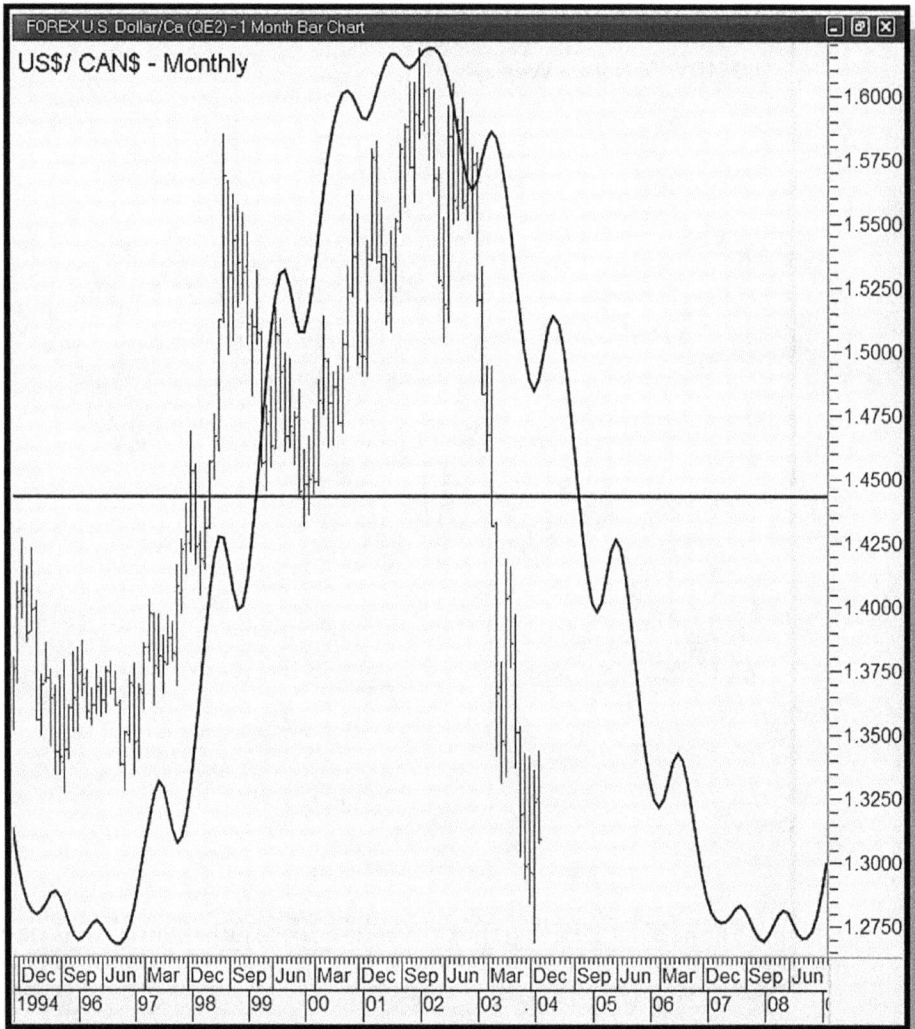

FOREX U.S. Dollar/Ca (QE2) - 1 Month Bar Chart

US$/ CAN$ - Monthly

Cycles: Gann Ingress Analysis

Cycles: Gann Planetary Degrees (Saturn 15)

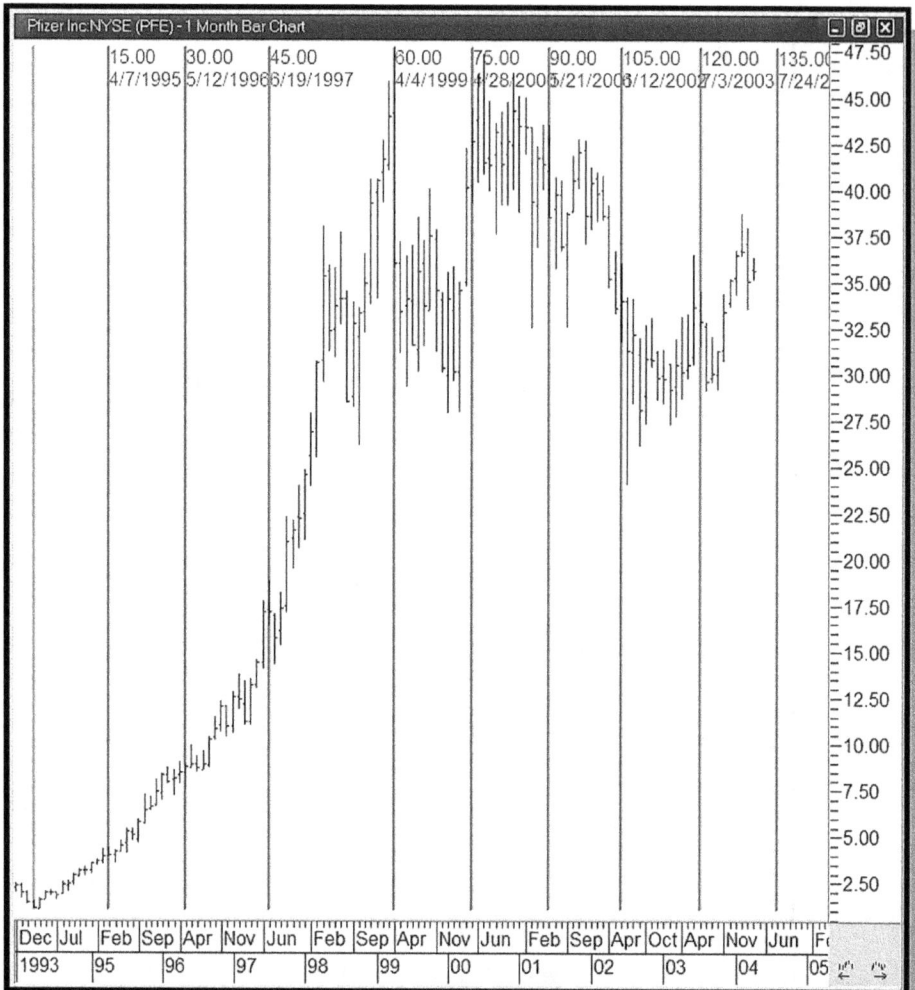

Pfizer Inc.NYSE (PFE) - 1 Month Bar Chart

Cycles: Harmonic Series

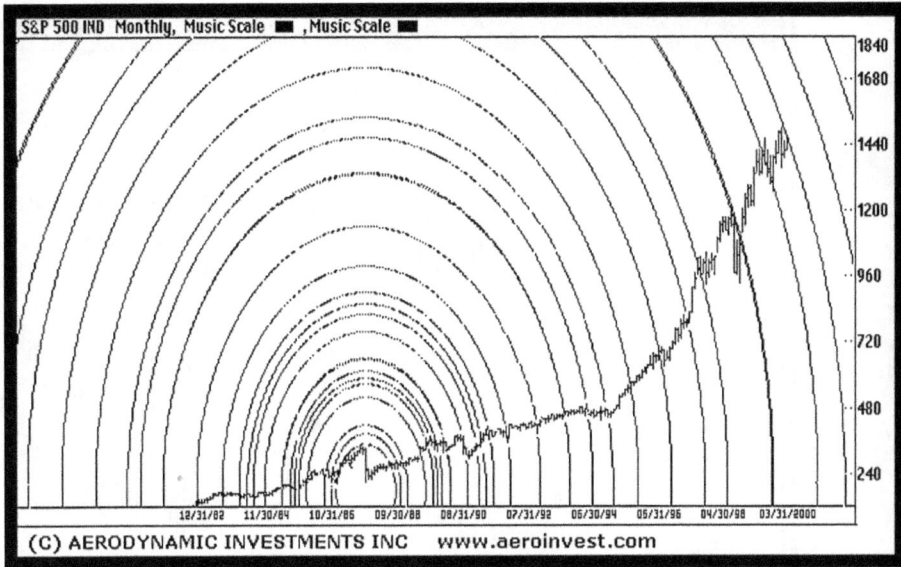

S&P 500 IND Monthly, Music Scale ■■ , Music Scale ■■

1840
1680
1440
1200
960
720
480
240

12/31/82   11/30/84   10/31/86   09/30/88   08/31/90   07/31/92   06/30/94   05/31/96   04/30/98   03/31/2000

(C) AERODYNAMIC INVESTMENTS INC   www.aeroinvest.com

Cycles: Historic Comparison Overlay

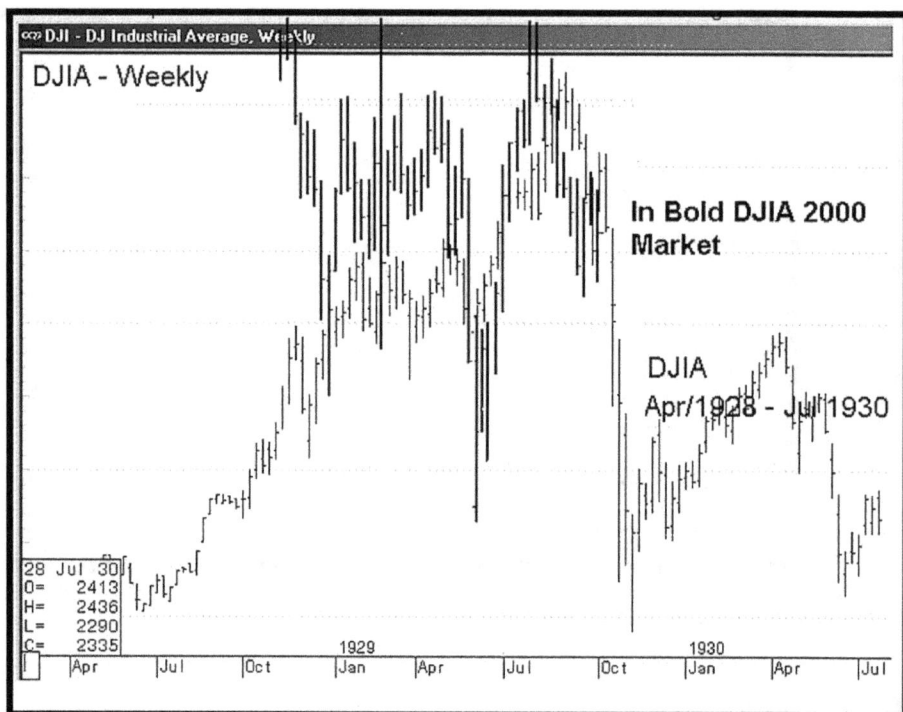

DJIA - Weekly

In Bold DJIA 2000 Market

DJIA
Apr/1928 - Jul 1930

28 Jul 30
O= 2413
H= 2436
L= 2290
C= 2335

1929   Apr   Jul   Oct   1930   Jan   Apr   Jul

Apr   Jul   Oct   Jan

Cycles: Multiple Fixed Period

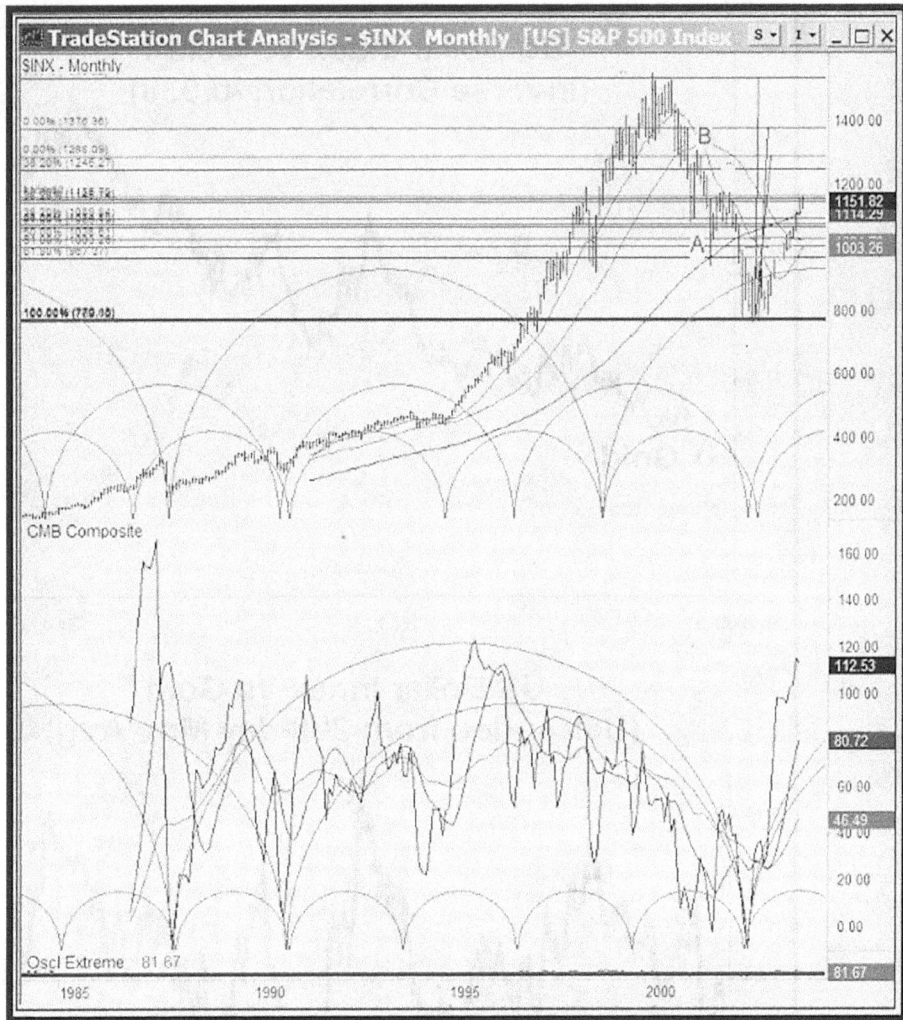

Detrended U.S. Dollar Index Versus Gold

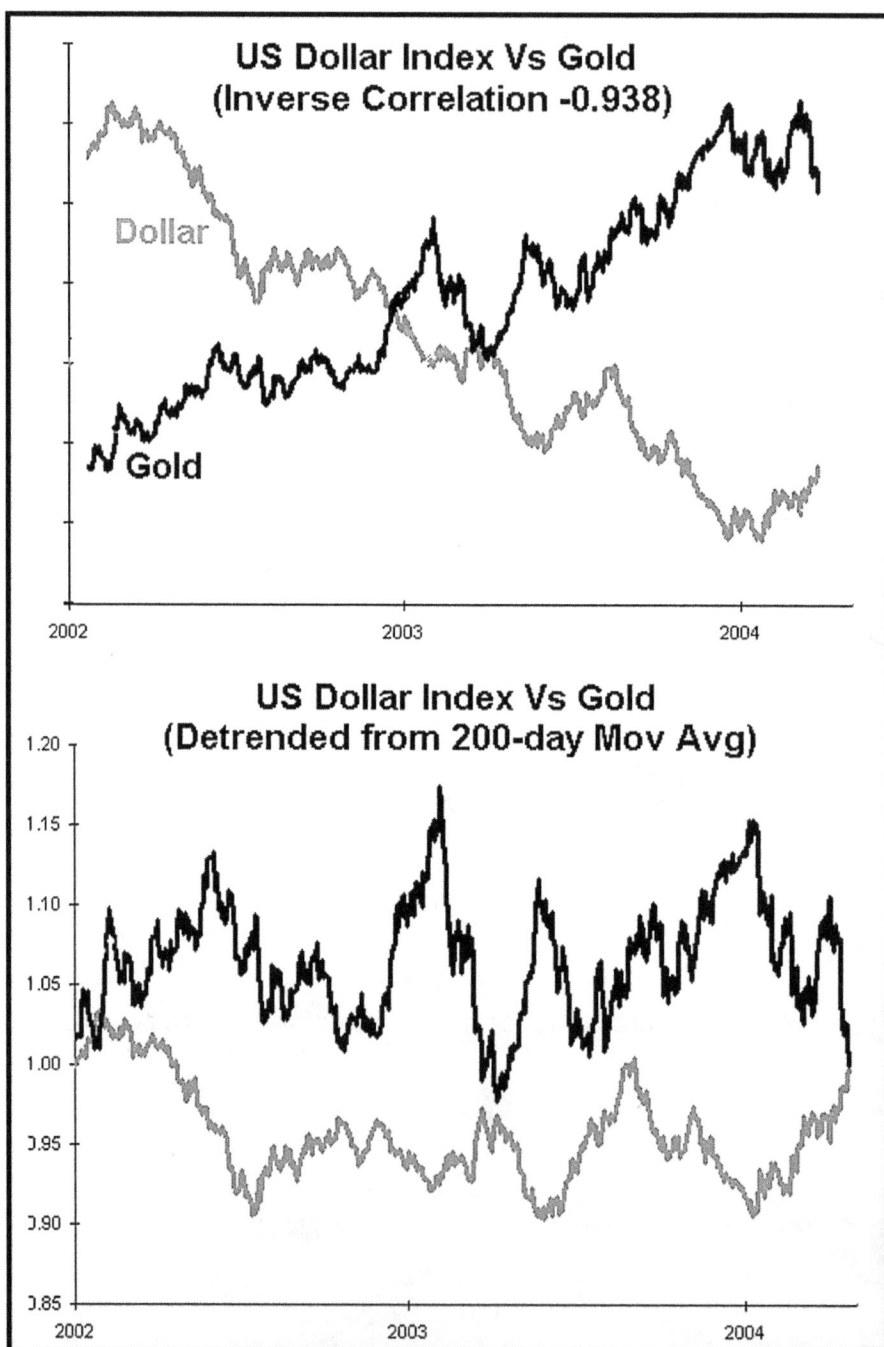

Directional Signal: Bearish RSI Negative Reversal

Directional Signal: Bullish RSI Positive Reversal

Directional Signal: Capitulation

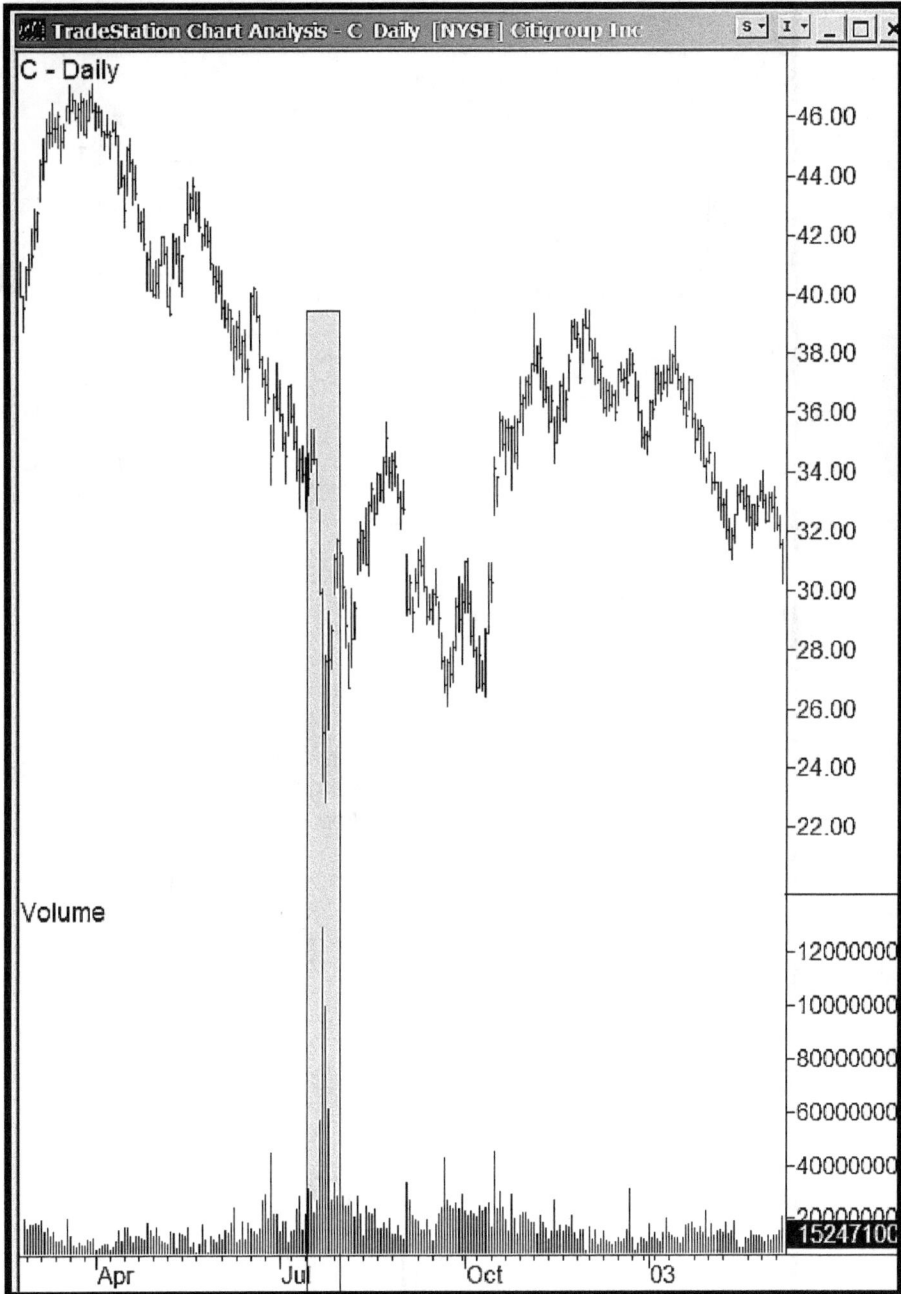

Directional Signal: Close above the High of the Low Day

TradeStation Chart Analysis - JNJ Daily [N... S ▾ I ▾ _ □

JNJ - Daily

close above
the high
of a low day

54.50

54.00
53.92

53.50

53.00

52.50

52.00

51.50

51.00

50.50

50.00

49.50

Mar   Apr

Directional Signal: Close below the Low of the High Day

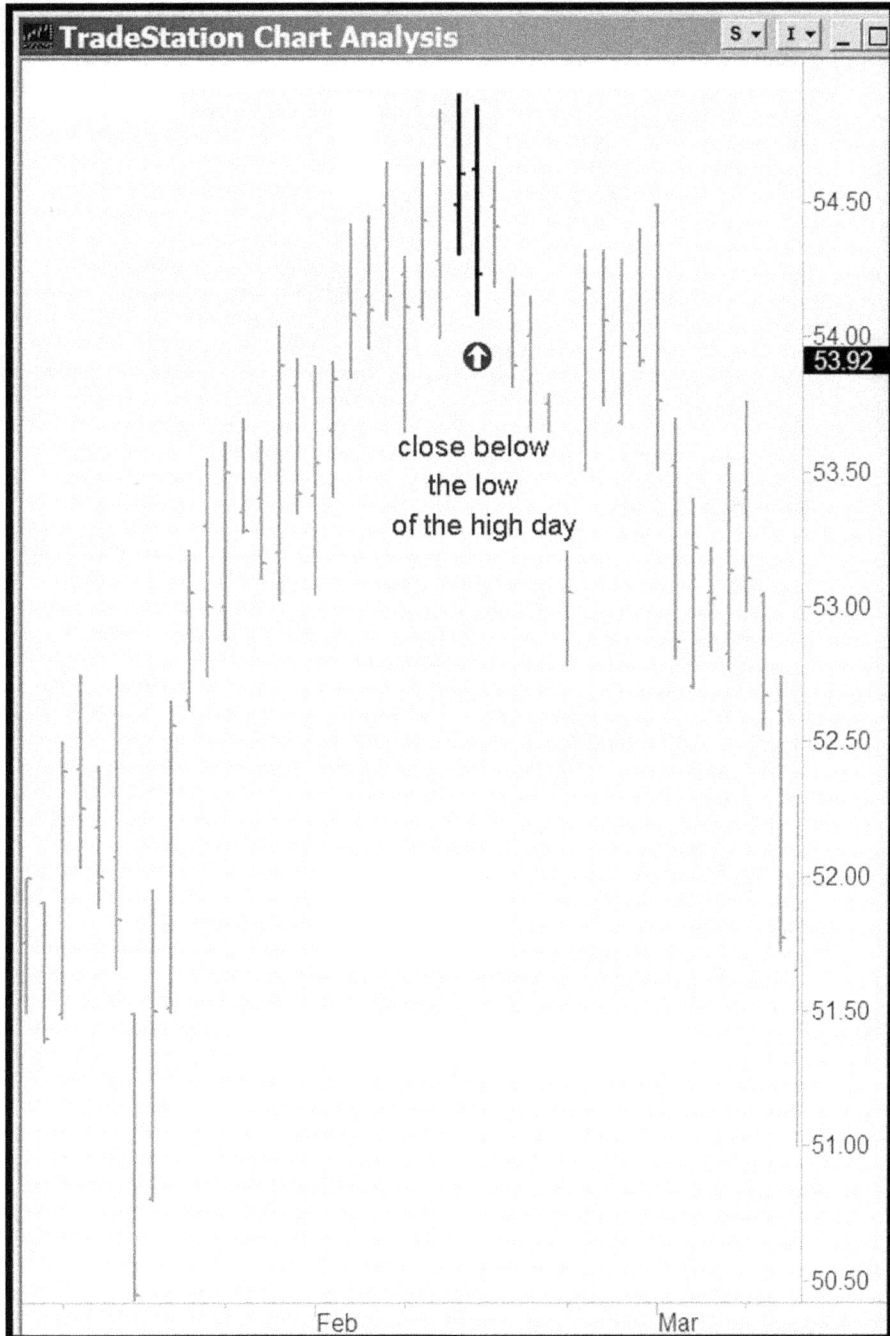

TradeStation Chart Analysis   S ▾ I ▾ _ □

close below
the low
of the high day

54.50

54.00
53.92

53.50

53.00

52.50

52.00

51.50

51.00

50.50

Feb   Mar

Directional Signal: Divergence between Oscillators

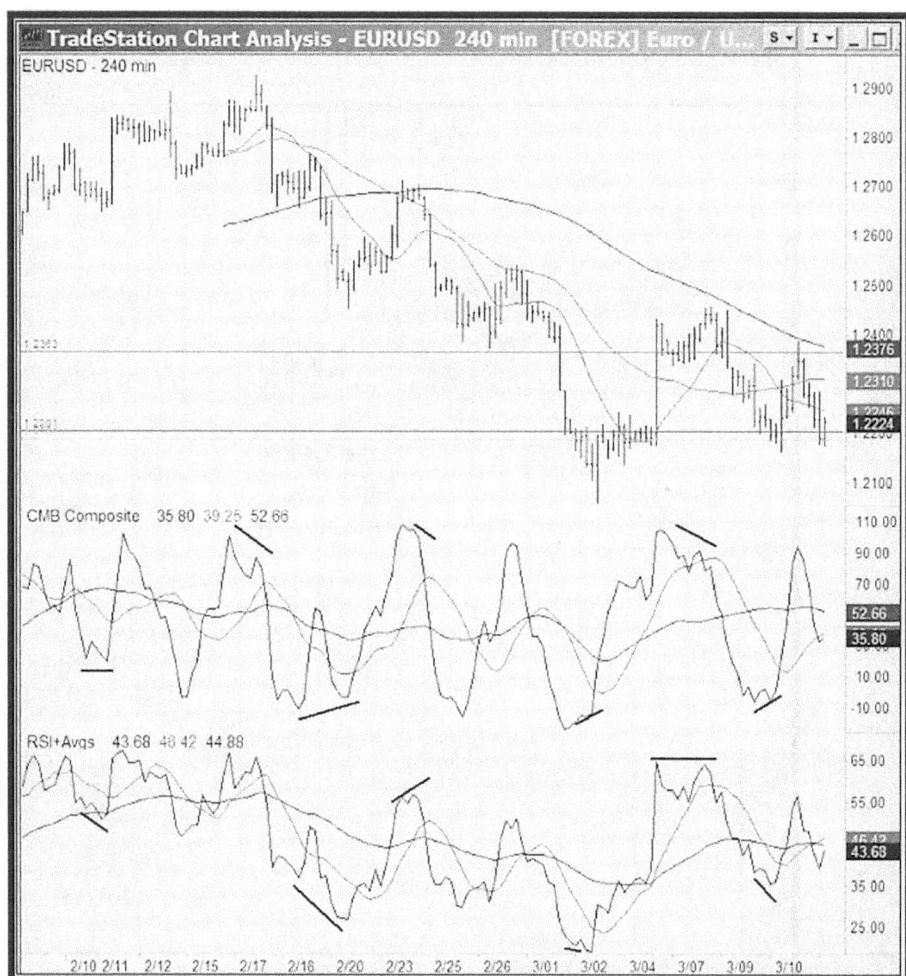

Directional Signal: Exhaustion Gap

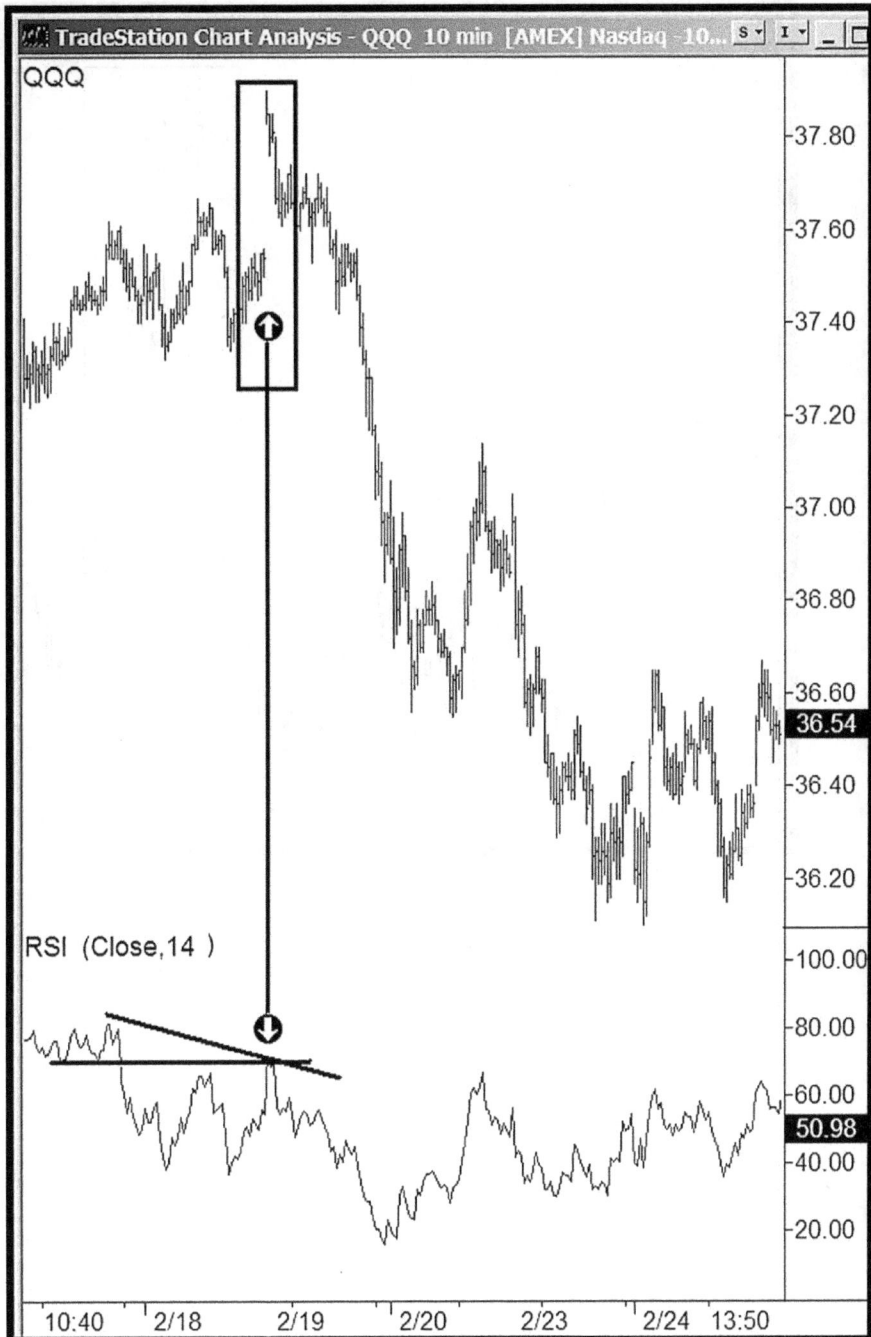

Directional Signal: Island Reversal (Bar or Candlesticks)

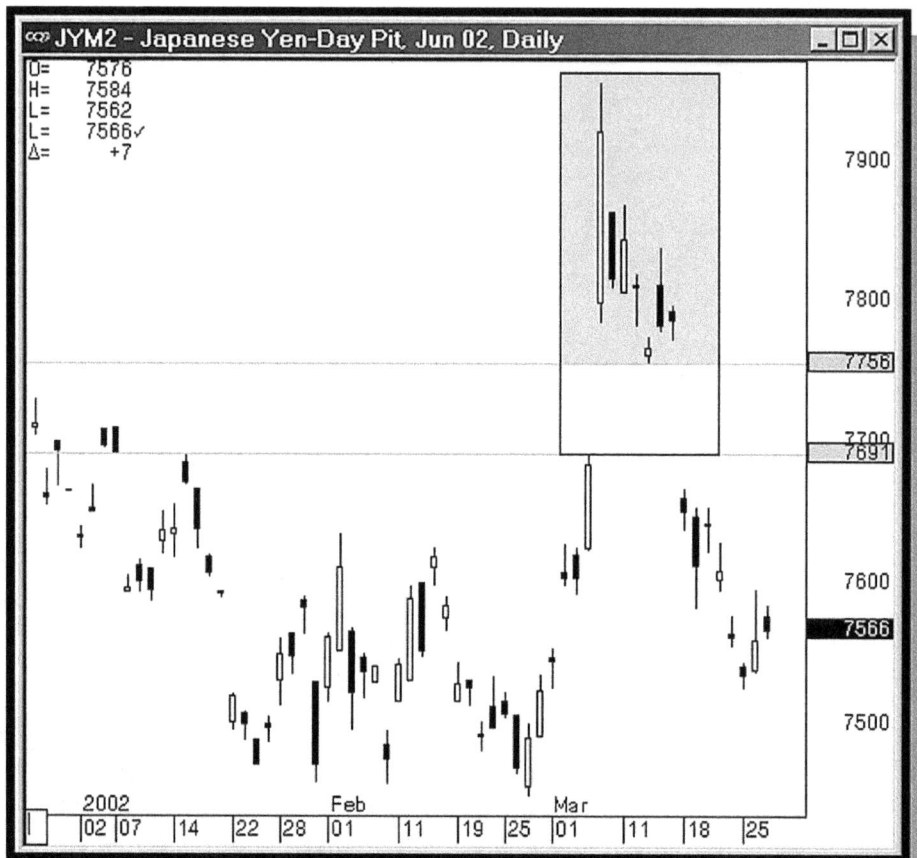

Directional Signal: Key Reversal

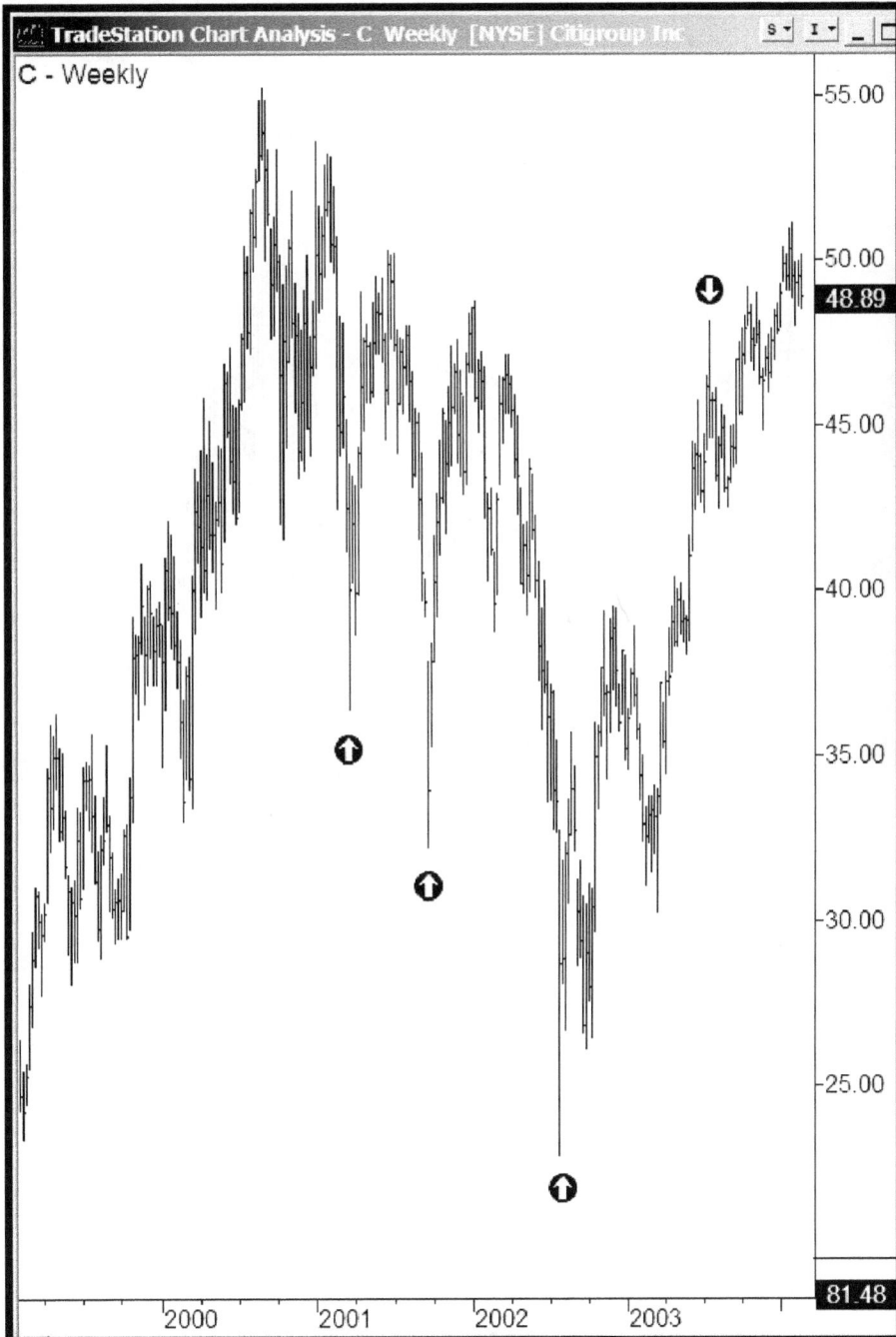

Directional Signal: Railway Tracks

Directional Signal: Reversal Day

TradeStation Chart Analysis - Daily [NY...

Elliott Wave Applied to Point-and-Figure

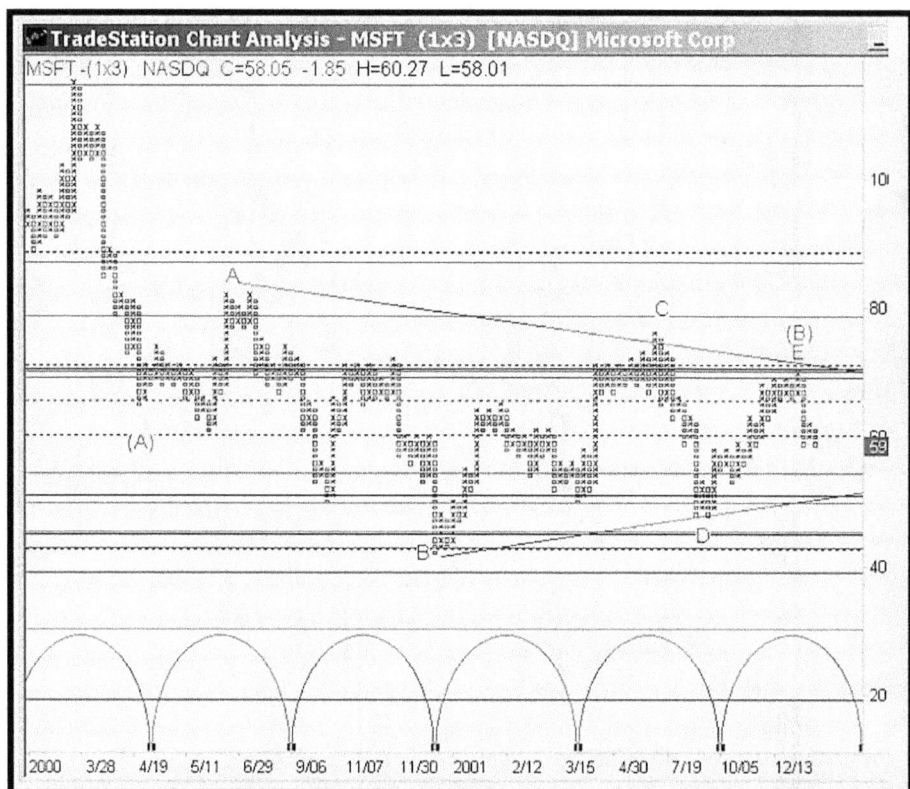

TradeStation Chart Analysis - MSFT (1x3) [NASDQ] Microsoft Corp

MSFT -(1x3) NASDQ C=58.05 -1.85 H=60.27 L=58.01

Elliott Wave: Corrective Waves in Five-Wave Rally

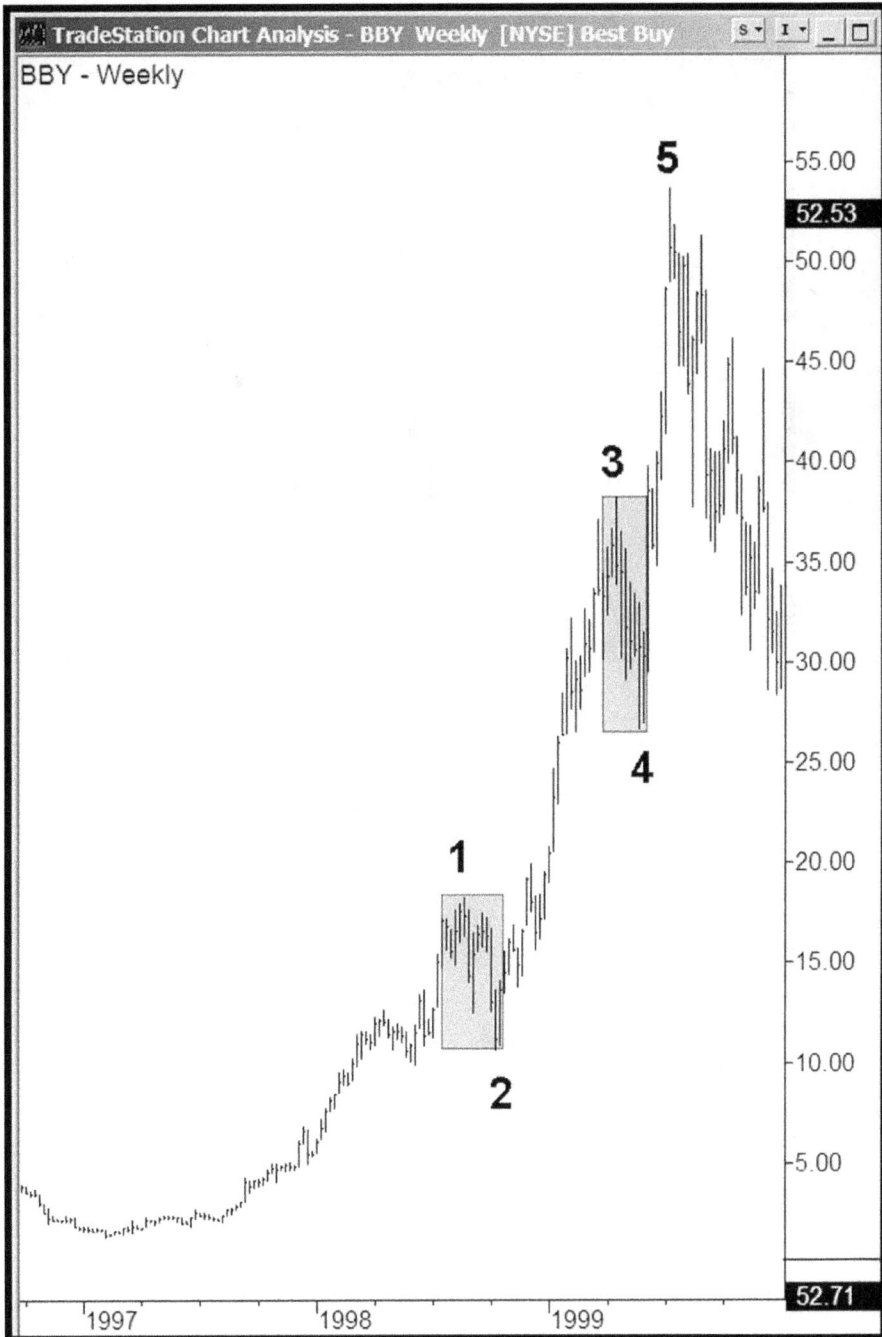

Elliott Wave: Expanded Flat Rally
within an Expanded Flat Correction

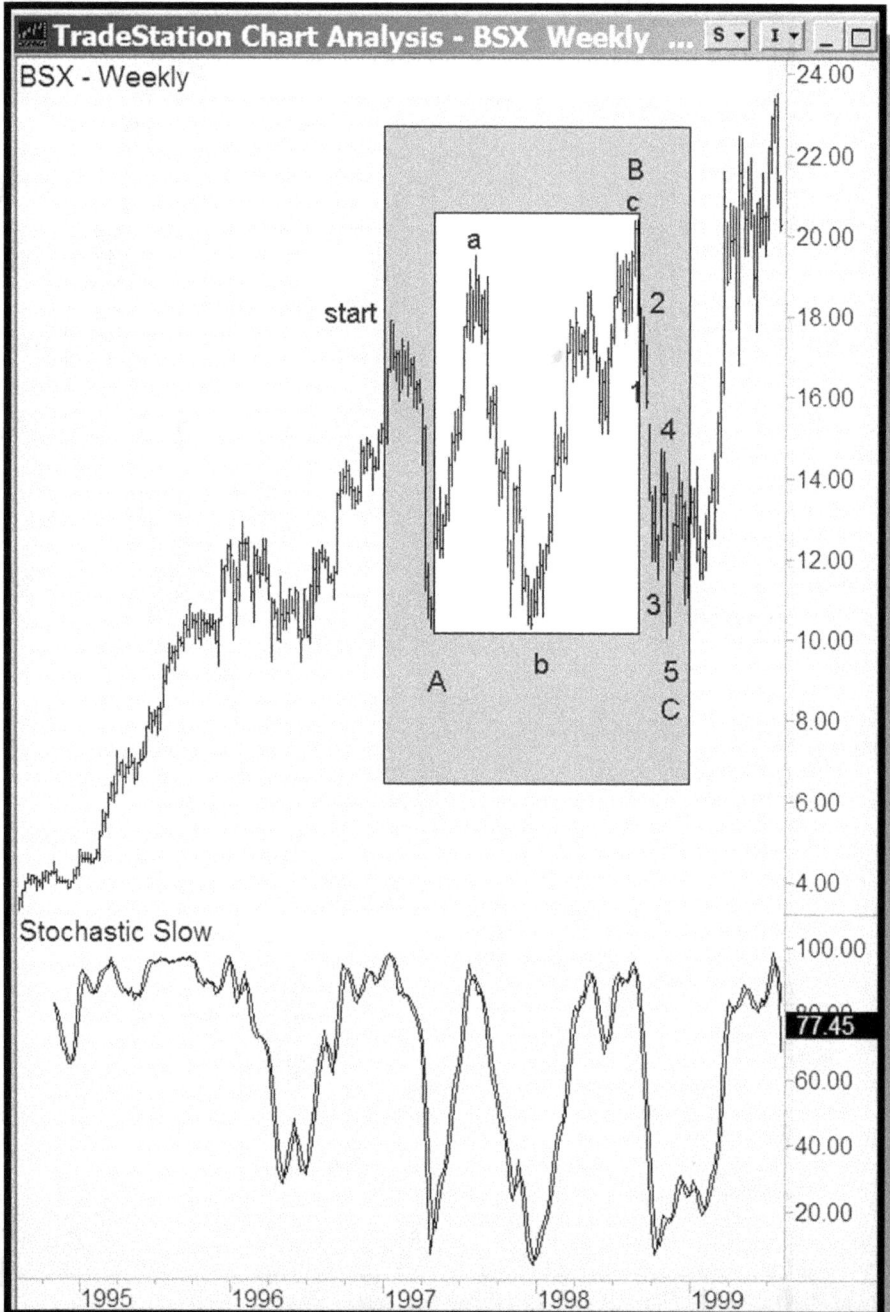

Elliott Wave: Impulsive Waves in Five-Wave Rally

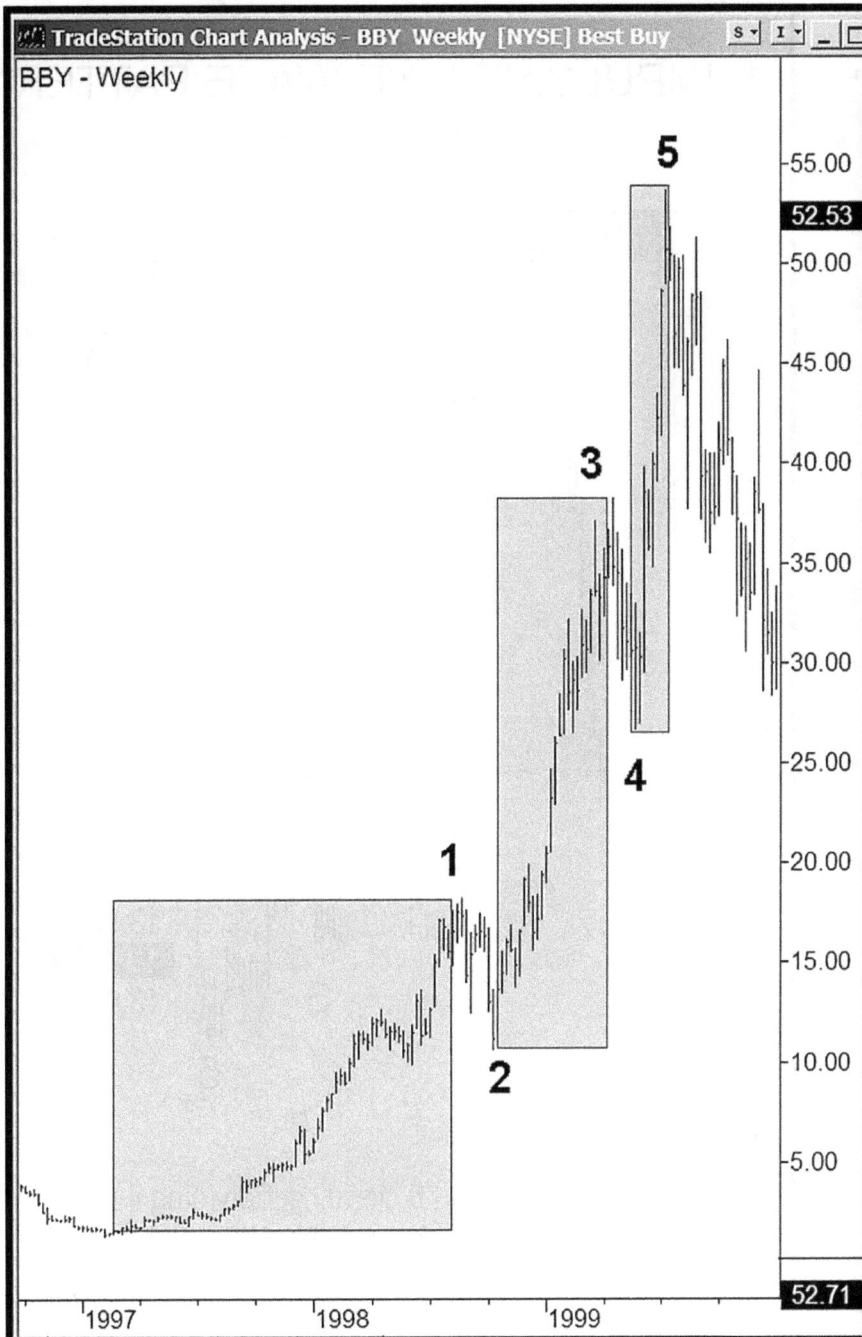

Elliott Wave: Pattern 1

1. IMPULSIVE FIVE WAVE PATTERN

WAVES 1, 3, and 5 clearly subdividing into the required simple five wave substructure.

Elliott Wave: Pattern 2

2. EXTENDING FIVE WAVE PATTERN

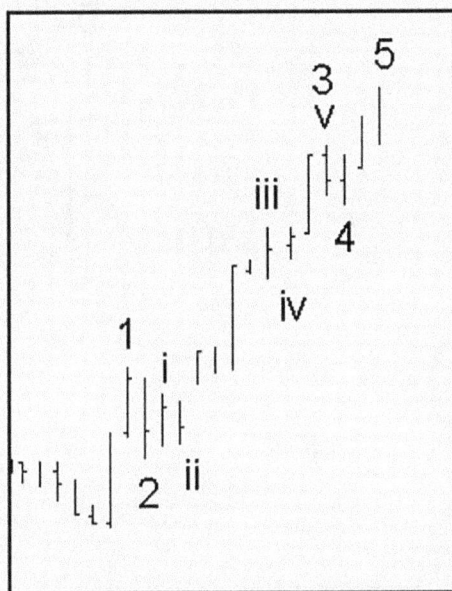

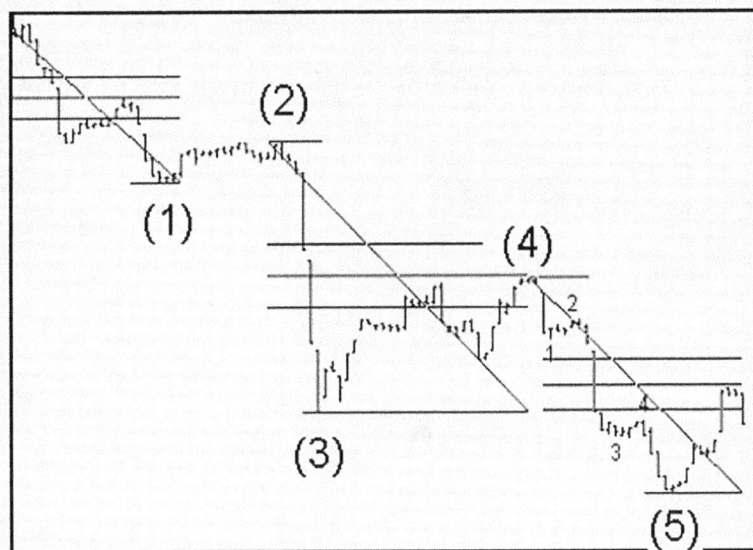

Elliott Wave: Patterns 3 and 4

3. A FAILURE FIFTH WAVE

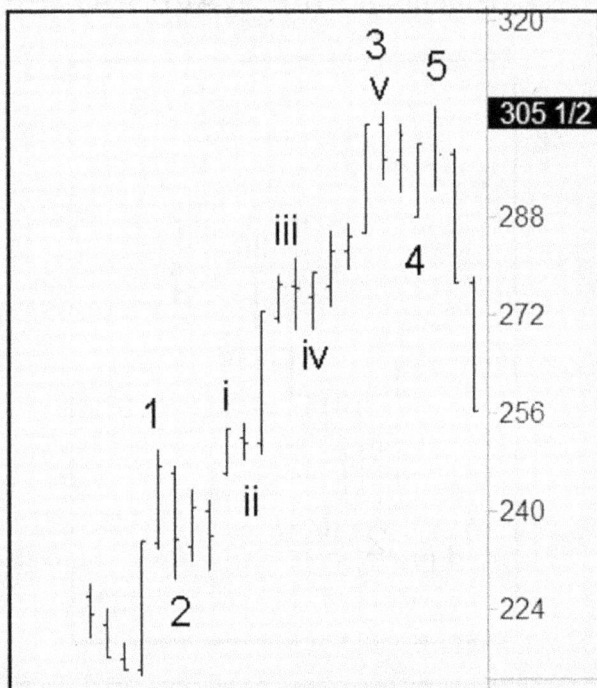

4. DIAGONAL TRIANGLE (Termination Wedge)

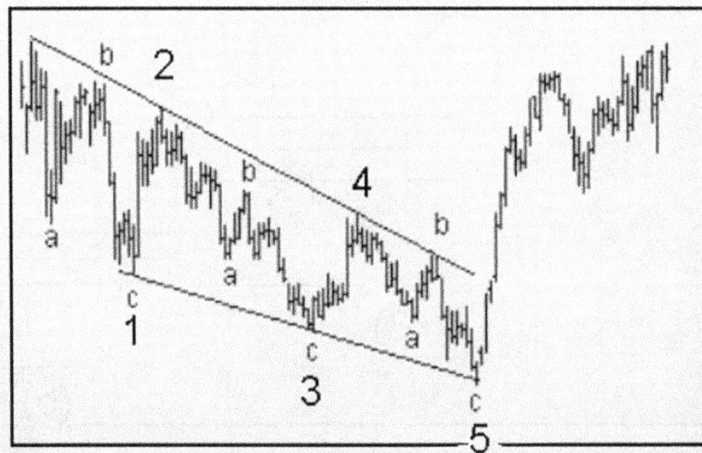

Elliott Wave: Pattern 5

5. CORRECTIVE ZIGZAG

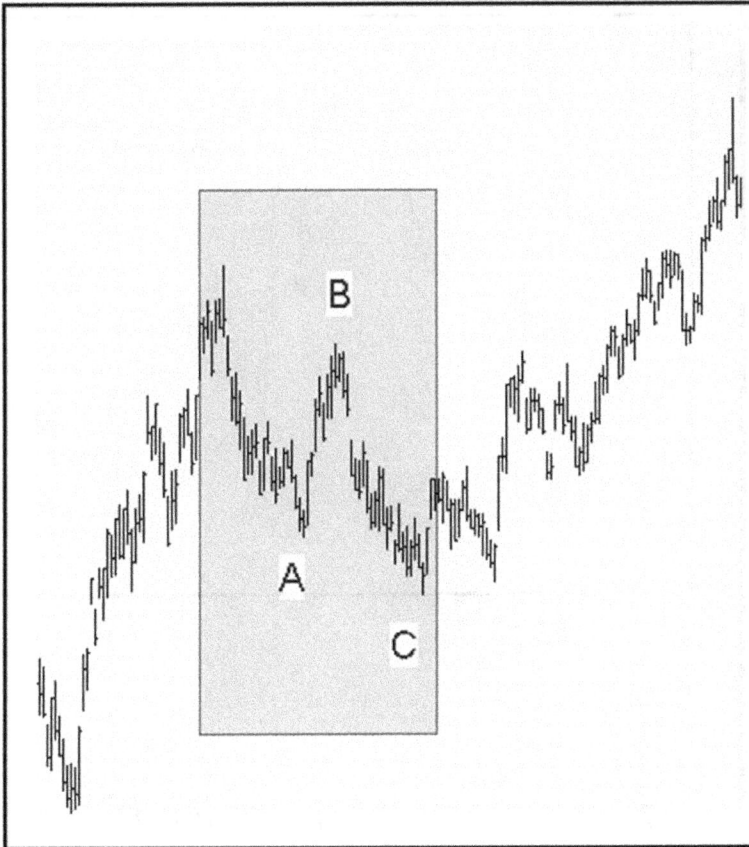

Elliott Wave: Patterns 6 and 7

6. CORRECTIVE DOUBLE ZIGZAG

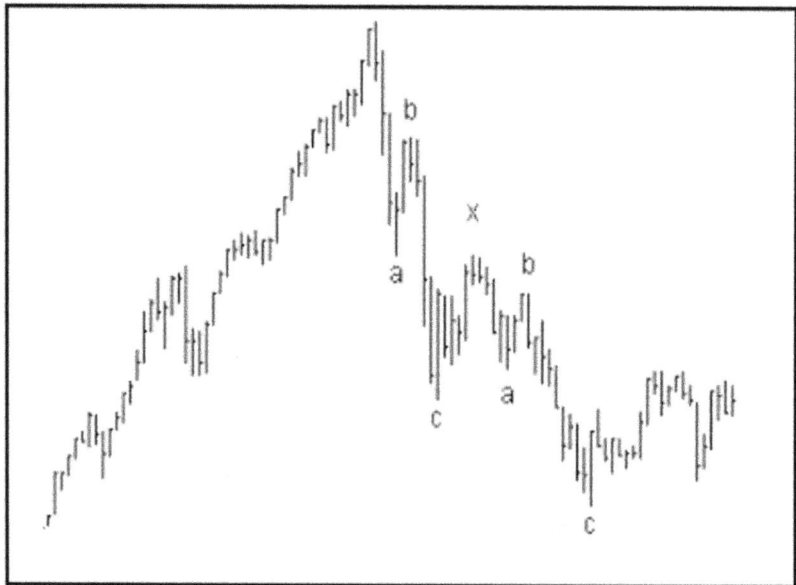

7. CORRECTIVE TRIPLE ZIGZAG
(Example: The Great Crash)

Elliott Wave: Pattern 8

8. CORRECTIVE EXPANDED FLAT

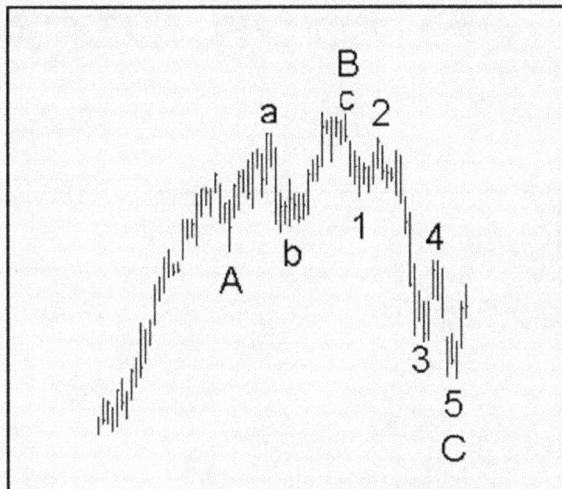

Wave A is an Expanded Flat within a larger Expanded Flat

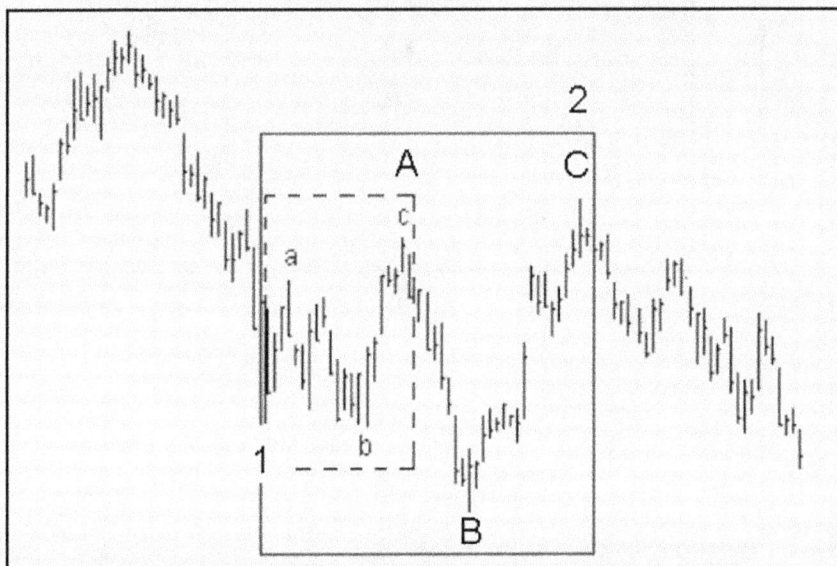

Elliott Wave: Pattern 9

9. CORRECTIVE FLAT

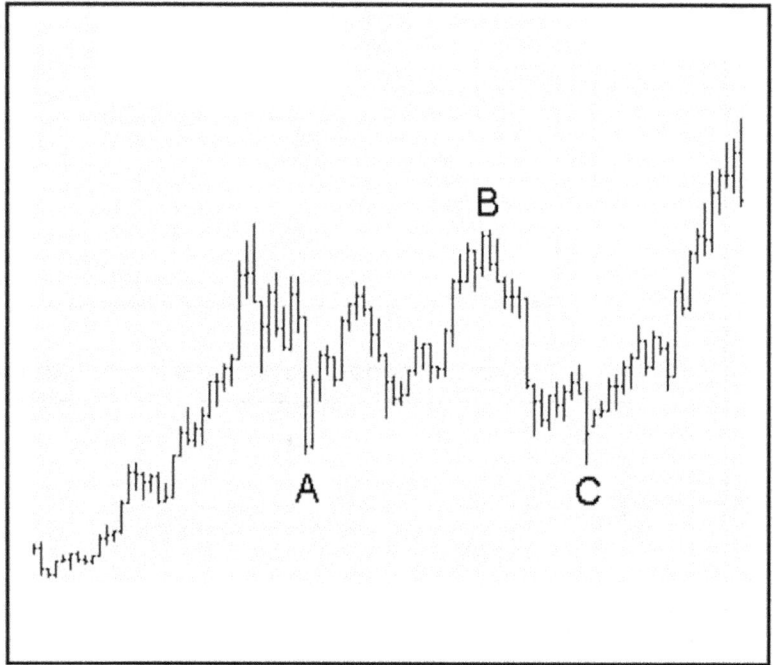

Elliott Wave: Patterns 10 and 11

10. CORRECTIVE EXPANDING TRIANGLE

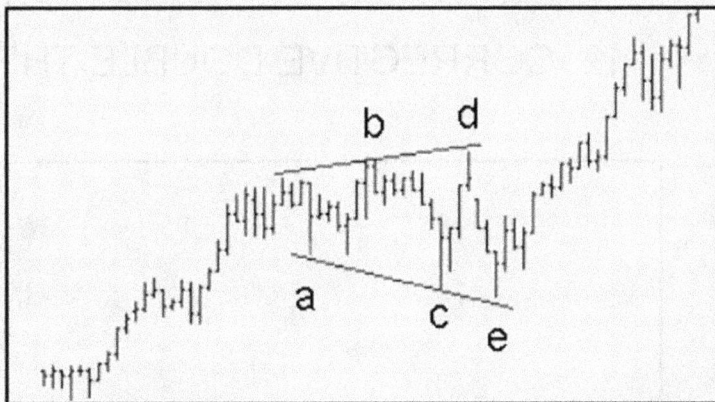

11. CORRECTIVE CONTRACTING TRIANGLE

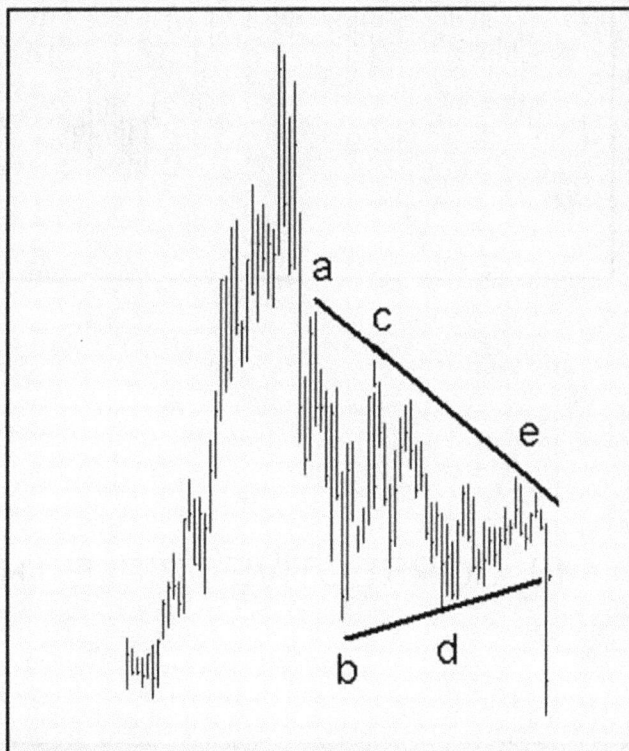

Elliott Wave: Patterns 12 and 13

12. CORRECTIVE DOUBLE THREES

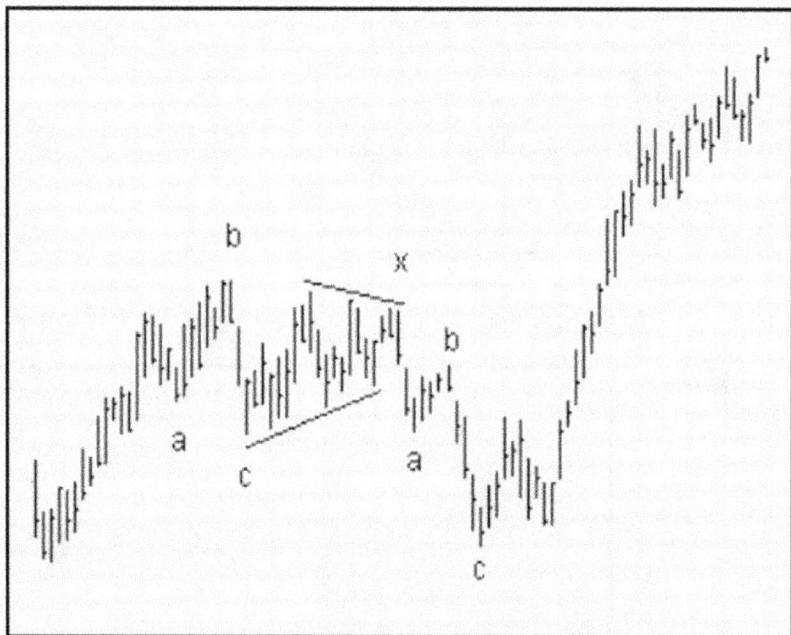

13. CORRECTIVE TRIPLE THREES

Elliott Wave: Retracement to the Vicinity of a Previous 4th Wave

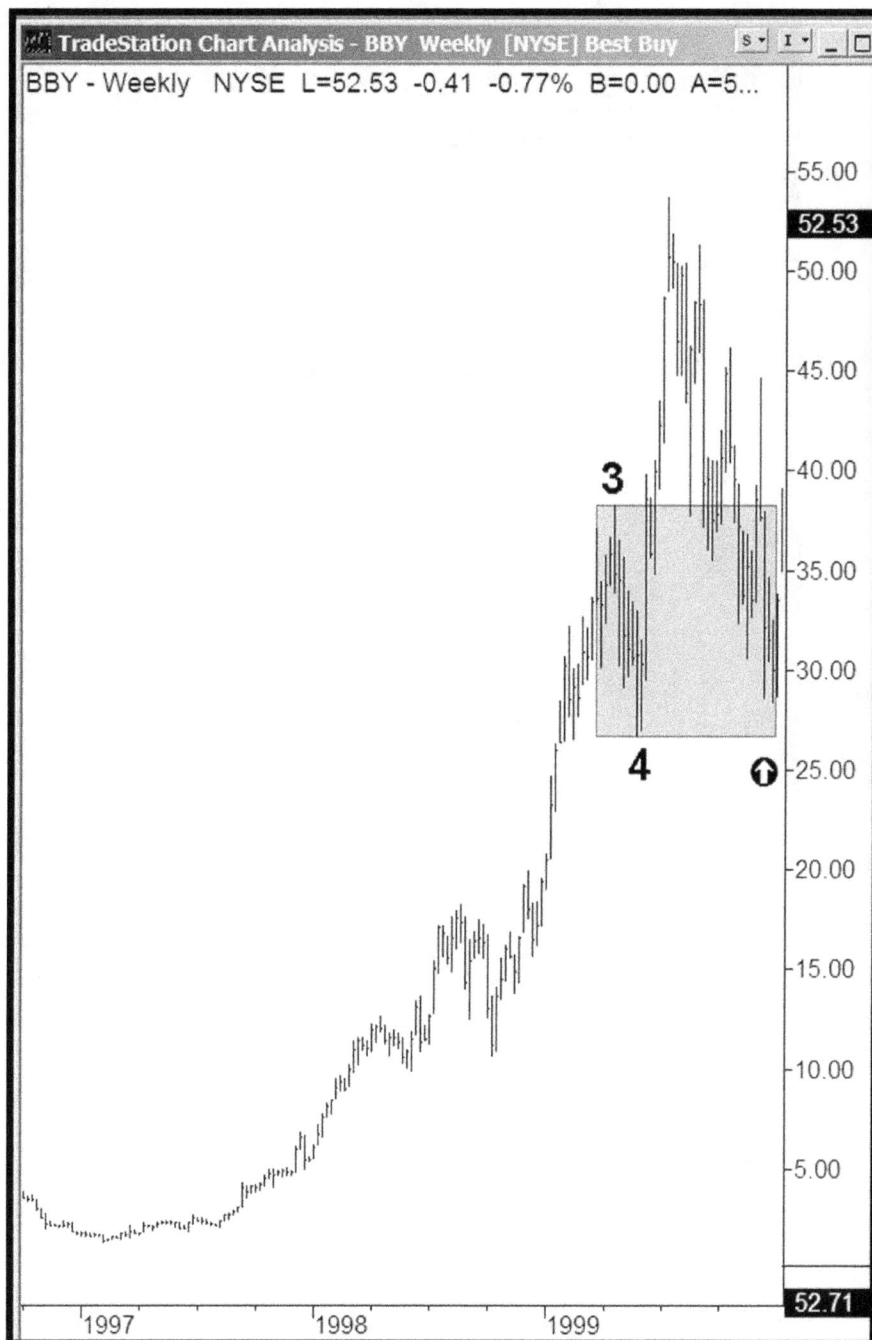

Elliott Wave: Strongest Global Stock Index

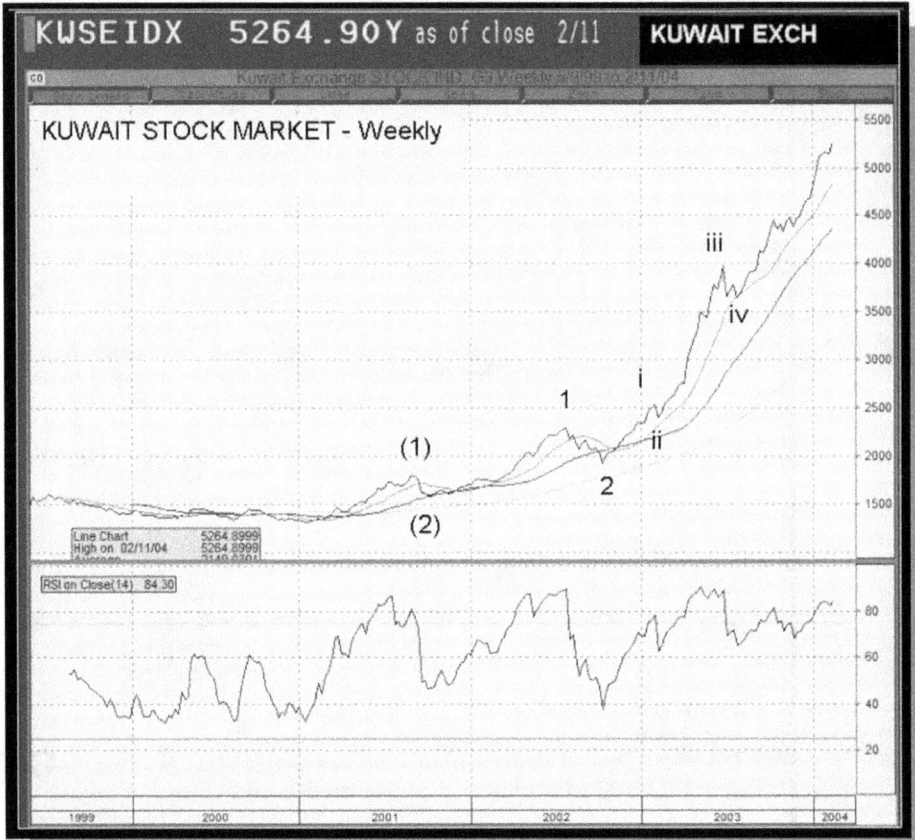

KWSEIDX   5264.90Y as of close 2/11   KUWAIT EXCH

KUWAIT STOCK MARKET - Weekly

Elliott Wave: Third-of-Third Wave

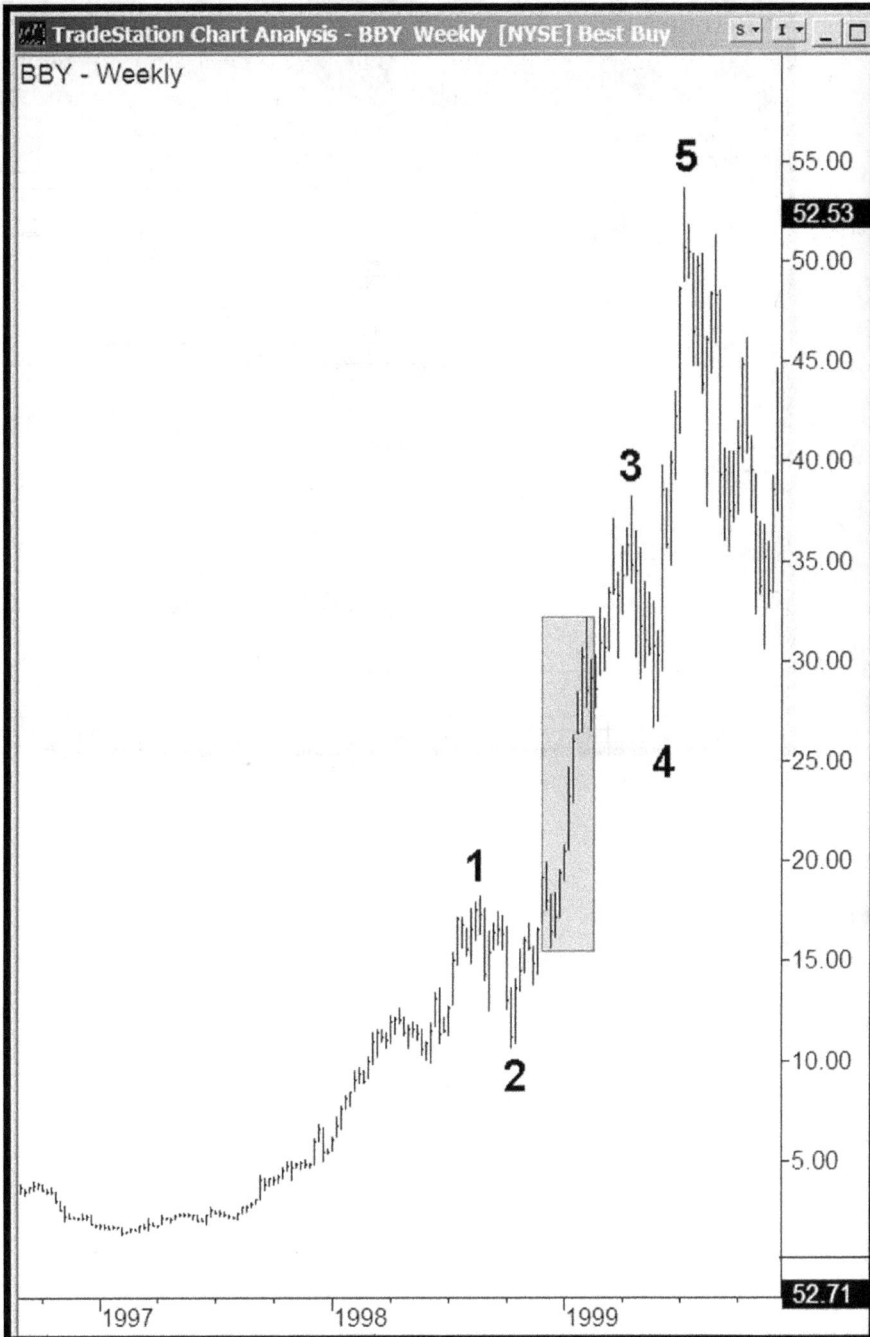

Entry Signal: Fibonacci Confluence Zone

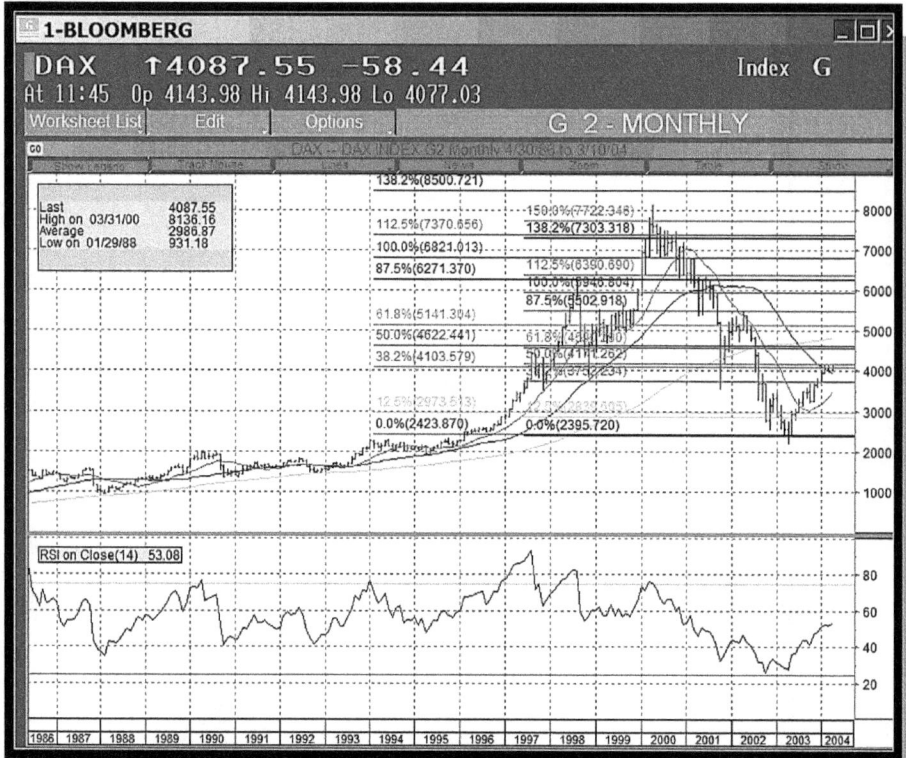

Entry Signal: Following Stochastic Flutter

Entry Signal: Head-and-Shoulder Lowest Risk

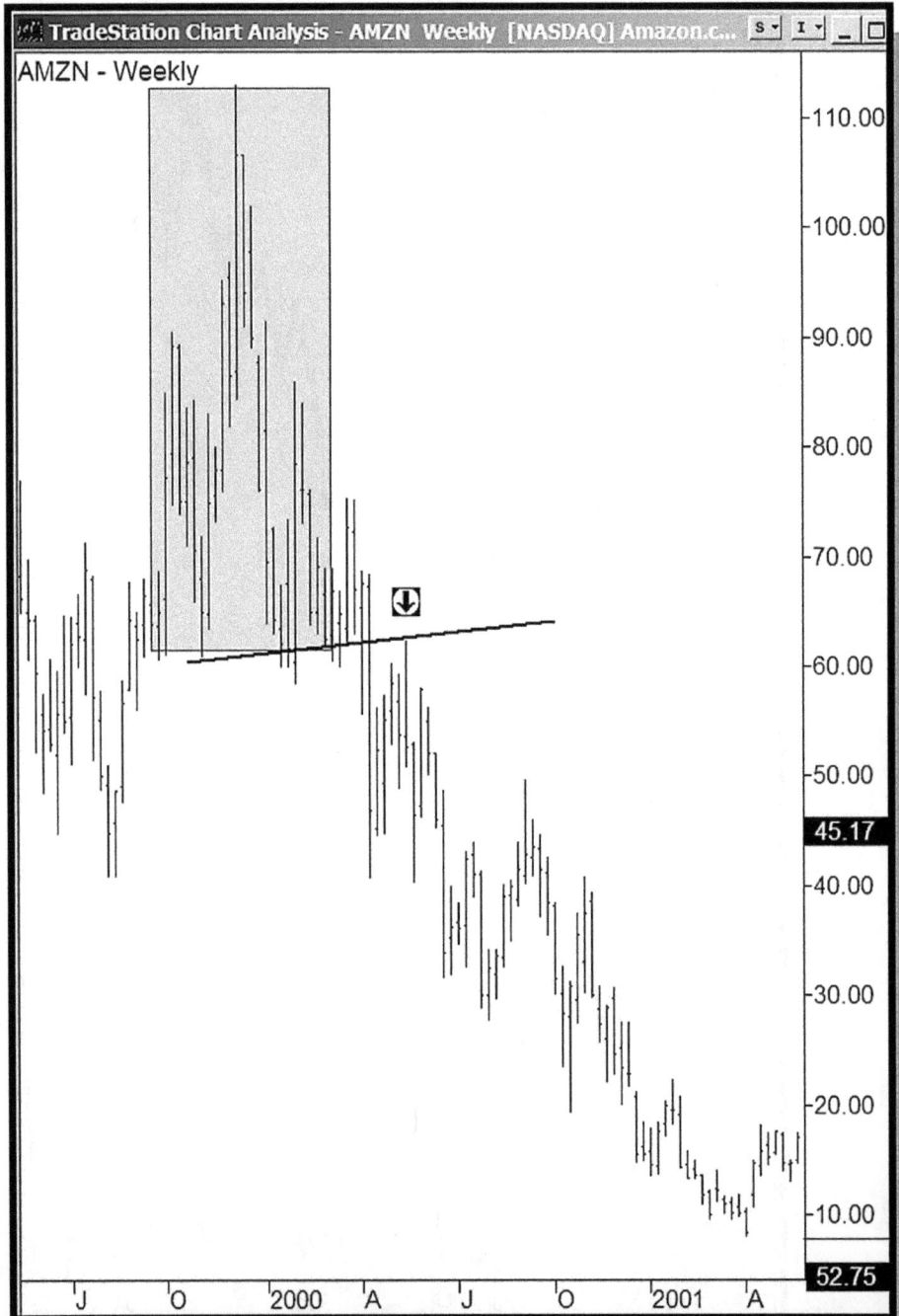

Entry Signal: Key Reversal Becomes Resistance

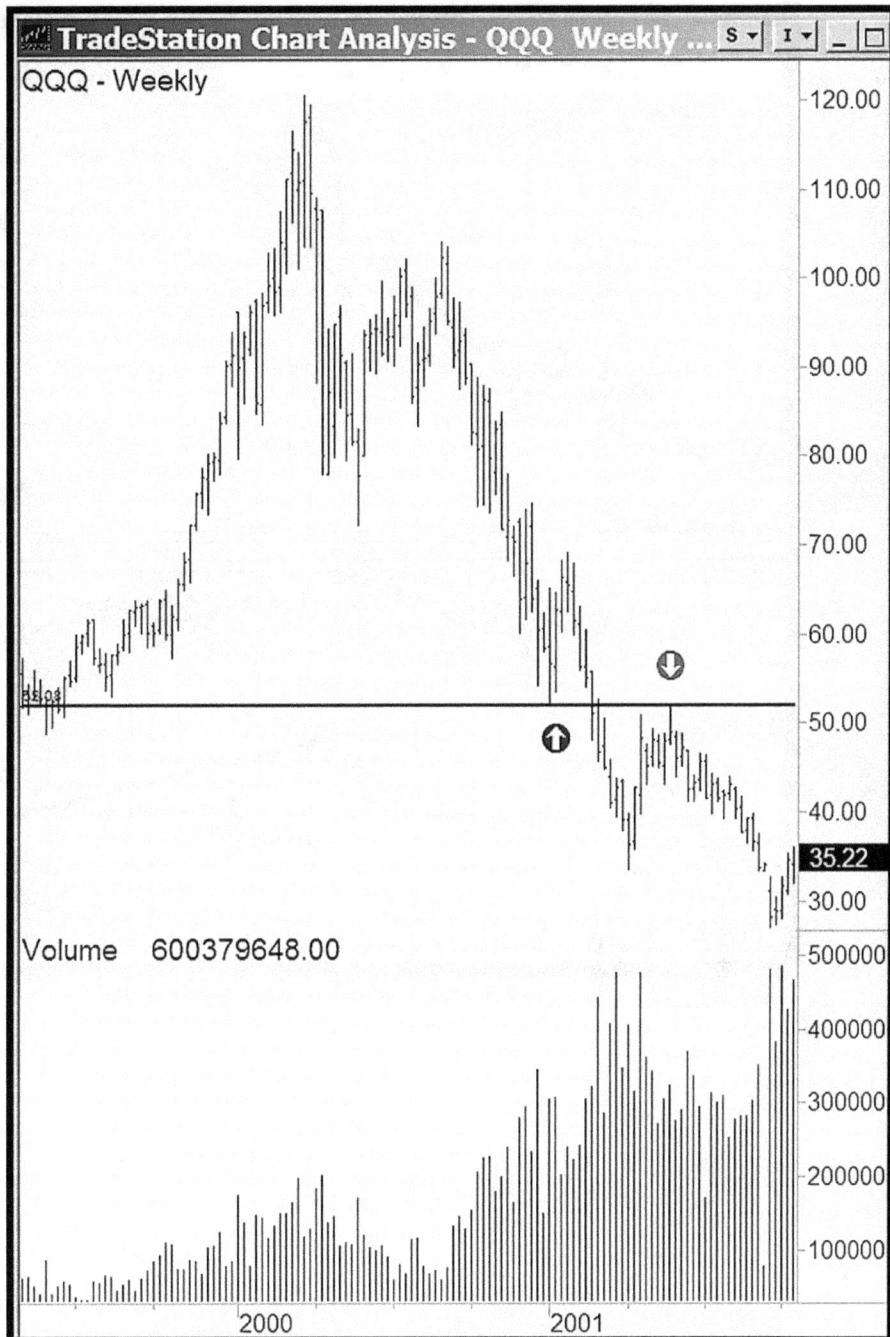

Entry Signal: Multiple Confluence Resistances

Entry Signal: Oscillator Confirmation in Different Time Charts 1

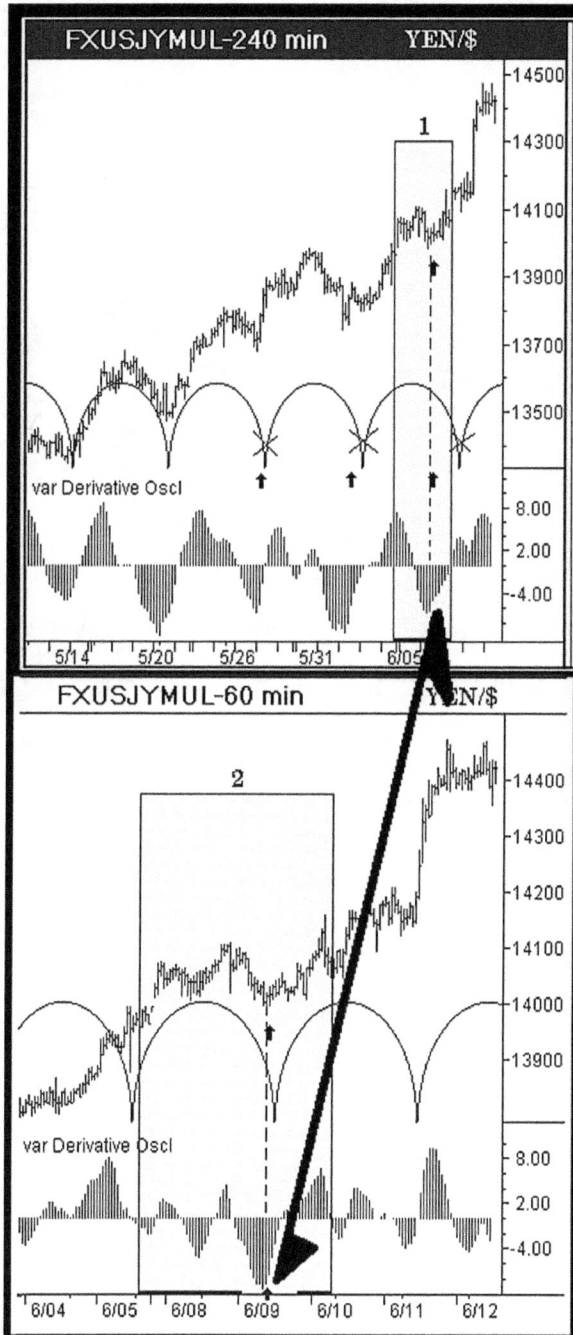

Entry Signal: Oscillator Confirmation in Different Time Charts 2

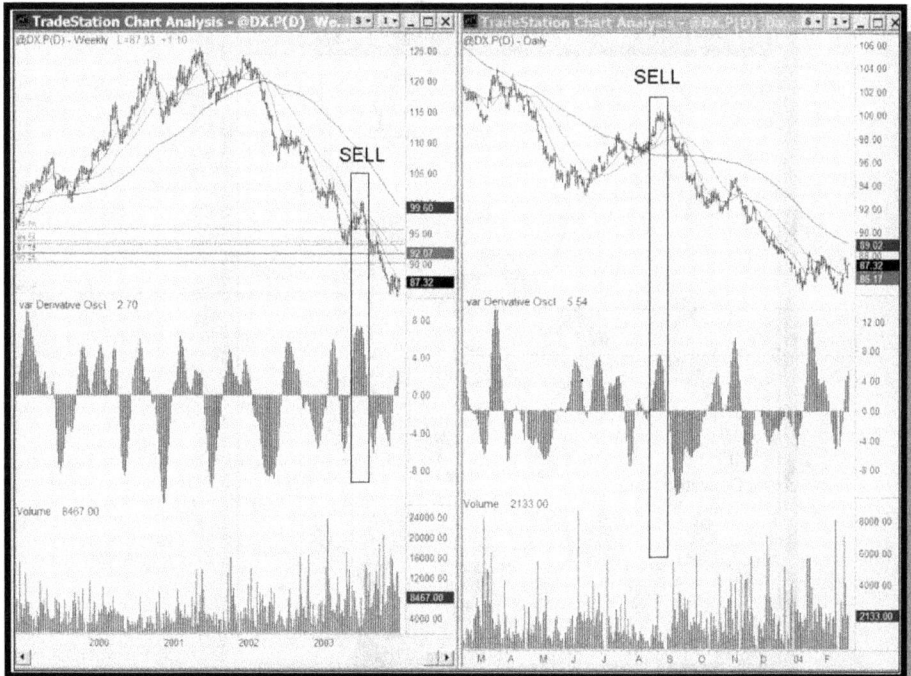

Entry Signal: Oscillator Confirmation in Different Time Charts 3

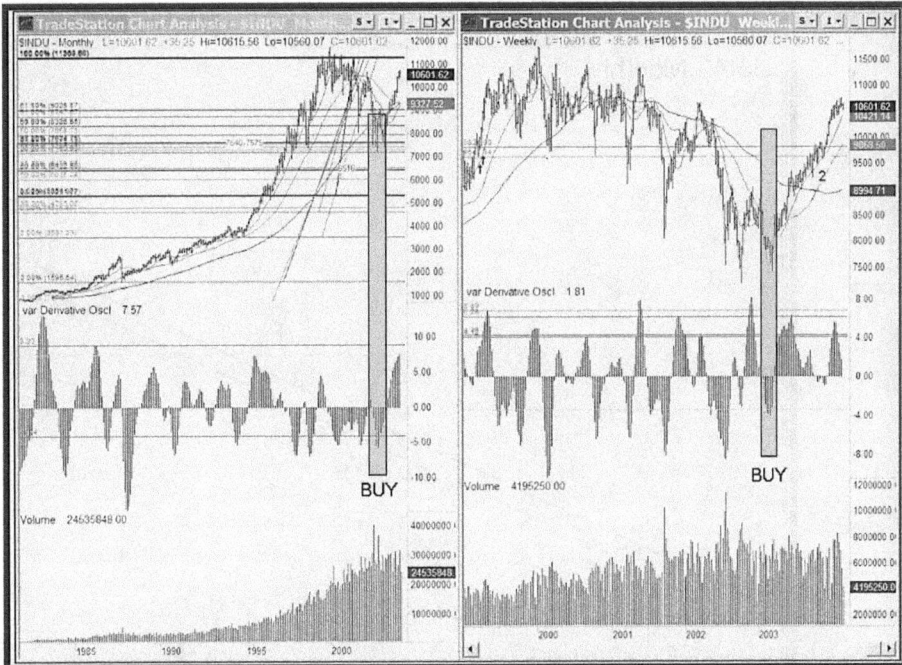

Entry Signal: Prior Horizontal Indicator Pivot

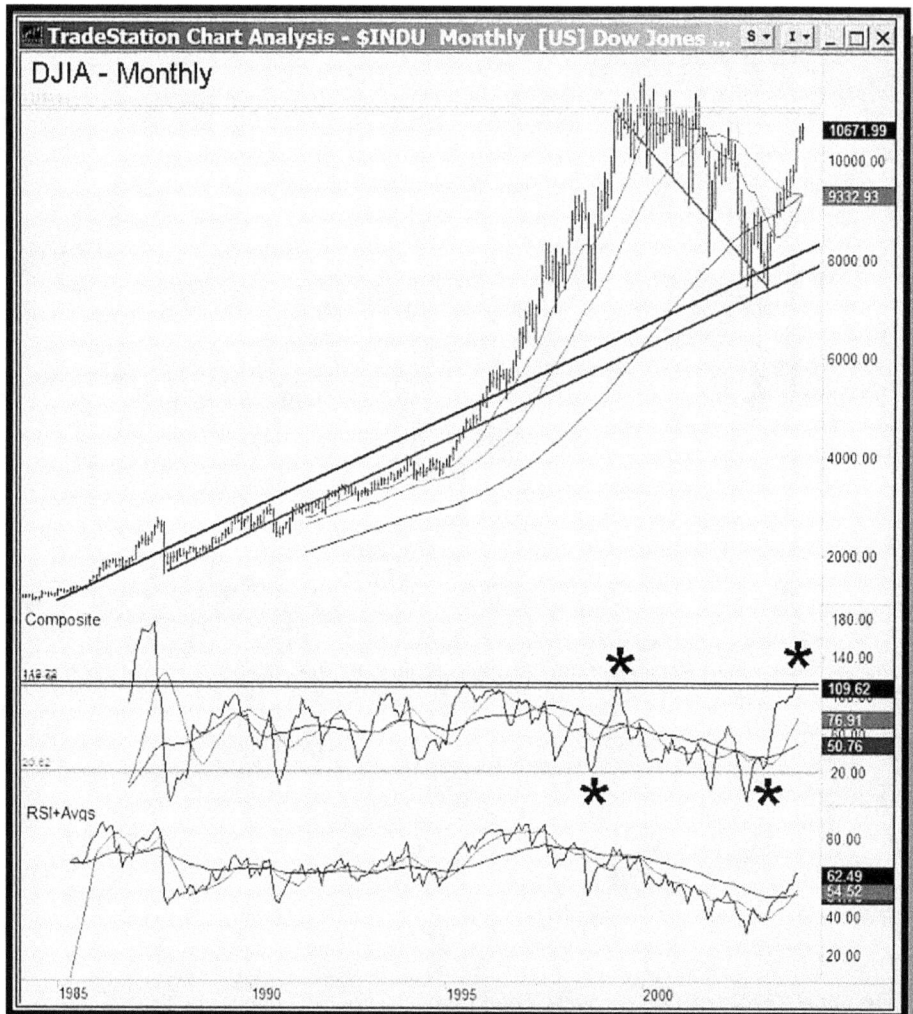

Entry Signal: Resistance Becomes Support

Entry Signal: Stochastic Buy at 80

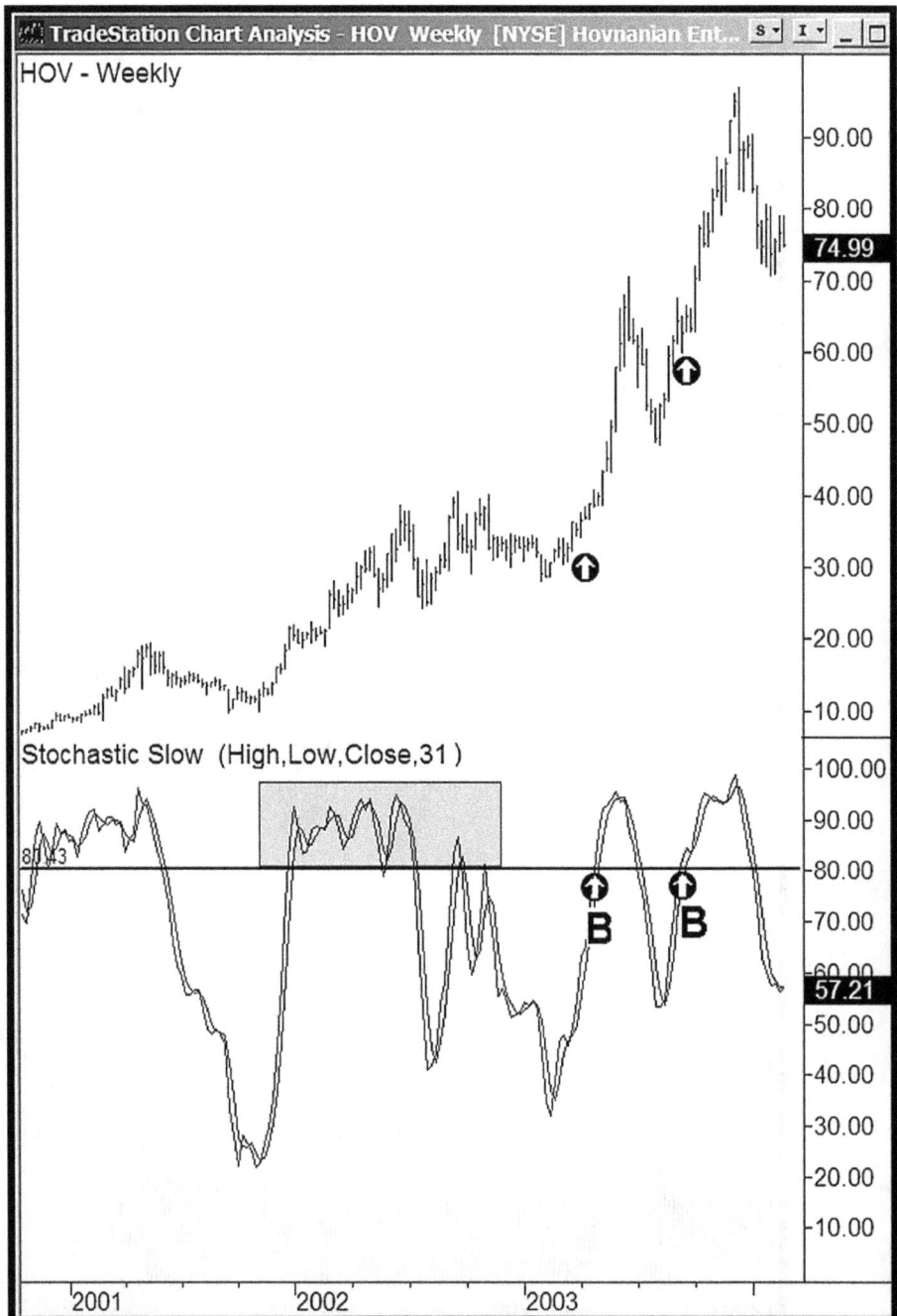

Entry Signal: Stochastic Sell at 20

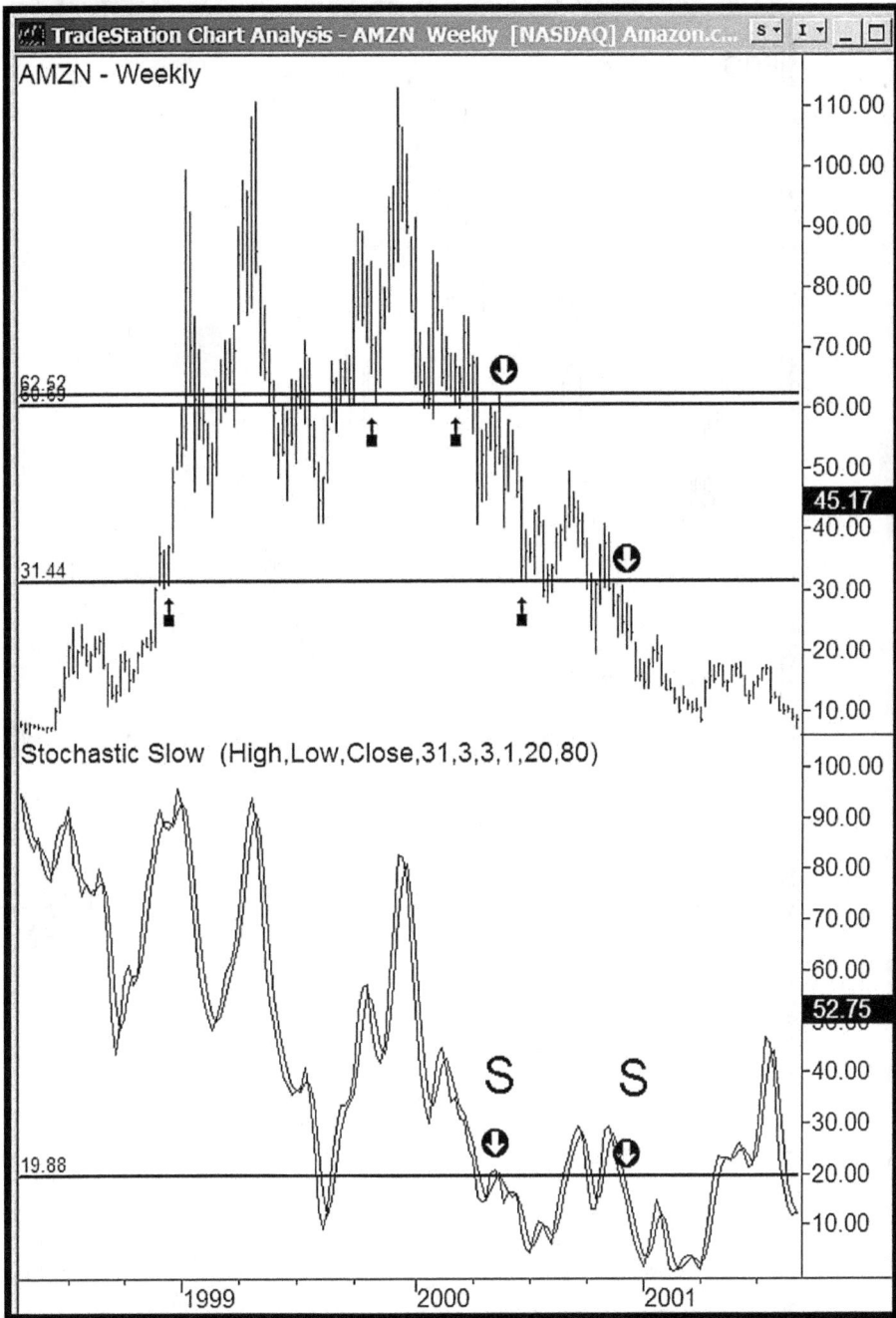

TradeStation Chart Analysis - AMZN Weekly [NASDAQ] Amazon.c...

AMZN - Weekly

Stochastic Slow (High,Low,Close,31,3,3,1,20,80)

Entry Signal: Stochastic Low Risk

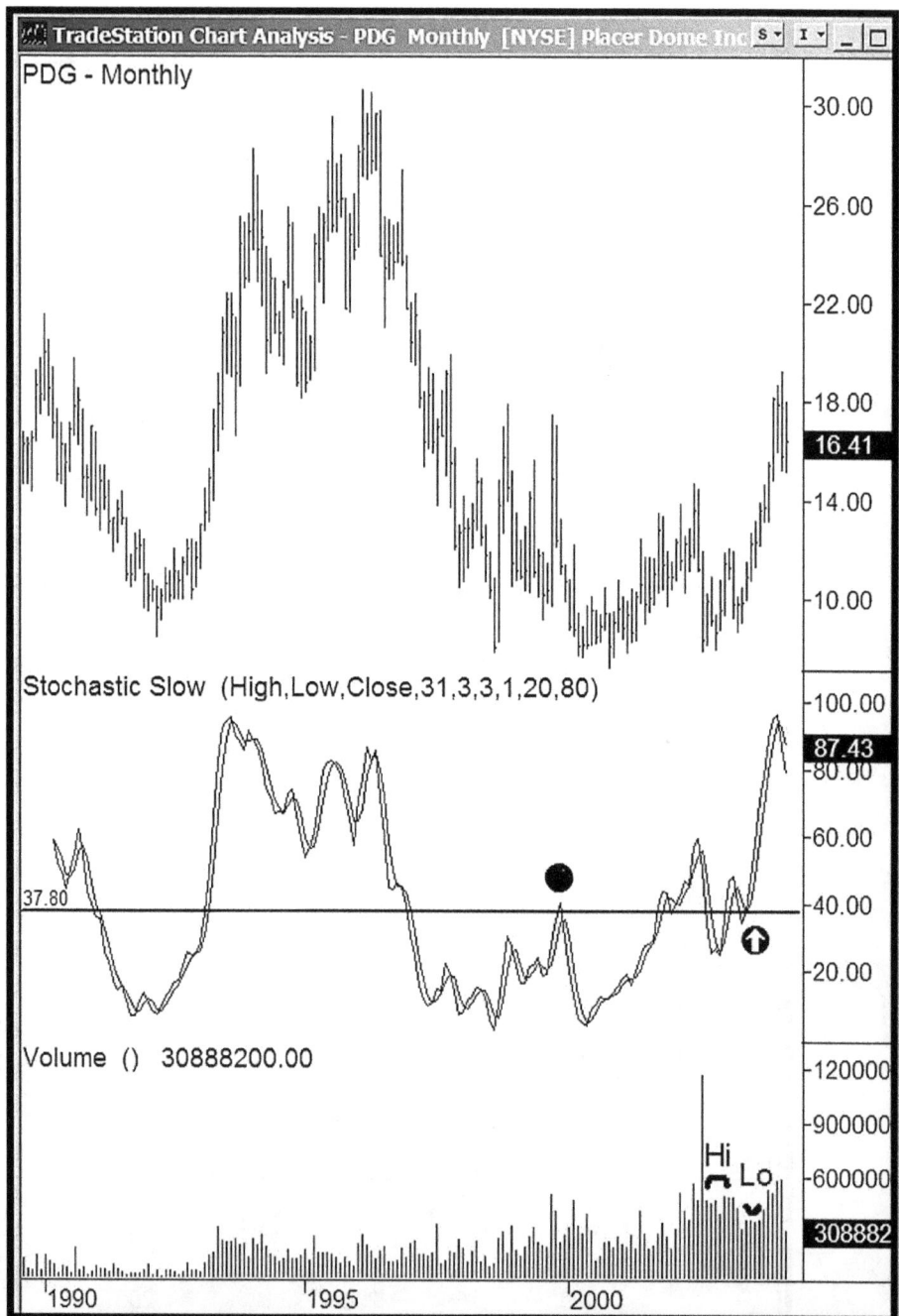

Entry Signal: Support Becomes Resistance

Entry Signal: Support within
Stochastics Confirmed by Lower Volume

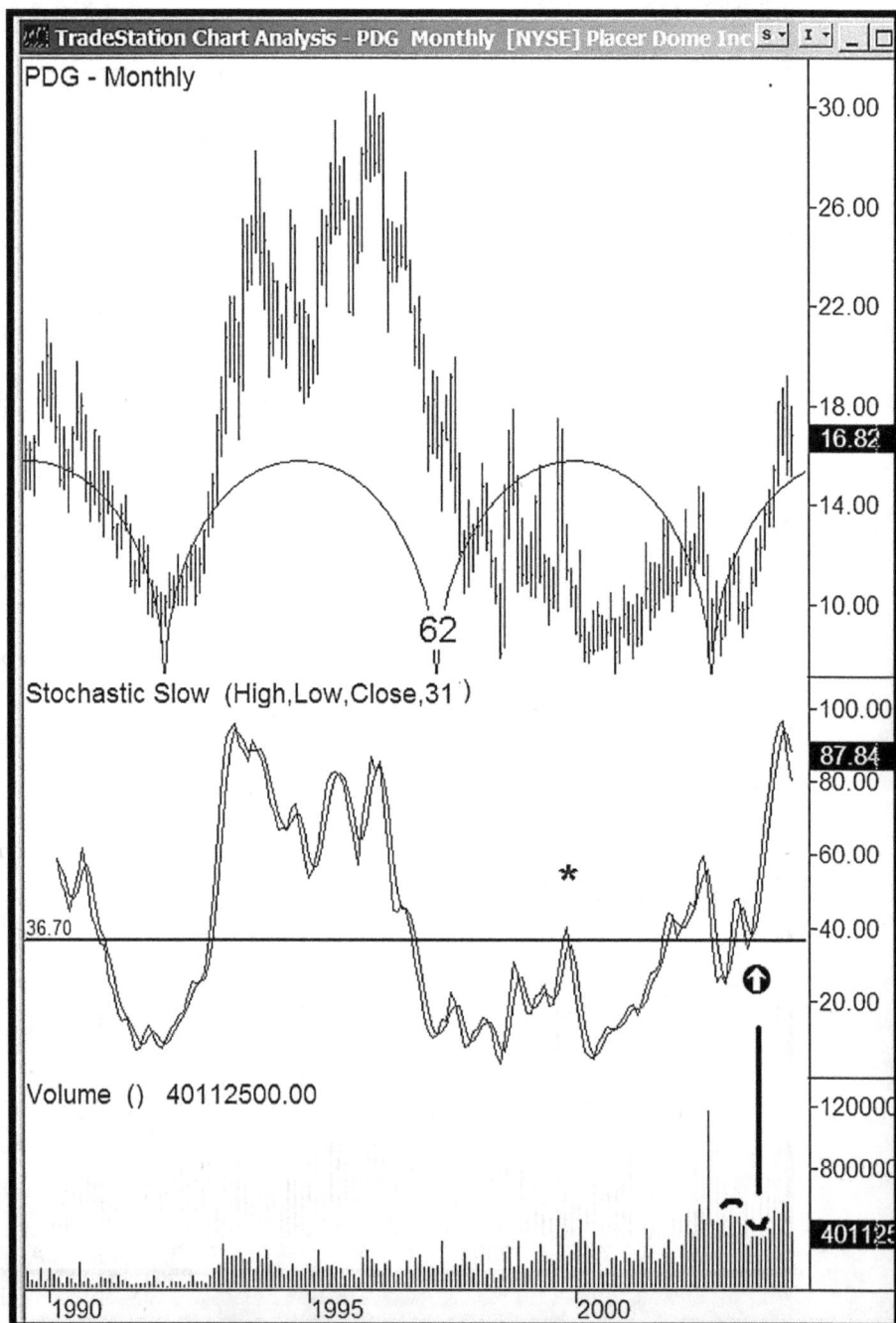

Entry Signal: Testing Converging Trendlines

Entry Signal: Testing Market Breakout

Entry Signal with Low Risk after Resistance Becomes Support

Exit Signal: Trailing Stop

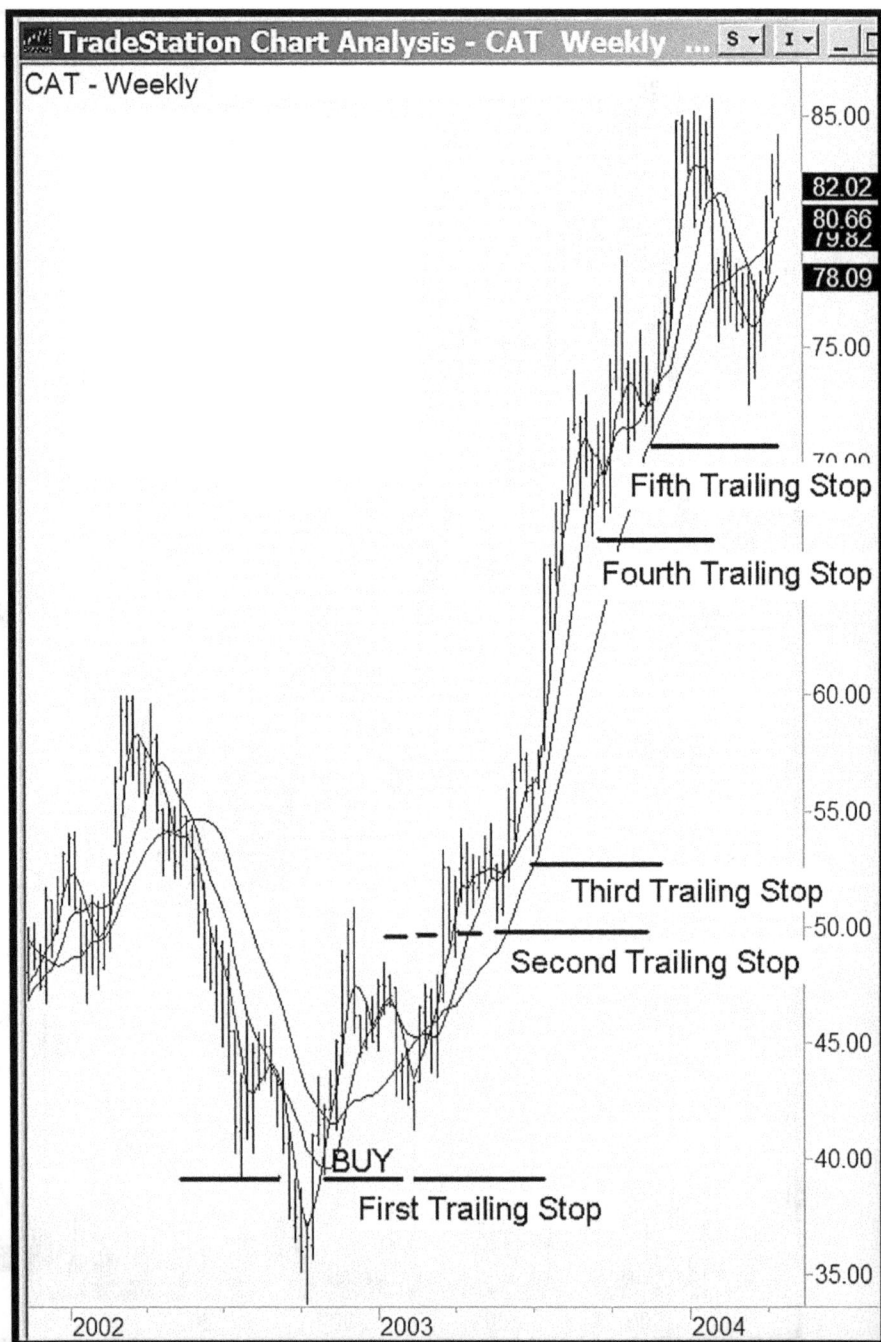

Fibonacci 50 Percent Retracement

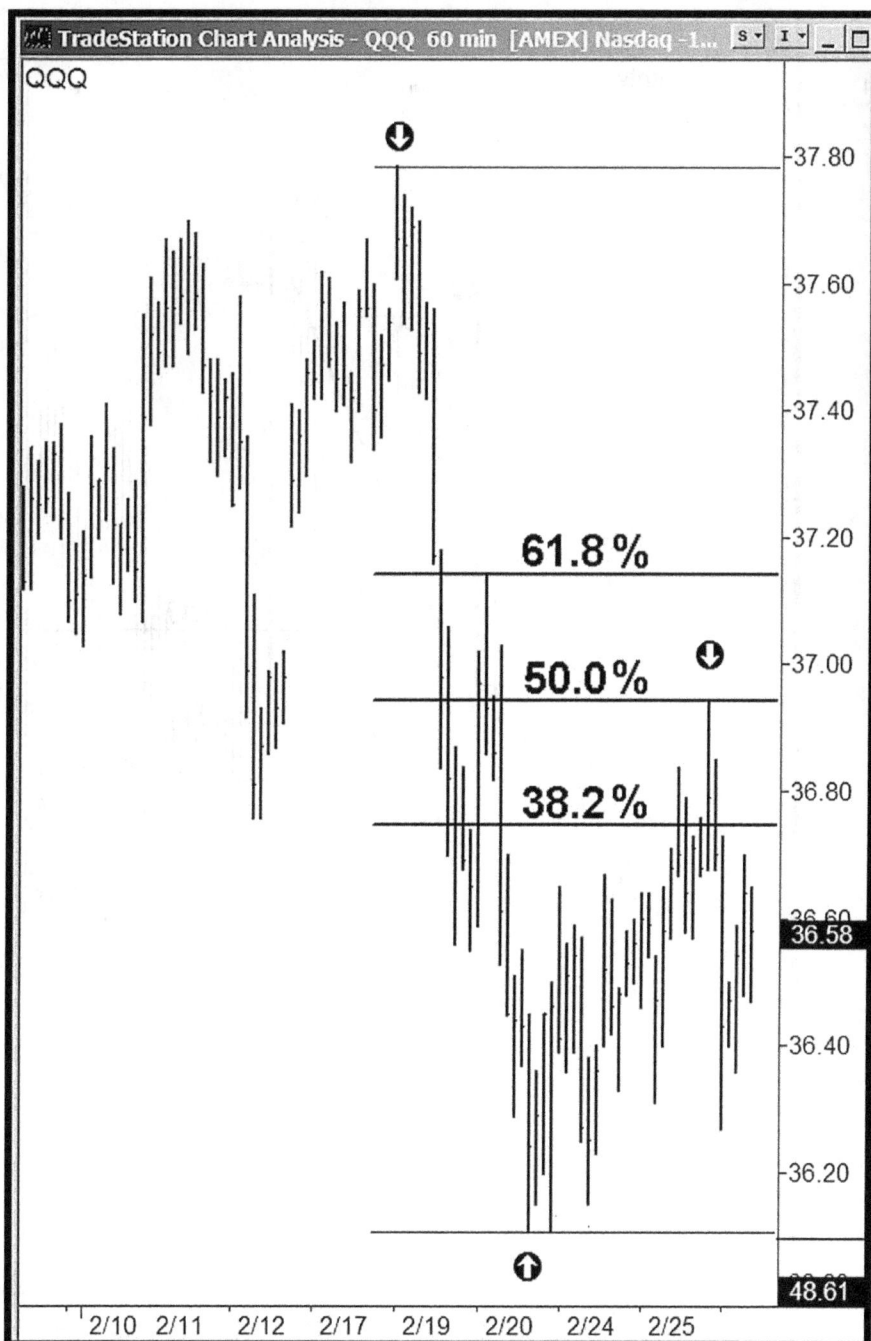

Fibonacci Price Projection: Bearish Extension Swing

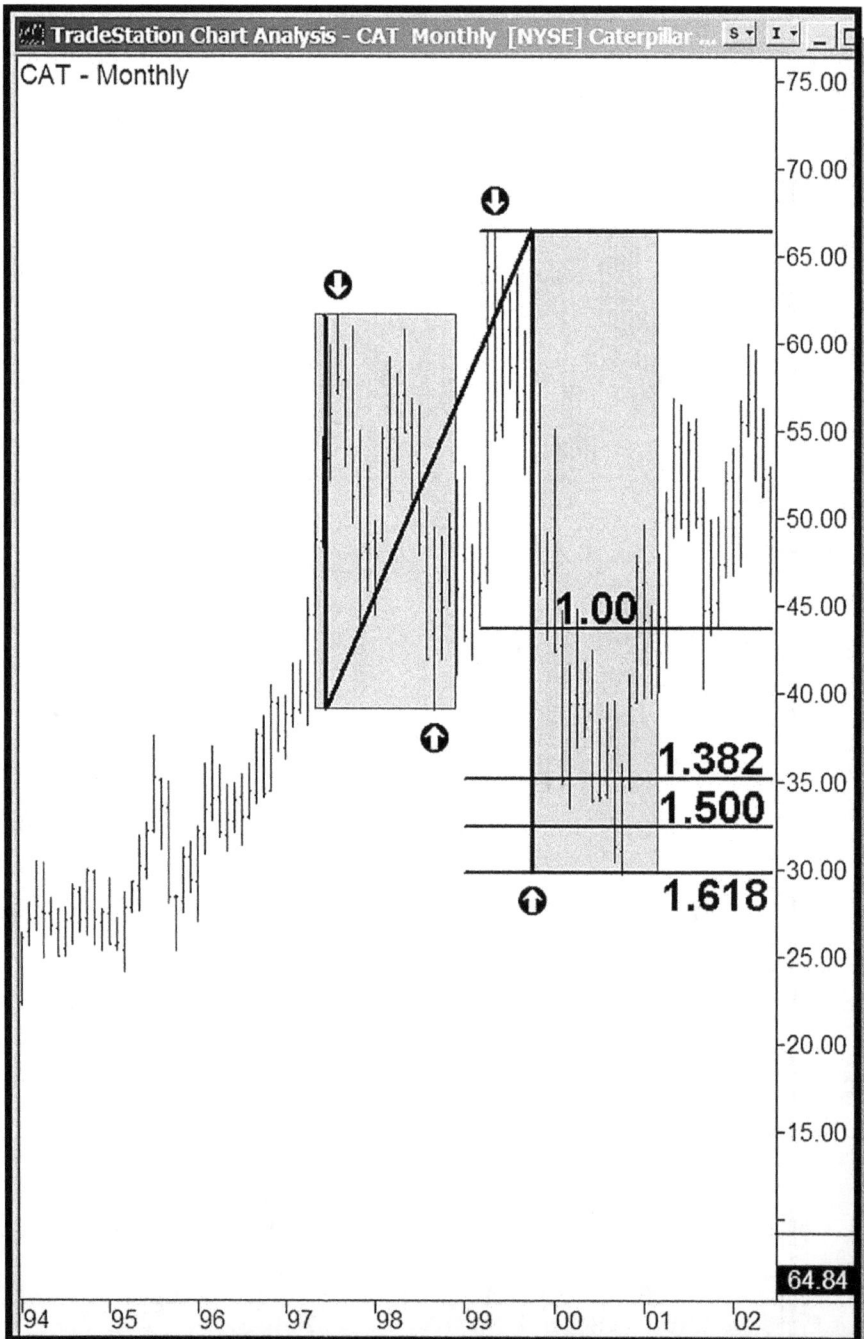

Fibonacci Price Projection: Bullish Extension Swing

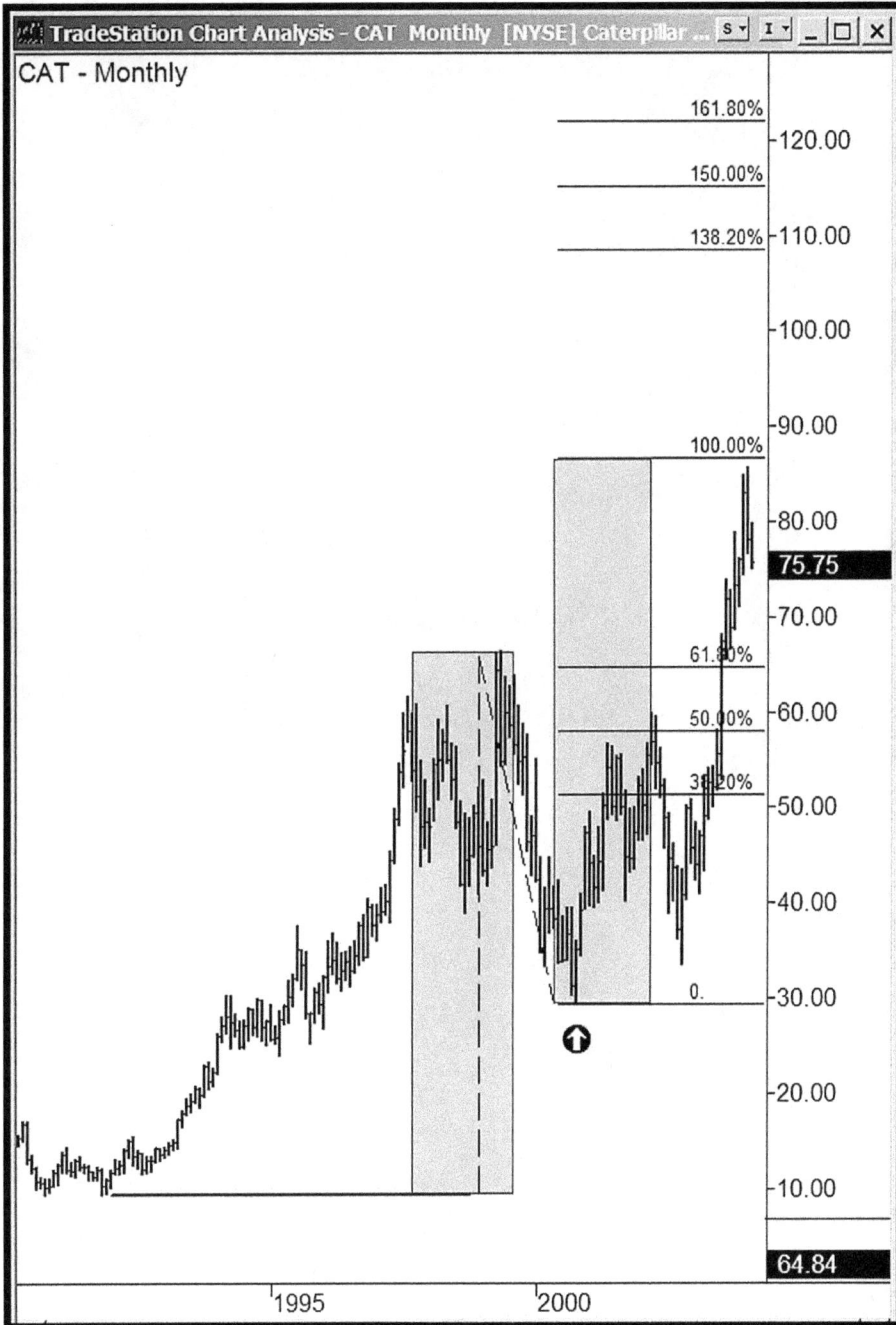

Fibonacci Ratios in Nature

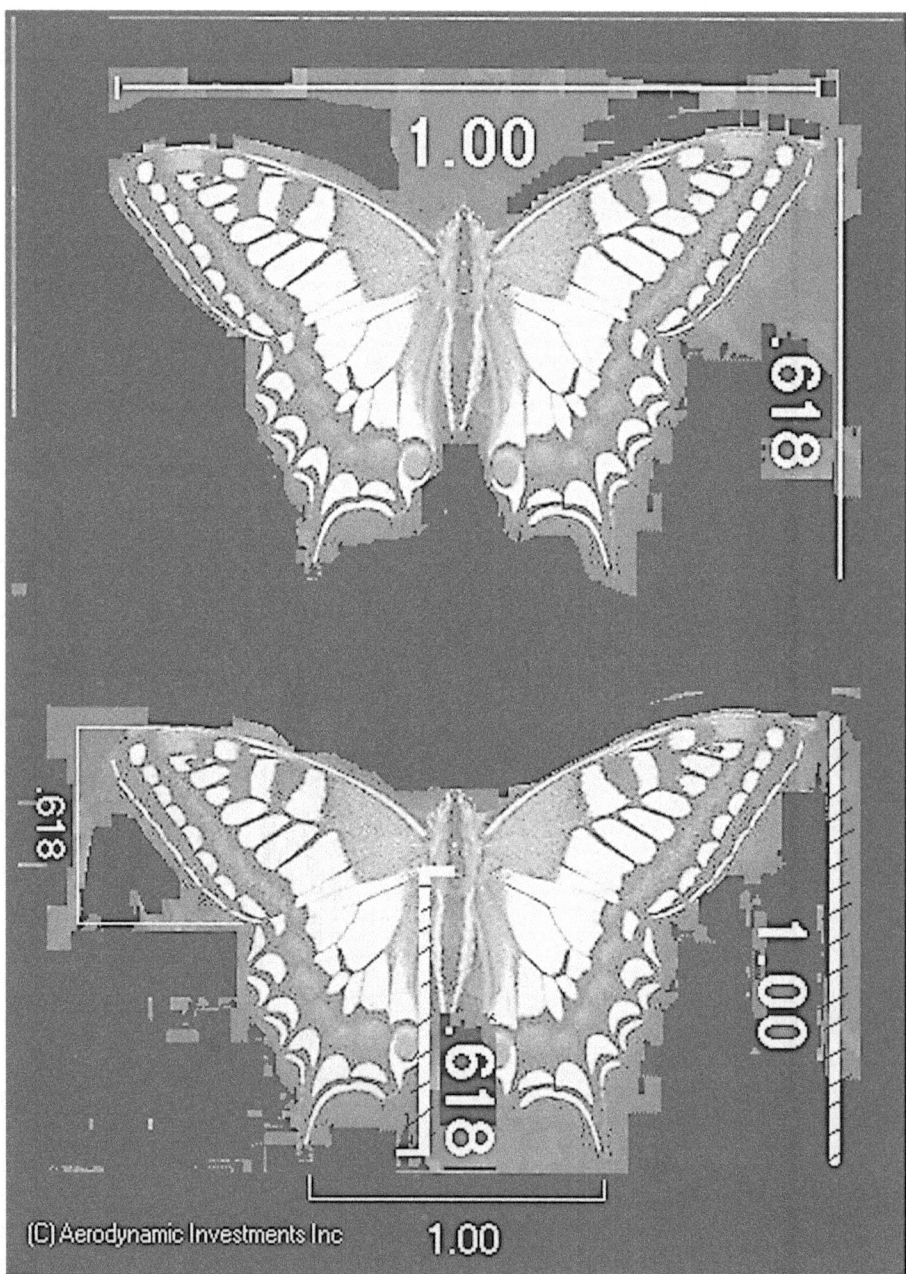

(C) Aerodynamic Investments Inc

Fibonacci Retracement (Beginner)

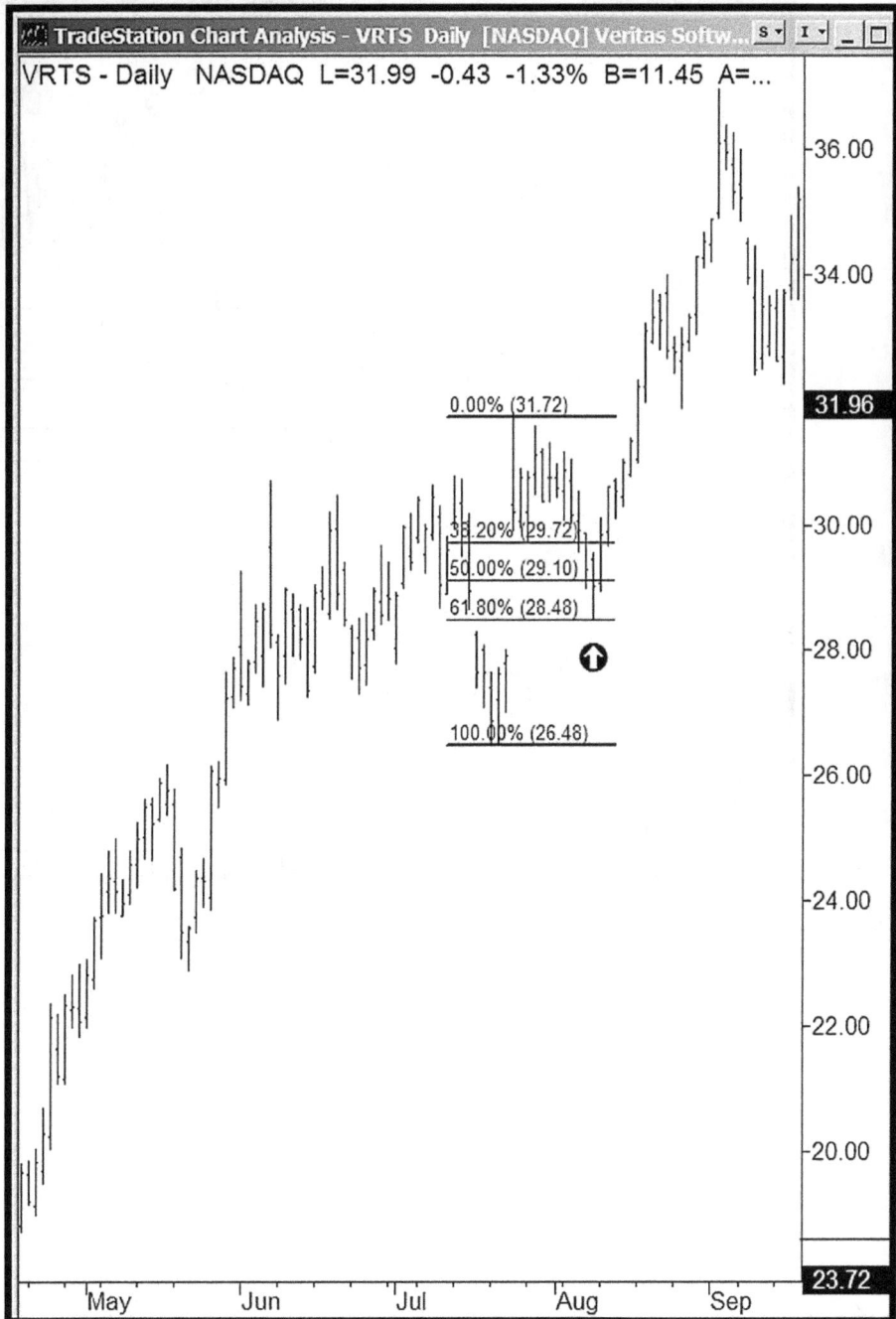

Fibonacci Retracement Confluence Zone (Intermediate)

Fibonacci Retracement with Gann Confluence Target (Advanced)

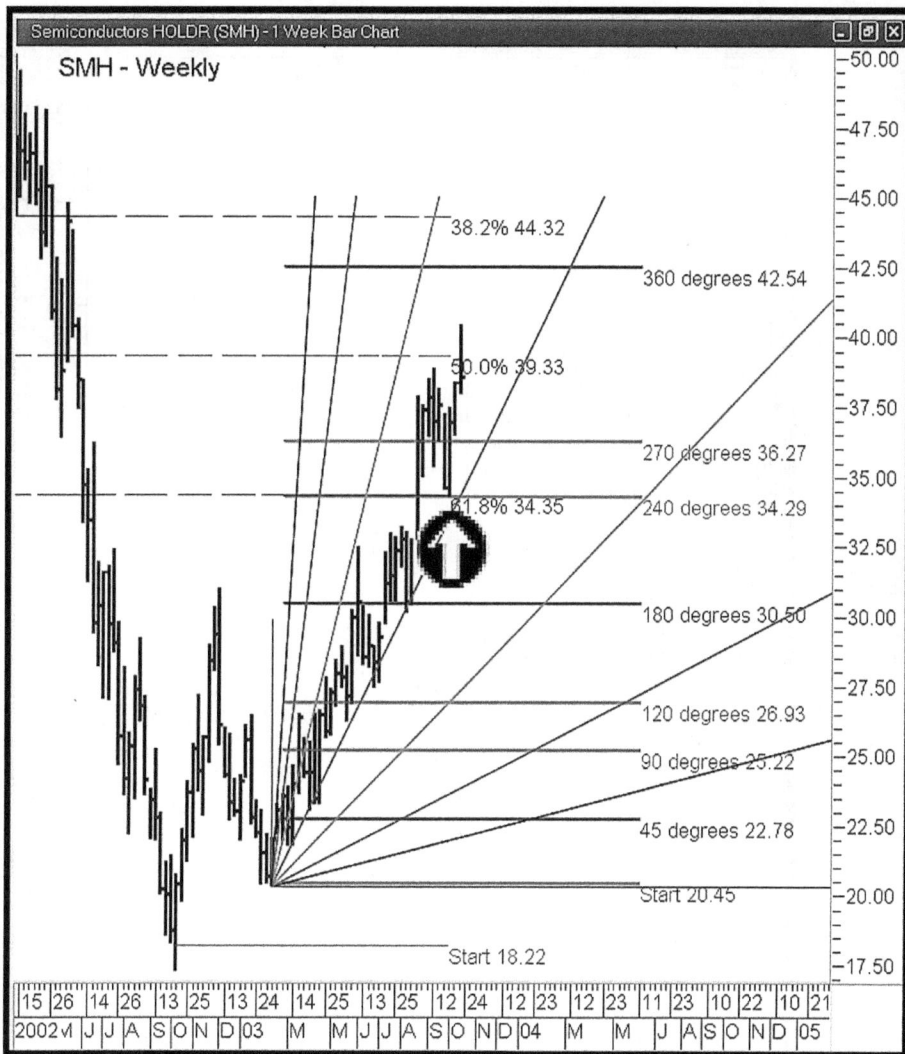

Semiconductors HOLDR (SMH) - 1 Week Bar Chart

SMH - Weekly

38.2% 44.32

360 degrees 42.54

50.0% 39.33

270 degrees 36.27

61.8% 34.35   240 degrees 34.29

180 degrees 30.50

120 degrees 26.93

90 degrees 25.22

45 degrees 22.78

Start 20.45

Start 18.22

Fibonacci Speed Lines

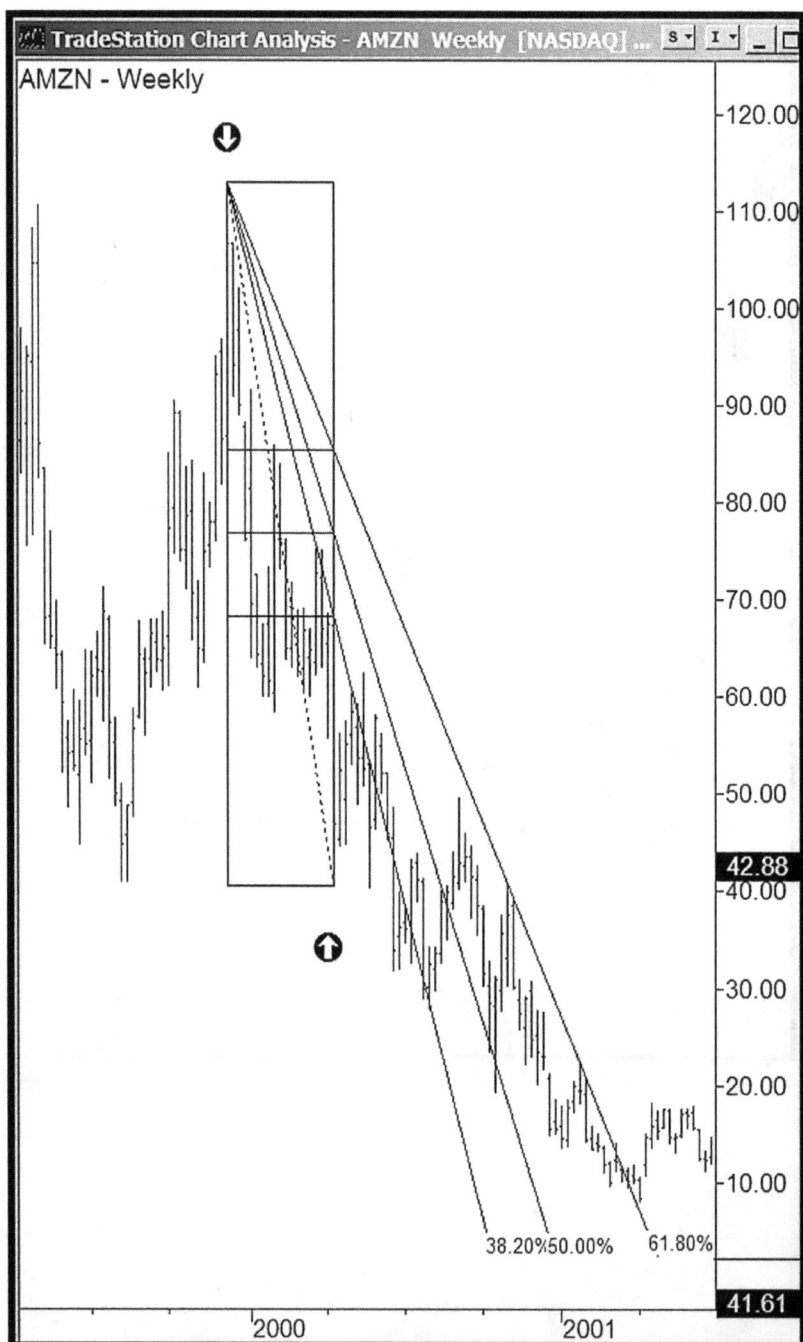

Fibonacci Speed Lines Angle Adjustment

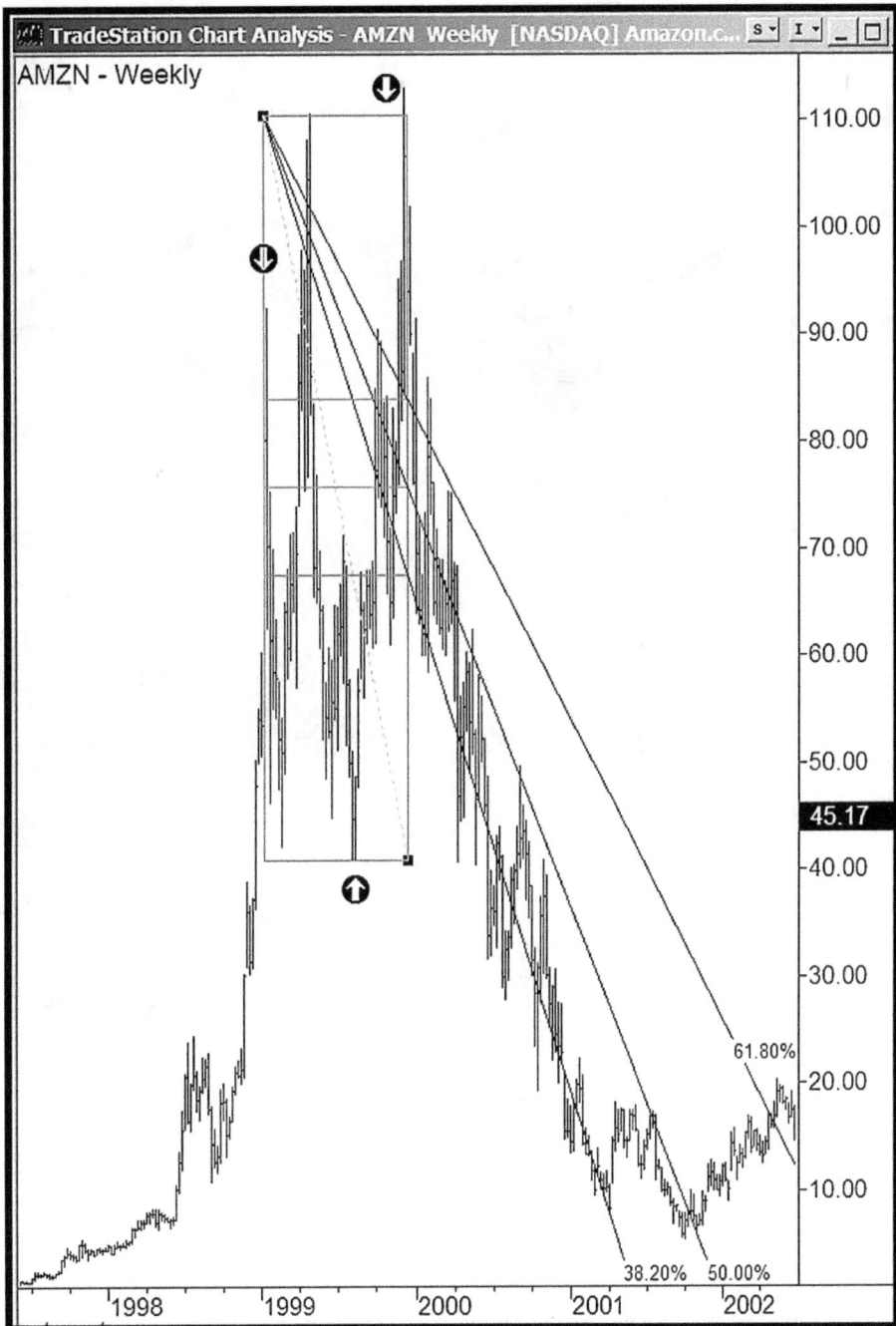

Fibonacci Spiral in Nature

Fibonacci Support Confluence Zone Confirmed by RSI Trendline

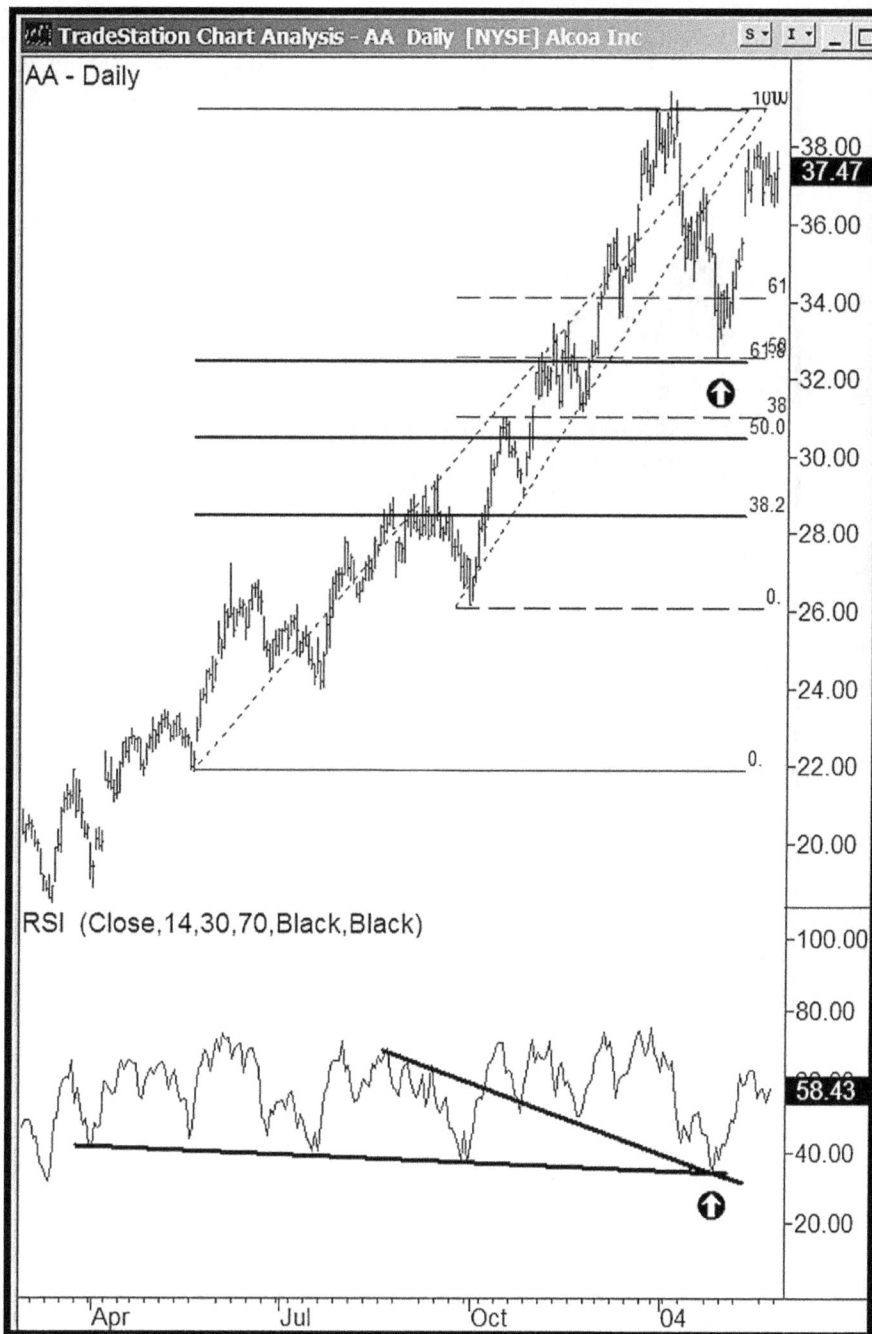

Fundamental Data with Gann Aspect Cycle Target Dates

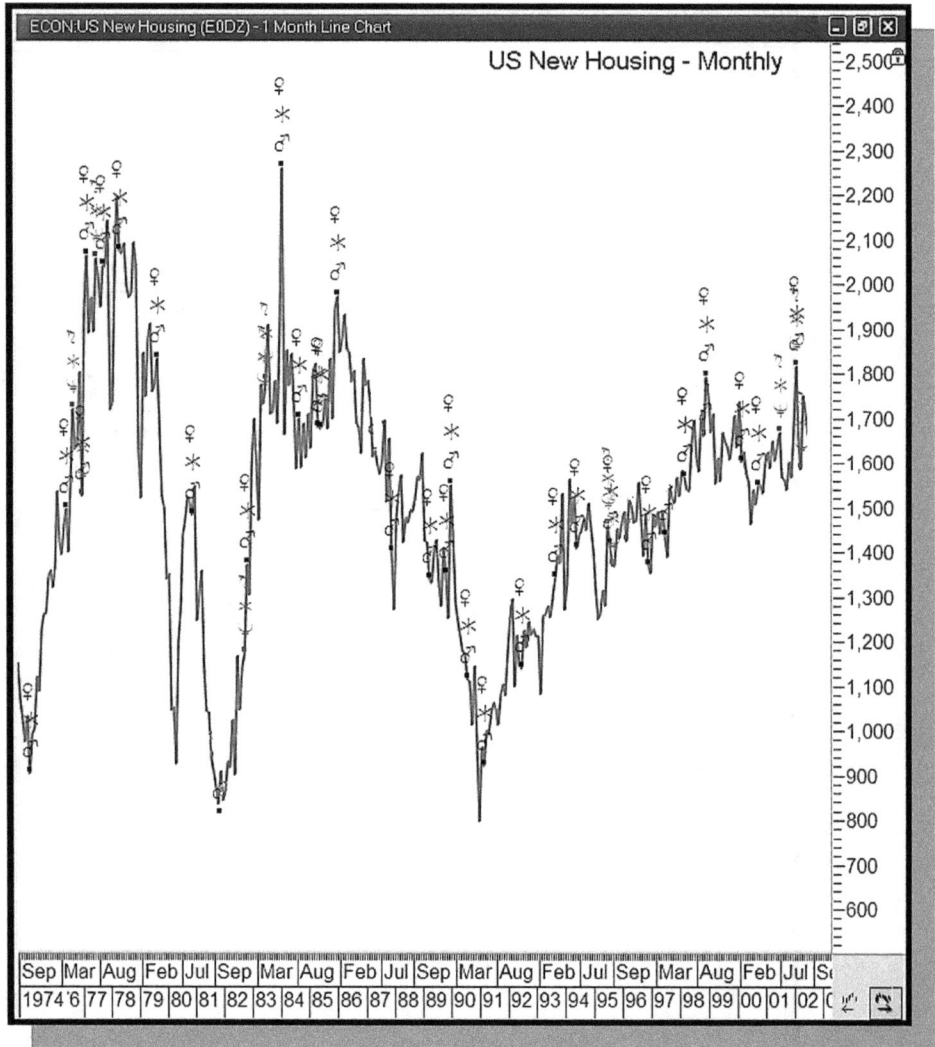

Fundamental Data with Momentum and Gann Analysis

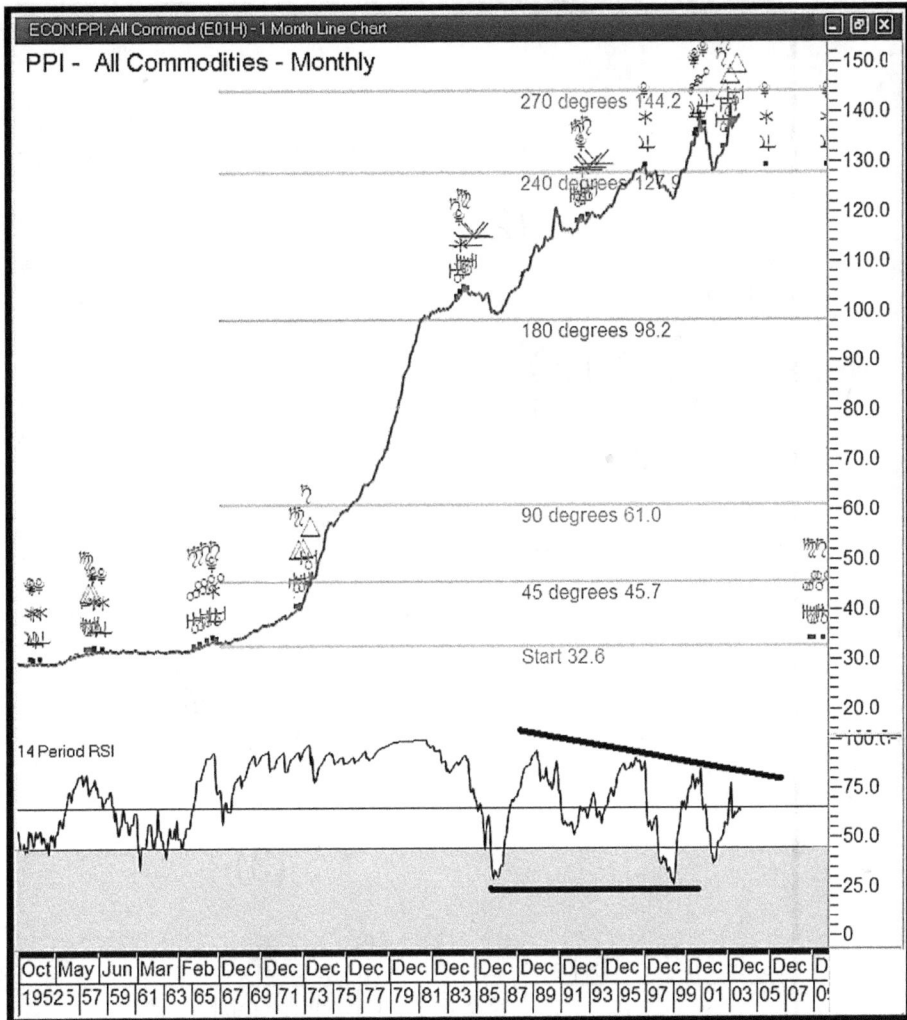

ECON:PPI: All Commod (E01H) - 1 Month Line Chart

PPI - All Commodities - Monthly

270 degrees 144.2

240 degrees 127.9

180 degrees 98.2

90 degrees 61.0

45 degrees 45.7

Start 32.6

14 Period RSI

Oct	May	Jun	Mar	Feb	Dec	Dec	Dec	Dec	Dec	Dec	Dec	Dec	Dec	Dec	Dec	Dec	Dec	D
1952	55	57	59	61	63	65	67	69	71	73	75	77	79	81	83	85	87	89	91	93	95	97	99	01	03	05	07	0!

Gann and Elliott Wave Analysis Applied

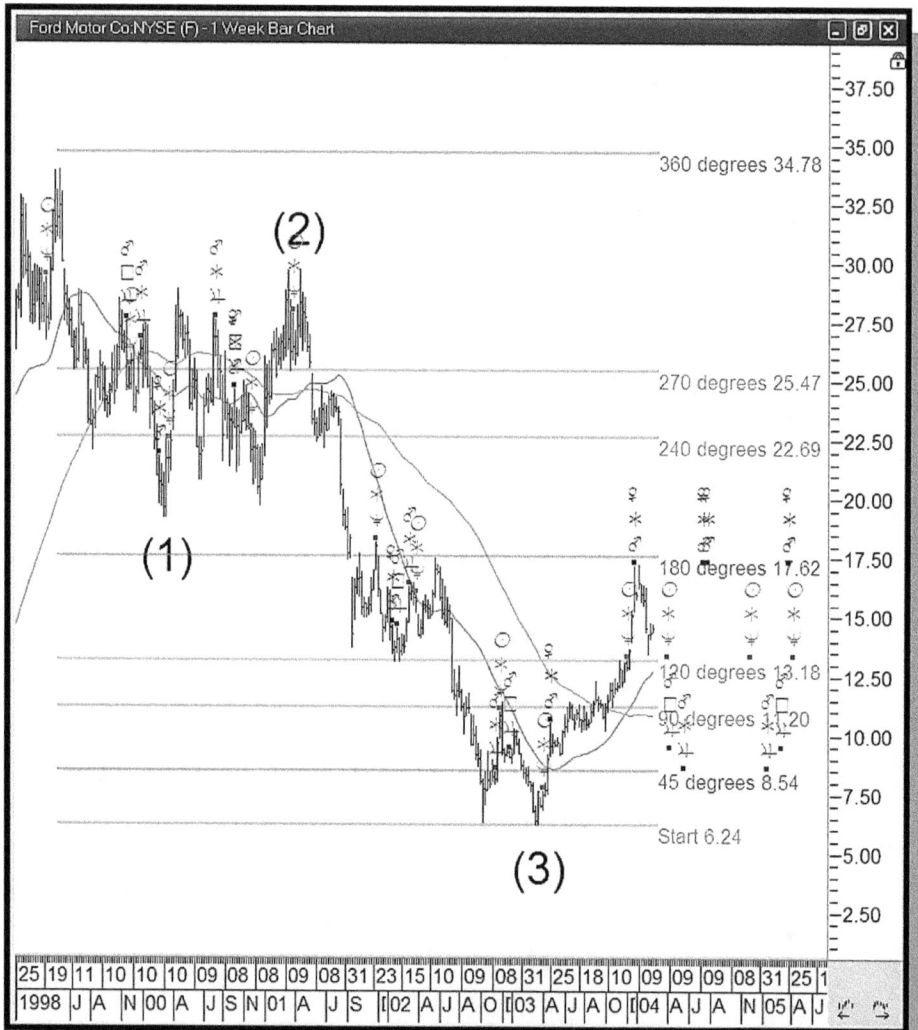

Gann Angles and Time Analysis

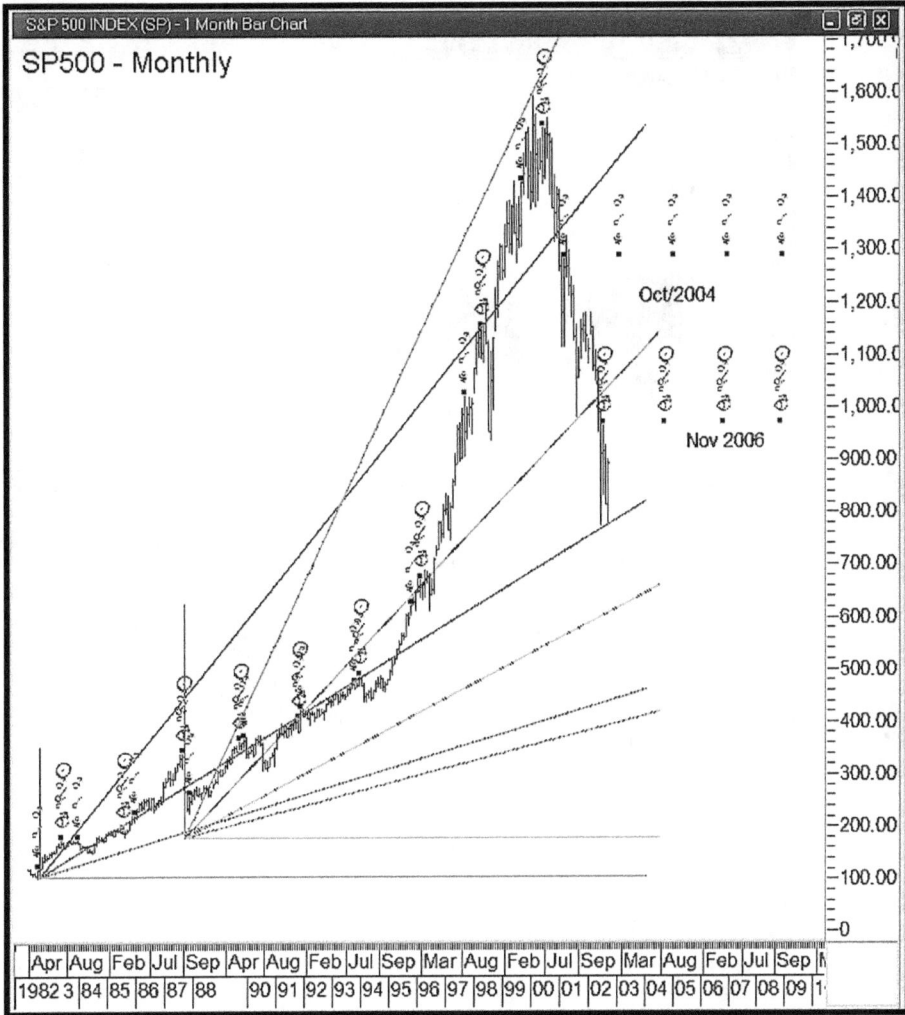

Gap Defining Support

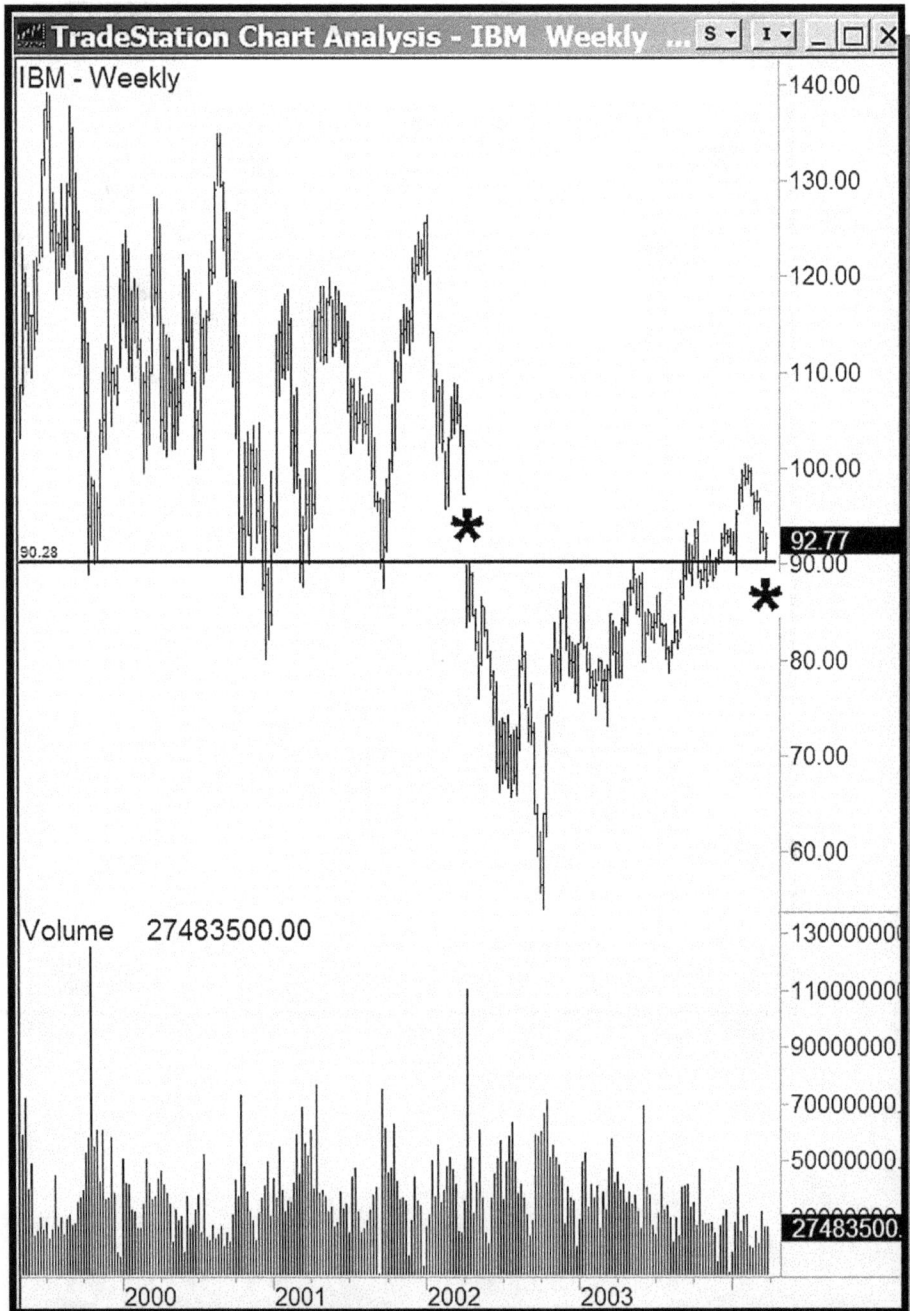

Gaps: Breakaway, Runaway, Exhaustion

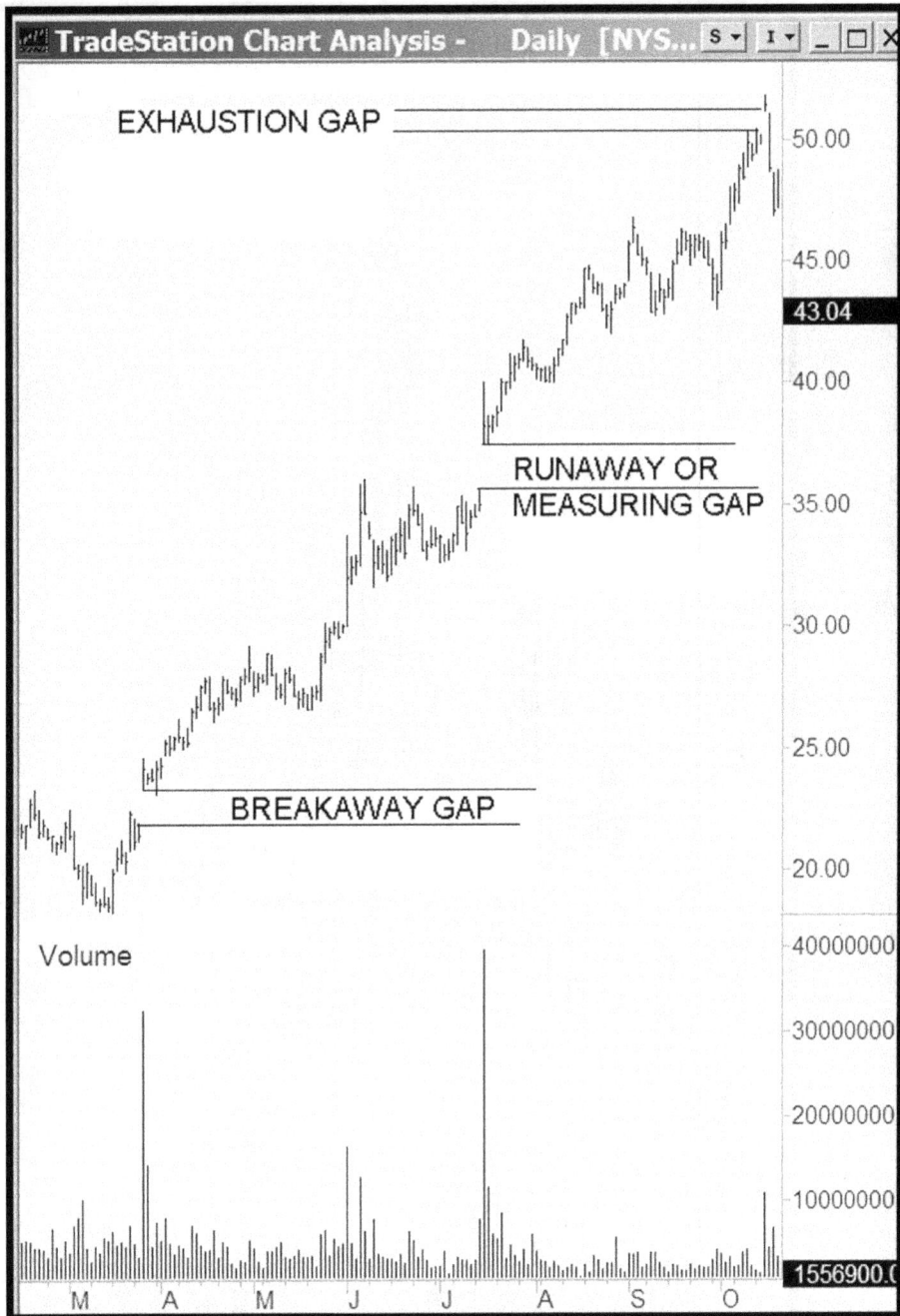

History: 1-Month Certificates of Deposit (CDs)

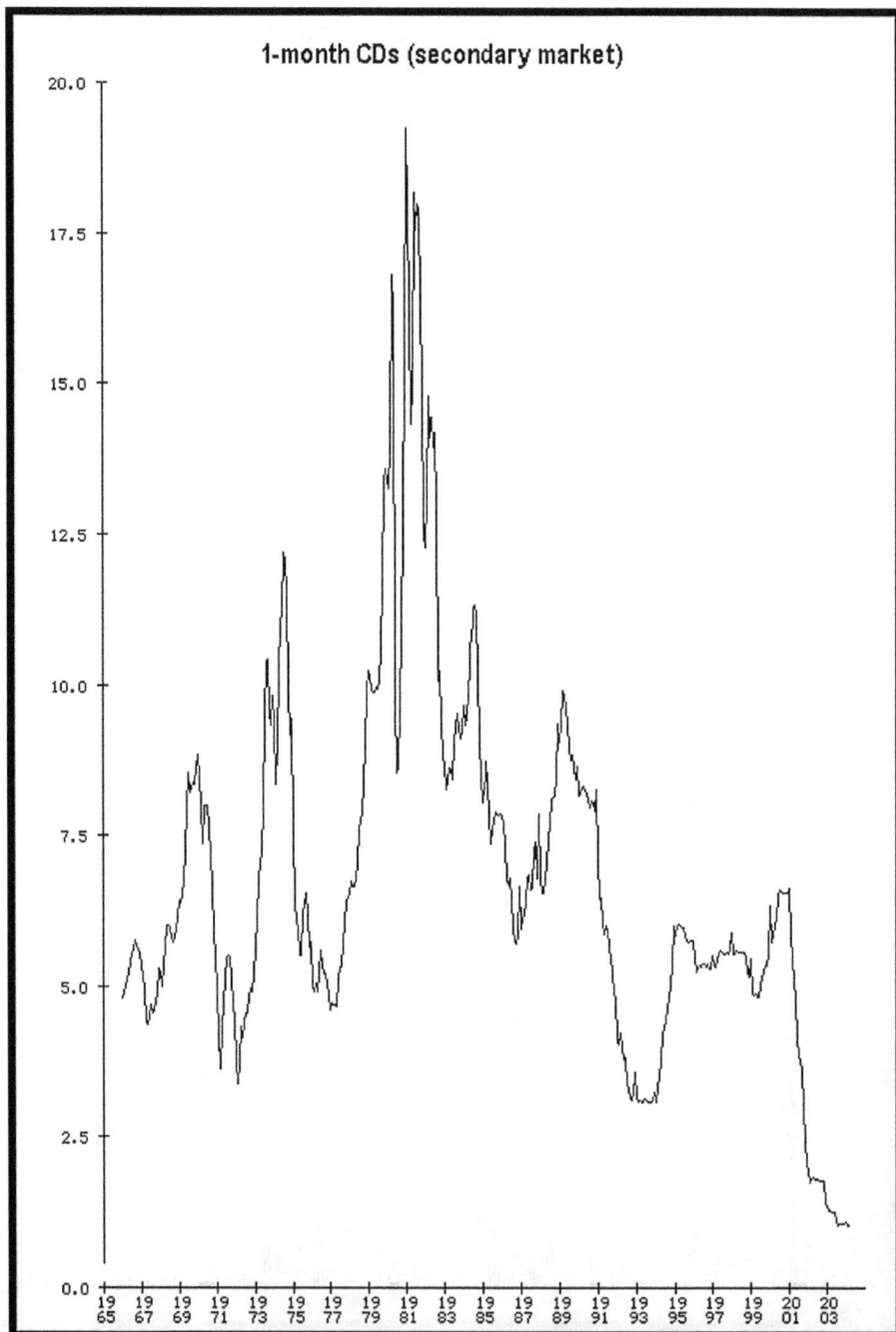

1-month CDs (secondary market)

History: 6-Month Certificates of Deposit (CDs)

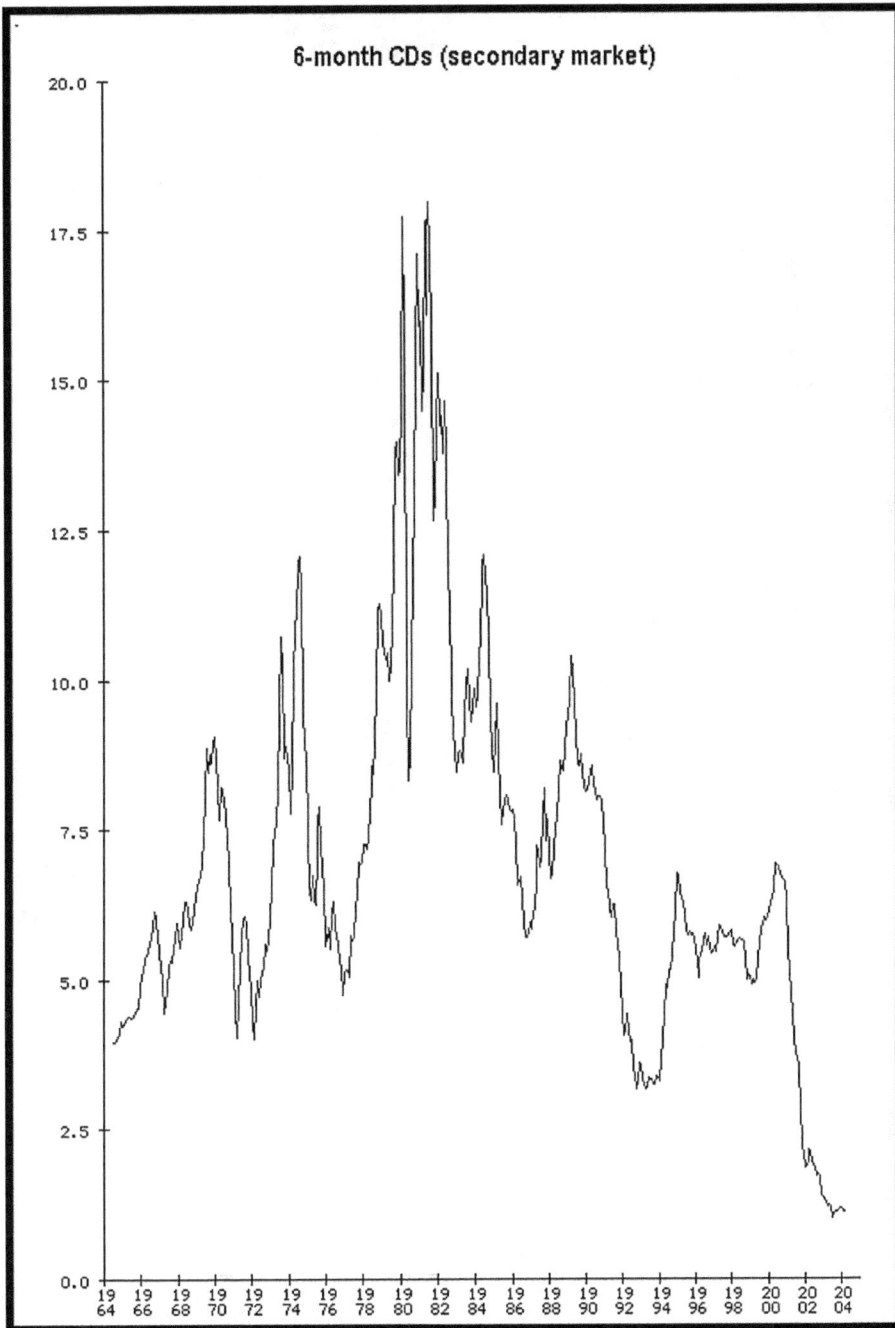

6-month CDs (secondary market)

History: 10-Year Treasury Constant Maturity

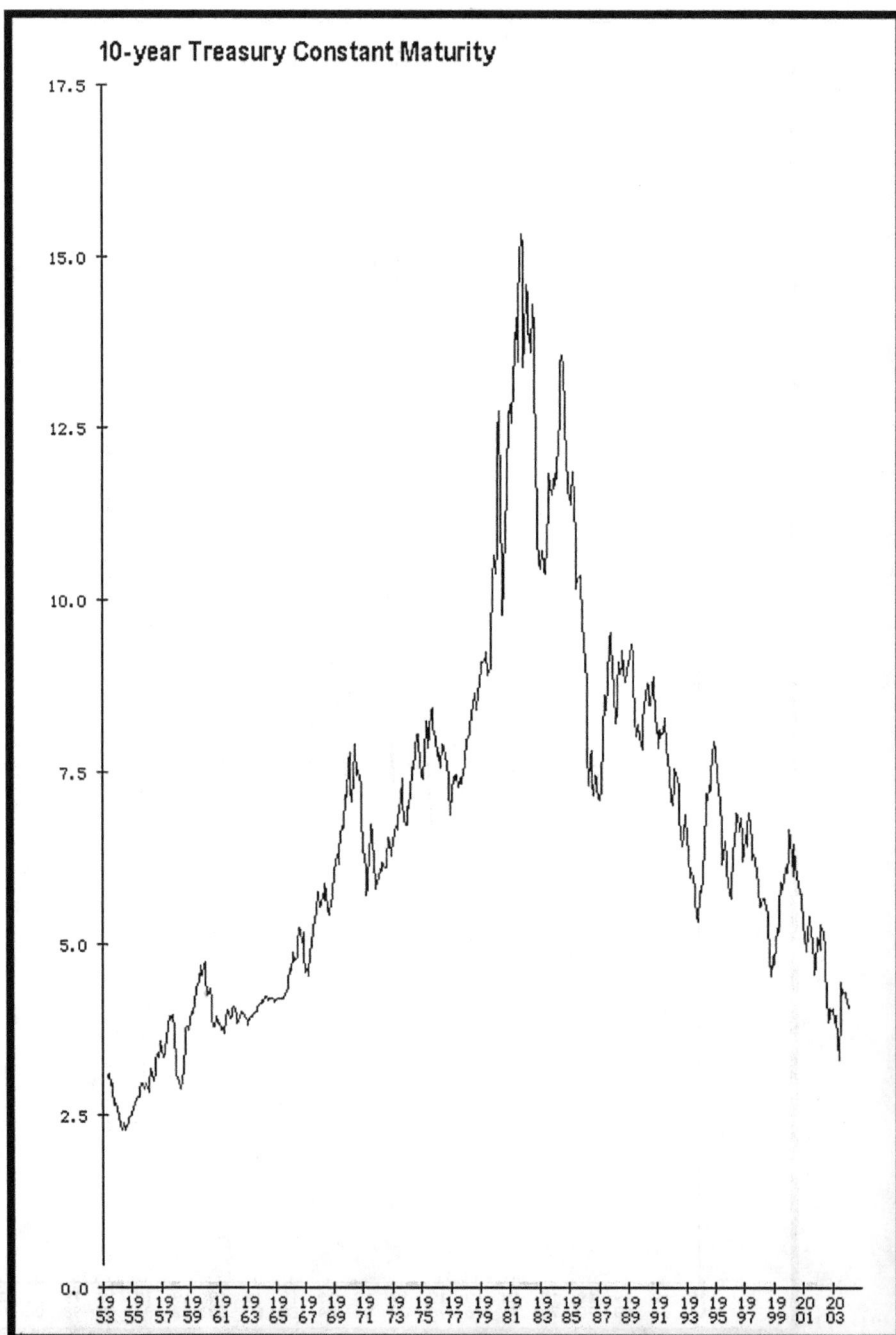

History: 10-Year Treasury
Constant Maturity Versus Unemployment

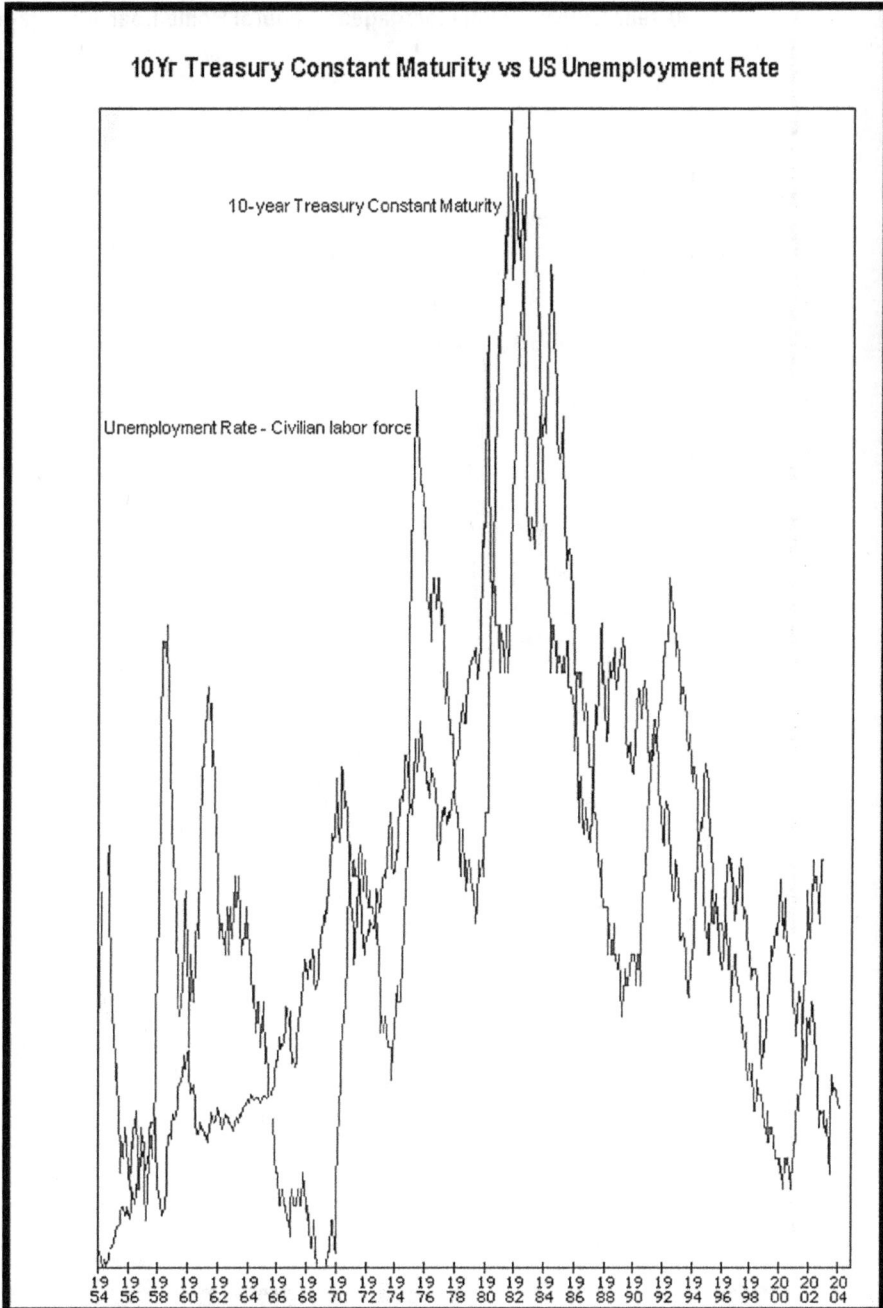

10Yr Treasury Constant Maturity vs US Unemployment Rate

History: 30-Year Conventional Mortgages

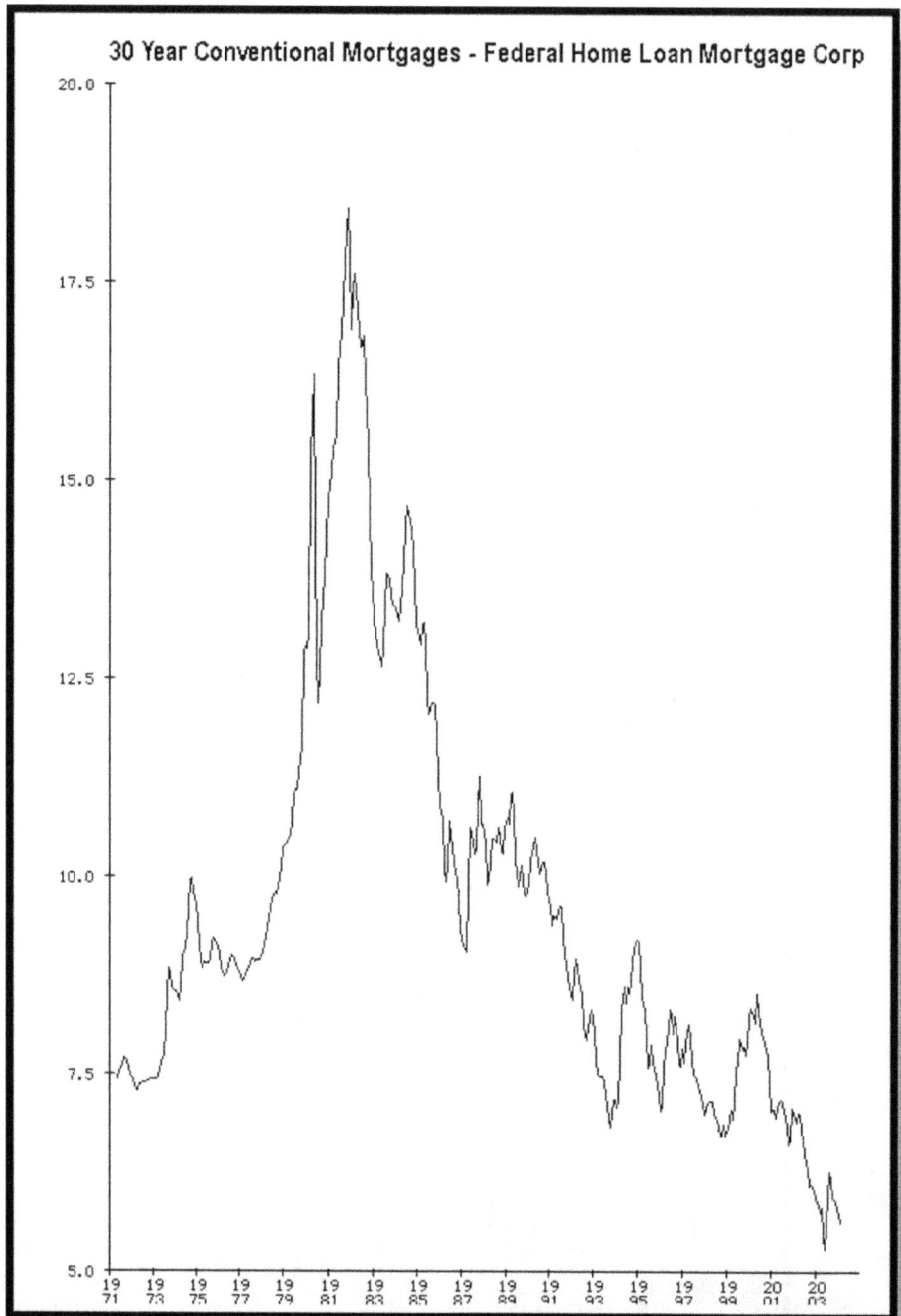

30 Year Conventional Mortgages - Federal Home Loan Mortgage Corp

History: 30-Year Treasury Bond Yield Constant Maturity

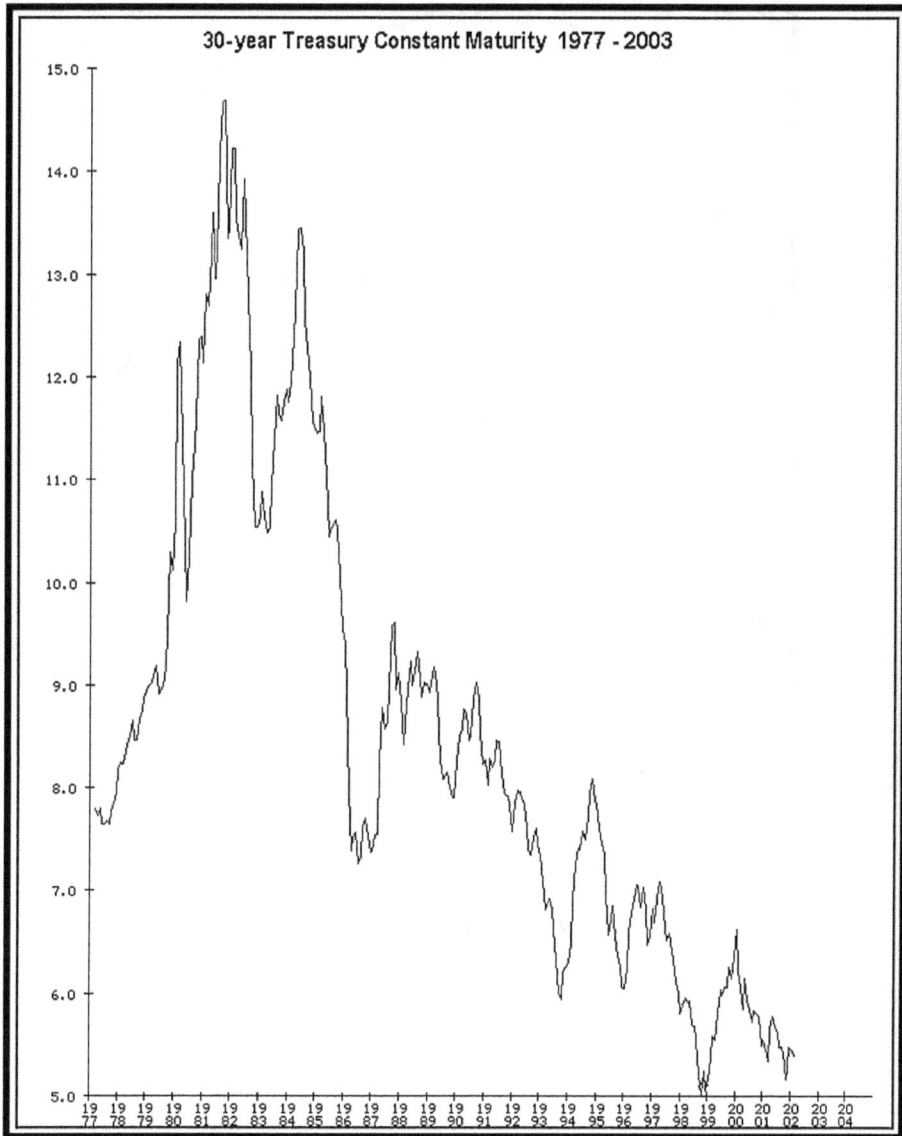

30-year Treasury Constant Maturity 1977 - 2003

History: Bank Prime Loan Rate

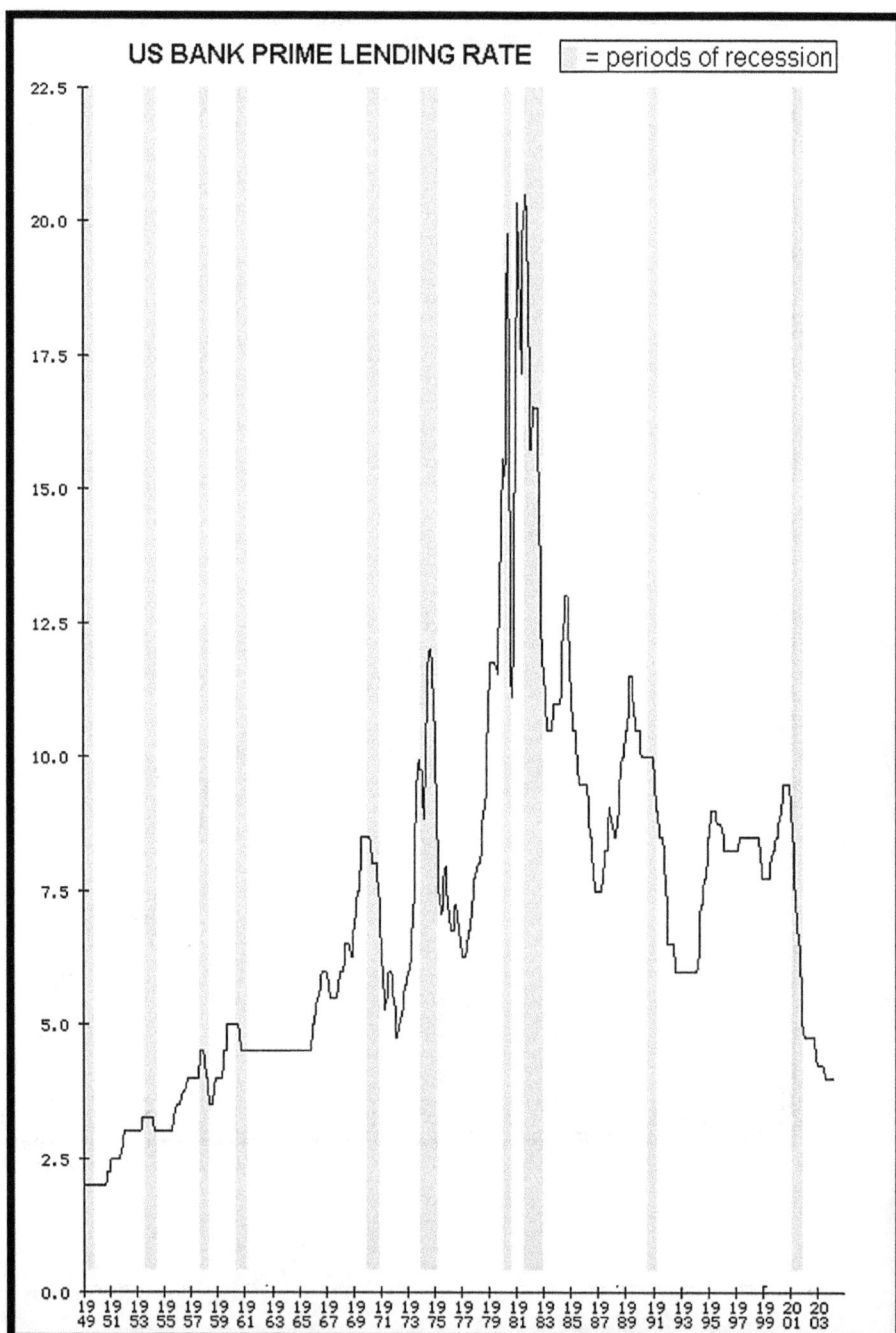

History: Inflation in Consumer Prices

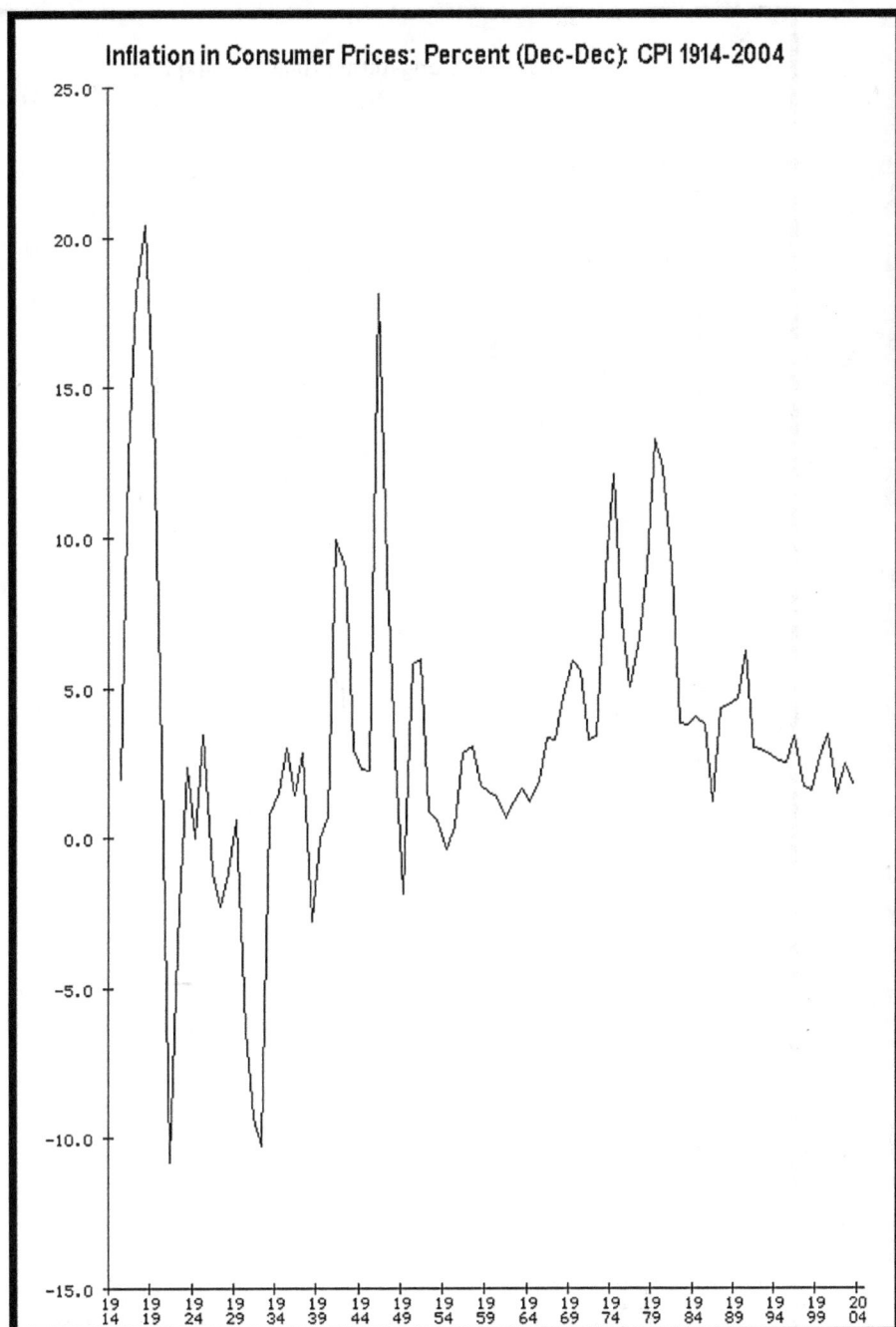

Inflation in Consumer Prices: Percent (Dec-Dec): CPI 1914-2004

History: Japanese Long-Term Prime Lending Rate

Japanese Long-term Prime Lending Rate

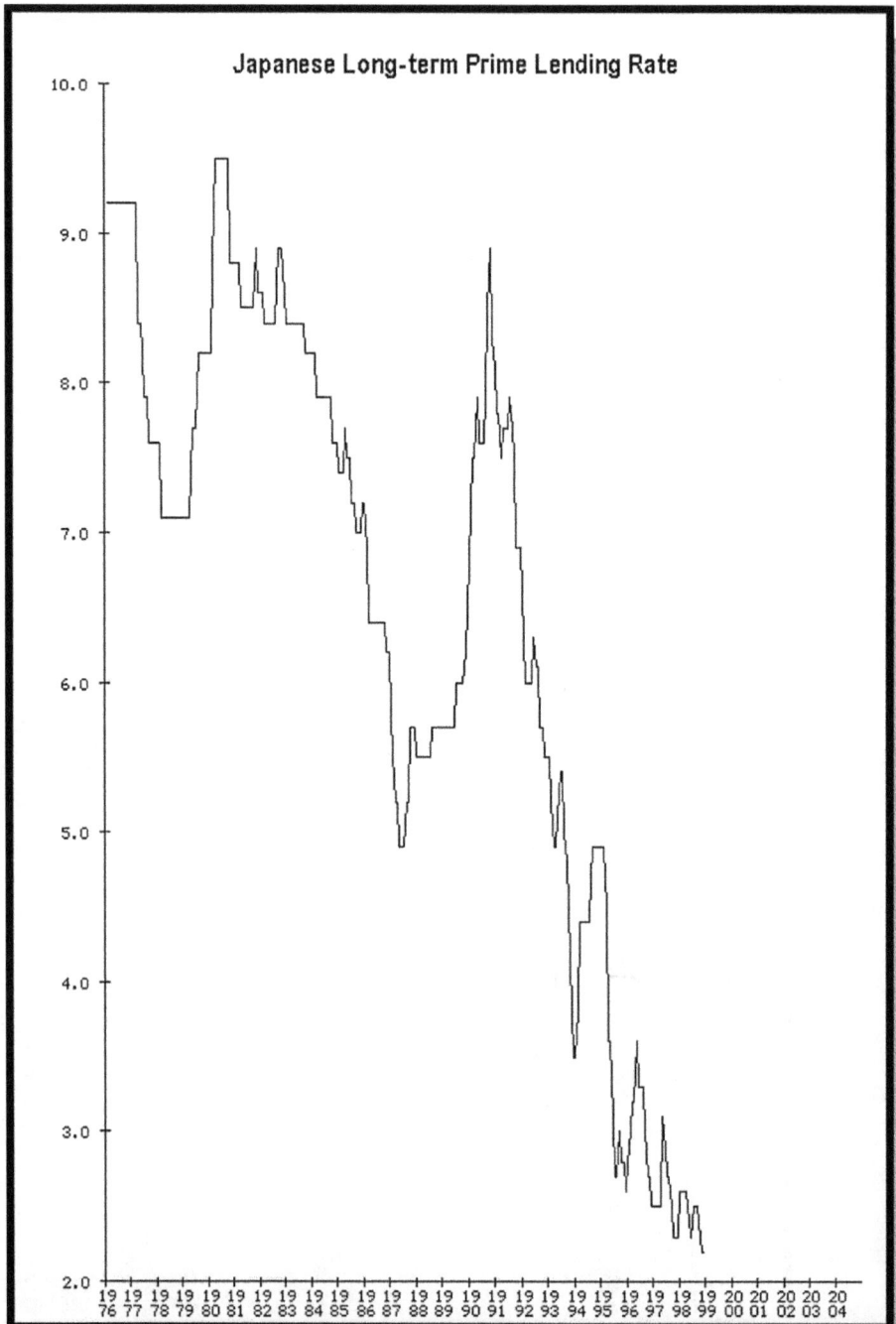

History: SP500 Total Return Versus Percent Change

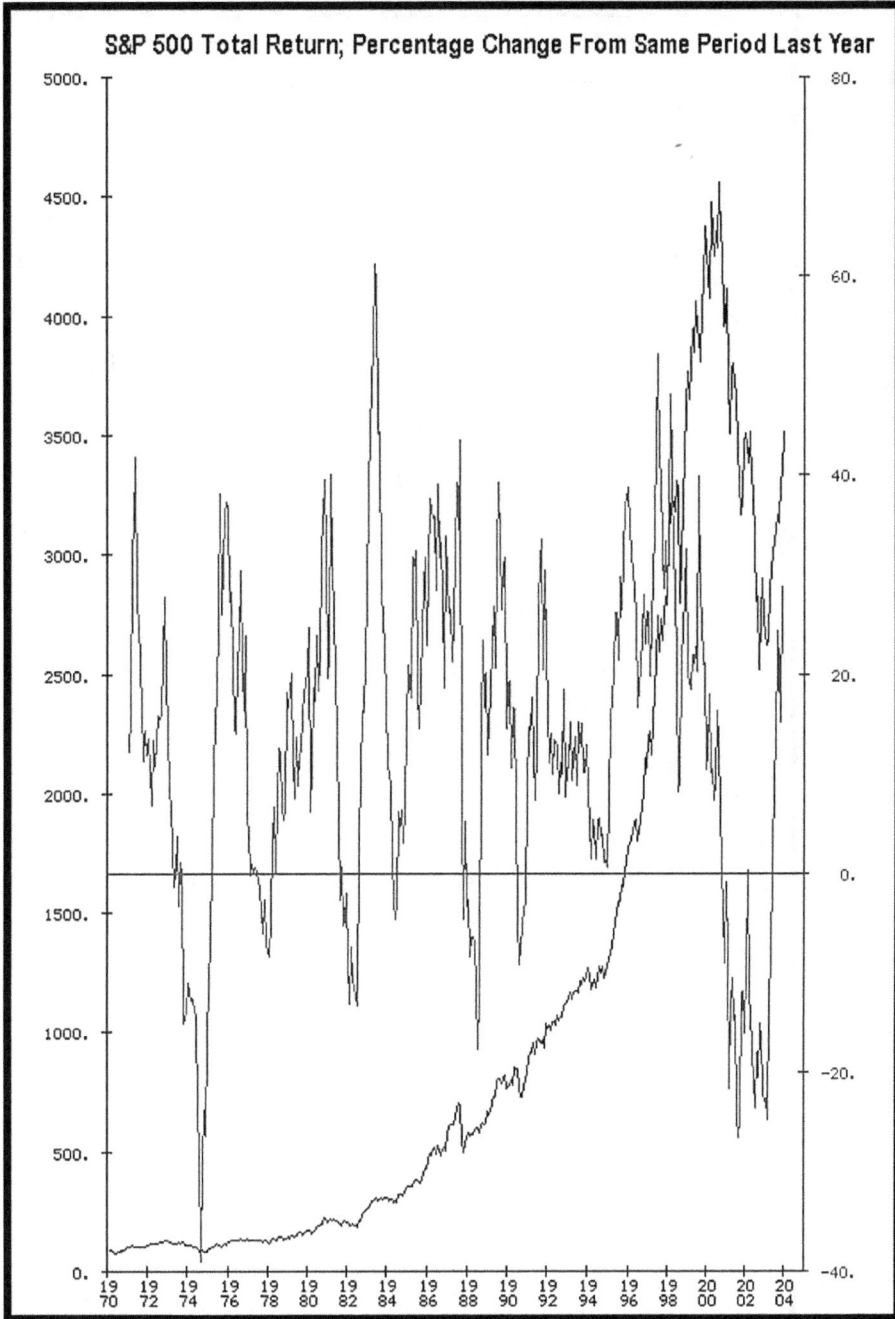

S&P 500 Total Return; Percentage Change From Same Period Last Year

History: SP500 Total Return Versus Smoothed Percent Change

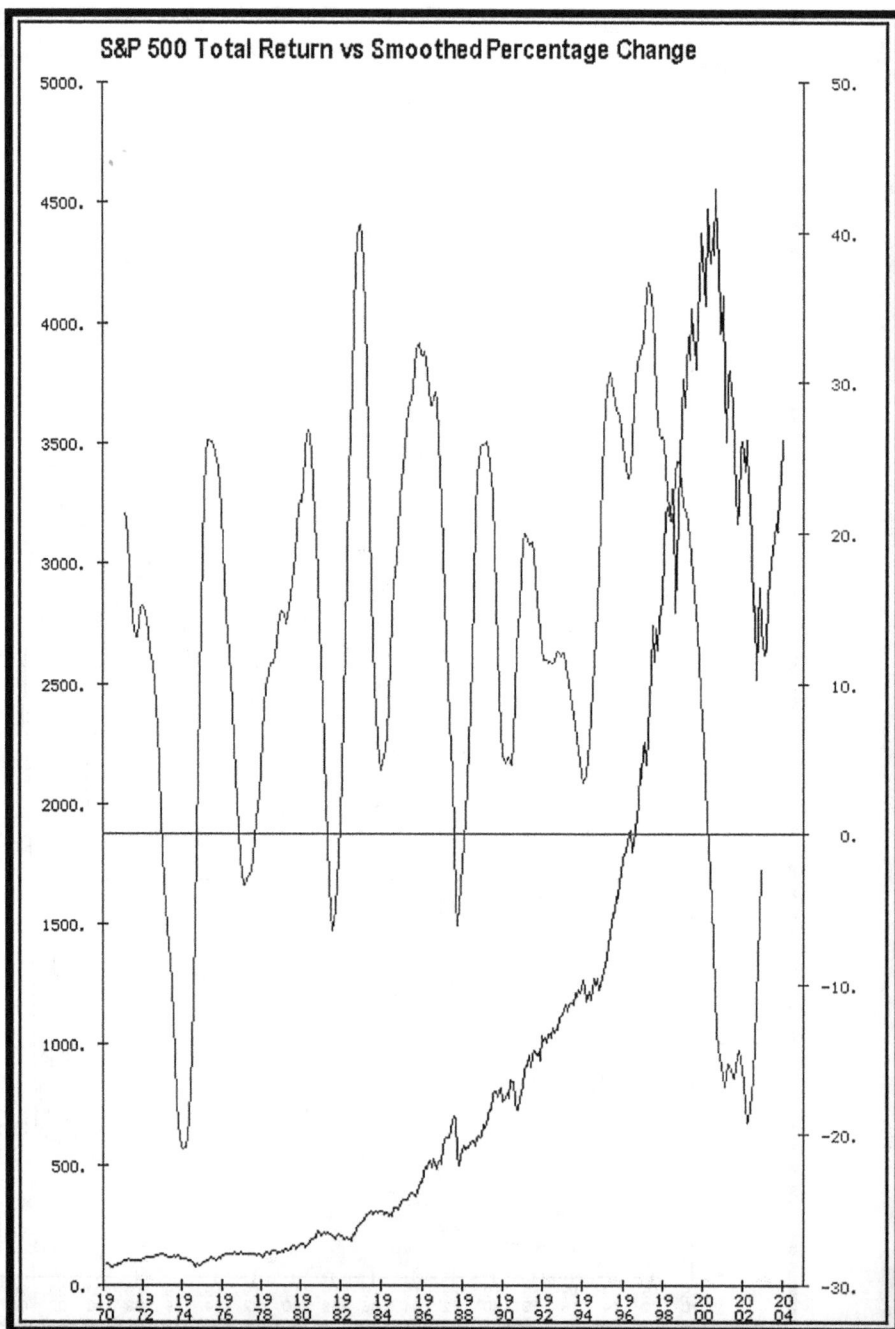

S&P 500 Total Return vs Smoothed Percentage Change

History: The Great Crash

History: Unemployment Rate

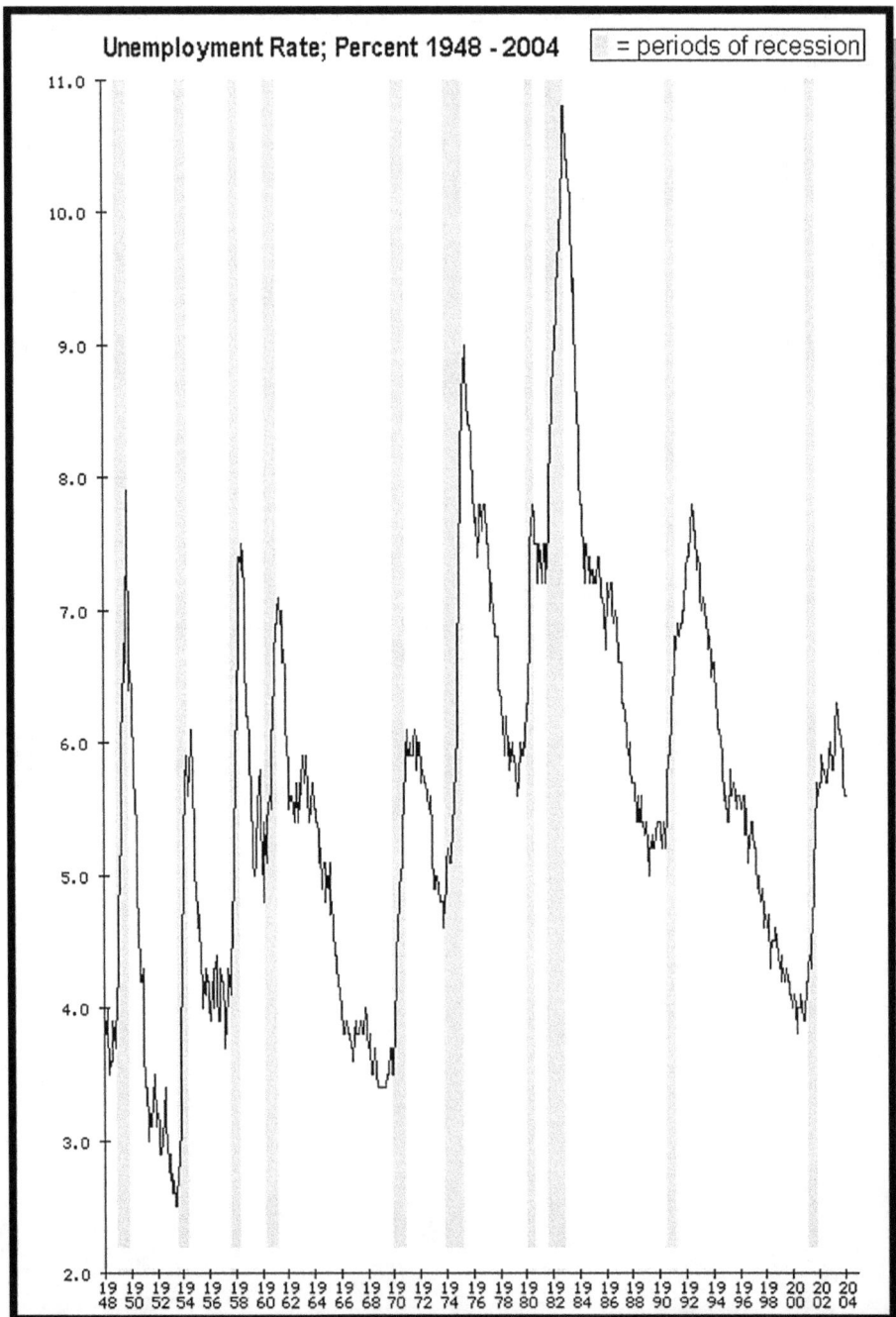

Unemployment Rate; Percent 1948 - 2004   = periods of recession

History: West Texas Intermediate Crude

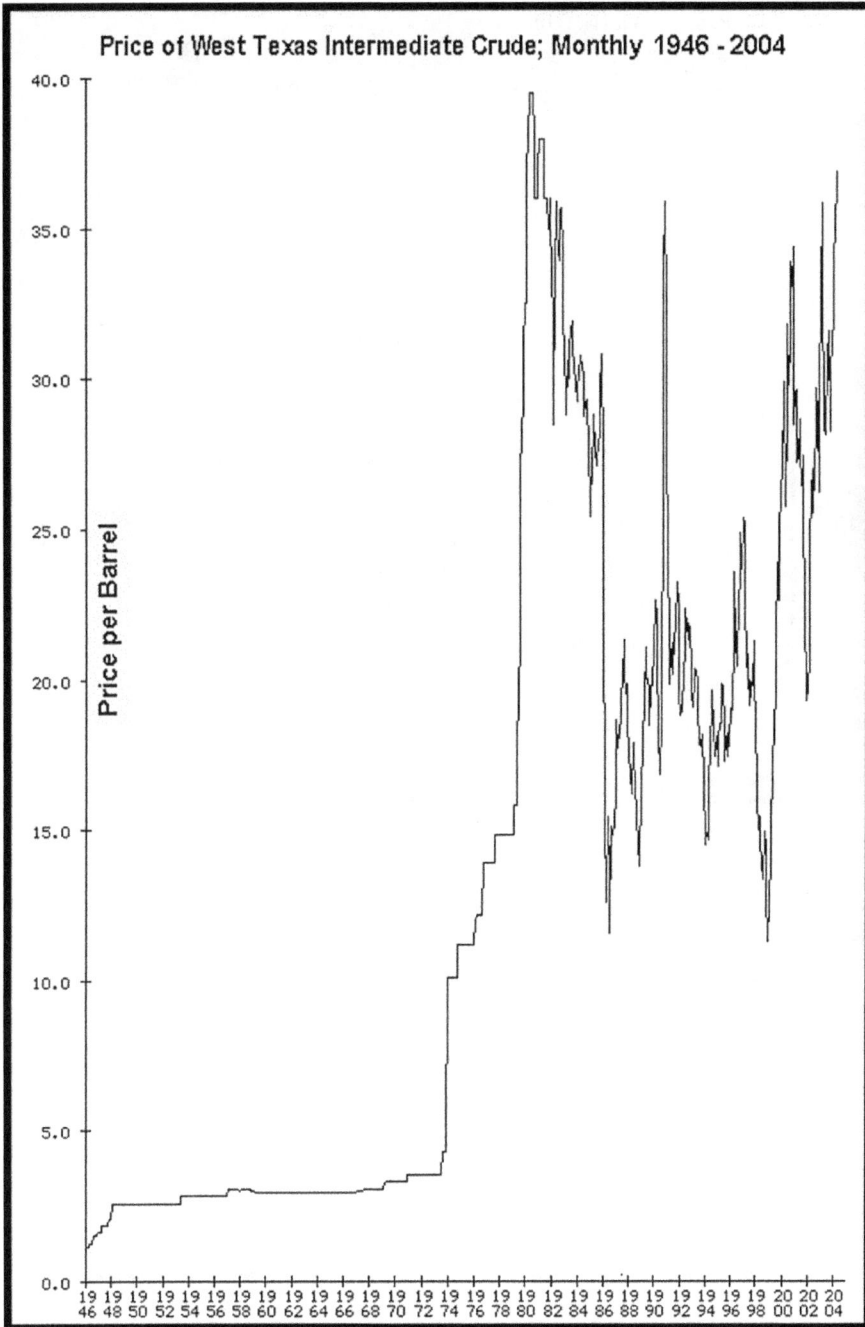

Price of West Texas Intermediate Crude; Monthly 1946 - 2004

Ichimoku Kinko Hyo

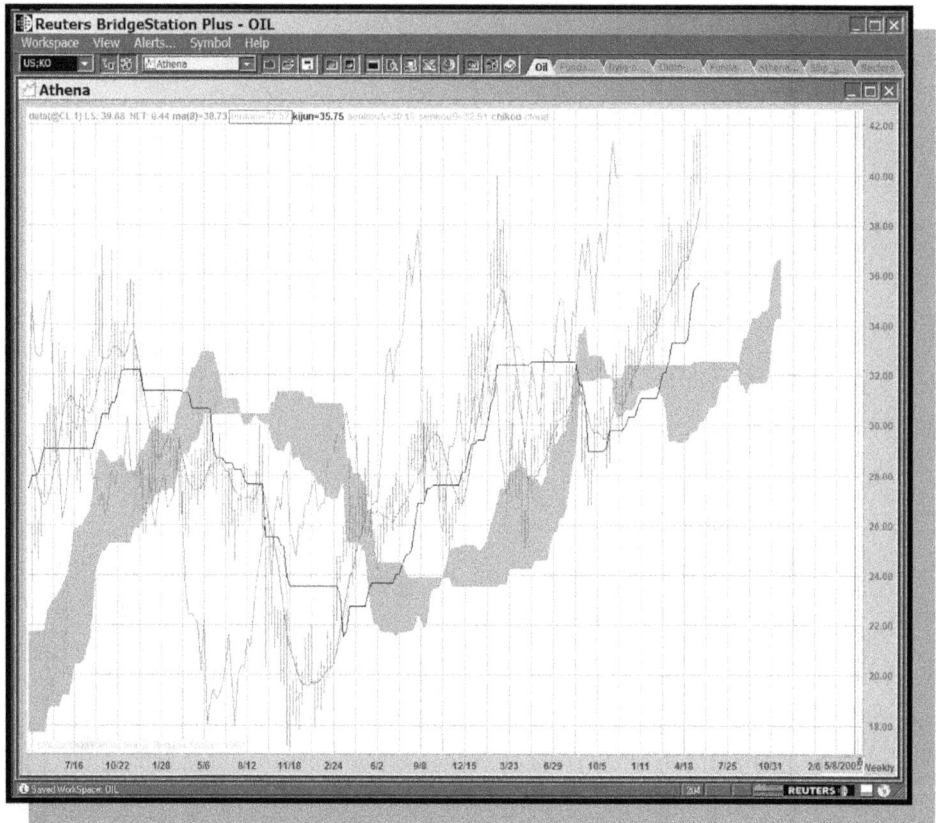

Intermarket Comparison: Nikkei 225 Versus Gold

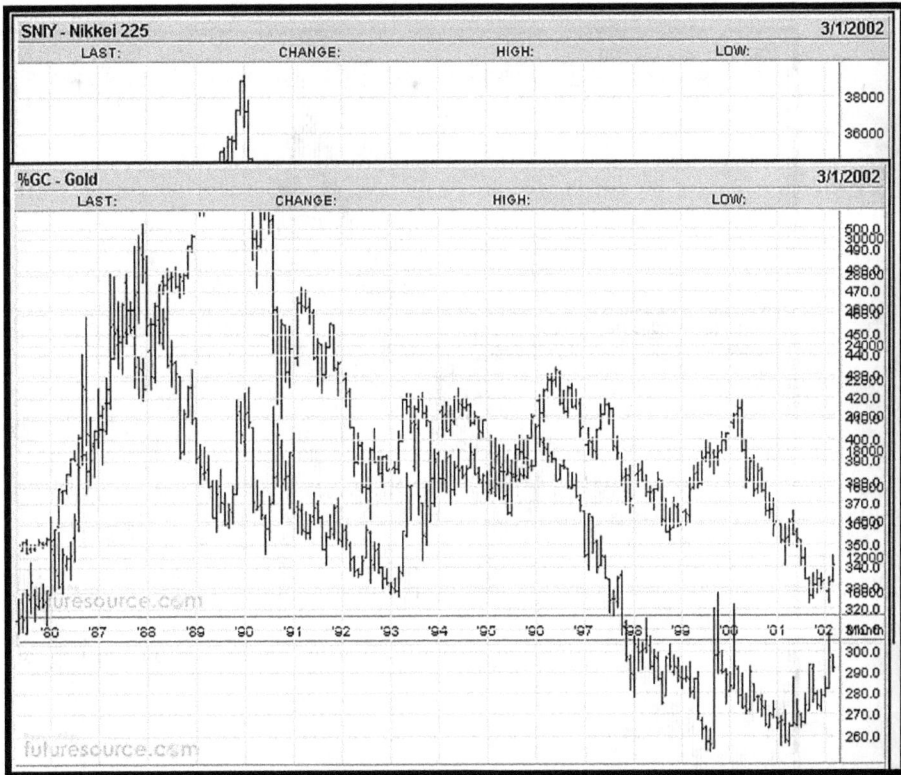

Intramarket Comparison: Toronto TSE 300 Versus Dow Jones Industrials

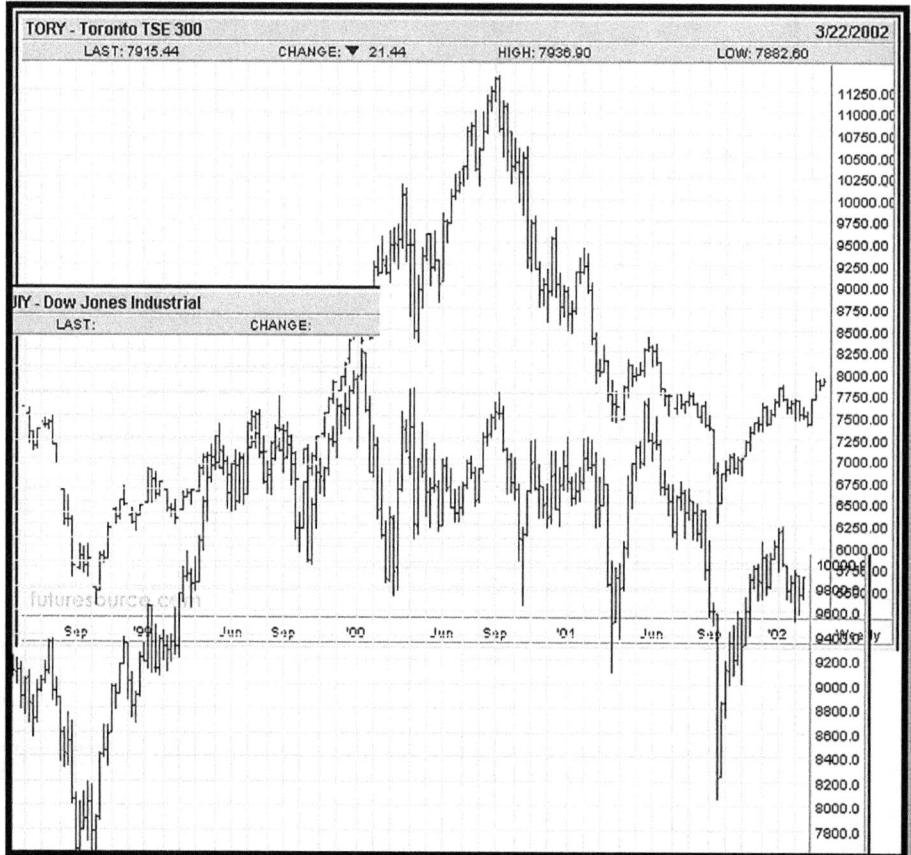

TORY - Toronto TSE 300			3/22/2002
LAST: 7915.44	CHANGE: ▼ 21.44	HIGH: 7936.90	LOW: 7882.60

JY - Dow Jones Industrial

LAST: CHANGE:

Leading Economic Index: Baltic Dry Index

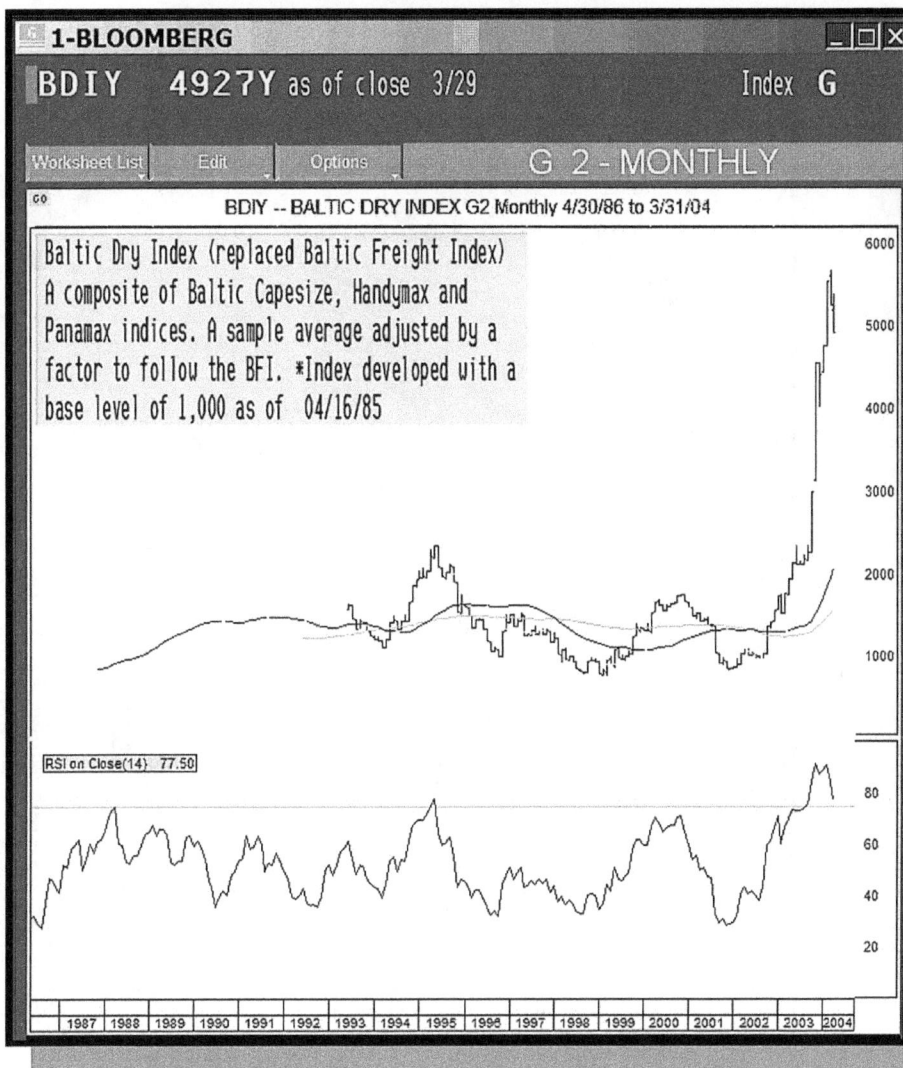

Most Active

TradeStation Chart Analysis - MSFT Daily [NASDA...

MSFT - Daily L=27.55 +1.60

27.54

25.66
25.33

0.19

TradeStation Hot Lists - ALL Most Active - Trades

Exchange ALL

Activity Most Active - Trades

	Symbol	Last	Net Chg	Net %Chg	High	Low	Close	Vol Tot	Trades
1	MSFT	27.55	1.60	6.17%	27.72	27.34	27.54	258,297,475	203,934
2	QQQ	37.19	0.27	0.73%	37.26	36.90	37.21	92,044,900	132,588
3	INTC	27.55	1.03	3.88%	27.57	26.65	27.53	65,231,230	93,538
4	CSCO	23.32	0.17	0.73%	23.44	22.87	23.32	51,370,184	80,711
5	TASR(HB)	81.70	4.55	5.90%	83.10	75.50	81.15	14,537,698	61,470
6	AMAT	19.92	0.19	0.96%	20.10	19.80	19.98	28,686,050	46,199
7	BRCM	42.15	1.35	3.31%	43.79	41.96	42.21	18,855,390	43,653
8	ORCL	12.51	0.14	1.13%	12.58	12.35	12.53	38,928,508	43,428
9	SPY	114.40	0.15	0.13%	114.57	113.79	114.36	29,422,500	37,343
10	AMZN	46.31	-2.55	-5.22%	46.89	45.51	46.29	14,602,911	35,750
11	AMGN	58.31	1.17	2.05%	58.98	58.06	58.31	15,418,576	31,328
12	EBAY	81.86	-0.73	-0.88%	82.90	81.19	82.14	10,346,918	31,151
13	SUNW	4.40	0.13	3.04%	4.43	4.28	4.39	38,203,847	30,772
14	DELL	35.96	0.56	1.58%	36.05	35.38	35.96	14,169,539	30,727
15	MCHP	32.65	4.32	15.25%	33.07	30.00	32.63	12,175,025	30,449
16	XLNX	36.56	-1.23	-3.25%	37.03	36.15	36.59	14,299,295	29,780
17	YHOO	56.75	-0.84	-1.46%	57.50	55.91	56.75	9,928,059	29,679
18	GILD	60.45	1.23	2.08%	63.85	59.11	60.12	10,865,784	26,072
19	JDSU	4.32	0.25	6.14%	4.26	4.11	4.25	28,650,471	24,688
20	SWIR	28.70	-5.65	-16.45%	34.93	27.23	28.80	8,719,929	24,534
21	QCOM	67.01	-0.87	-1.28%	68.09	66.52	66.98	9,535,415	23,948

Moving Averages Compared

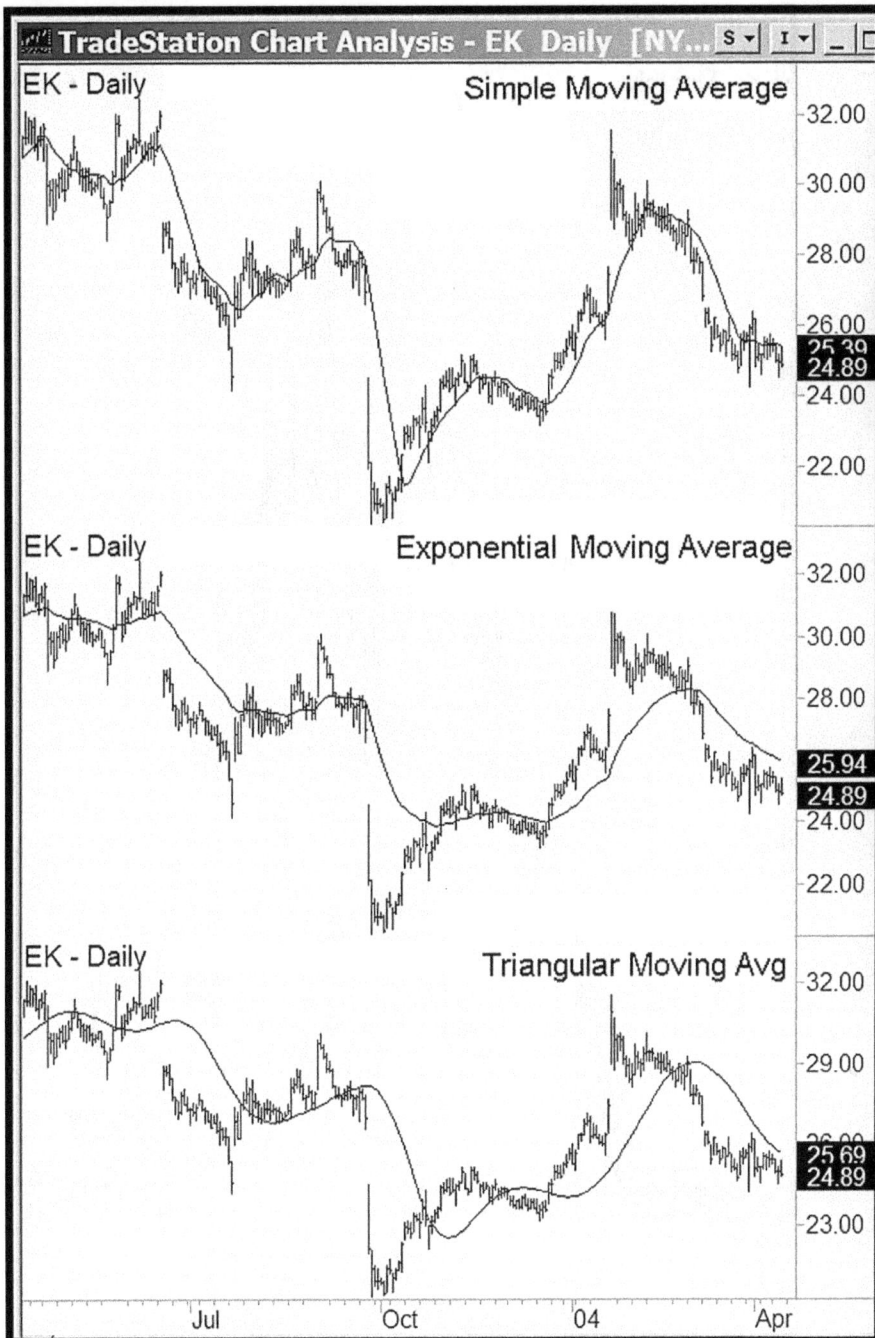

Moving Averages Setup Simple with Exponential

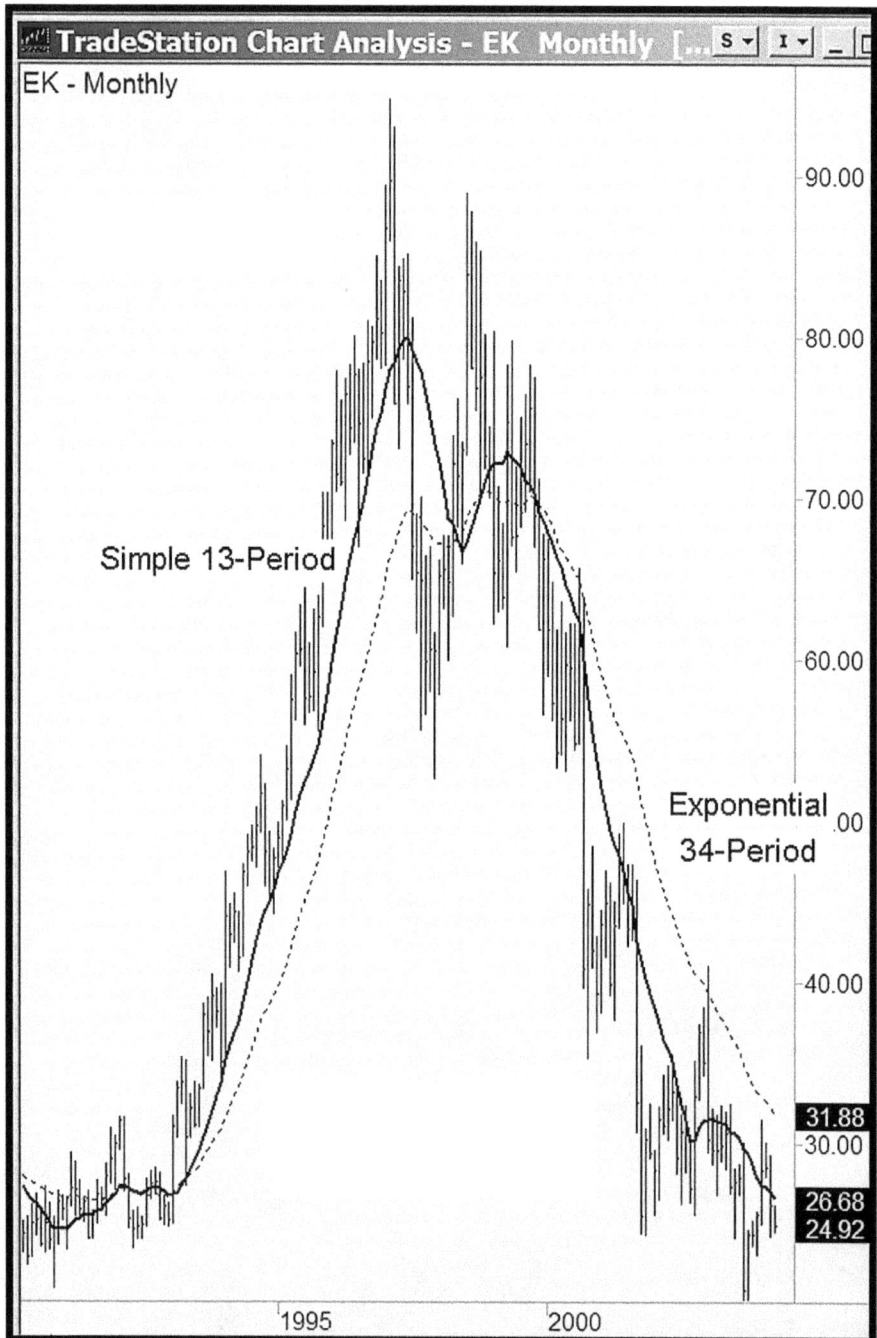

Moving Averages Setup Simple Versus Displaced

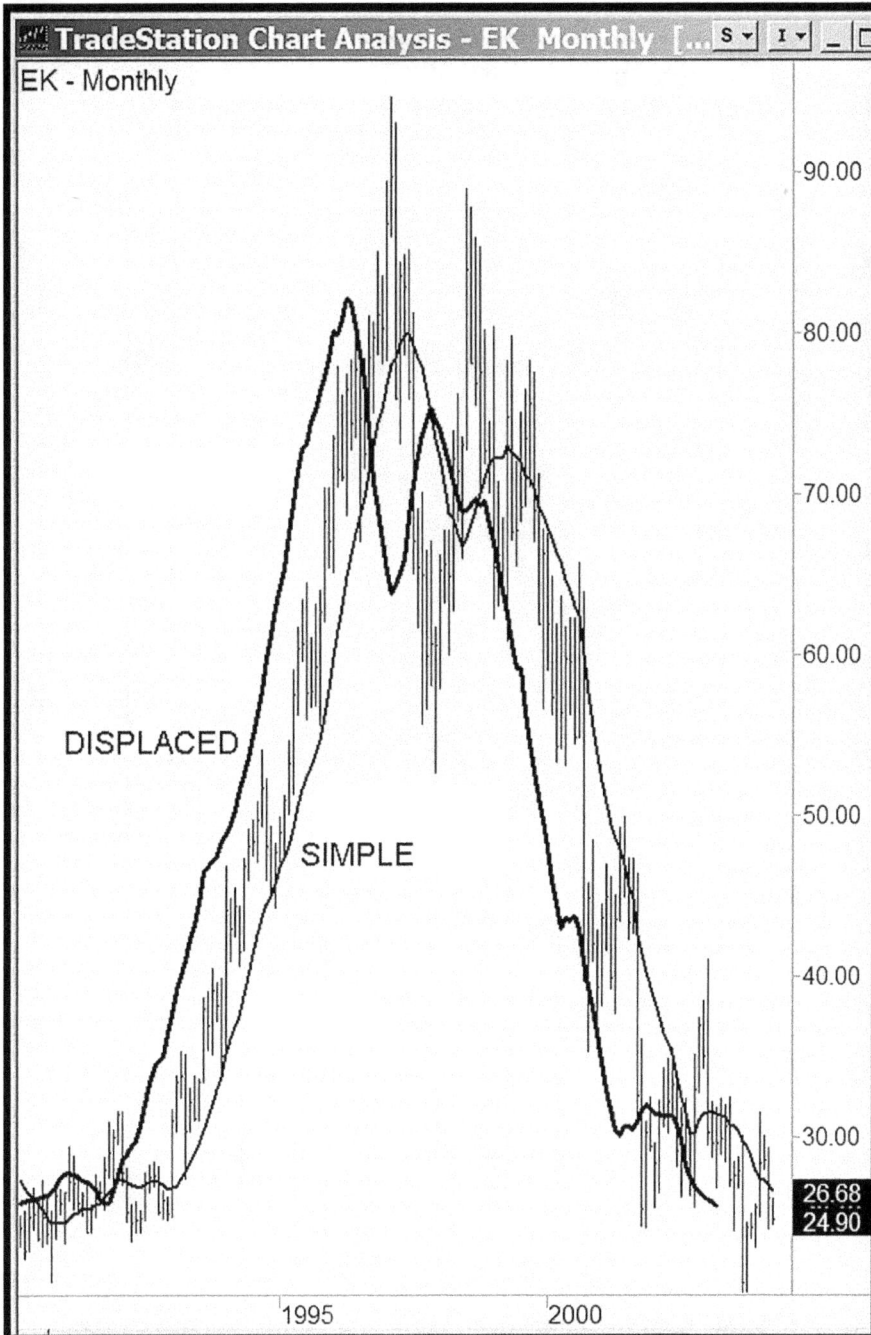

Open Interest Declining with Volume Decline, and Price Is Corrective

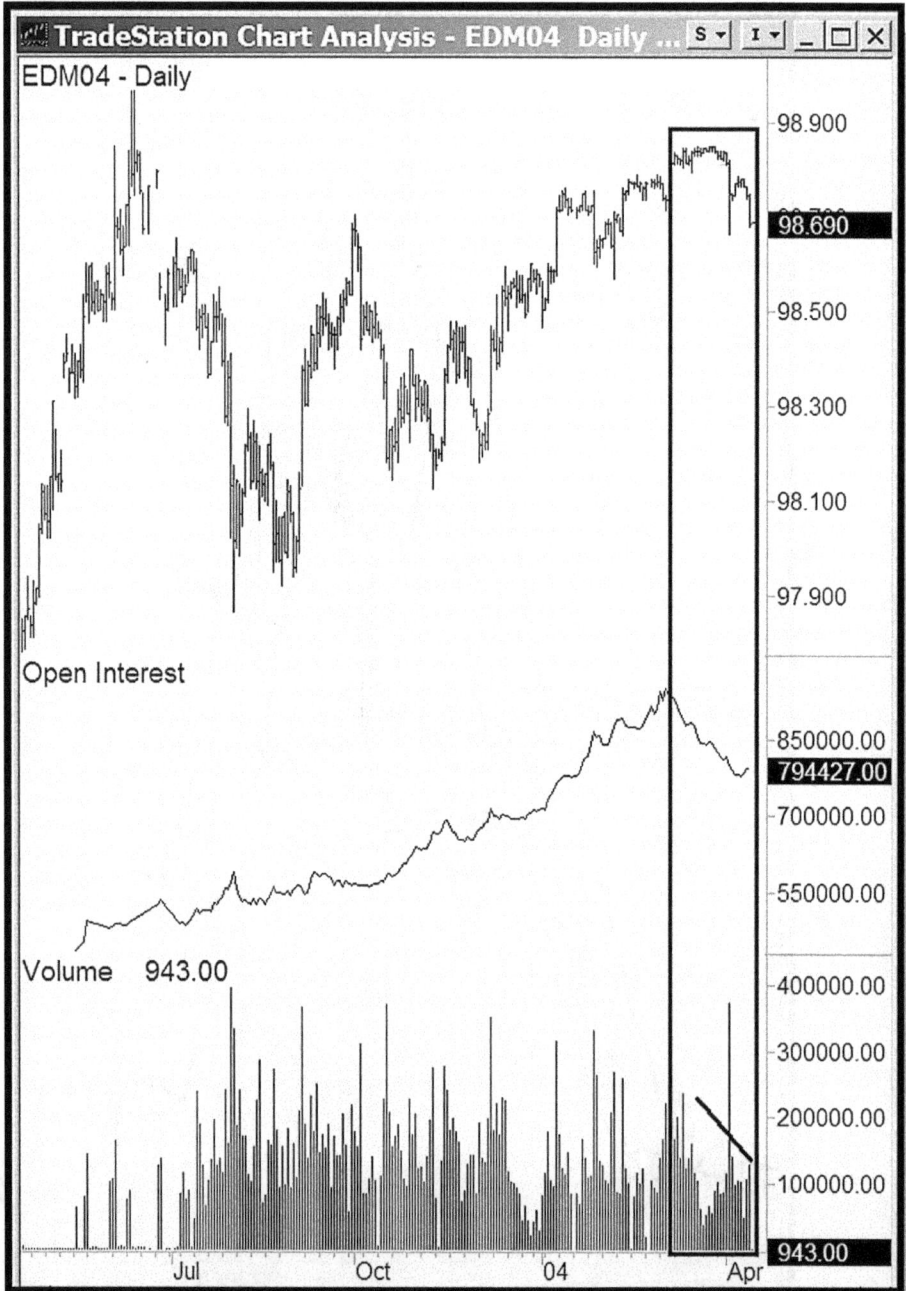

Open Interest Rising with Volume
Increase in Downtrend Confirms Weak Market

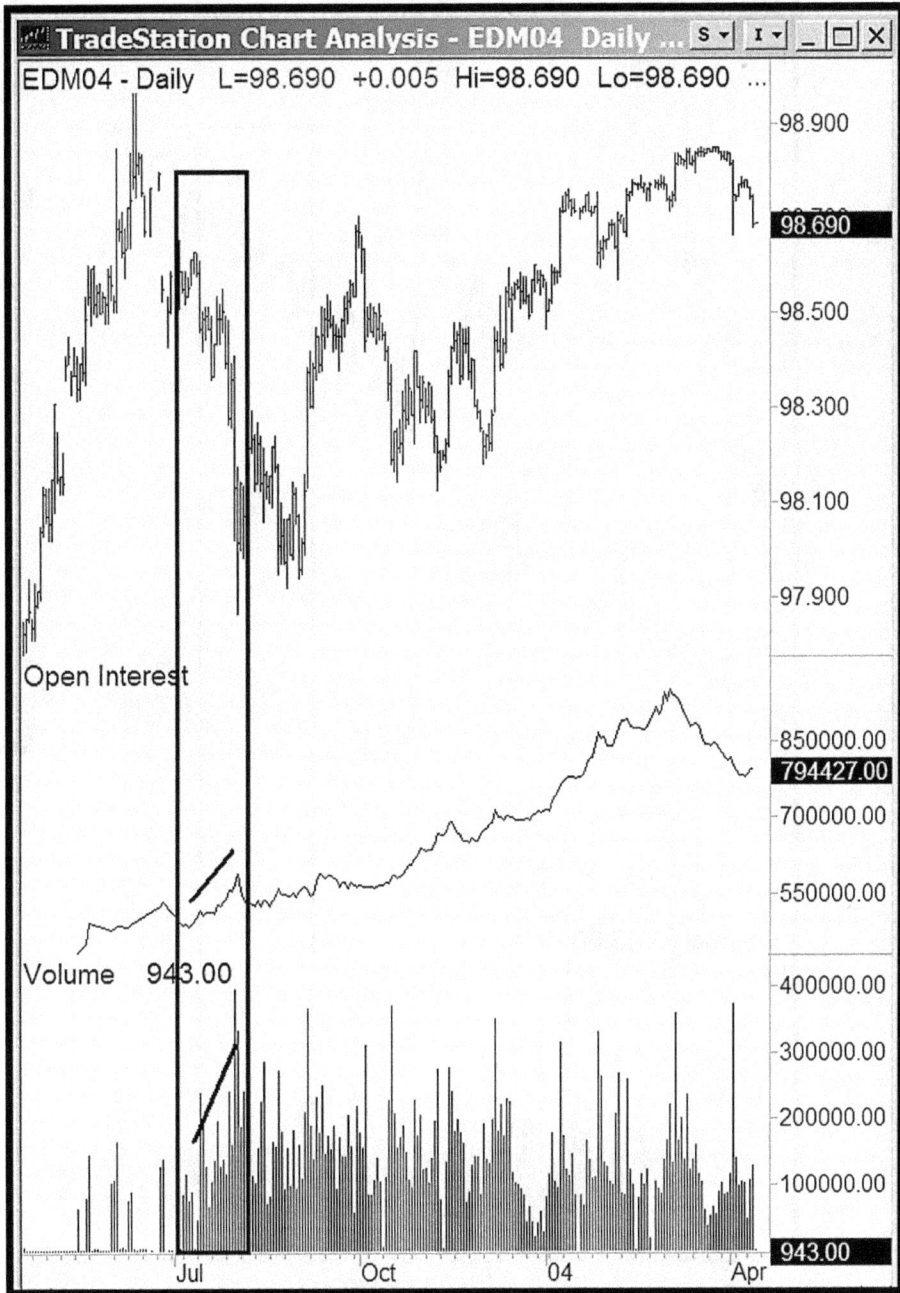

Open Interest Rising with Volume Increase Is Trend Confirmation

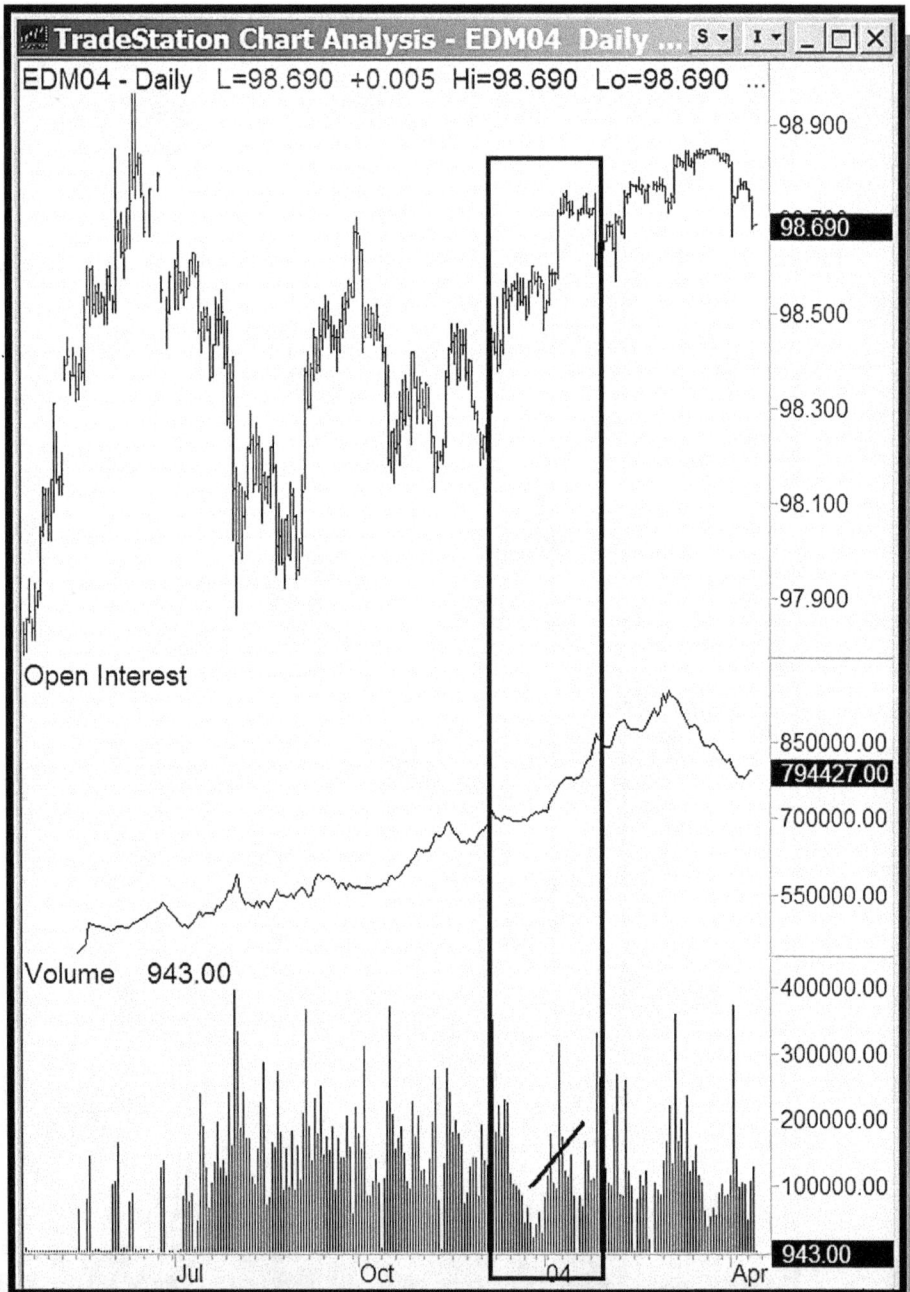

Oscillator Comparison: RSI Versus MACD

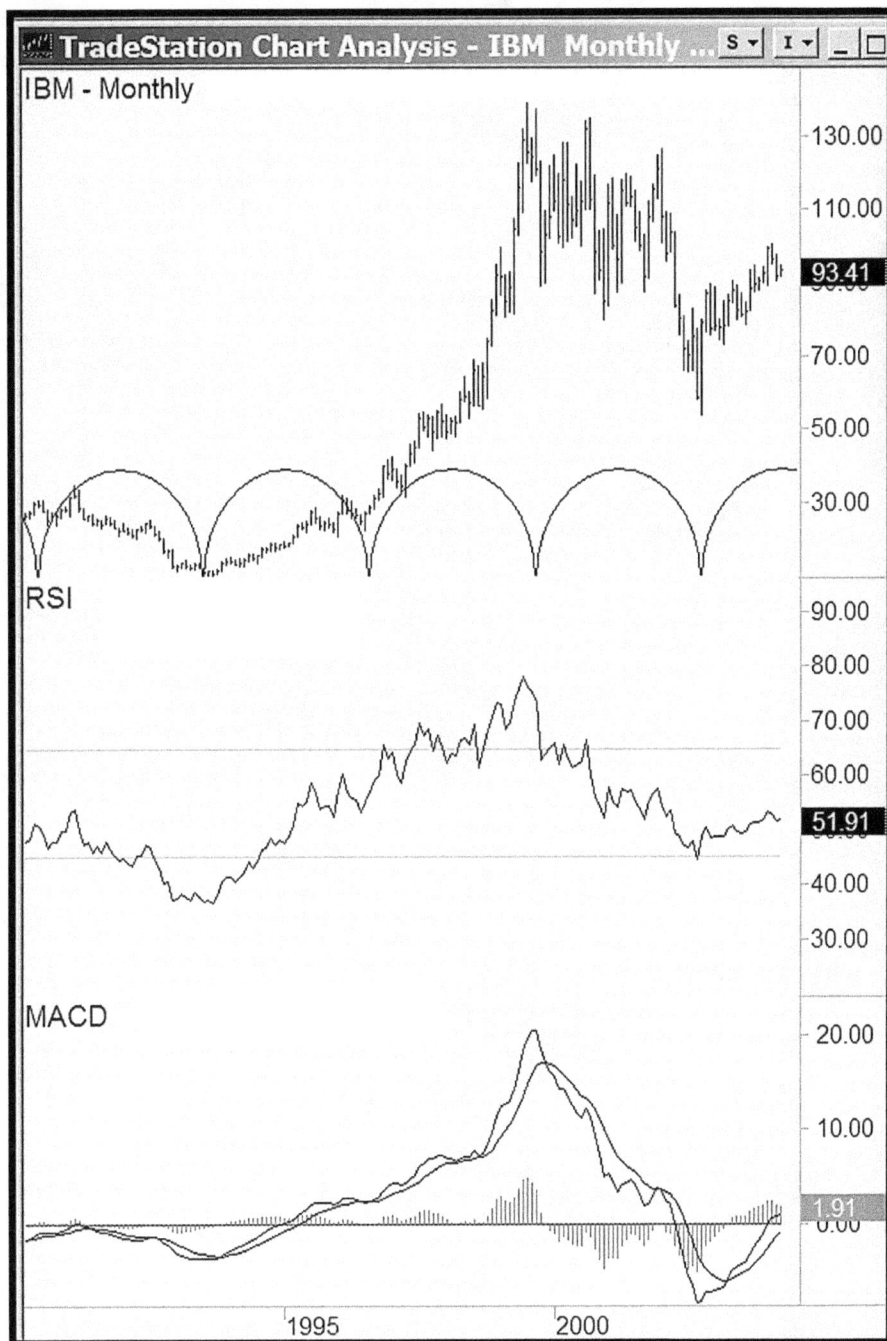

Oscillator Comparison: RSI Versus Stochastic

Oscillator Comparison: RSI Versus Ultimate Oscillator

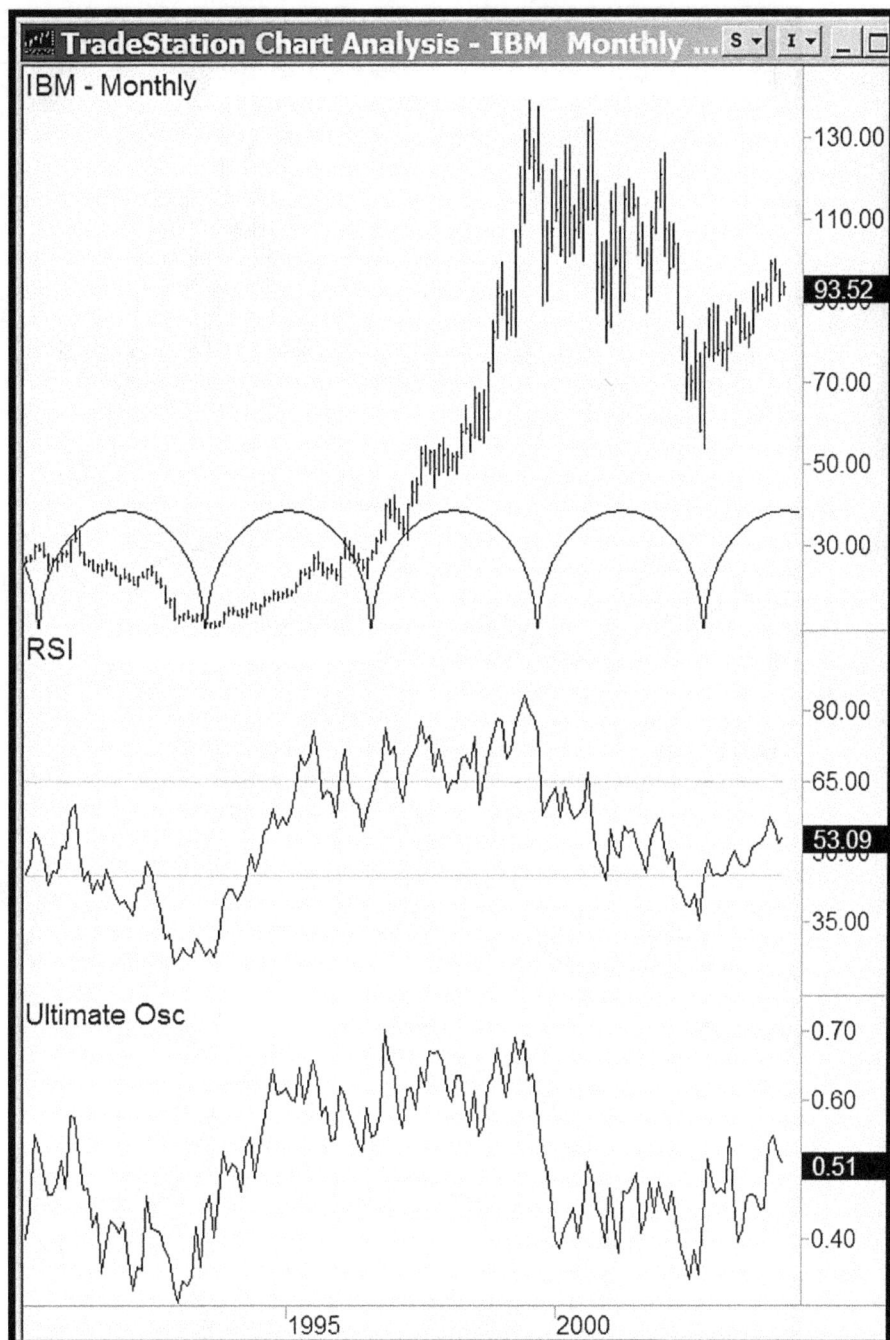

Oscillator Comparison: RSI with Averages Versus MACD

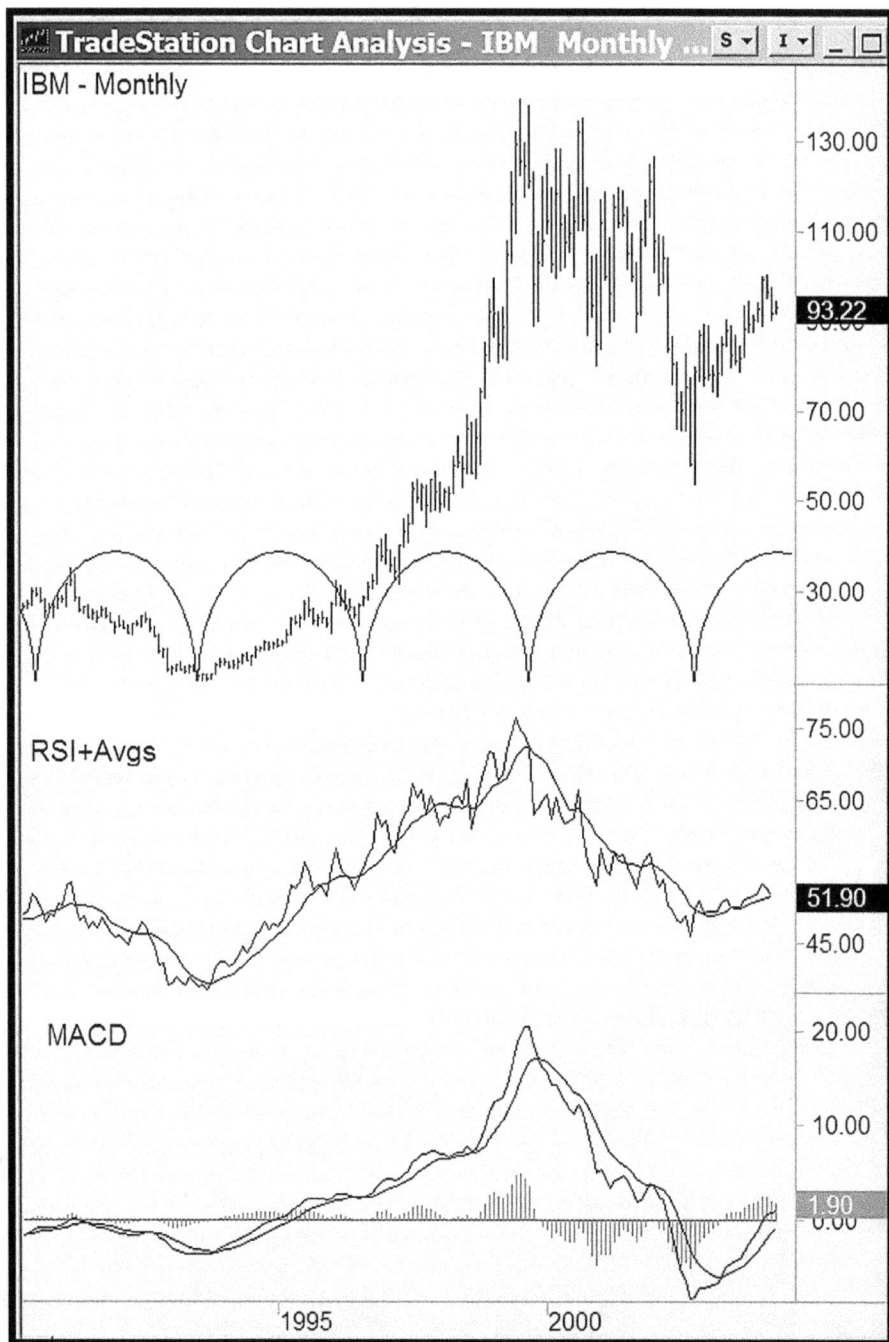

Oscillator Comparison: RSI with Averages Versus Stochastic with Averages

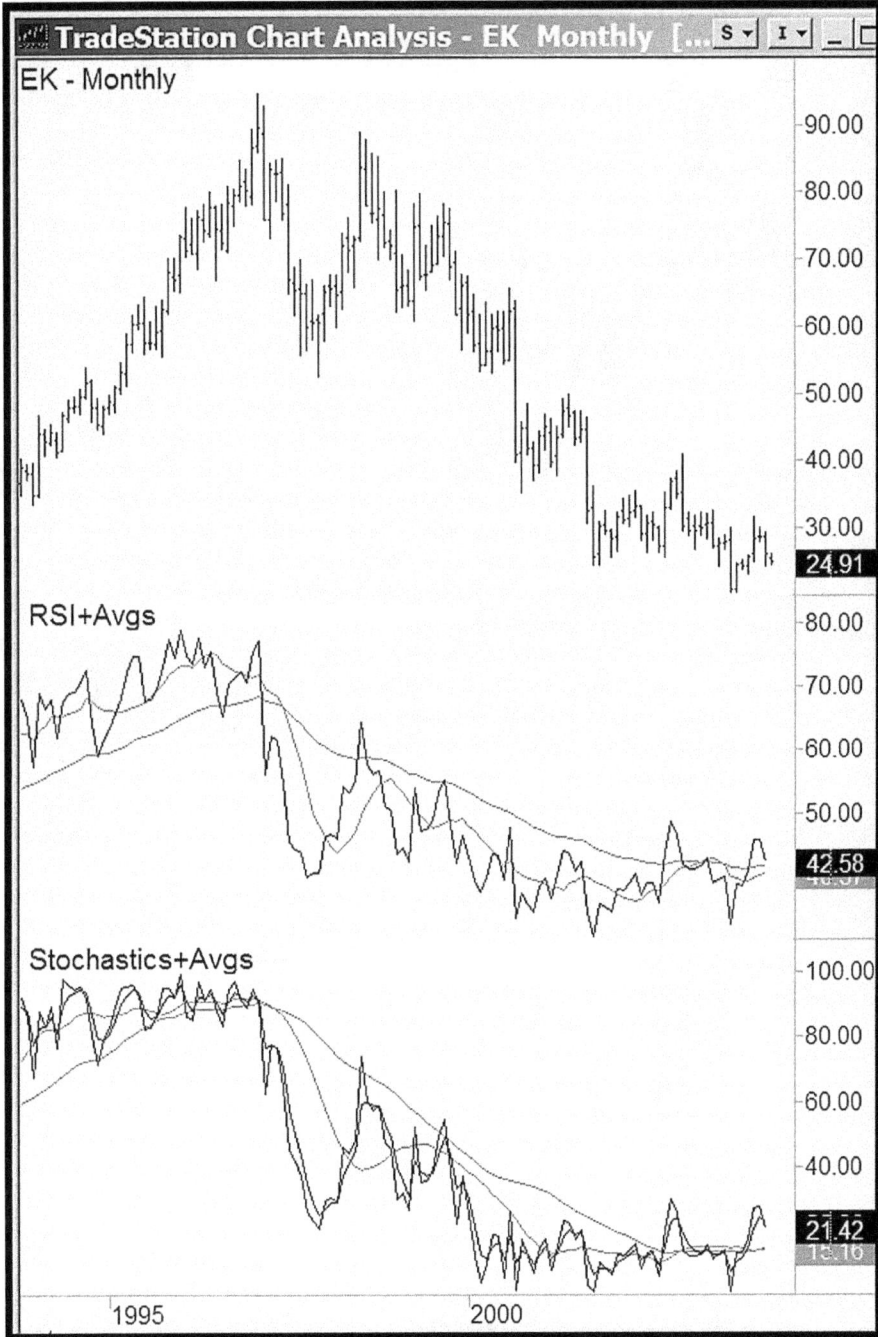

Oscillator Comparison: Stochastic with Averages Versus RSI with Averages

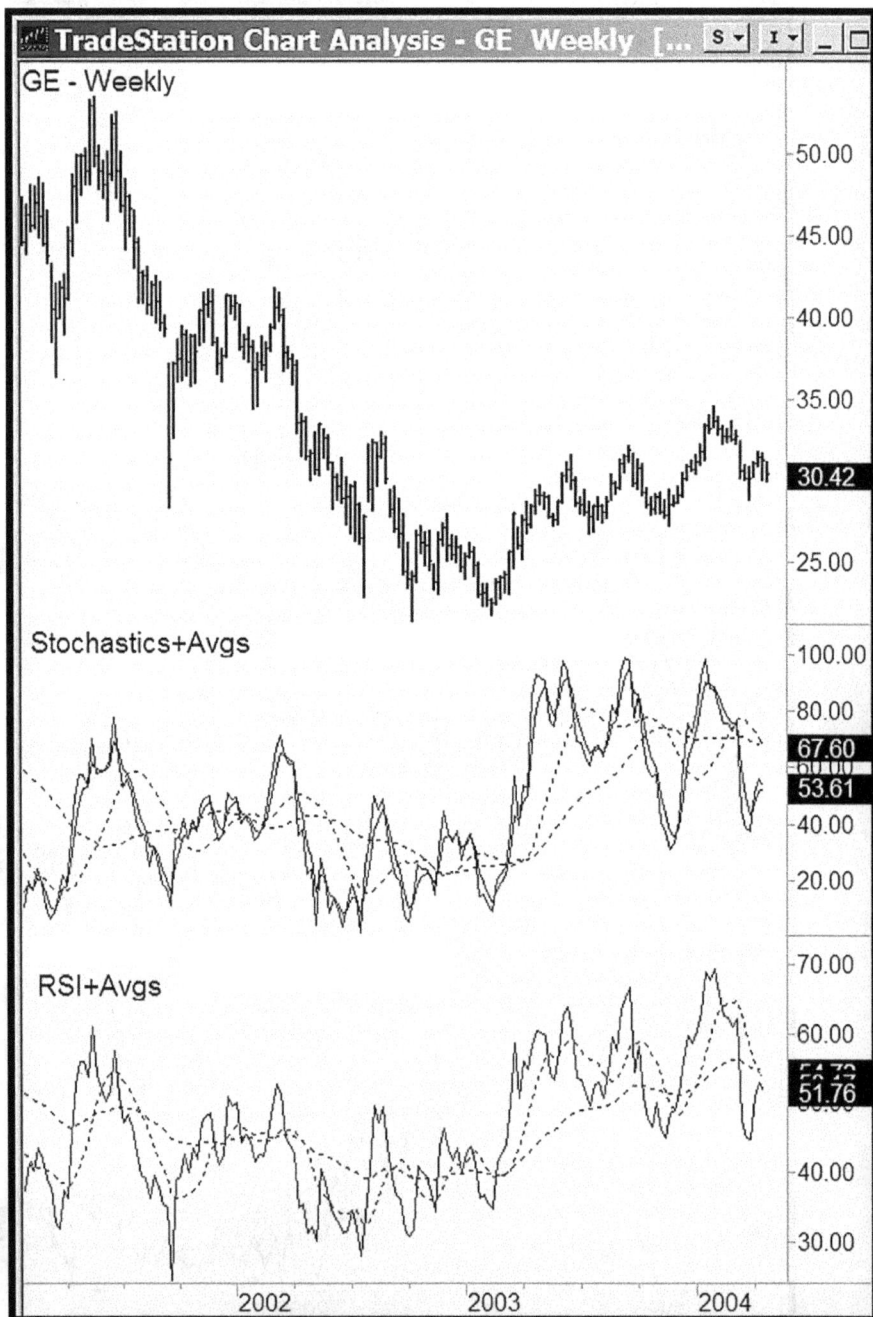

Oscillator Comparisons Not Normalized (Not Bound within Zero to 100)

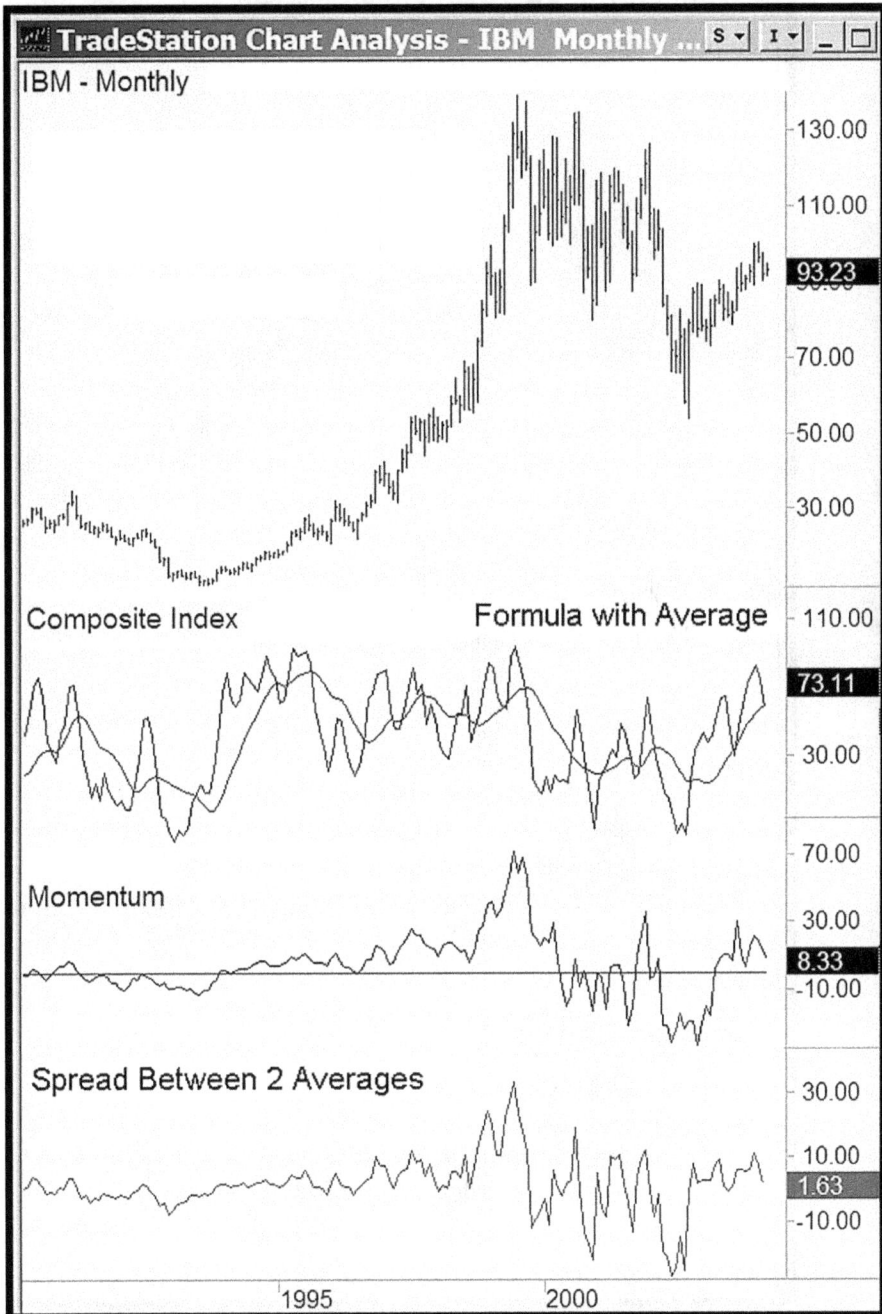

Oscillator Comparisons of Histograms

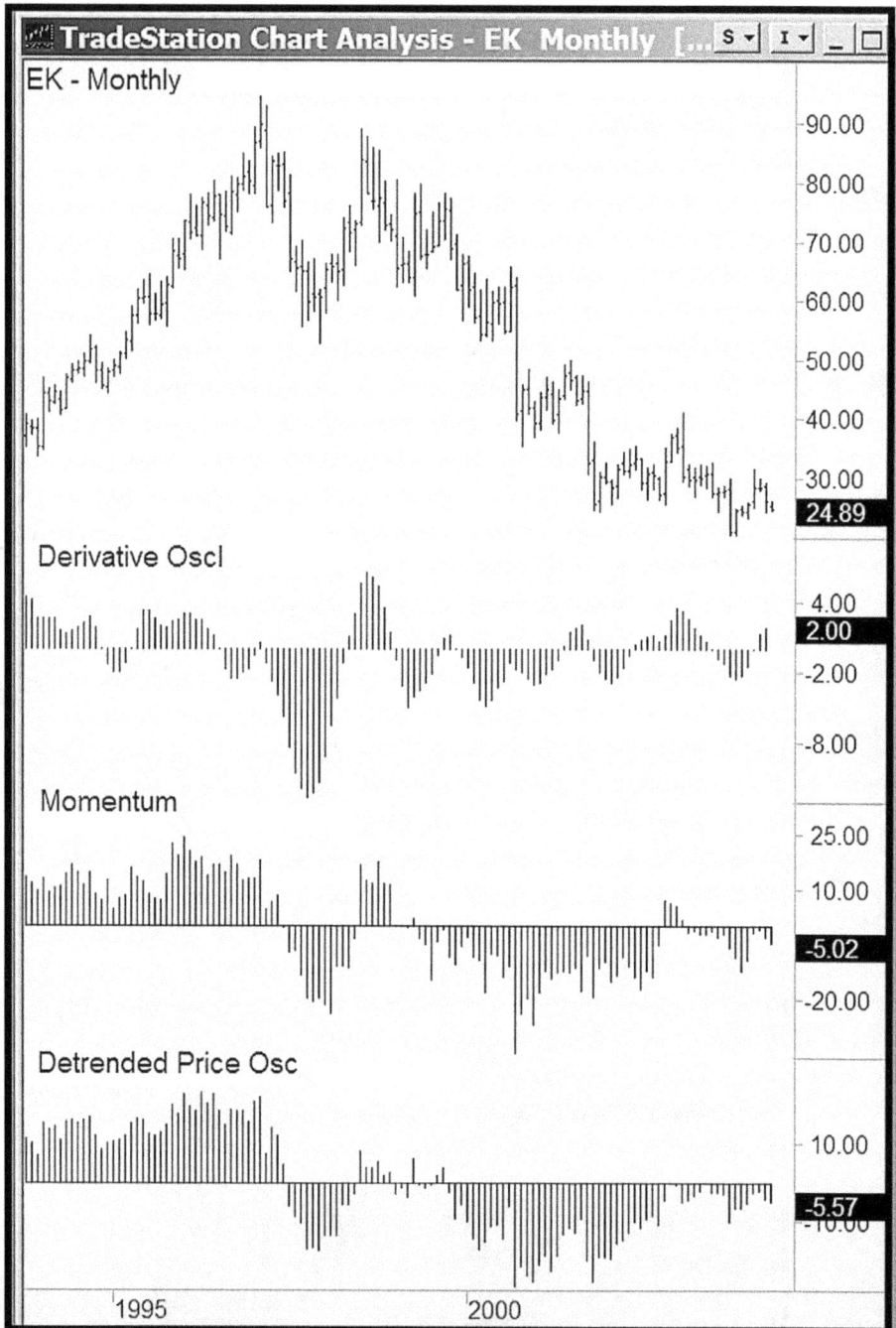

Oscillator Reverse Engineering*

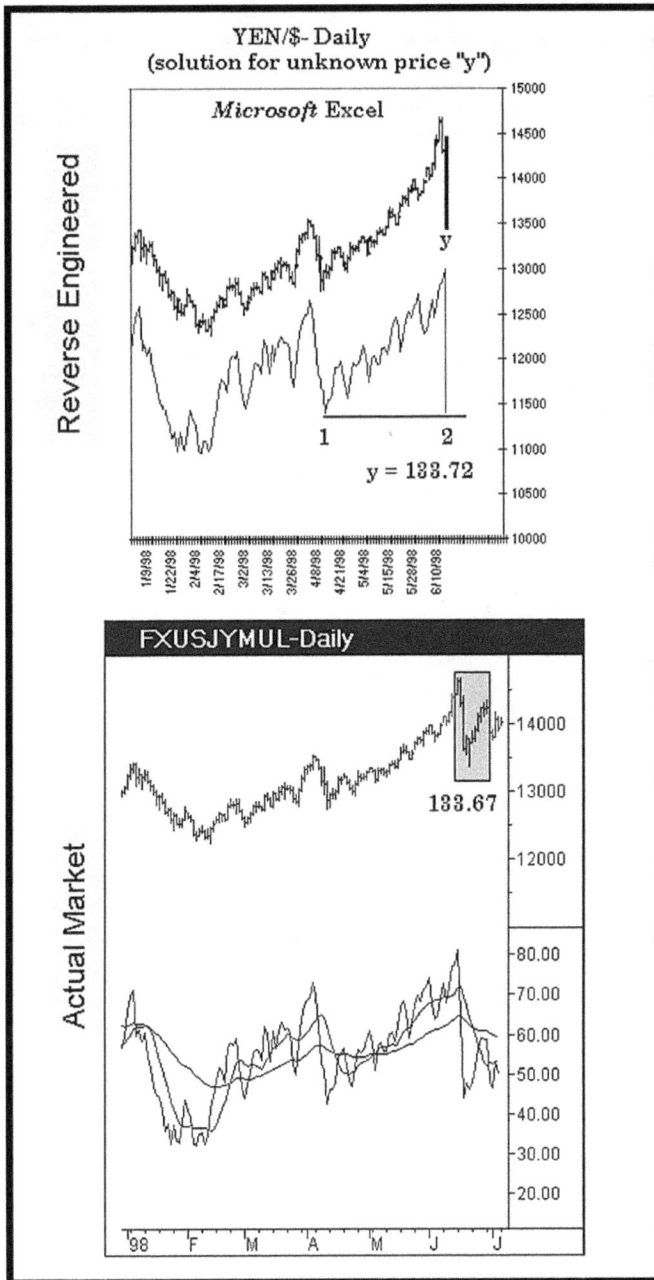

*For more information, please refer to *Technical Analysis for the Trading Professional* by Constance Brown (New York: McGraw-Hill), 1999.

Overlay Chronological
Comparison: Nikkei Versus Displaced SP500

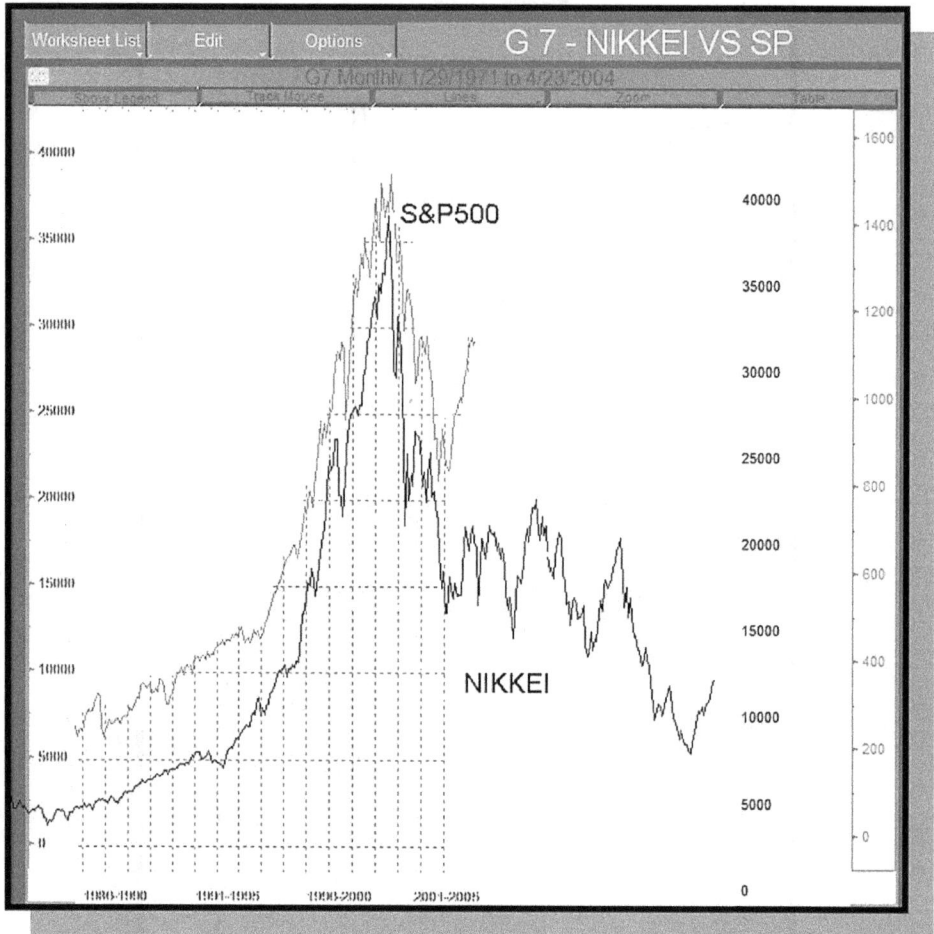

Overlay Chronological Comparison: Nikkei Versus SP500

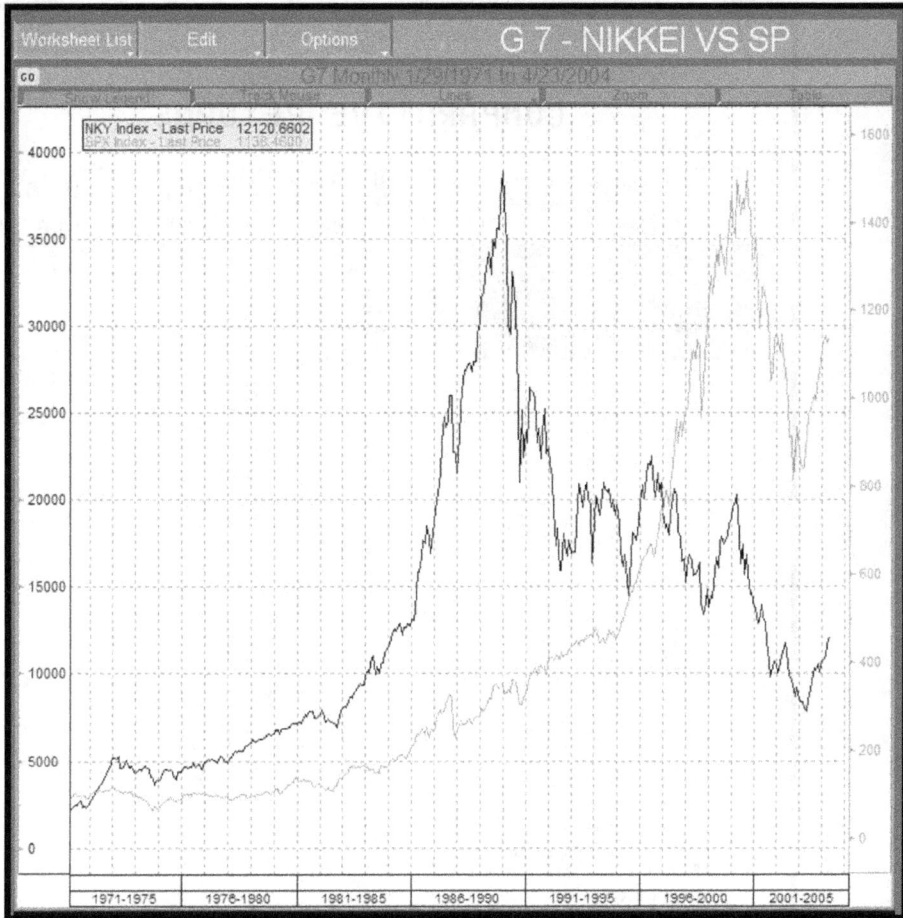

Overlay Comparative Returns

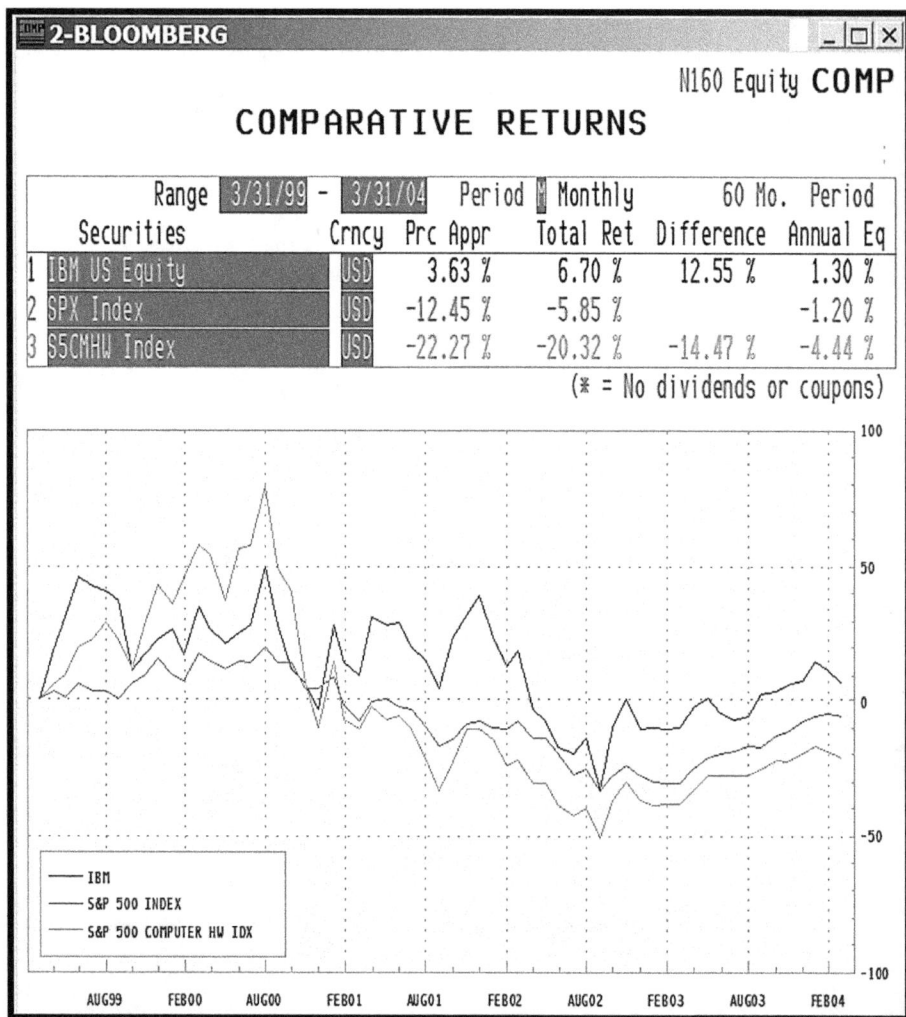

```
┌─────────────────────────────────────────────────────────────────────┐
│ ▨ 2-BLOOMBERG                                          _ □ ×          │
│                                                   N160 Equity COMP    │
│                    COMPARATIVE RETURNS                                │
│                                                                       │
│       Range  3/31/99 - 3/31/04   Period ⩔ Monthly    60 Mo. Period    │
│      Securities          Crncy  Prc Appr  Total Ret Difference Annual Eq│
│  1 IBM US Equity          USD    3.63 %    6.70 %    12.55 %   1.30 %  │
│  2 SPX Index              USD  -12.45 %   -5.85 %             -1.20 %  │
│  3 S5CMHW Index           USD  -22.27 %  -20.32 %   -14.47 %  -4.44 %  │
│                              (* = No dividends or coupons)            │
```

Securities	Crncy	Prc Appr	Total Ret	Difference	Annual Eq
1 IBM US Equity	USD	3.63 %	6.70 %	12.55 %	1.30 %
2 SPX Index	USD	-12.45 %	-5.85 %		-1.20 %
3 S5CMHW Index	USD	-22.27 %	-20.32 %	-14.47 %	-4.44 %

(* = No dividends or coupons)

Legend:
IBM
S&P 500 INDEX
S&P 500 COMPUTER HW IDX

X-axis: AUG99 FEB00 AUG00 FEB01 AUG01 FEB02 AUG02 FEB03 AUG03 FEB04
Y-axis: 100 / 50 / 0 / -50 / -100

Overlay Comparison: DJIA 1929 High Versus Nasdaq 2000 High

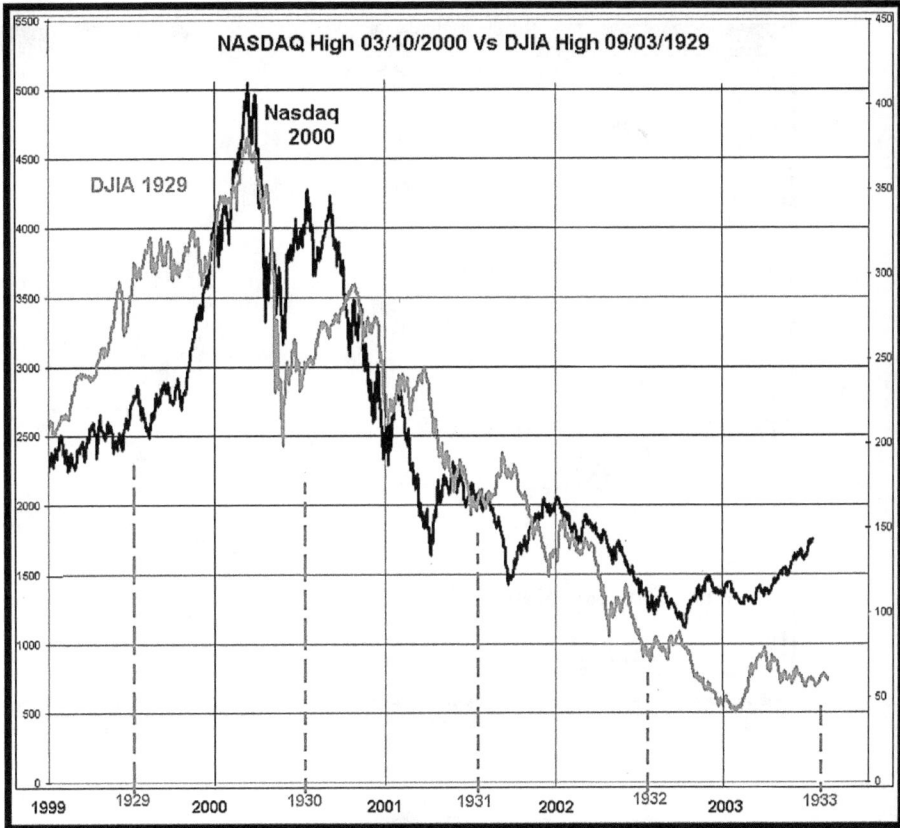

NASDAQ High 03/10/2000 Vs DJIA High 09/03/1929

Overlay Comparison: North American Stock Markets

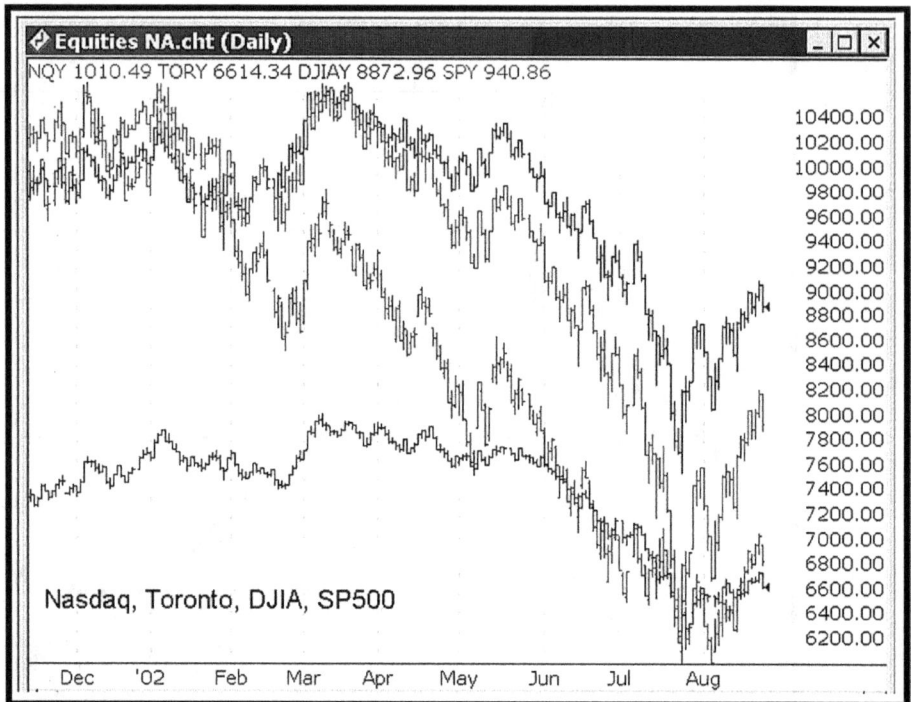

Nasdaq, Toronto, DJIA, SP500

Overlay Comparison: Relative Performance

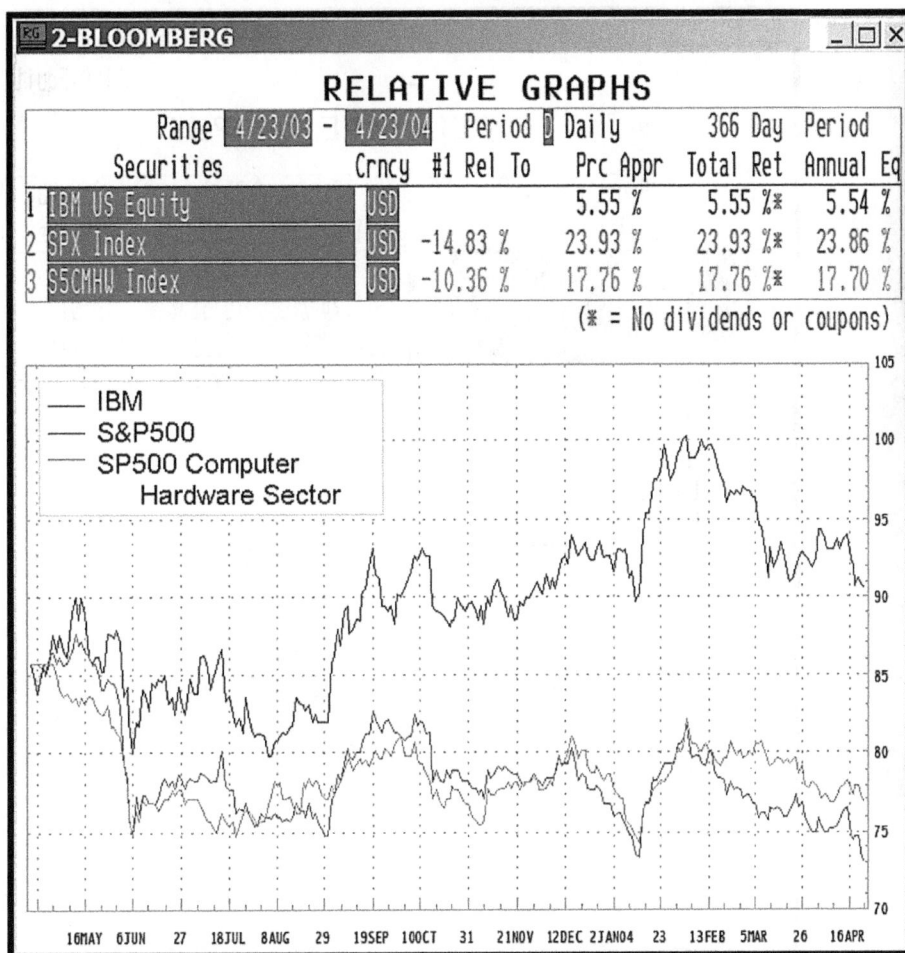

Overlay Comparison: Relative Stock Performance

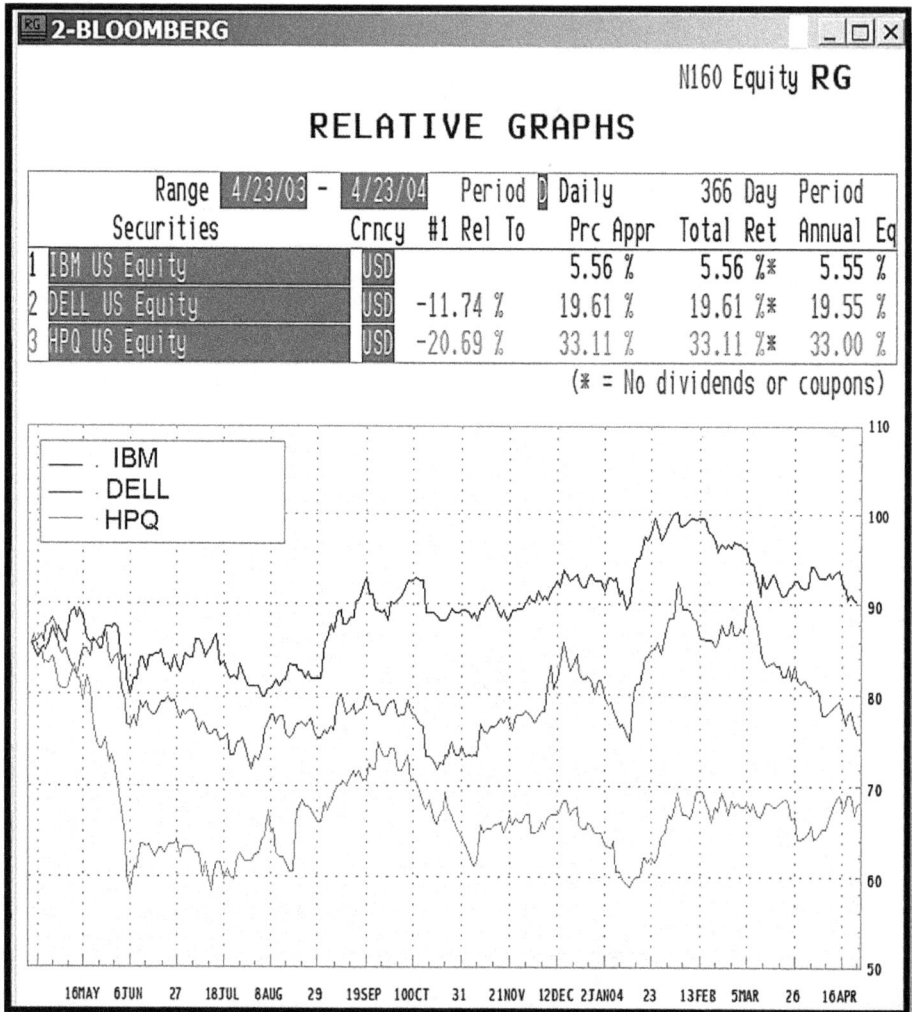

Overlay Comparison: World Stock Markets (Daily)

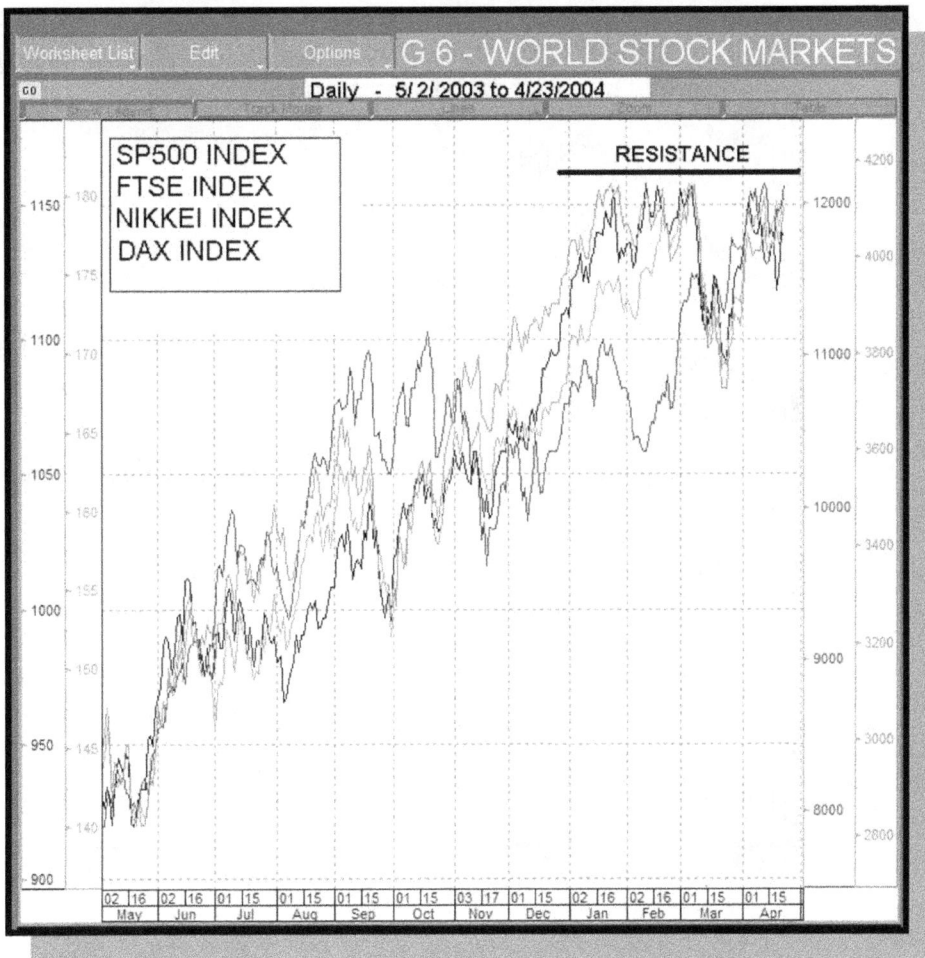

Overlay Comparison: World Stock Markets (Weekly)

Pattern Continuation: Bearish Flag

Pattern Continuation: Bullish Pennant

Pattern Continuation: Contracting Triangle

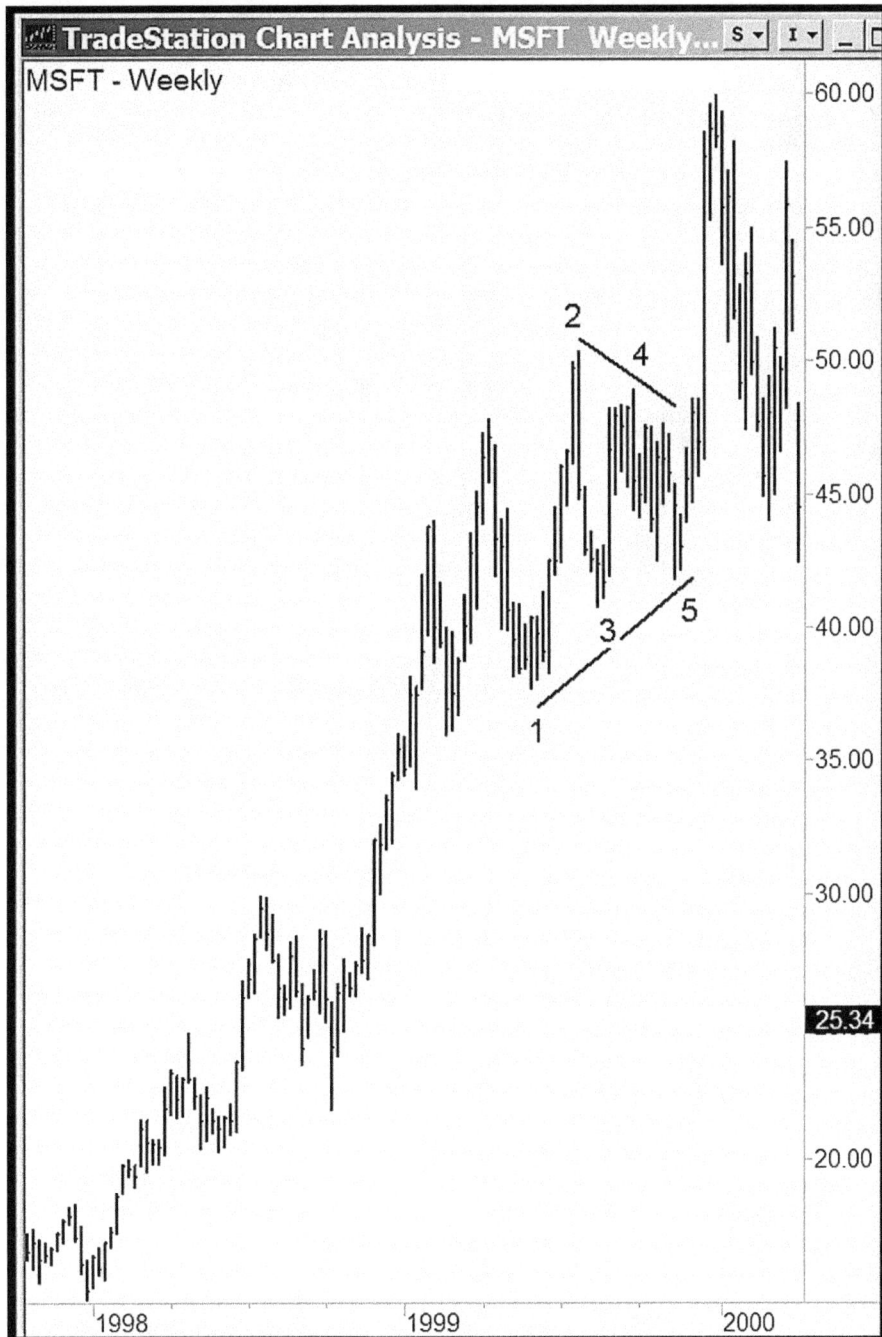

Pattern Continuation: Expanding Triangle

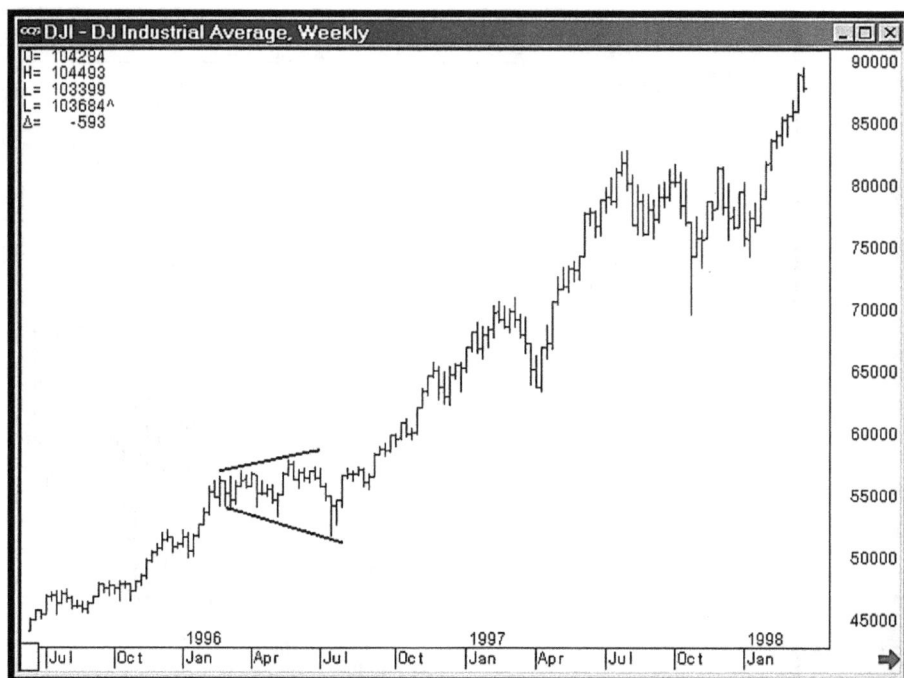

Pattern Resolution: "Thrust out of a Triangle"

Pattern Reversal: Diamond

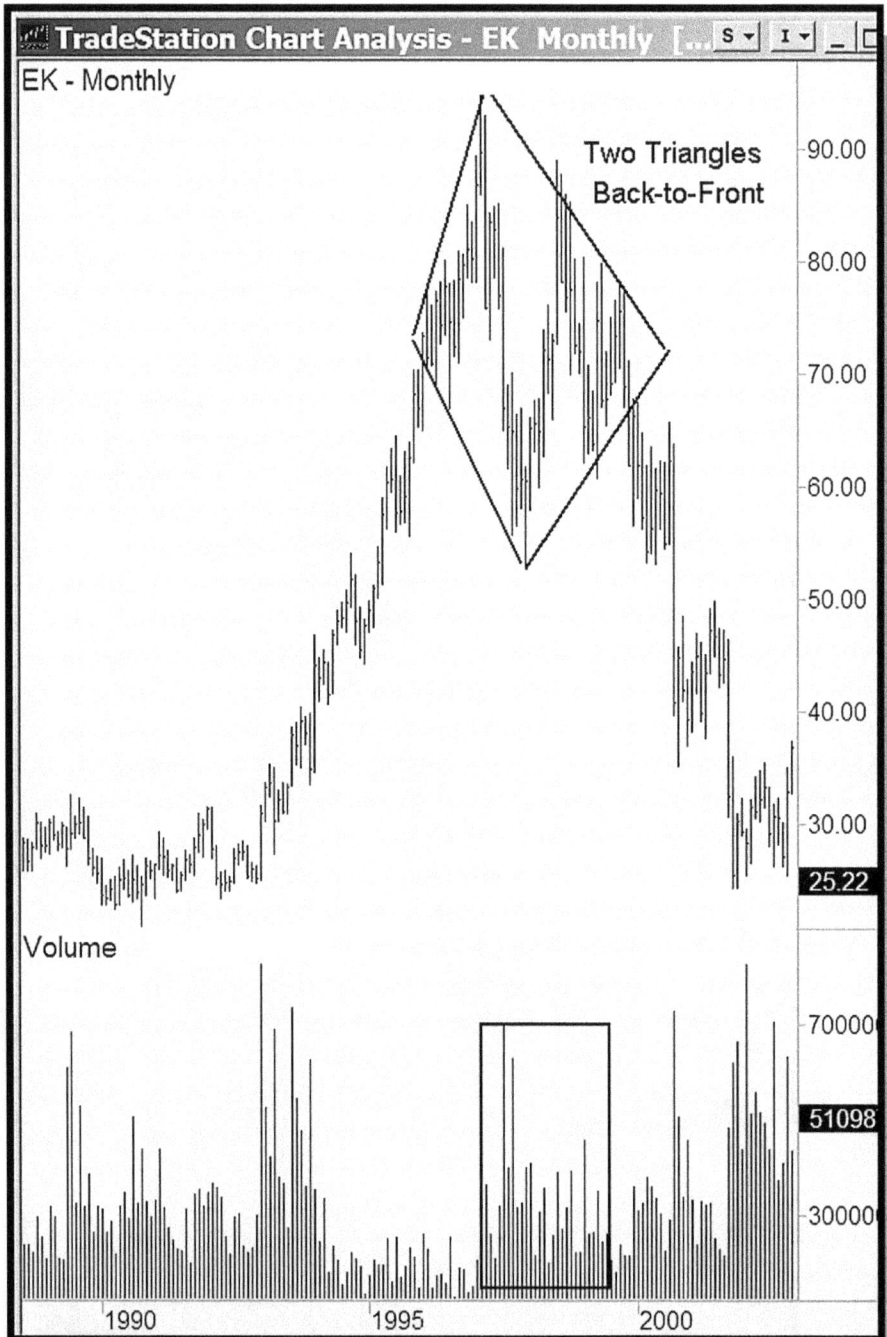

TradeStation Chart Analysis - EK Monthly [...]

EK - Monthly

Two Triangles
Back-to-Front

Volume

Pattern Reversal: Double Top

Pattern Reversal: Falling Termination Wedge

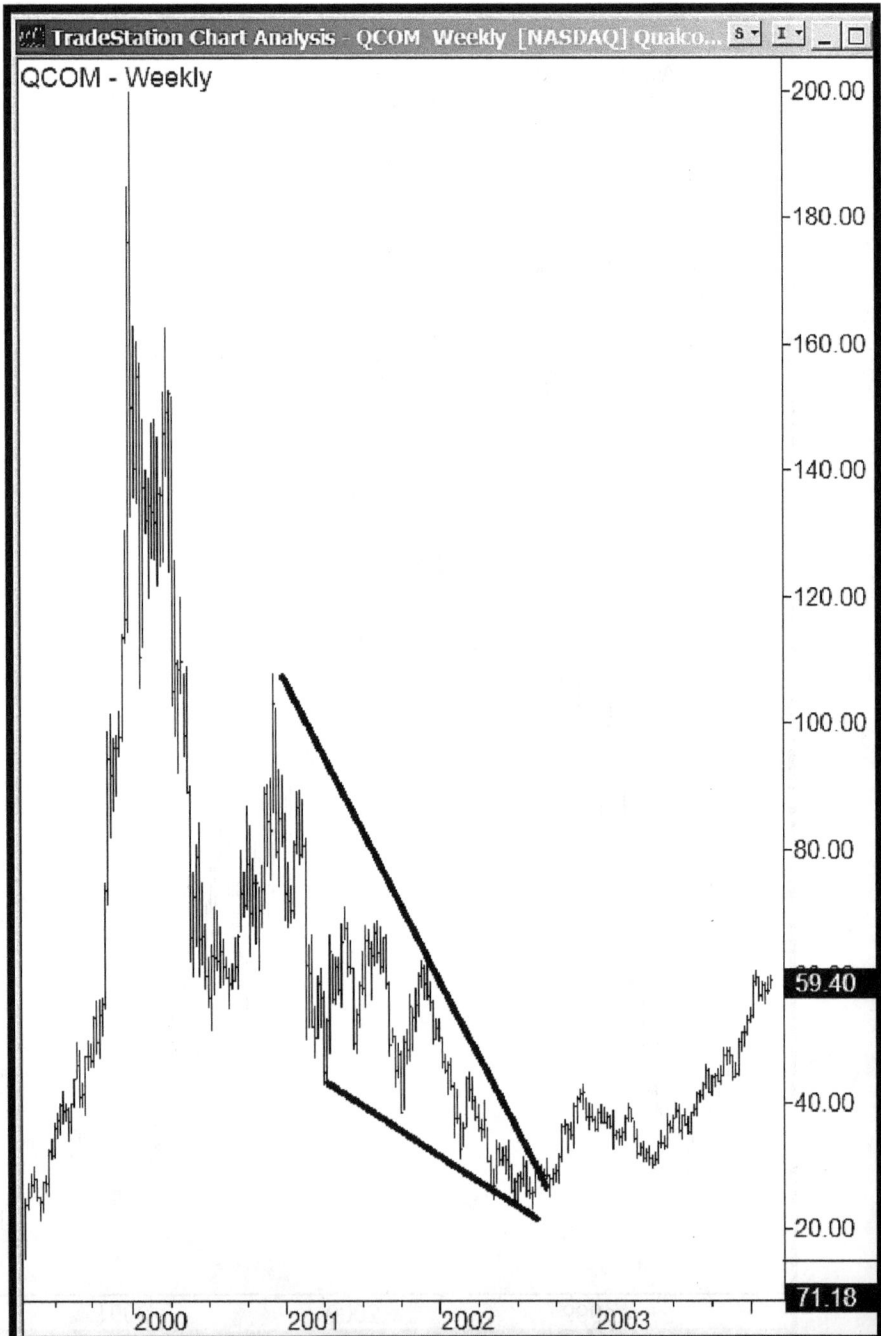

Pattern Reversal: Inside Day

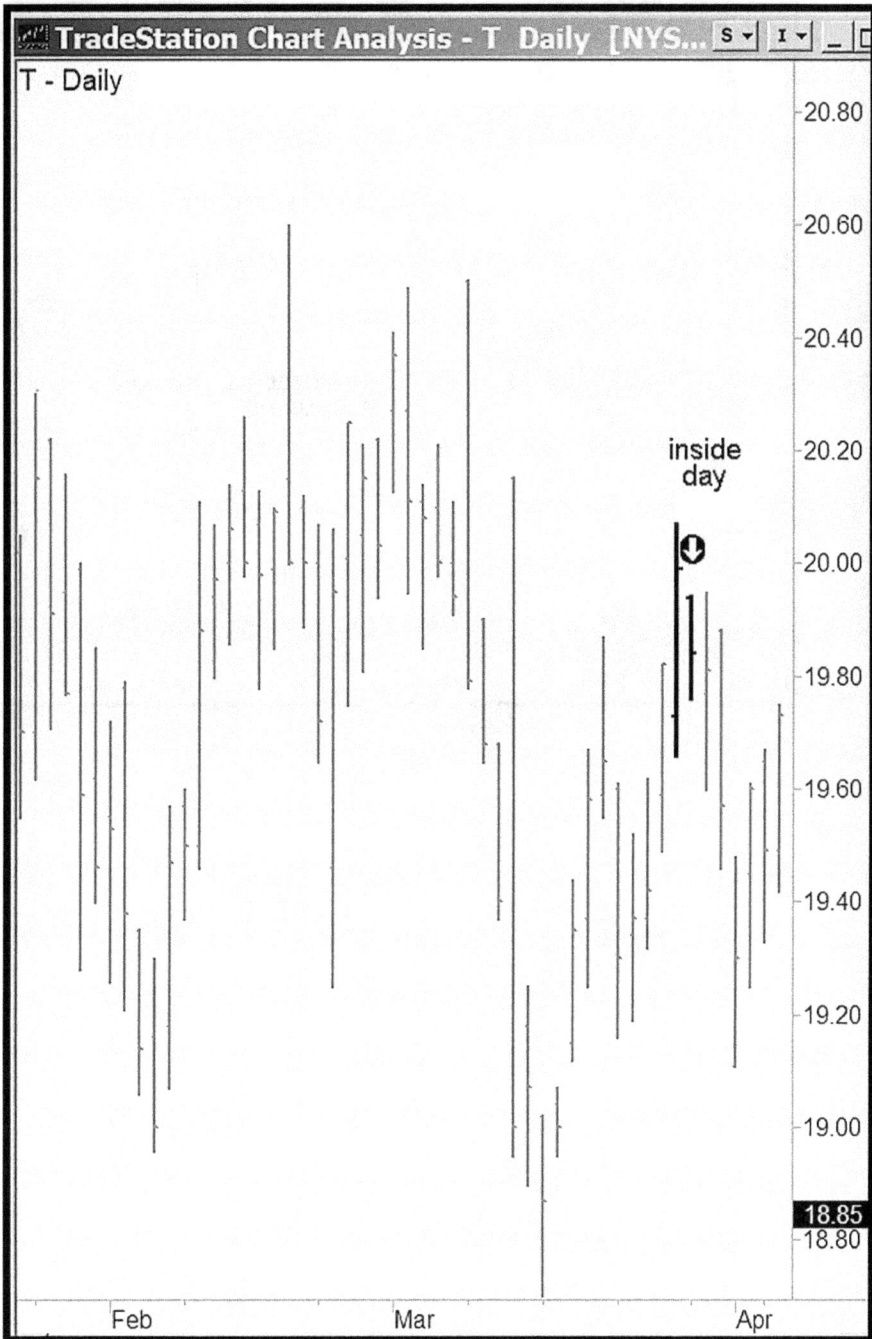

Pattern Reversal: Inverted Head and Shoulders

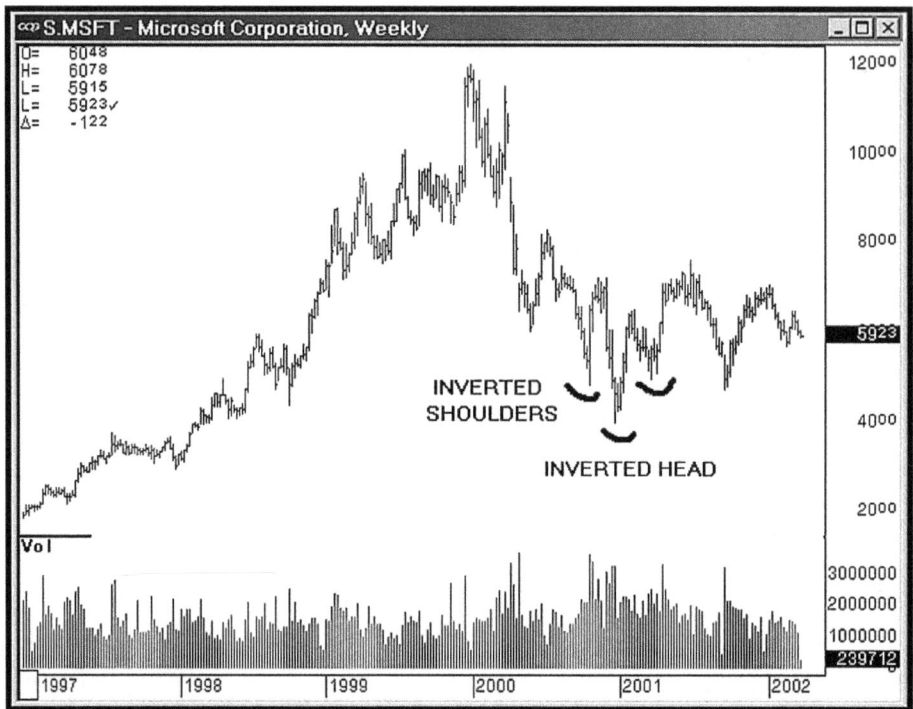

Pattern Reversal: Outside Day

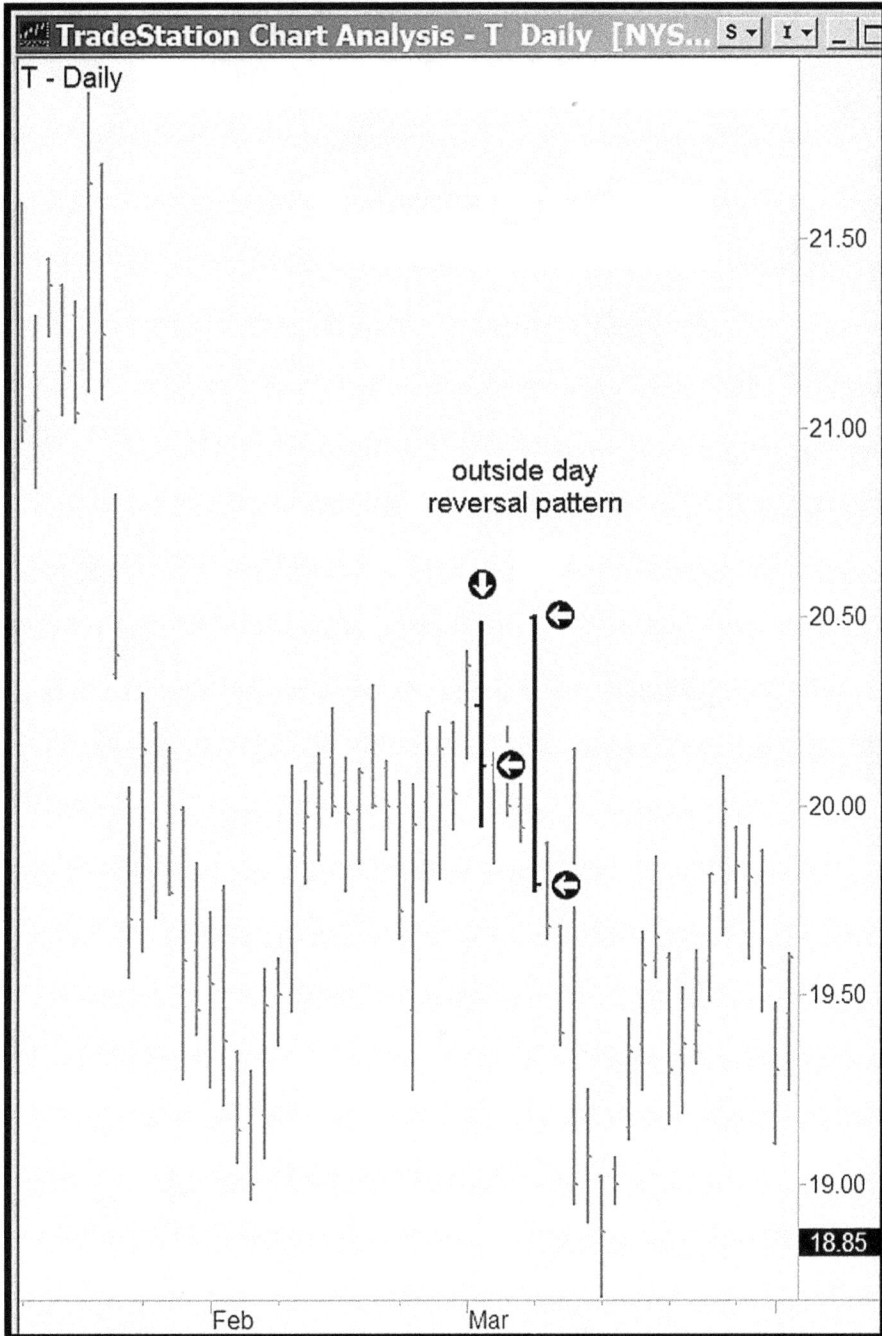

Pattern Reversal: Rounding Bottom

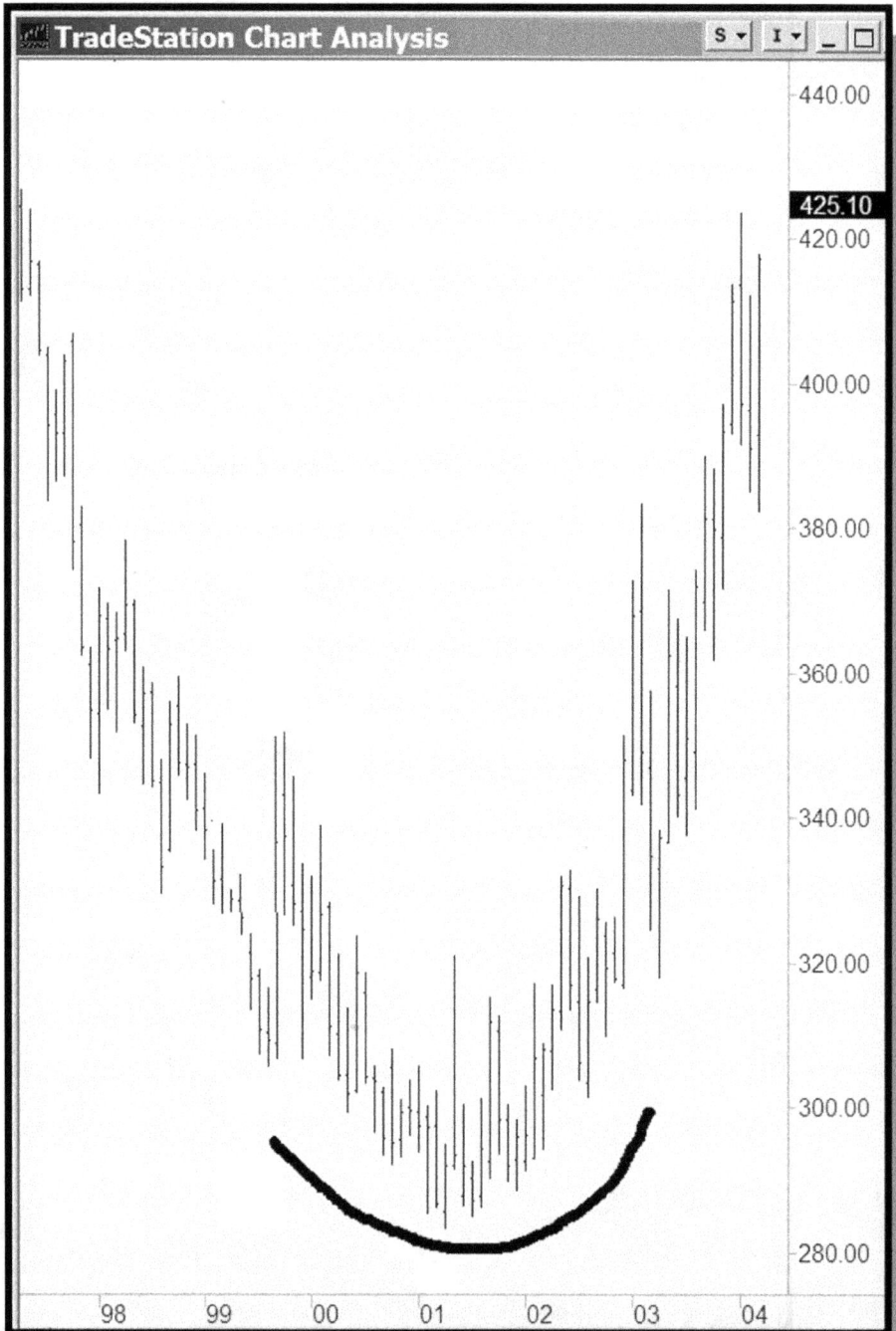

Pattern Reversal Triple Bottom

Pattern Reversal: Triple Top

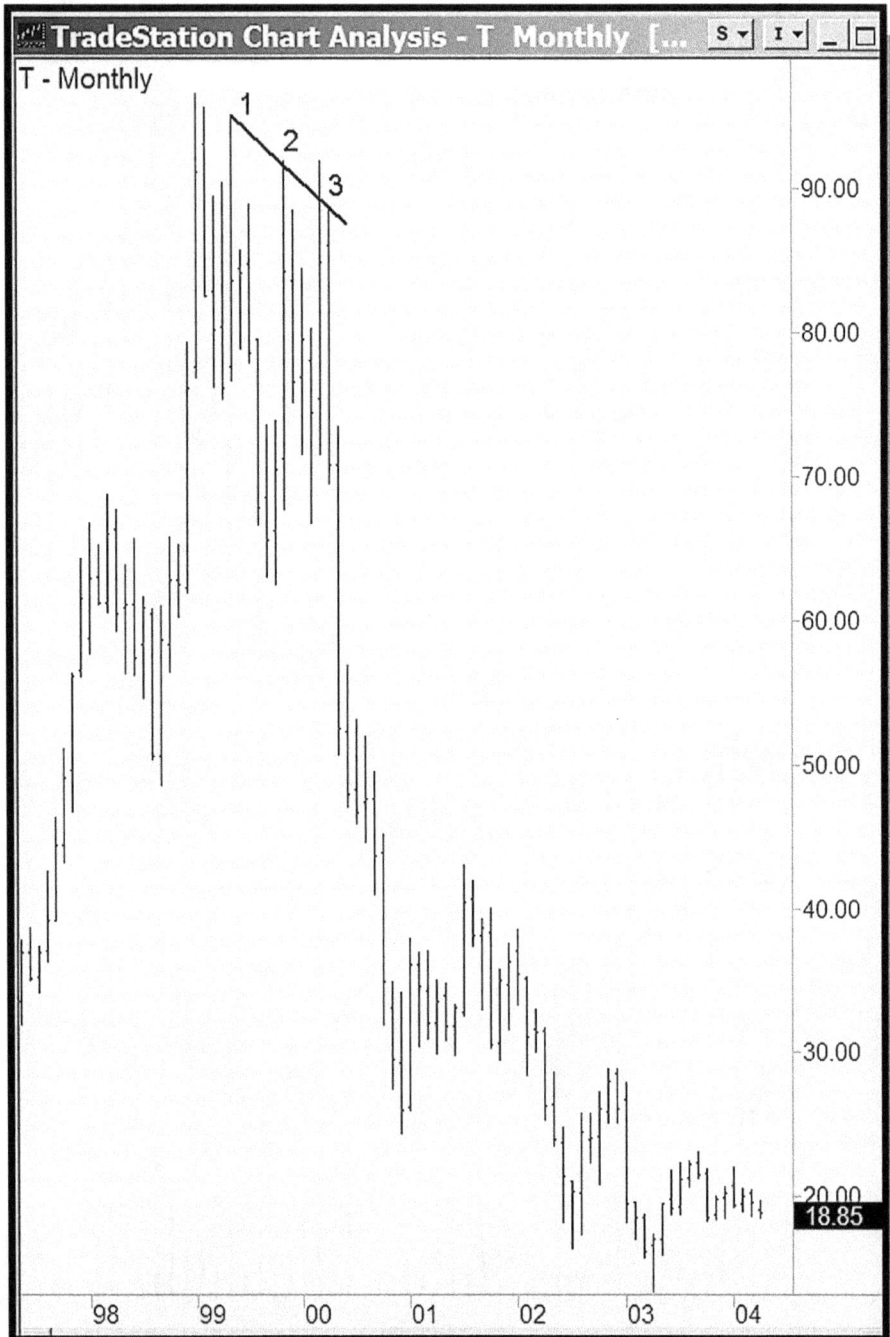

Pattern Reversal: V Bottom

Point-and-Figure Bearish Broadening Formation

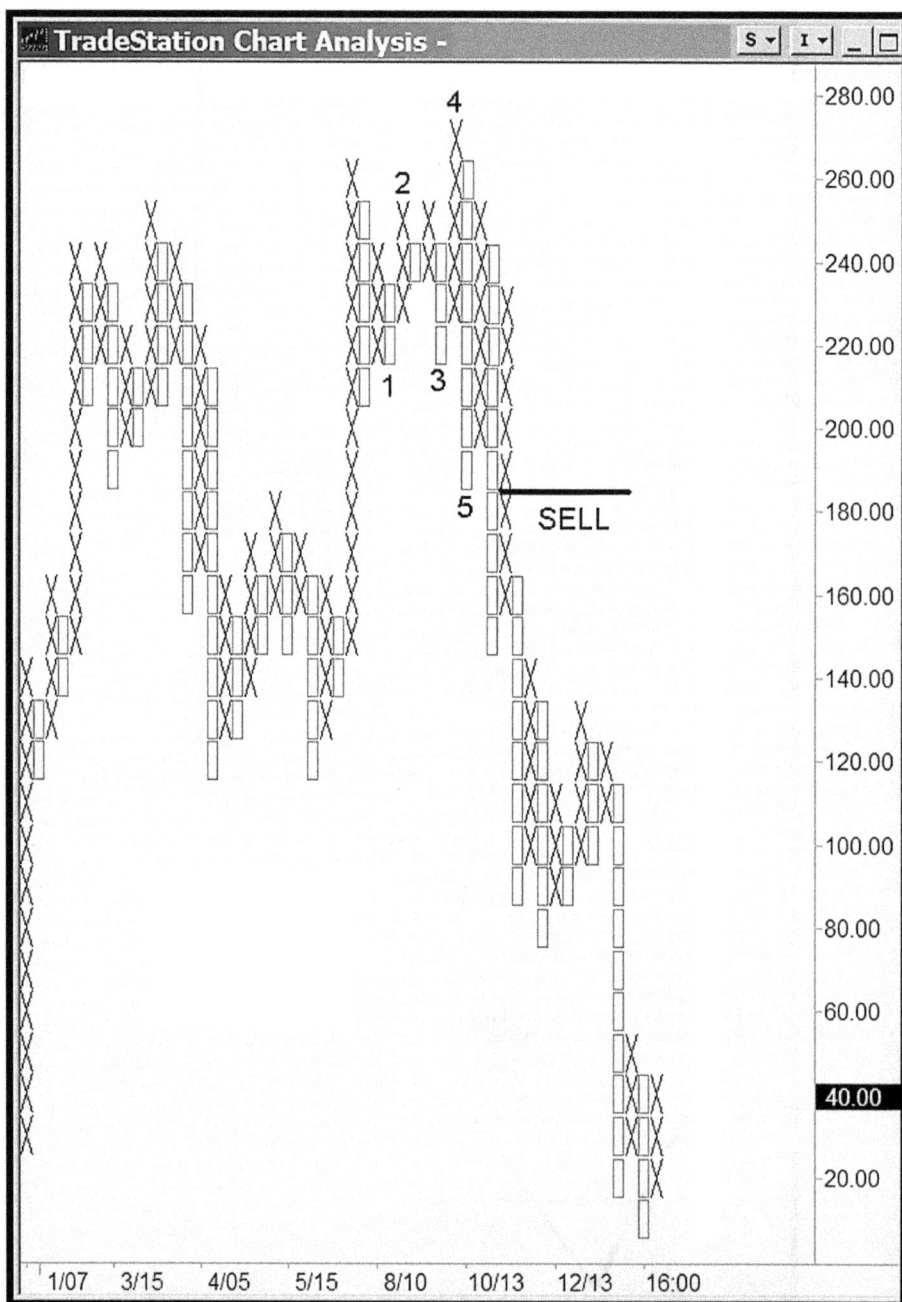

Point-and-Figure Bearish Trendlines

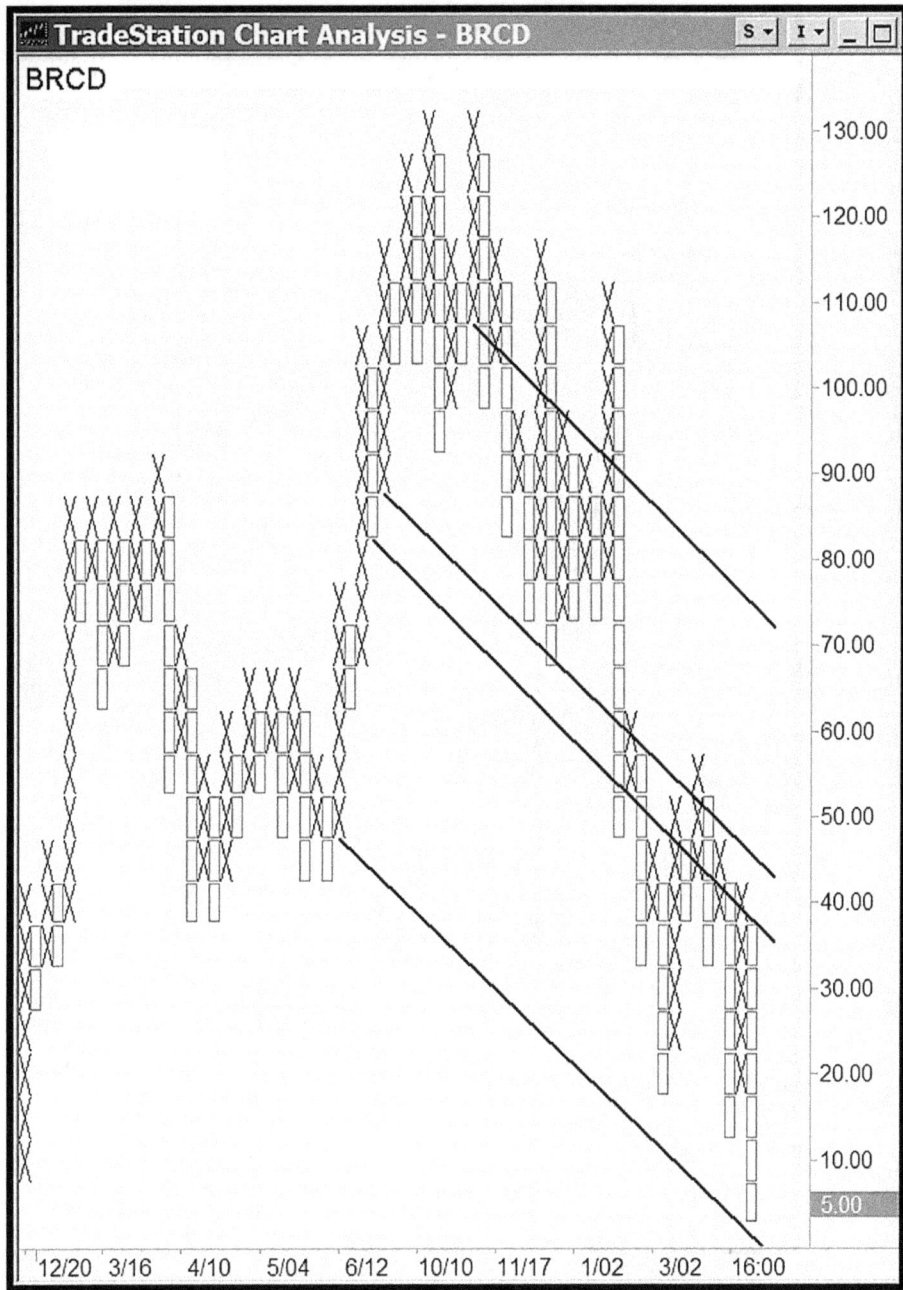

Point-and-Figure Bullish Broadening Formation

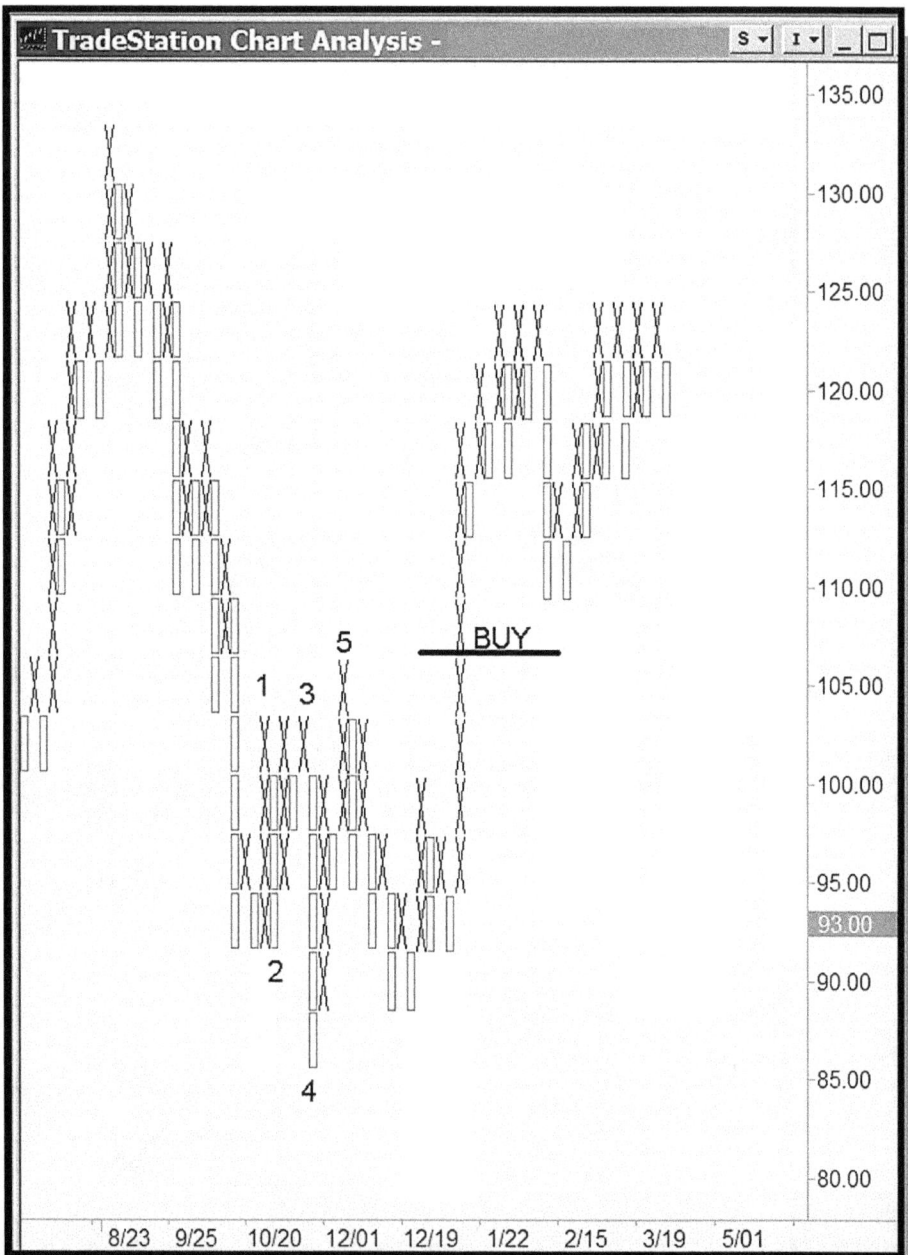

Point-and-Figure Bullish Trendlines

Point-and-Figure Buy Signal

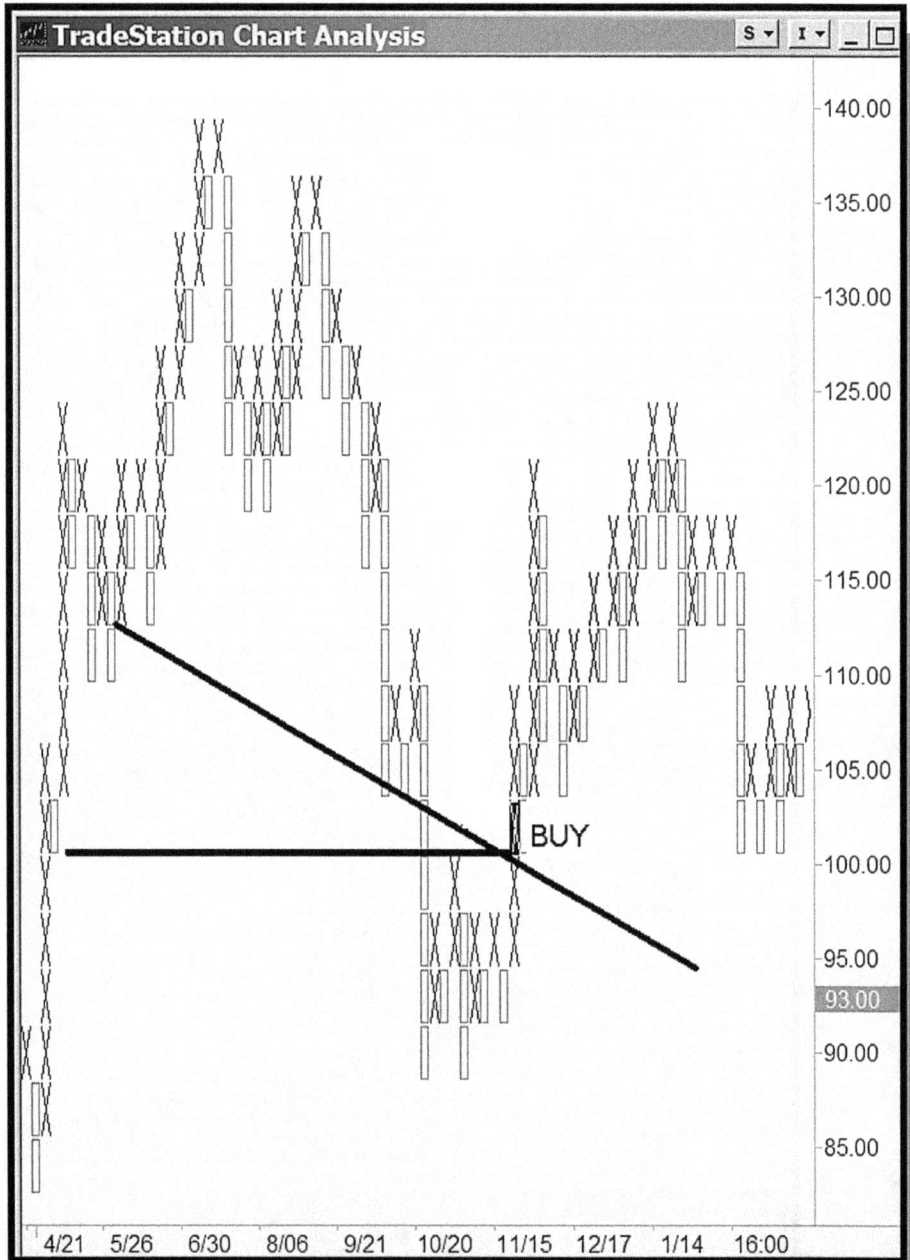

Point-and-Figure Sell Signal

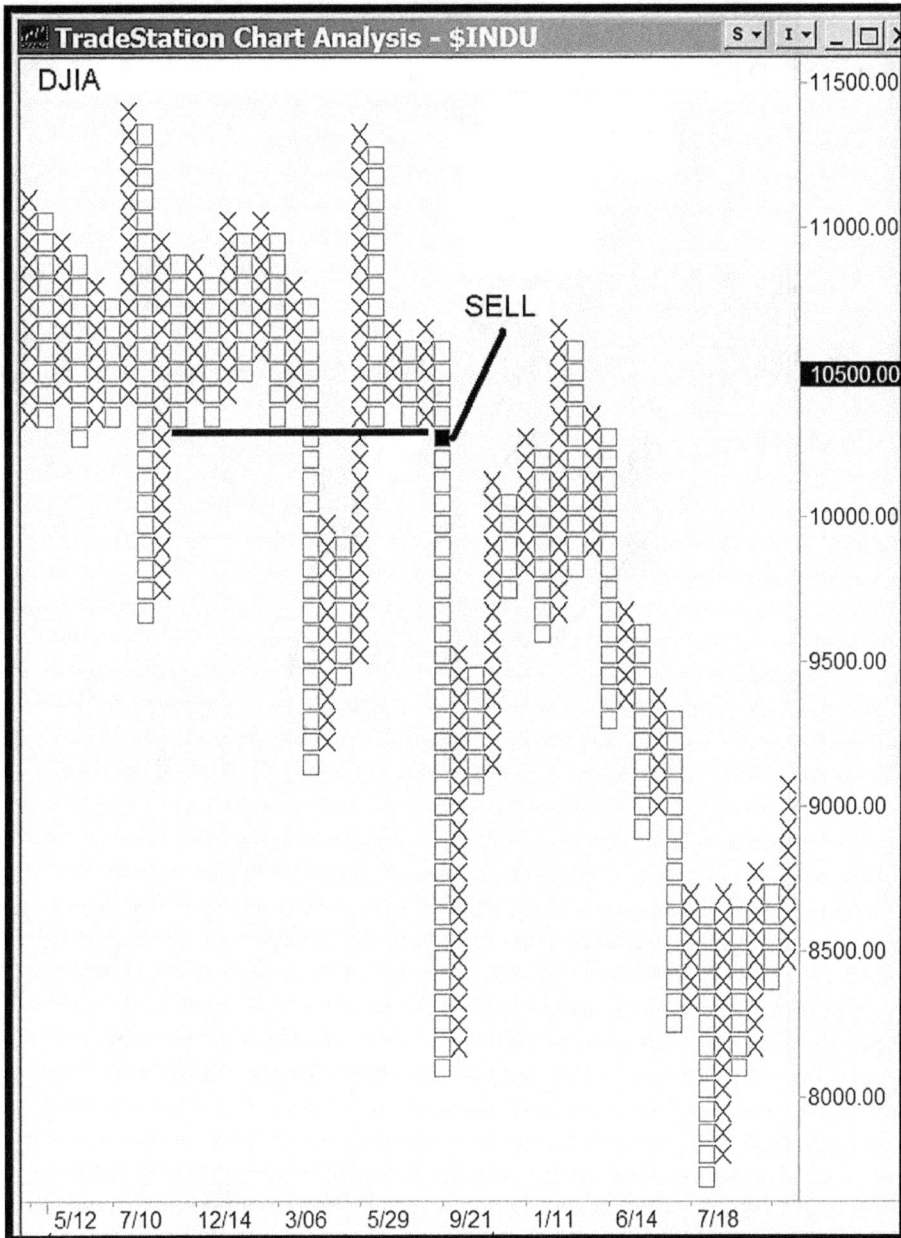

Point-and-Figure Trendlines

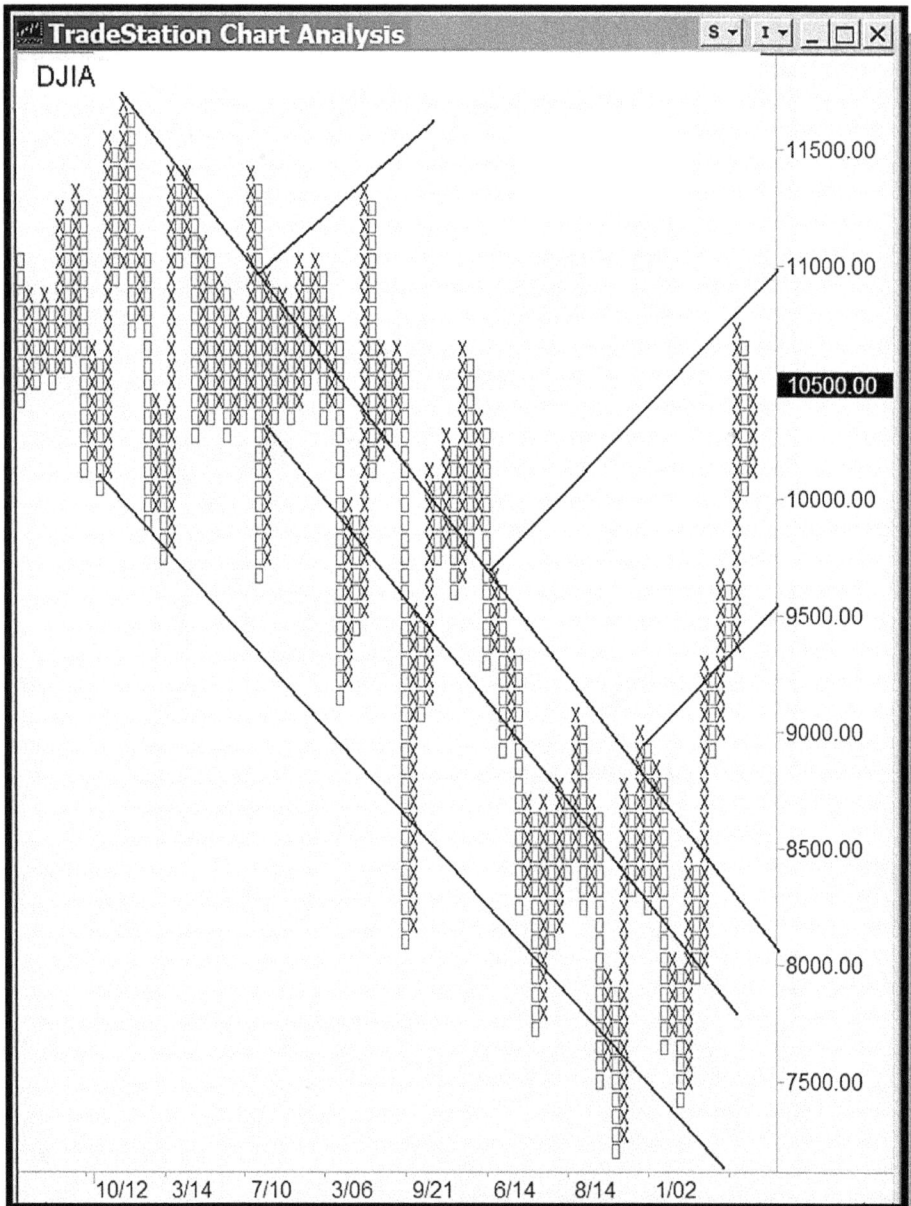

Price Action: Bear Trap

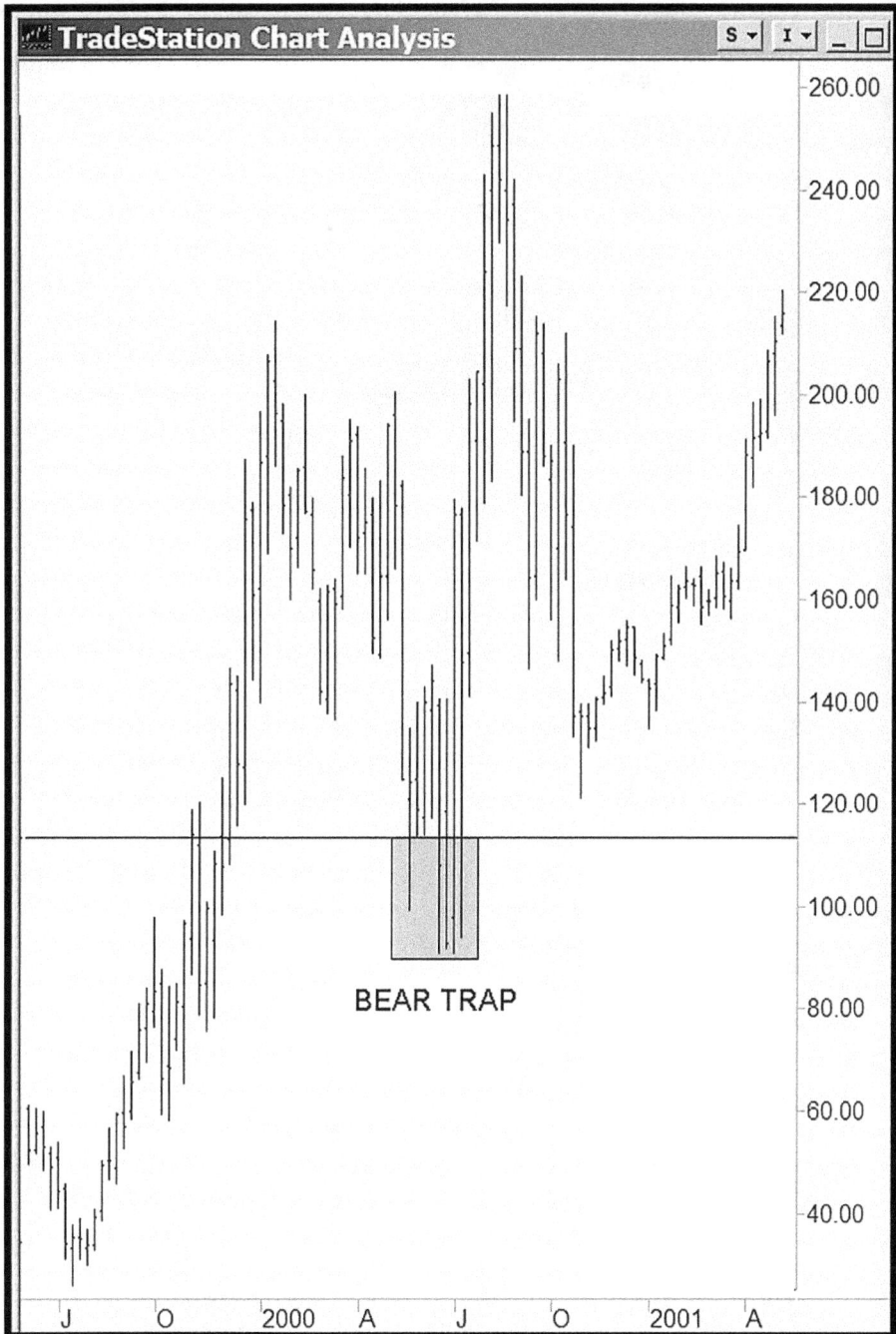

Price Action: Bull Trap

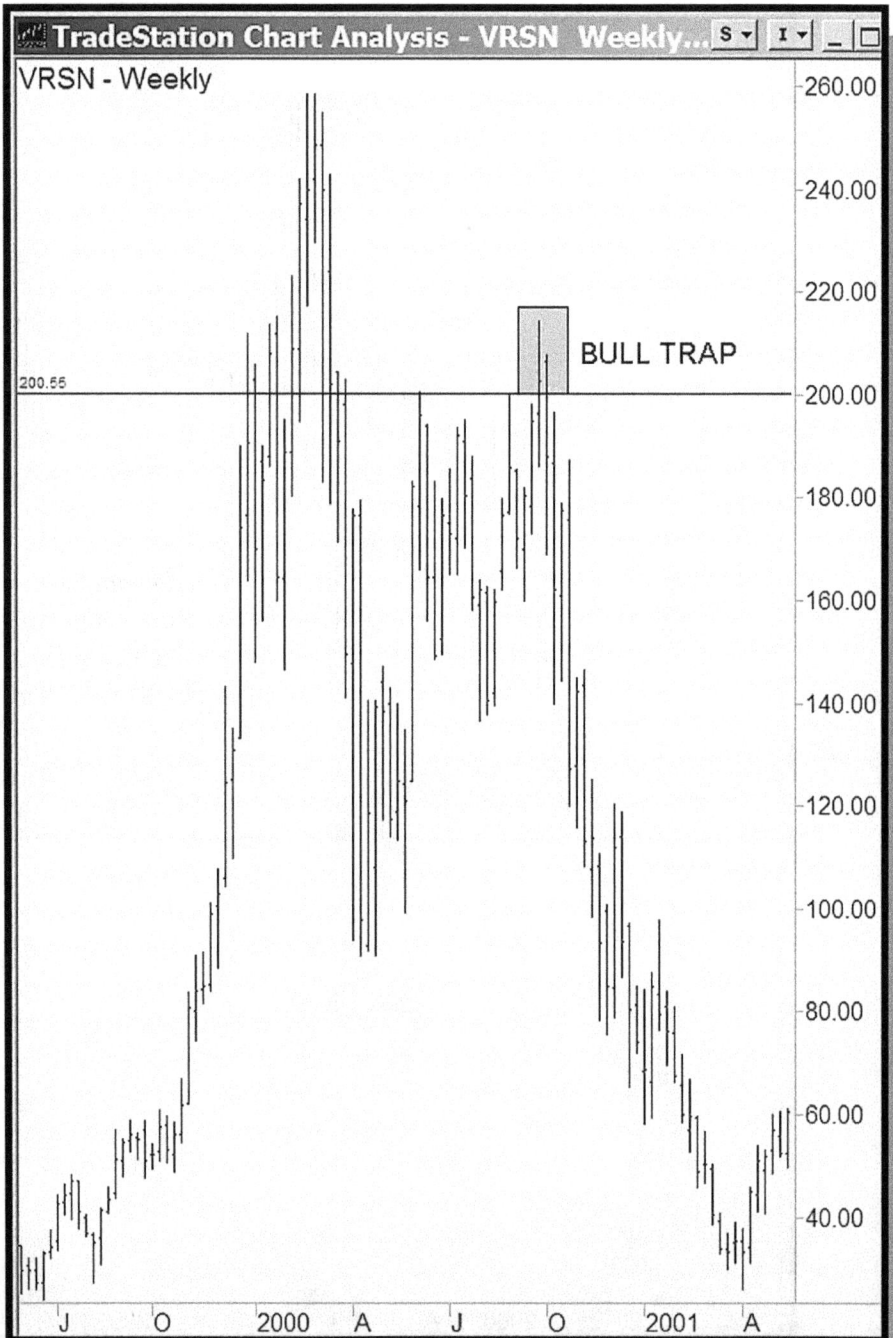

VRSN - Weekly

BULL TRAP

200.55

Price Action: Coiling Sideways Market

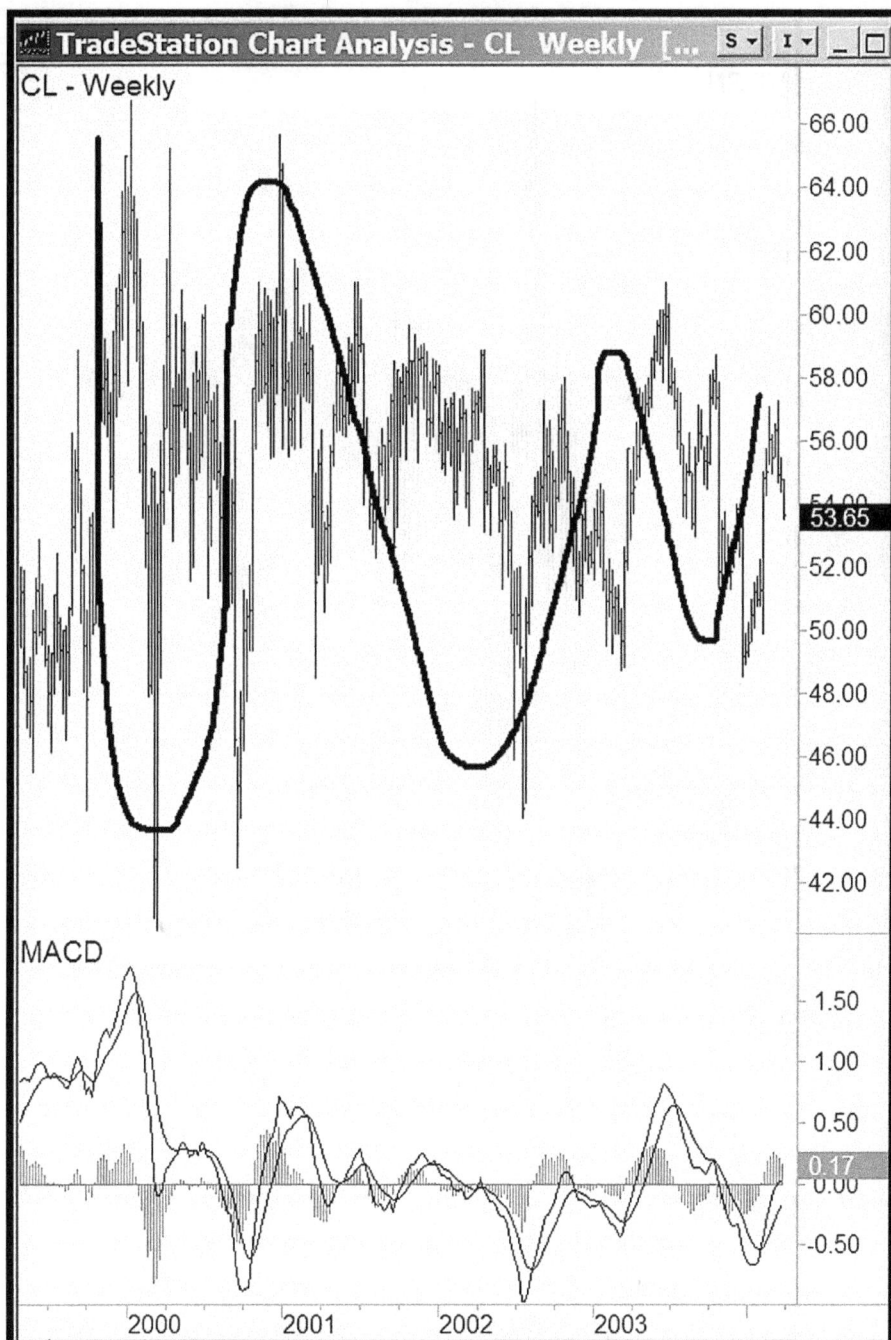

Price Action: Countertrend Rally

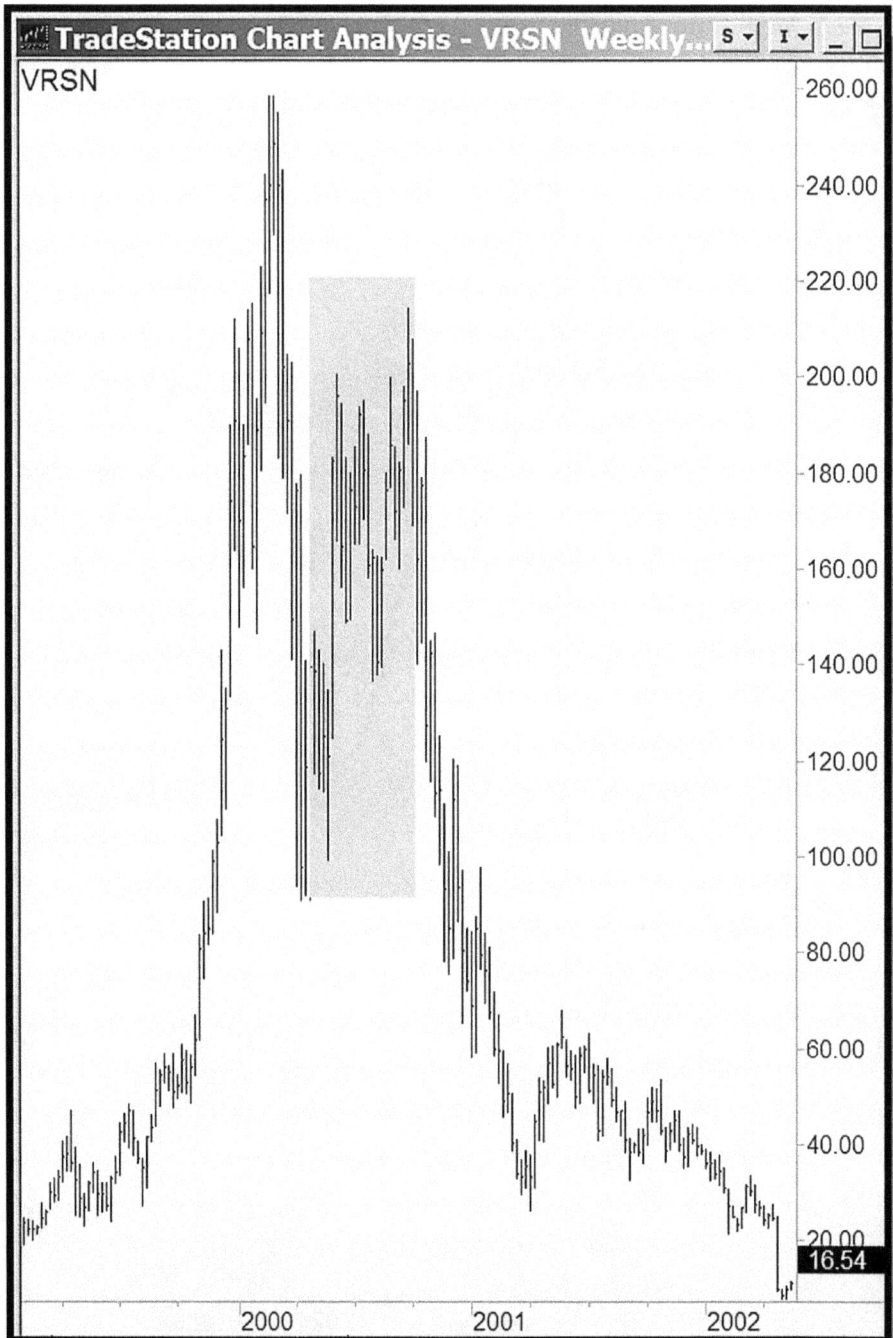

Price Action: Market Accumulation

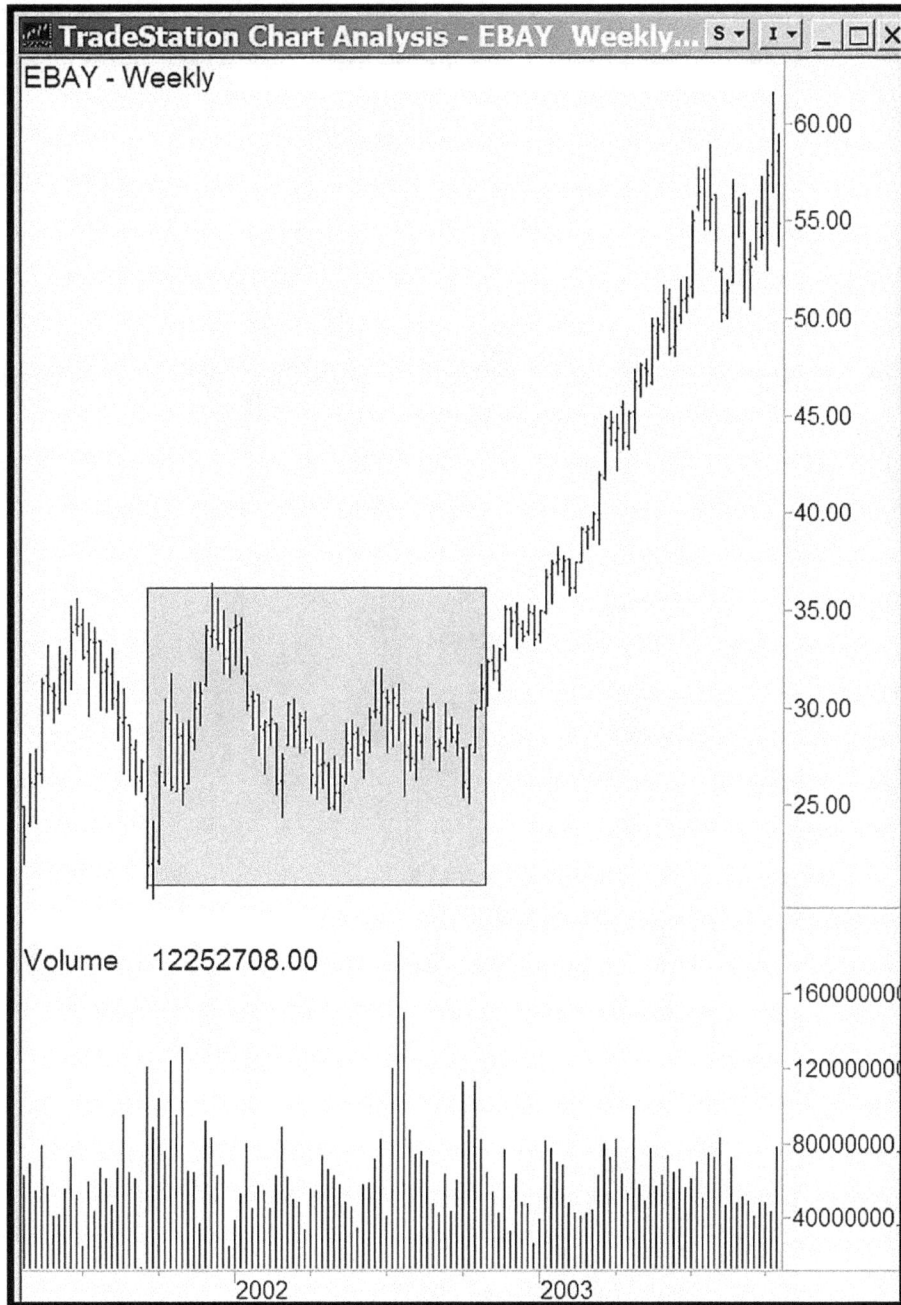

Price Action: Market Distribution

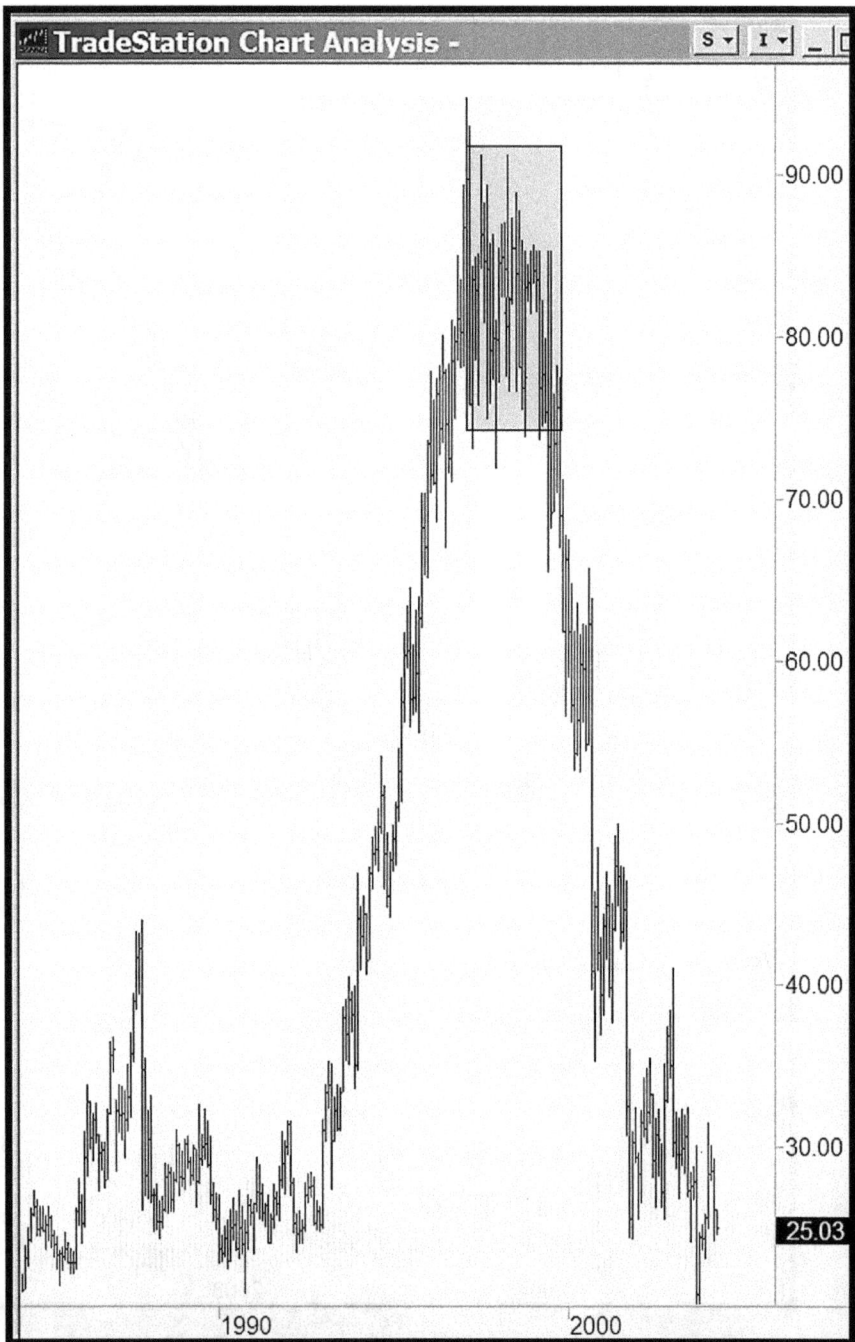

Price Action: Mirror Image

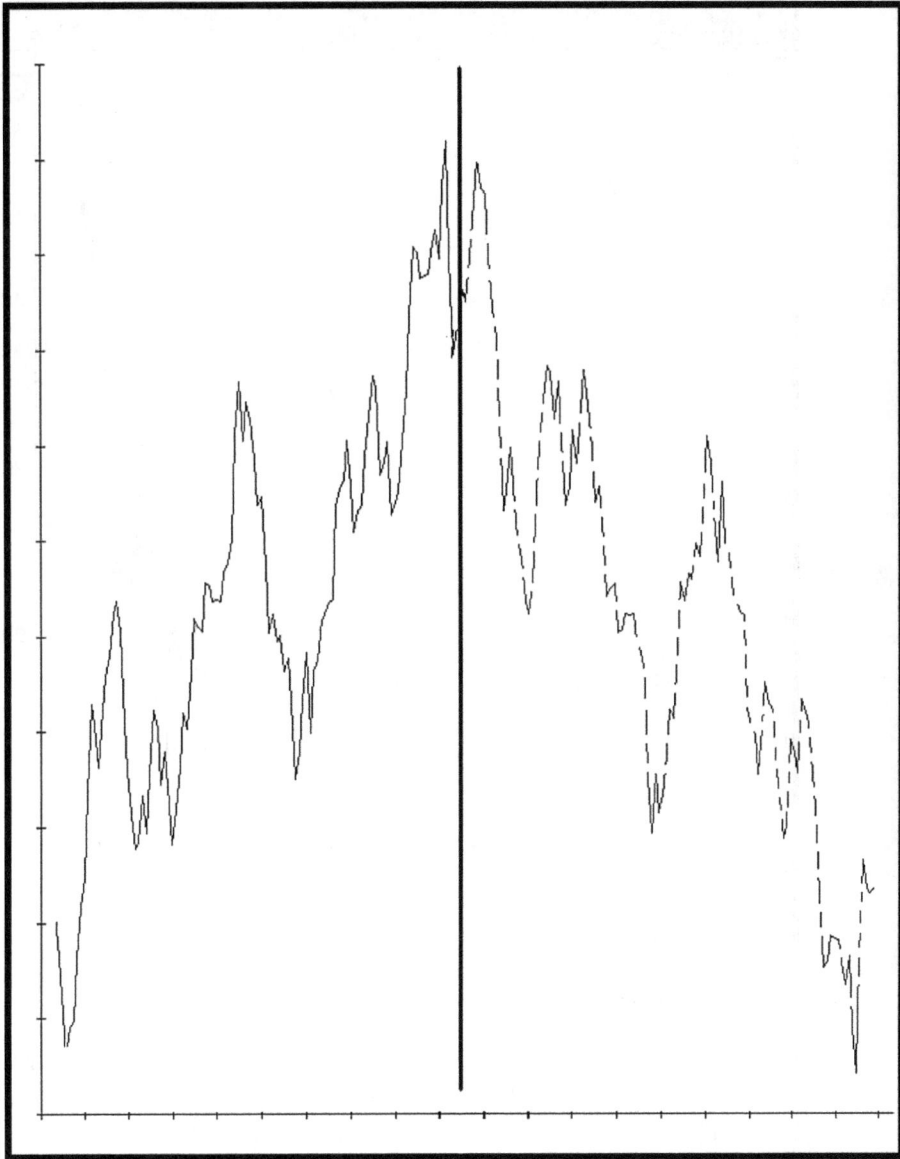

Price Action: Parabolic Rise (also Developing Market Bubble)

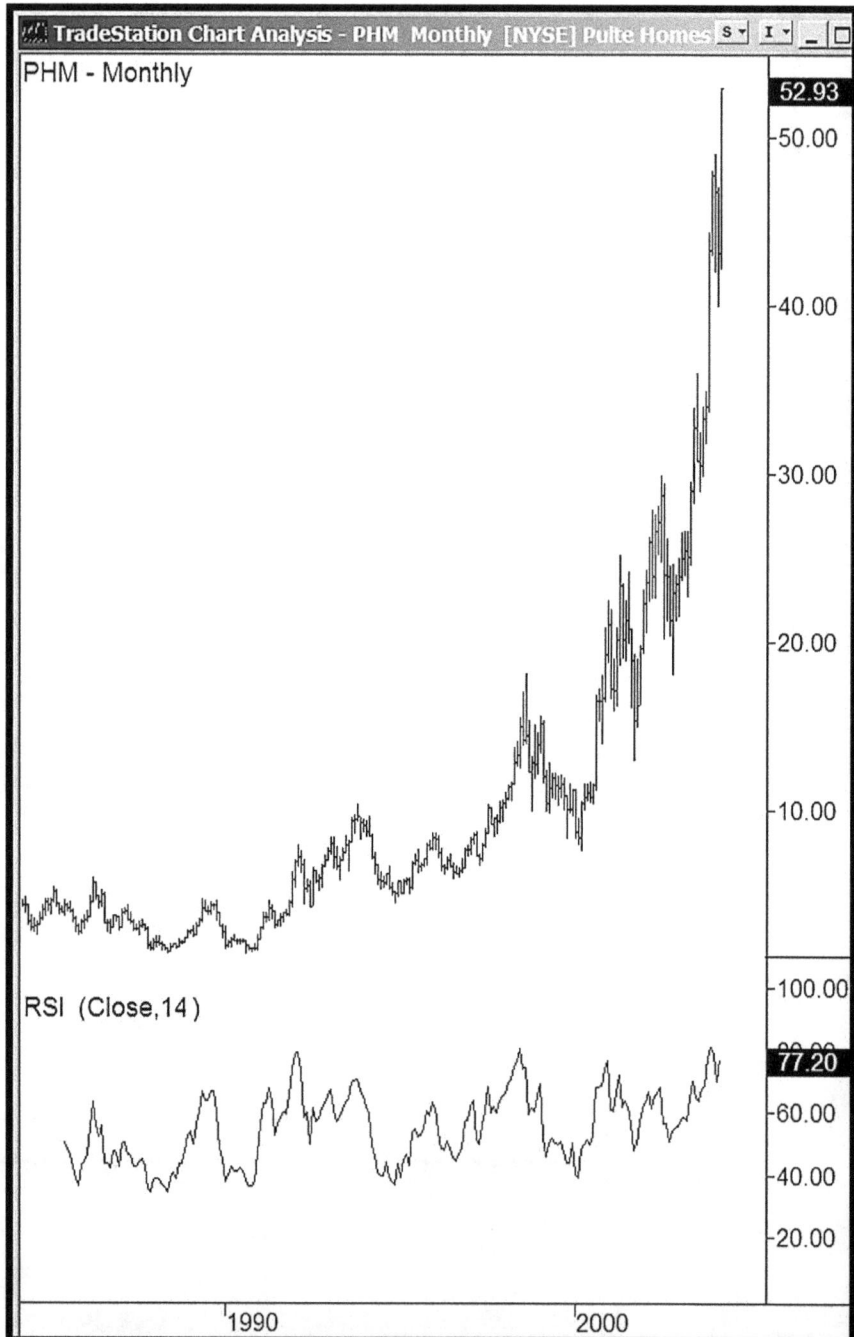

Price Action: Range-Bound or Sideways Market

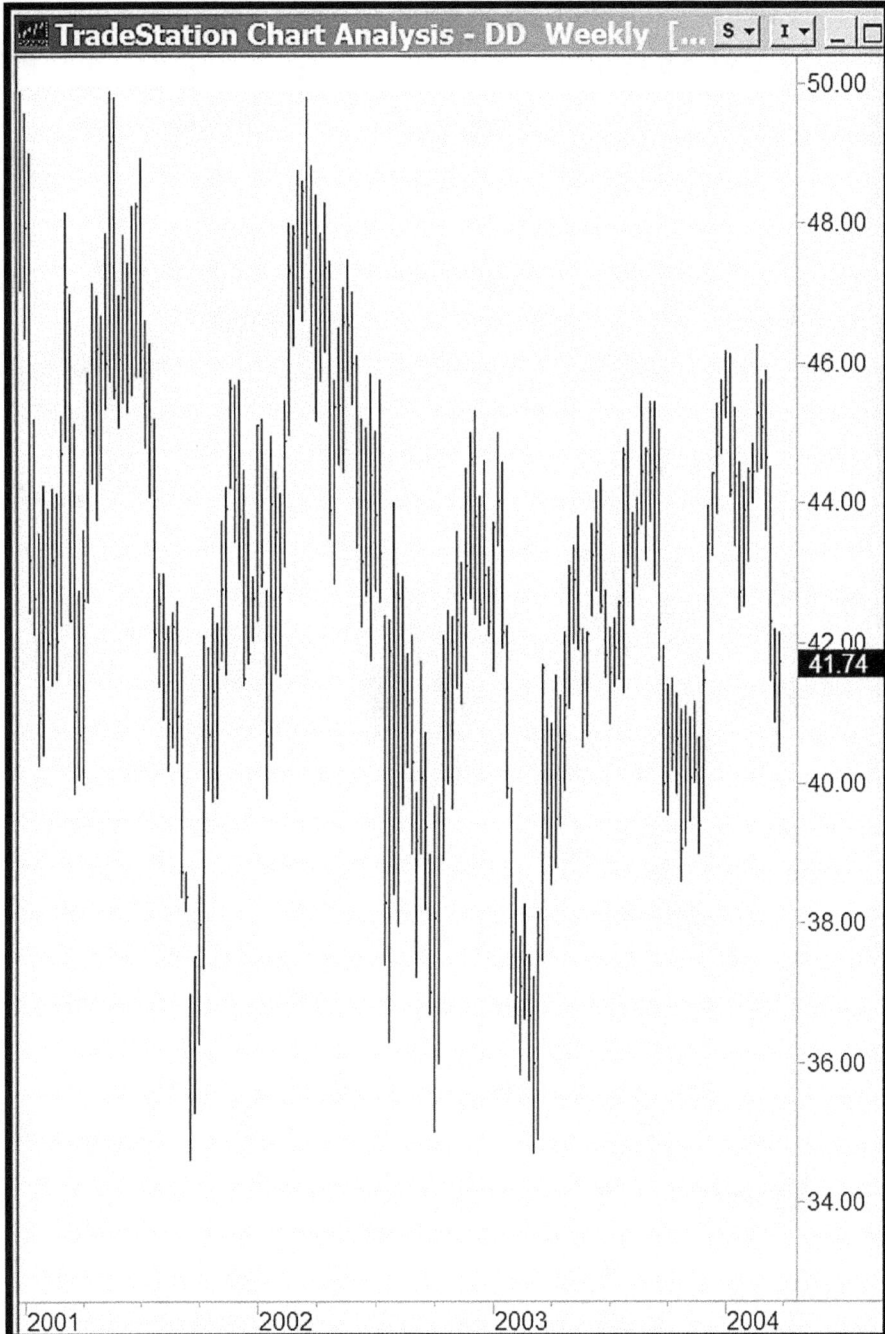

Price Action: Whipsaw Rally

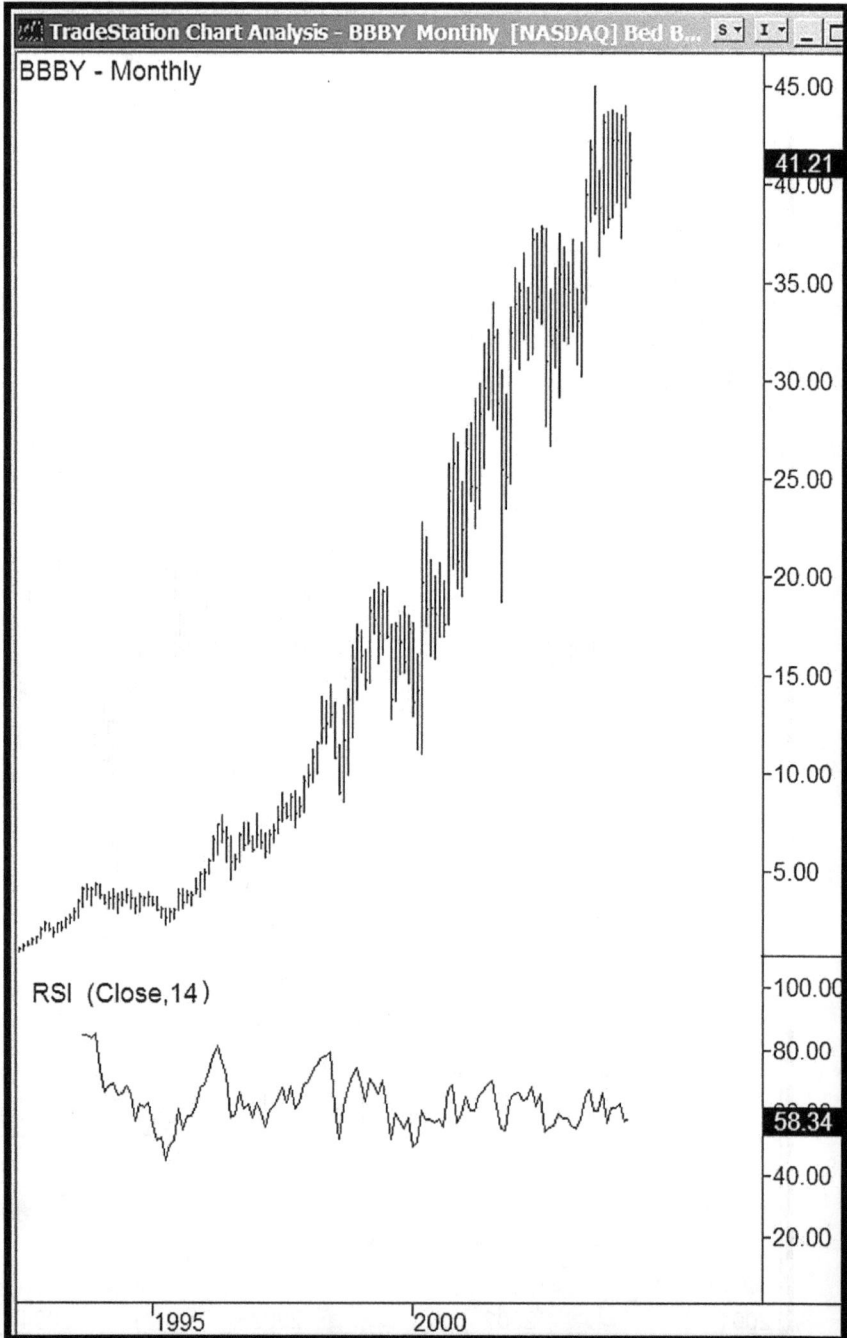

Price Projection: Equality from a Midpoint

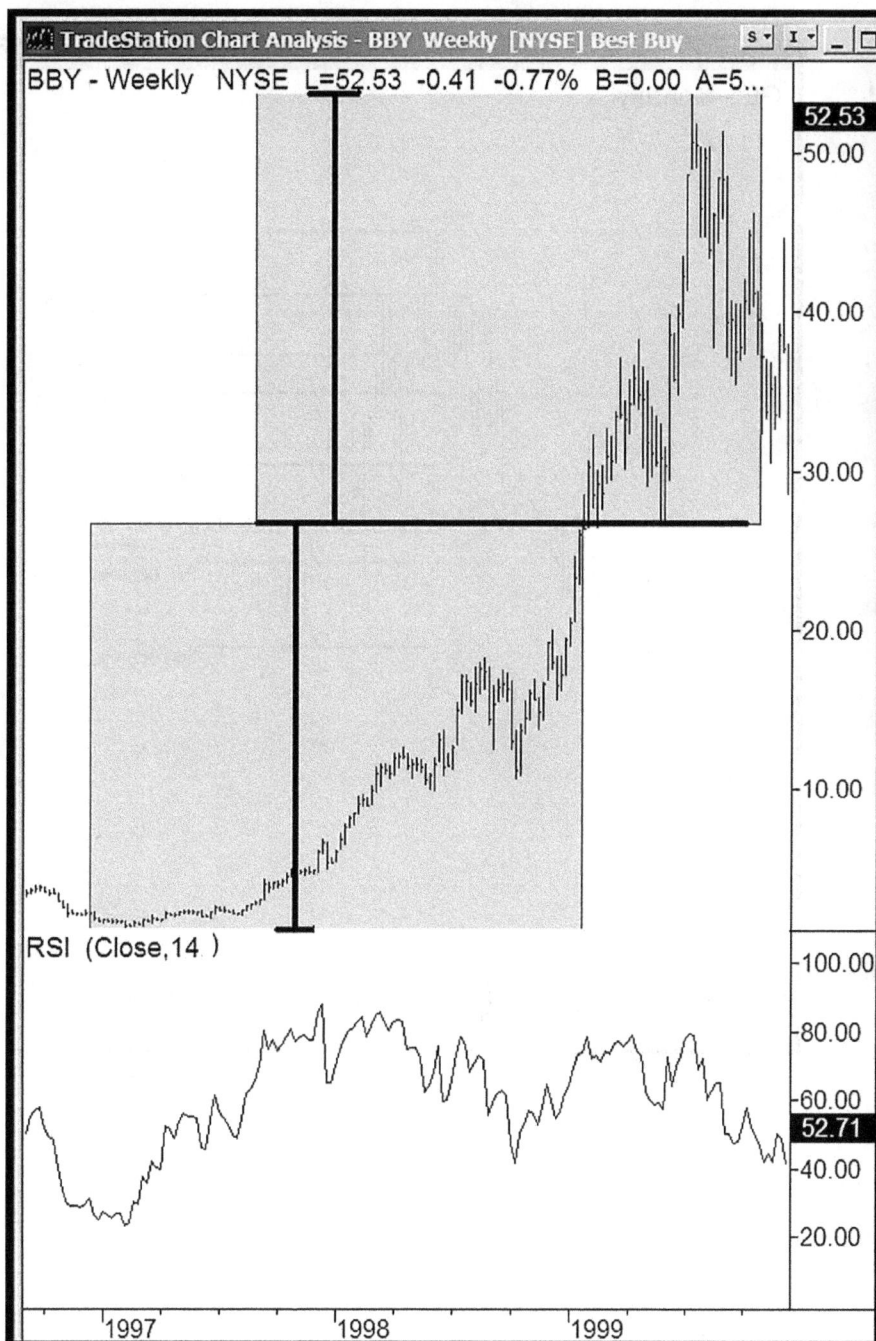

Price Projection: Exact 360-Degrees or Natural Square Retracement

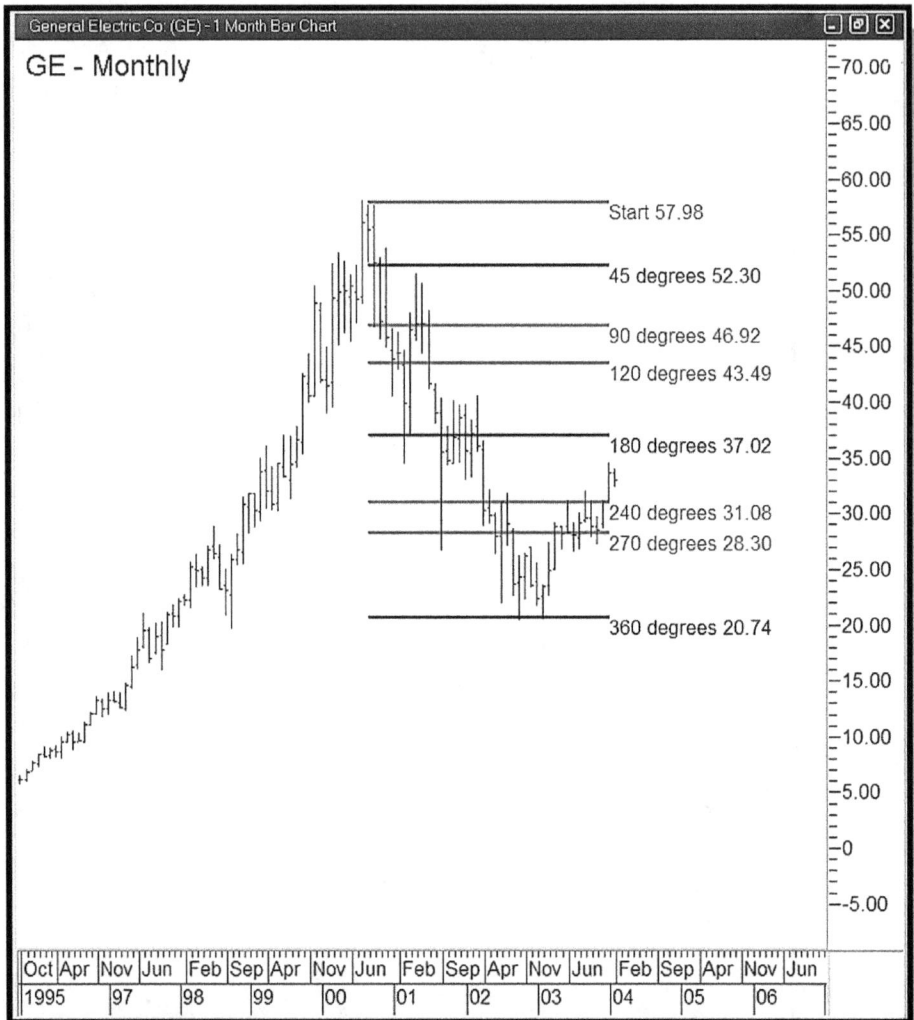

Price Projection following Stochastic Flutter

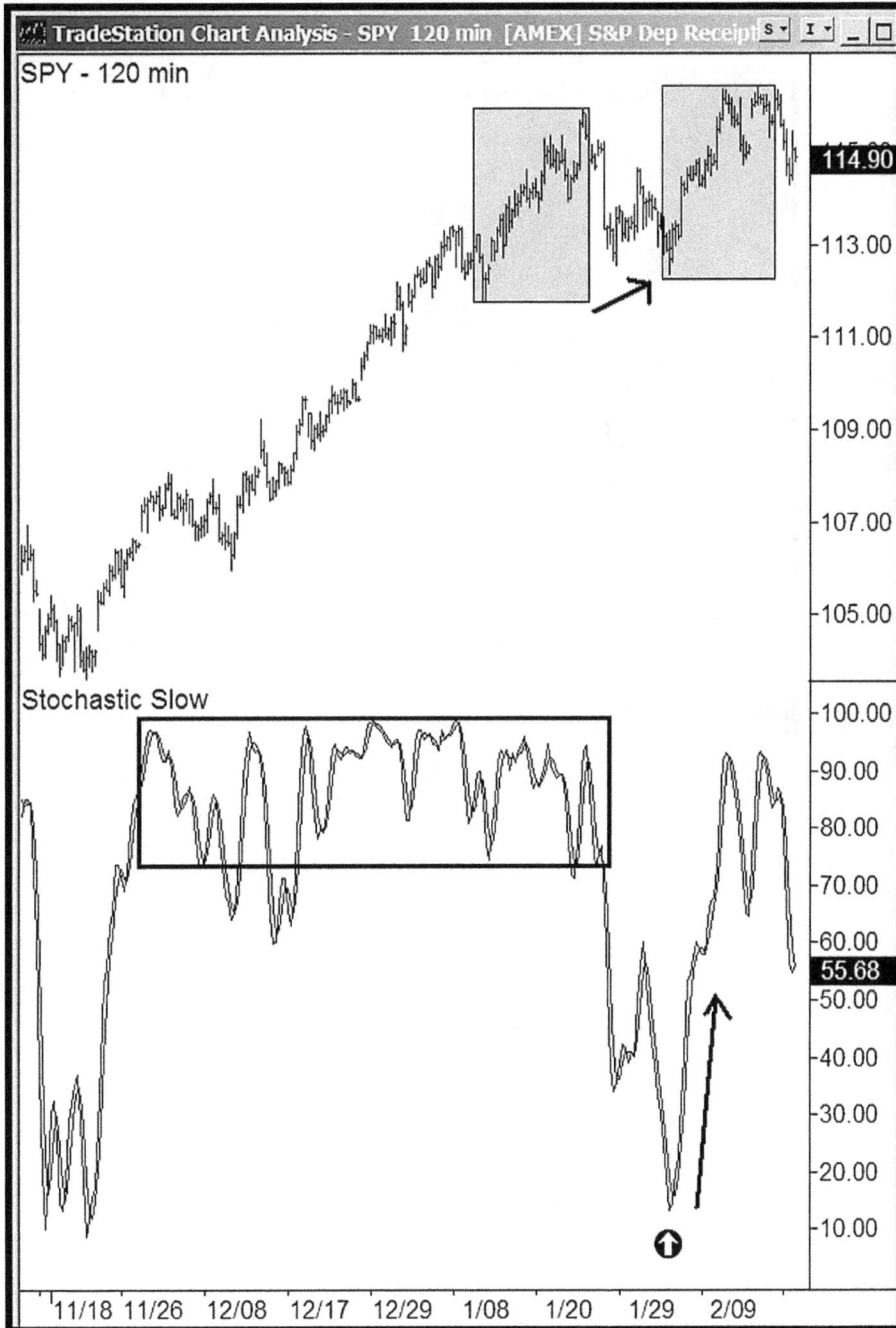

Price Projection from Head-and-Shoulders Pattern

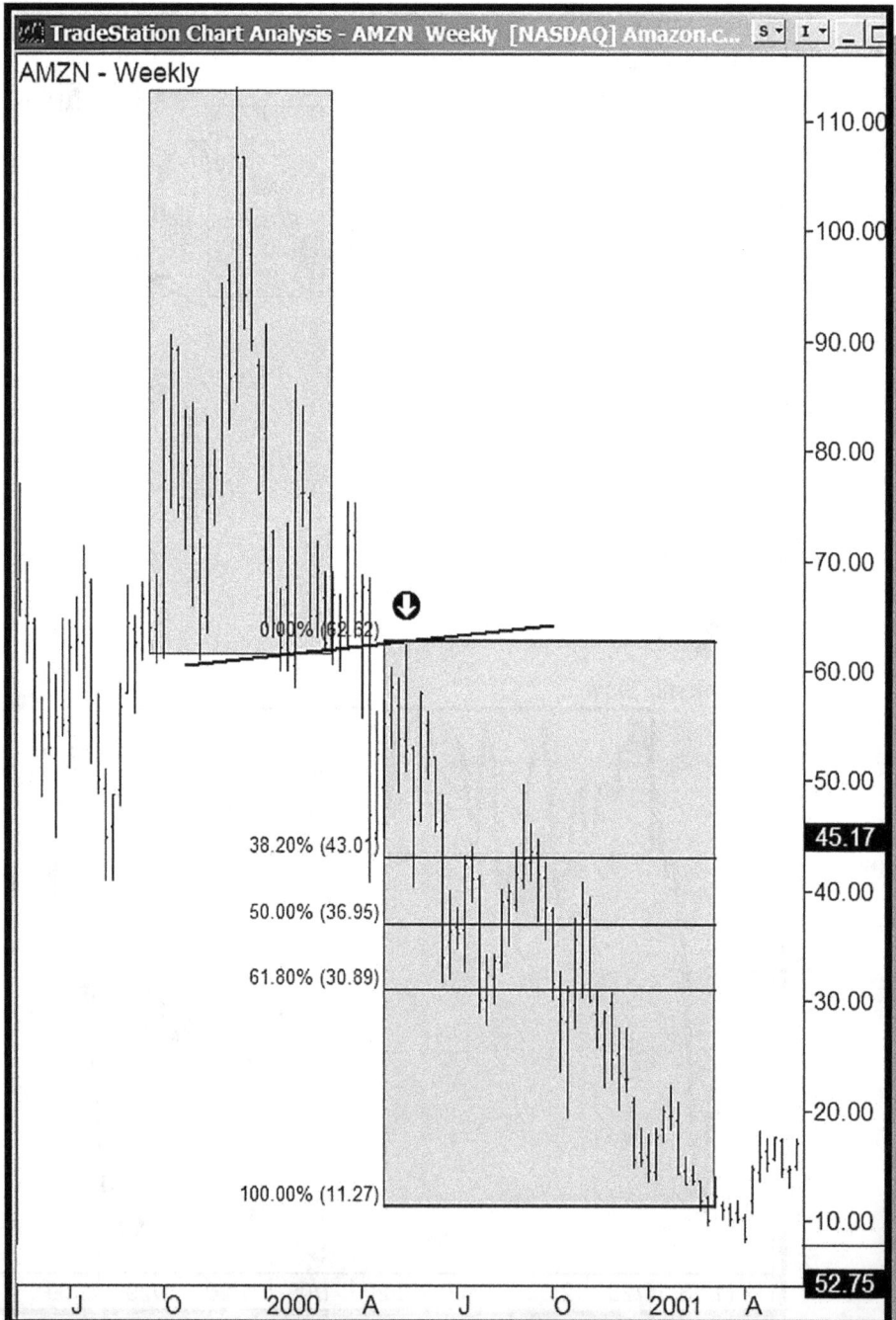

Price Projection from the Midpoint of a Gap

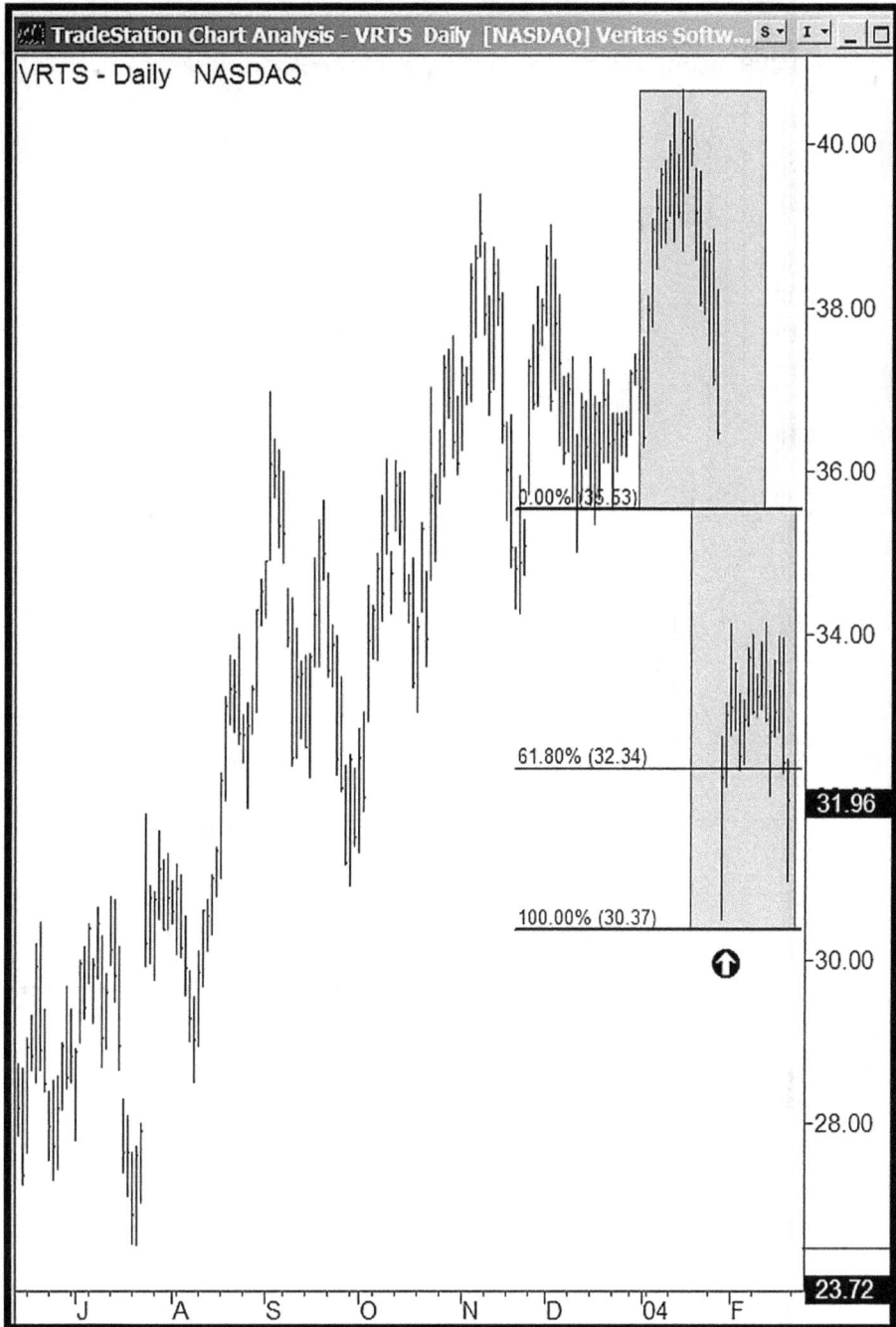

Price Projection: Market Geometry

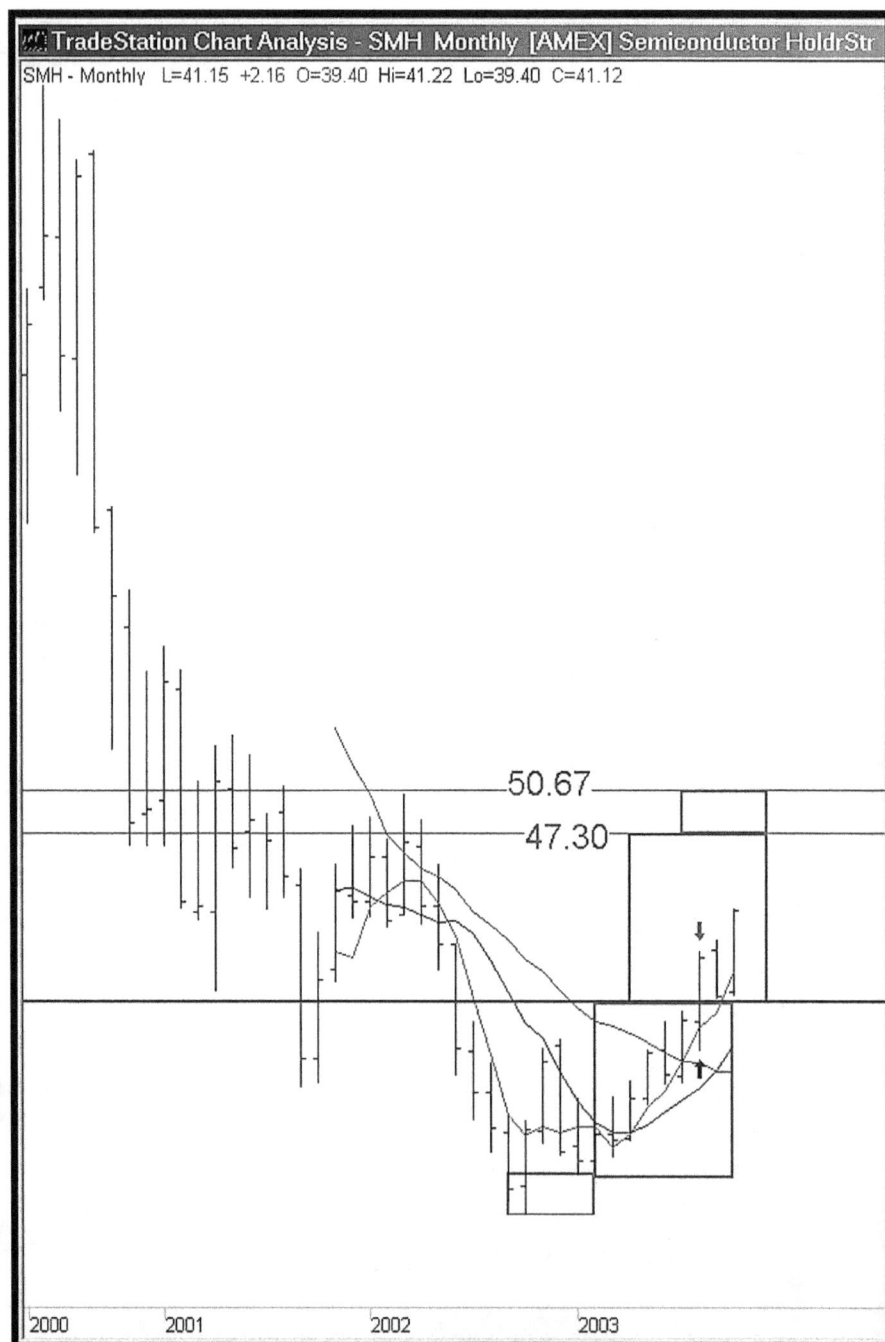

TradeStation Chart Analysis - SMH Monthly [AMEX] Semiconductor HoldrStr

SMH - Monthly   L=41.15 +2.16 O=39.40 Hi=41.22 Lo=39.40 C=41.12

50.67

47.30

2000   2001   2002   2003

Price Projection: RSI Negative Reversal

BRCM - Daily

Target = 77.50 - (142.81 - 133.44)

142.81

133.44

77.50

ALWAYS WITH A 14 PERIOD RSI

Price Projection: RSI Positive Reversal

TradeStation Chart Analysis - VTS Daily [N...

VTS - Daily

Target = 12.88 + (12.20 - 10.48) using closes

ALSO SEE "POSITIVE REVERSAL"

12.88

12.20

10.48

16.00

14.00

10.00

8.00

ALWAYS WITH A 14 PERIOD RSI

100.00

80.00

70.47

60.00

Positive
Reversal

40.00

20.00

Apr   Jul   Oct   04

Price Smoothing: Bollinger Bands

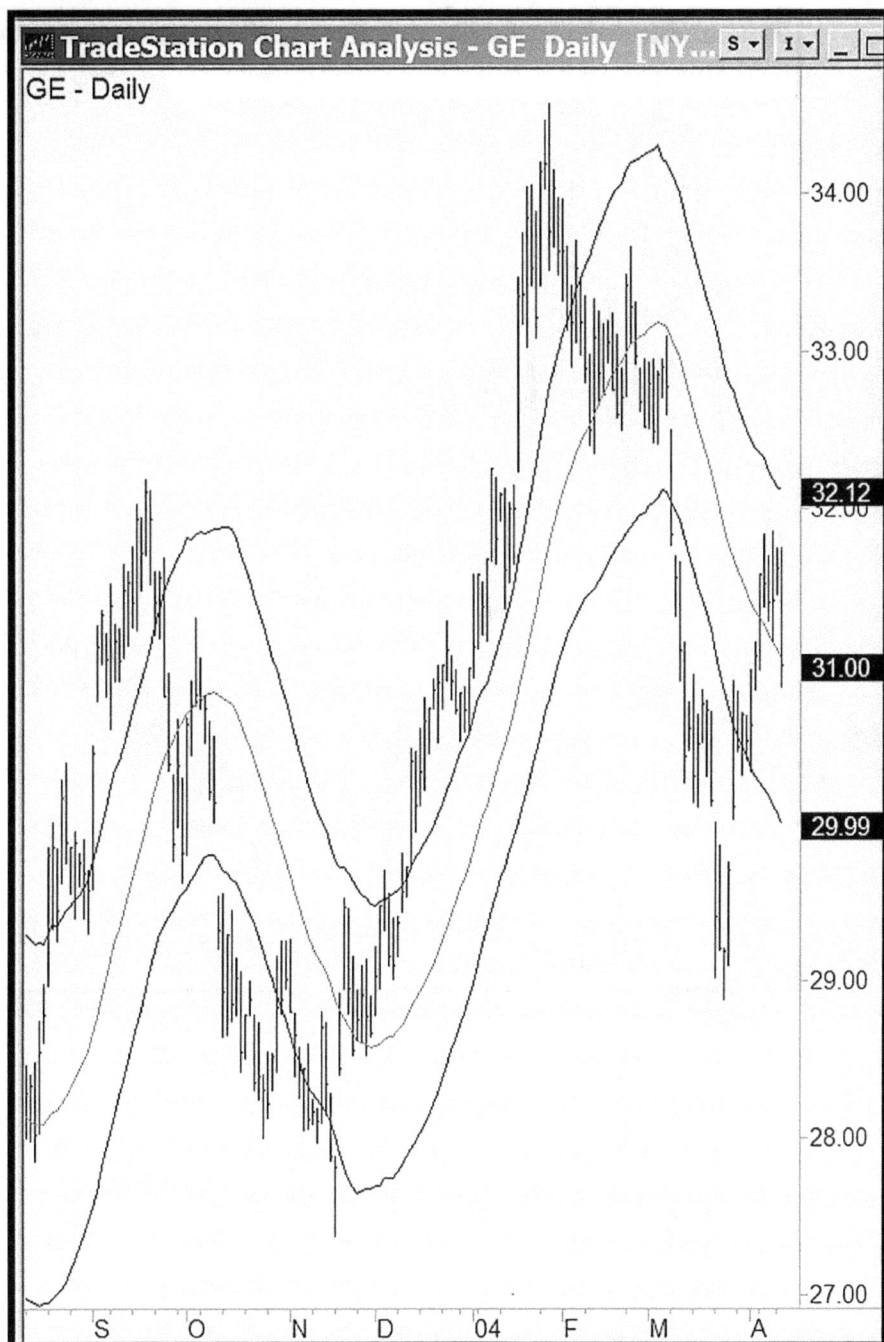

Price Smoothing: Gann Swing Overlay

Price Smoothing: Keltner Channel

CBOE 10-year Yield:I (TNX-I) - 1 Month Bar Chart

Price Smoothing: Percentage Change

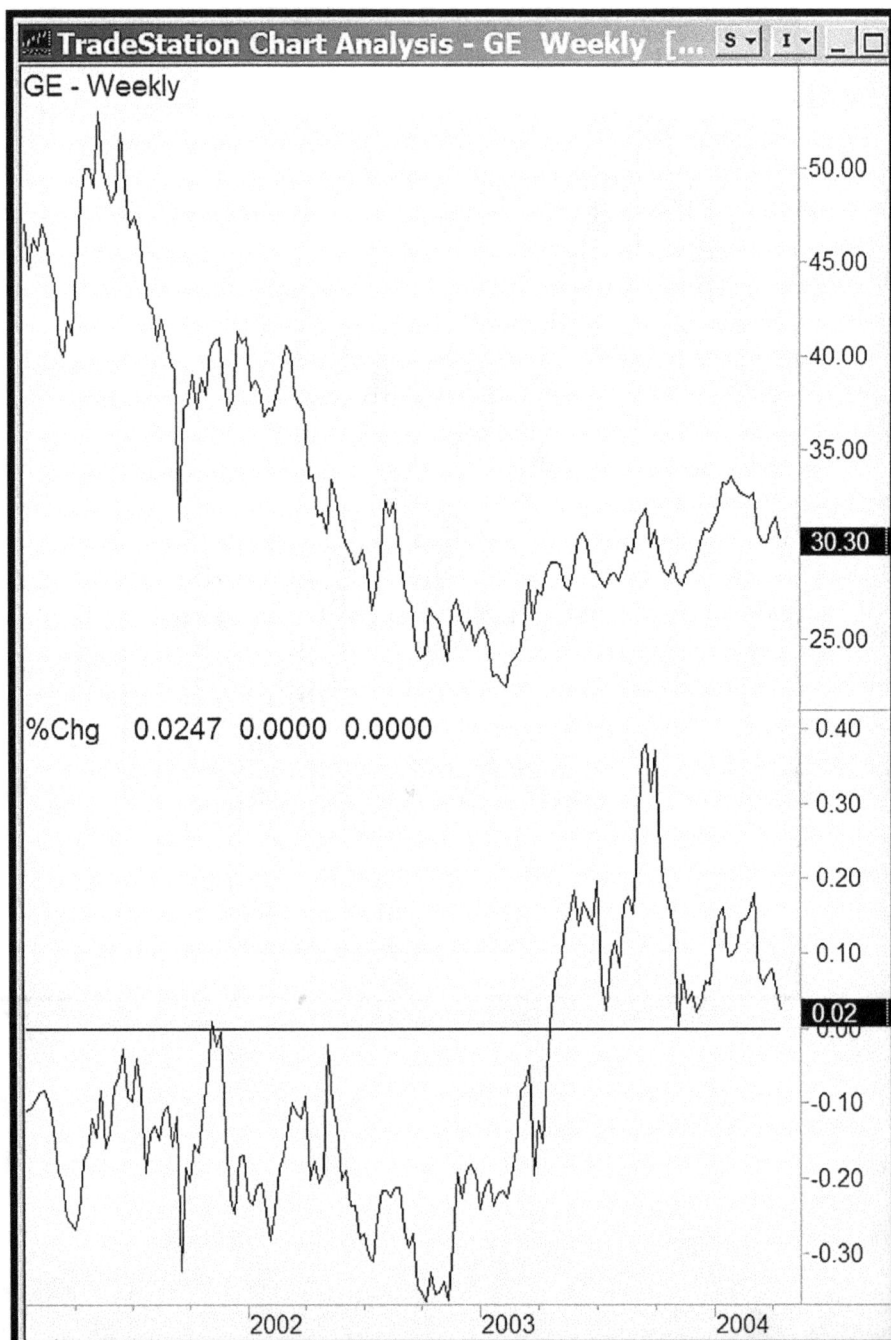

Price Smoothing: Percentage Displacement

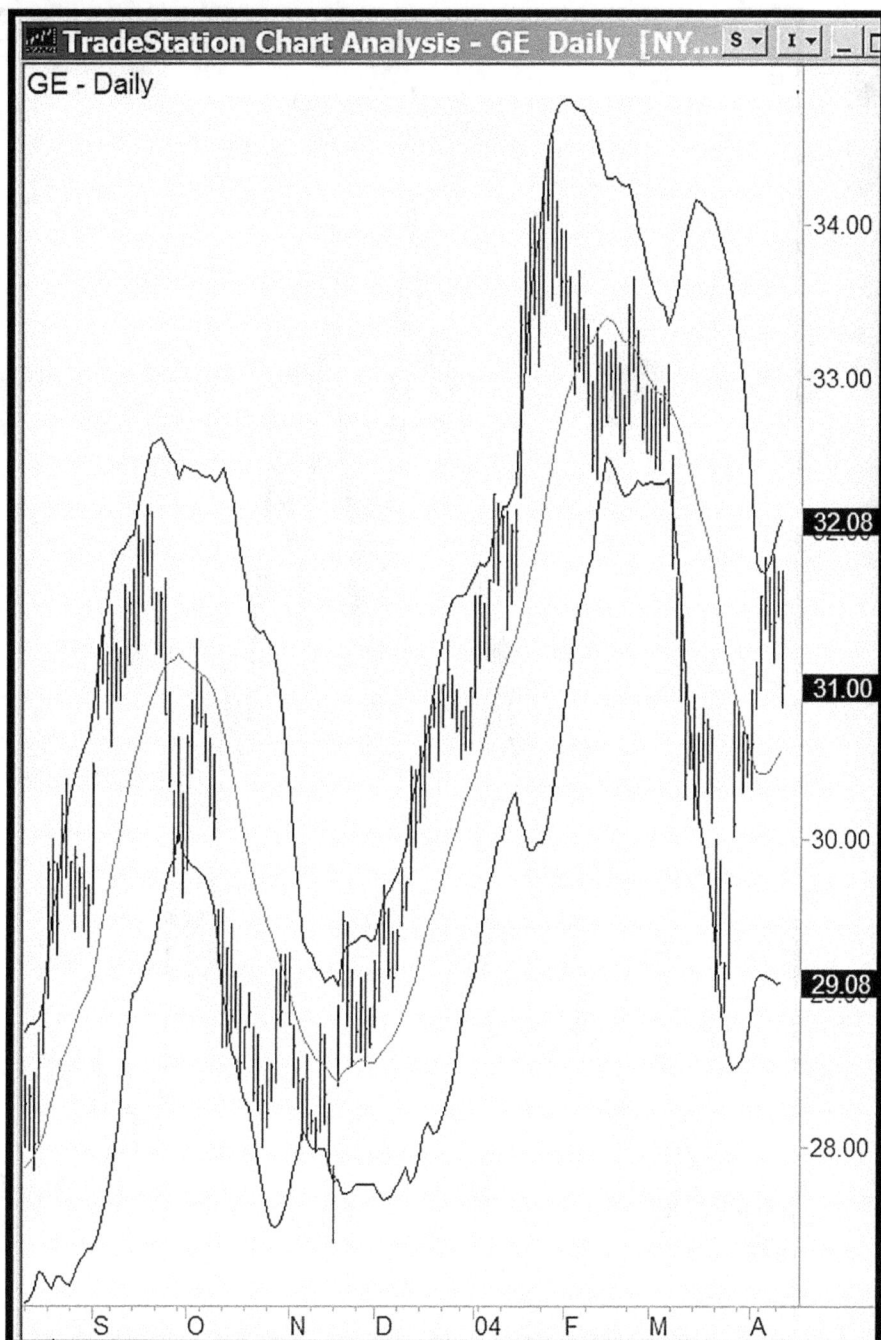

Price Smoothing: Regression Line

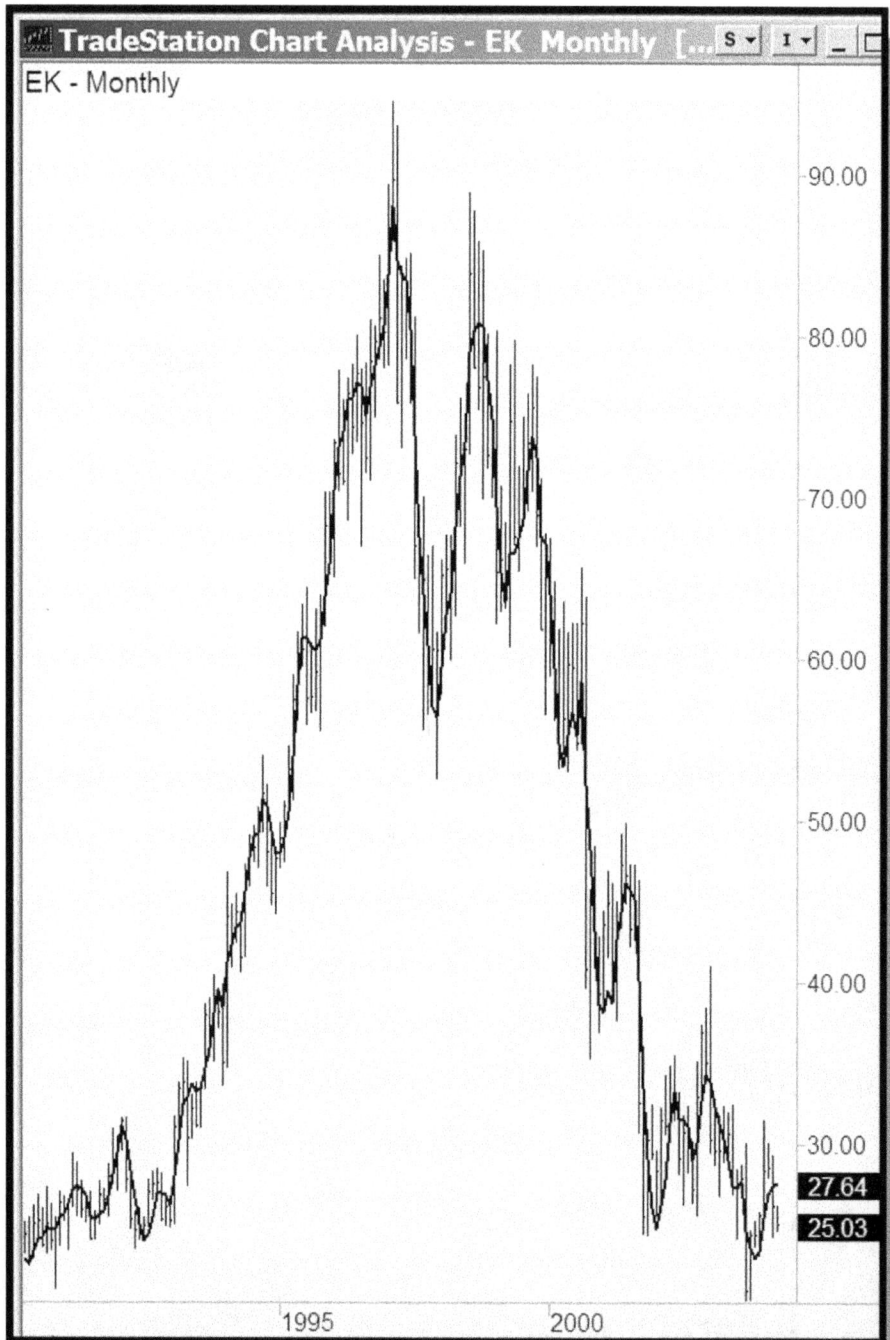

Price Smoothing: Simple Moving Average

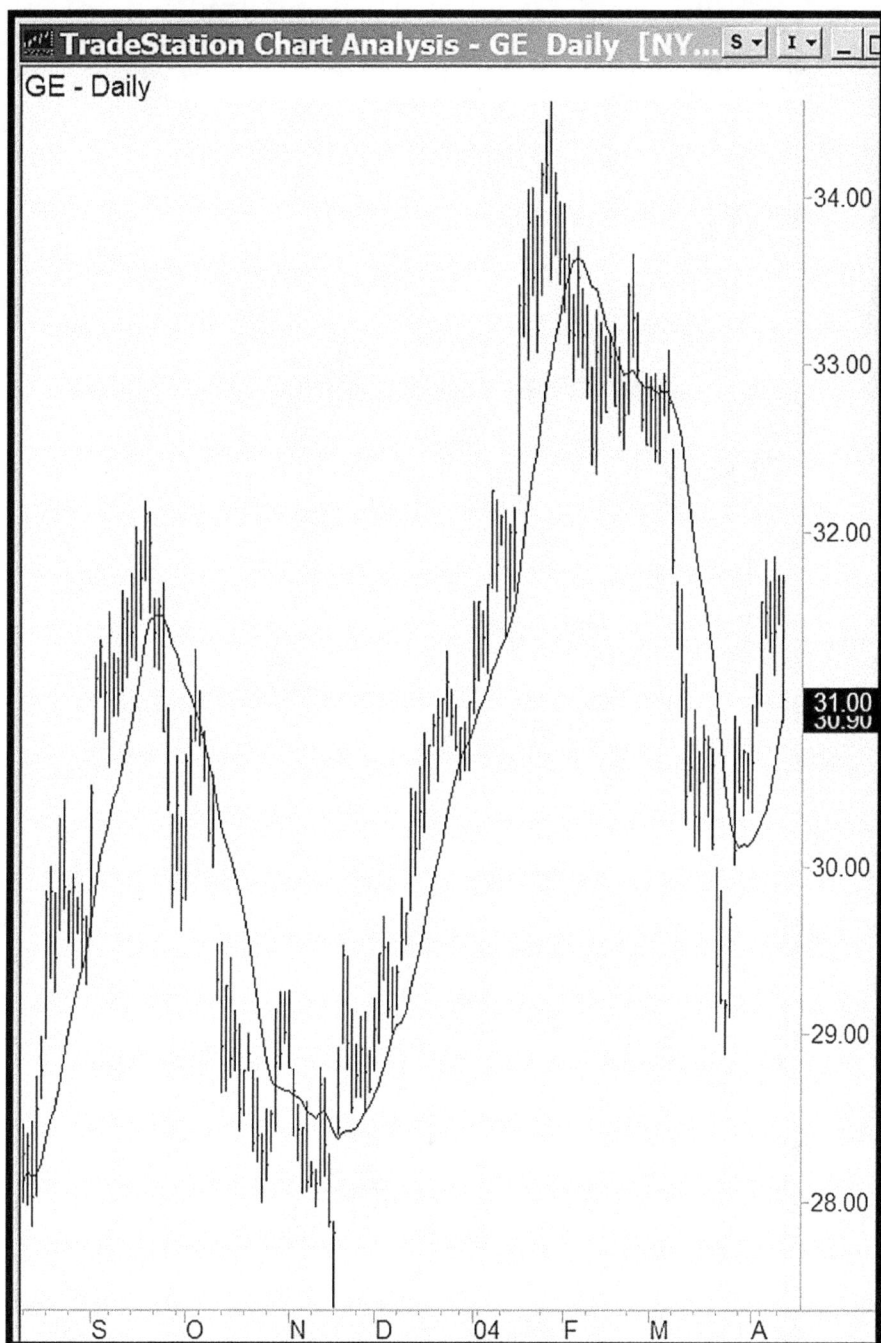

Price Smoothing: Simple Moving Average Envelope

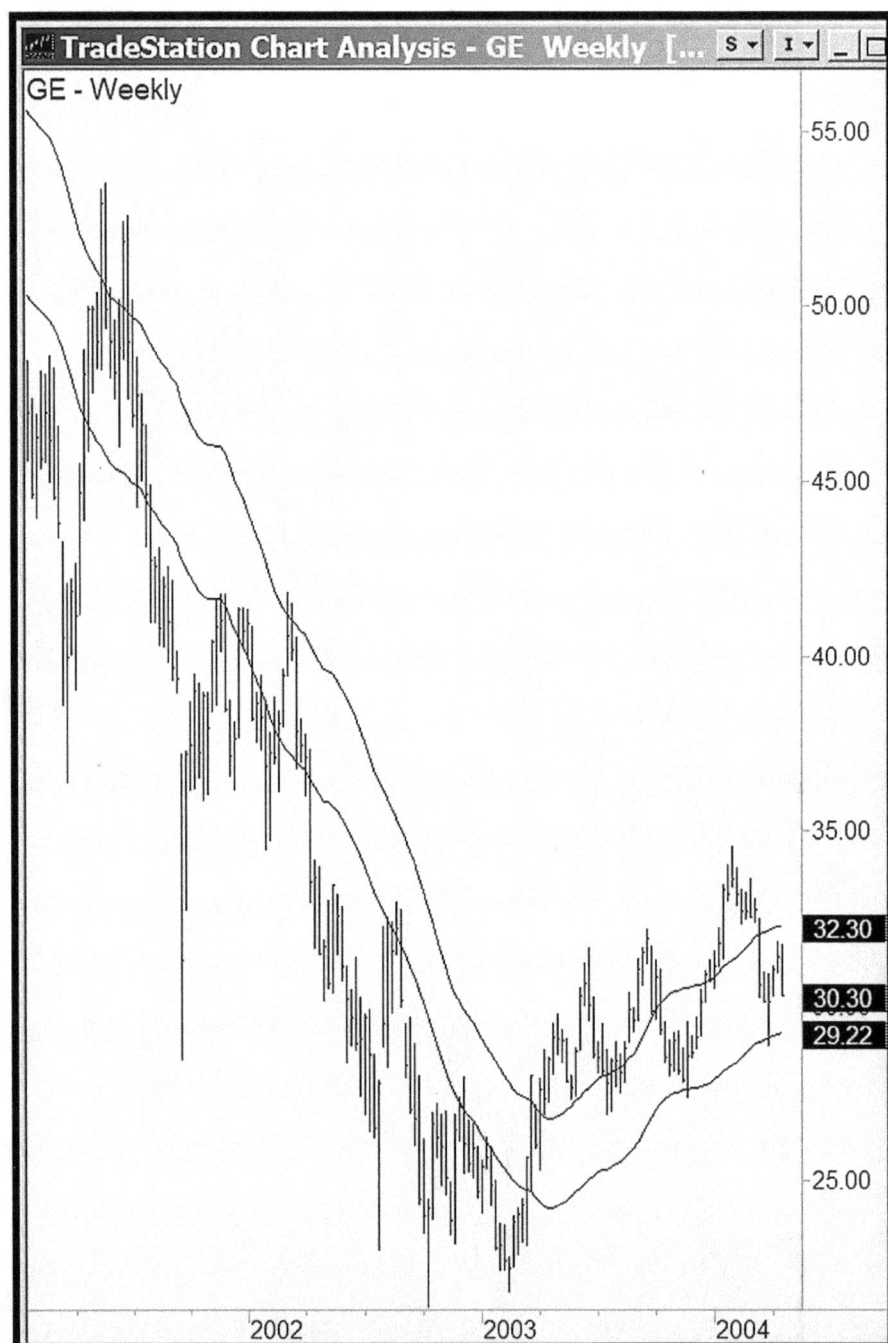

Price Smoothing: Spread between Two Averages Detrended

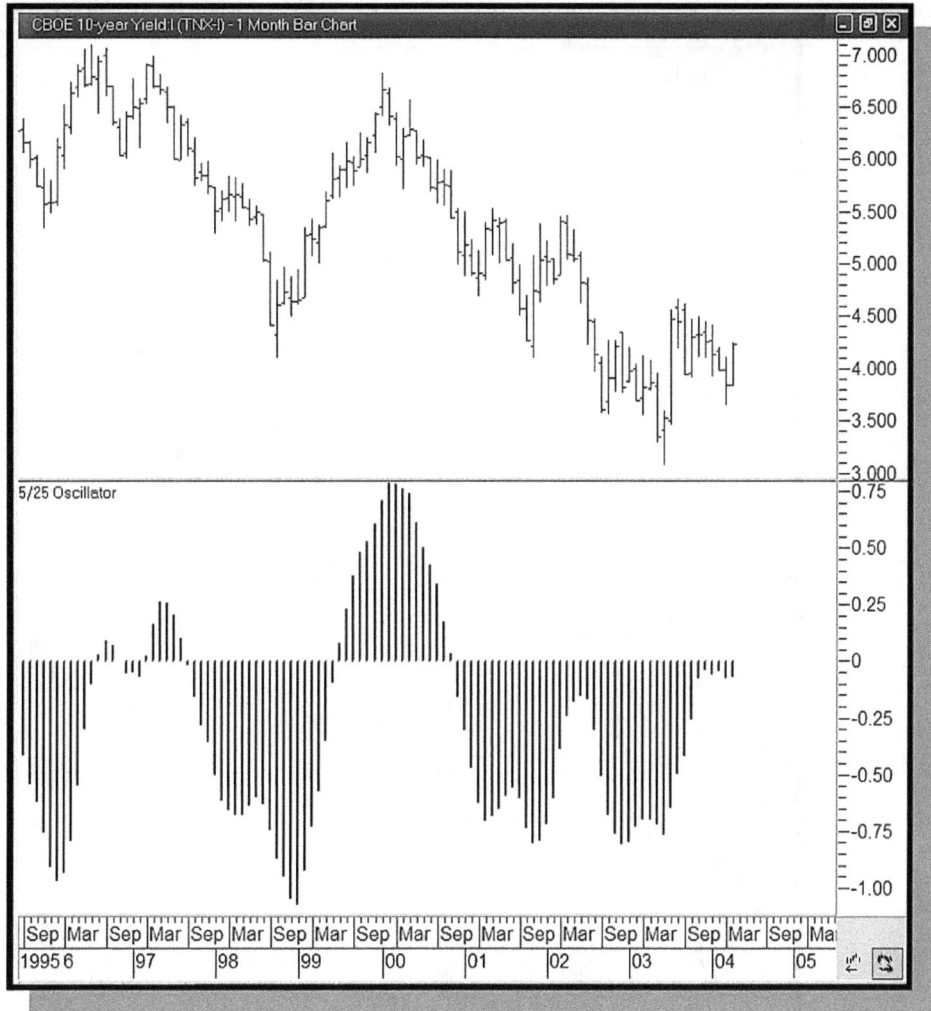

Price Smoothing: Starc or Stoller Bands

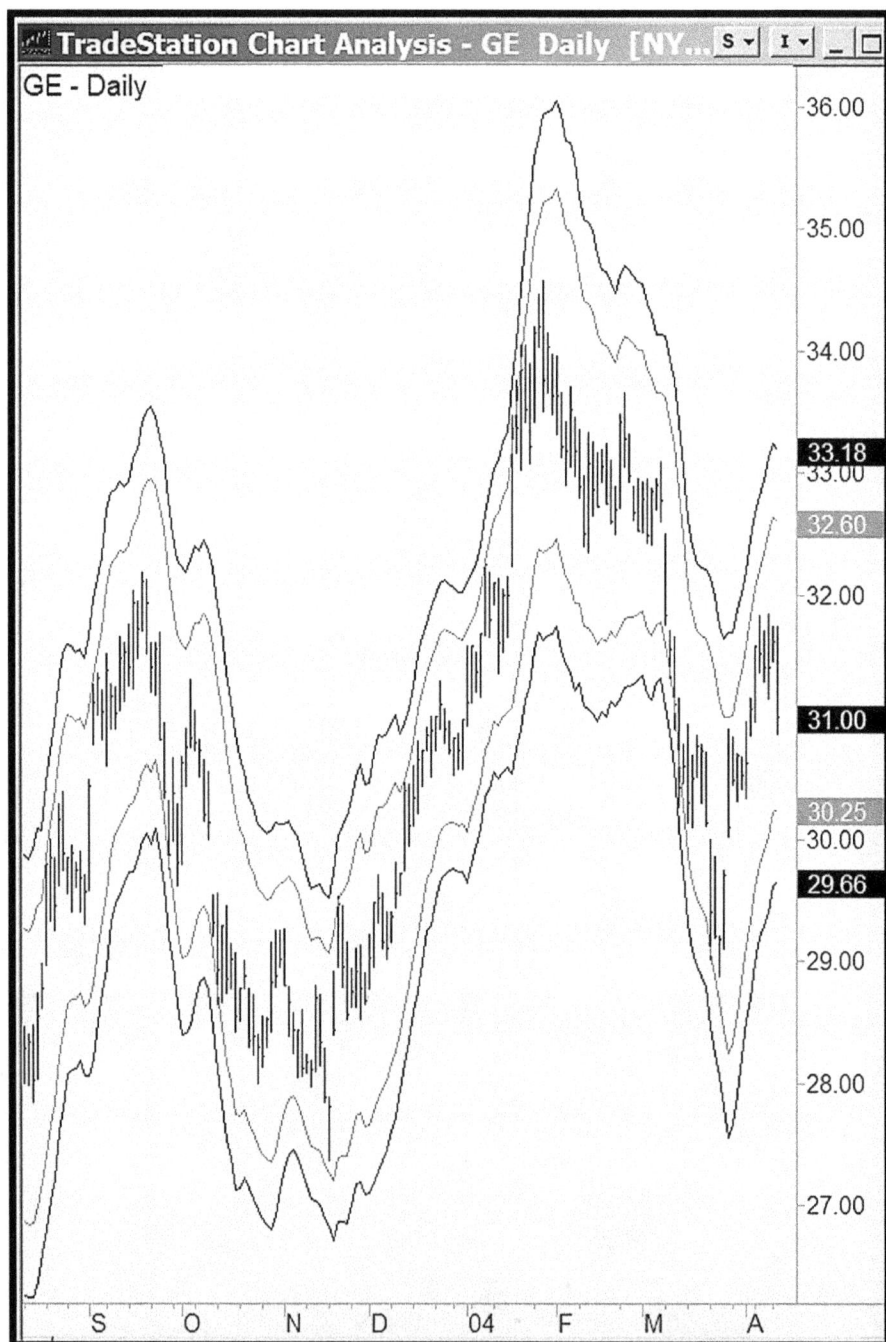

Psychological Support

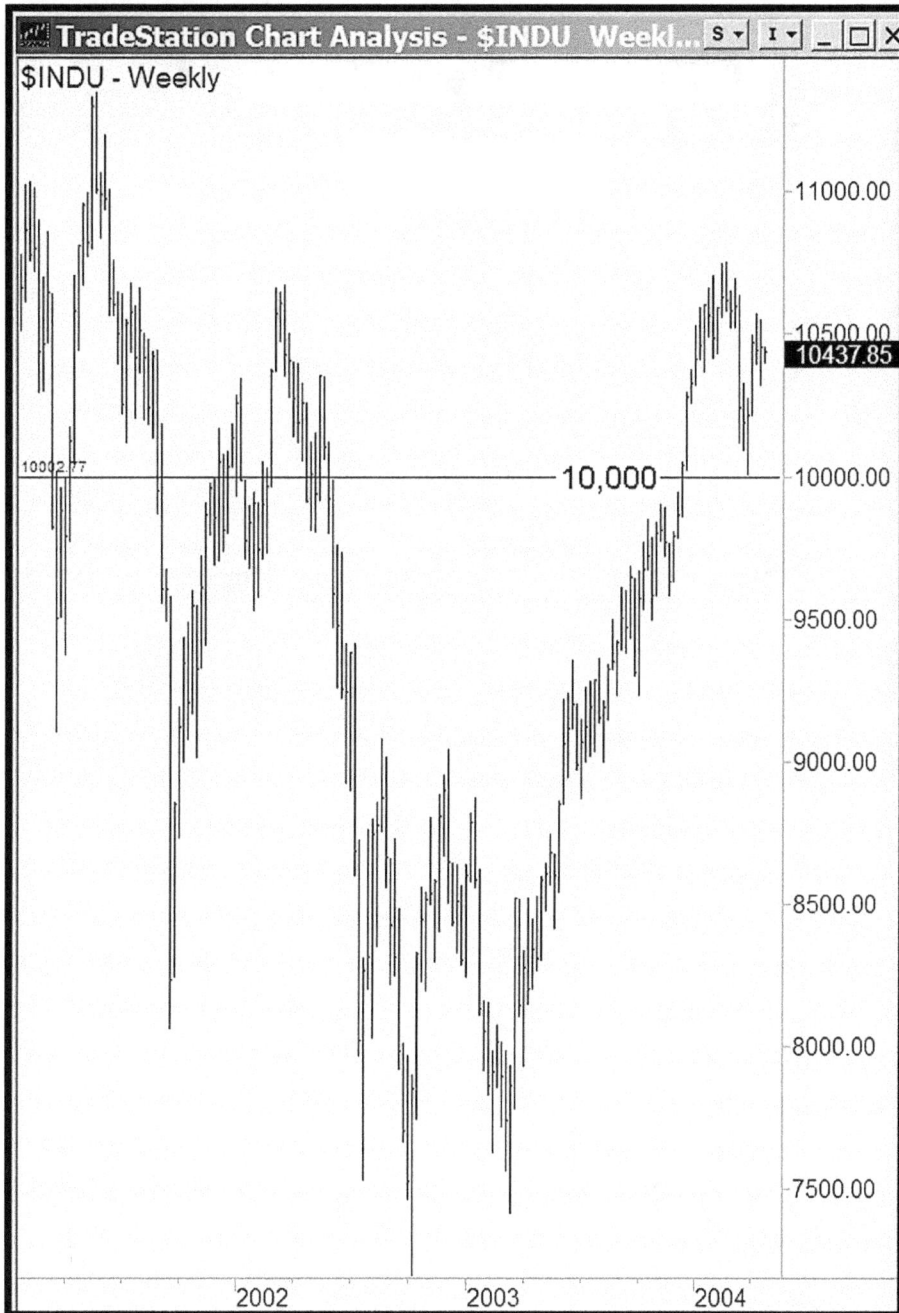

Relative Strength

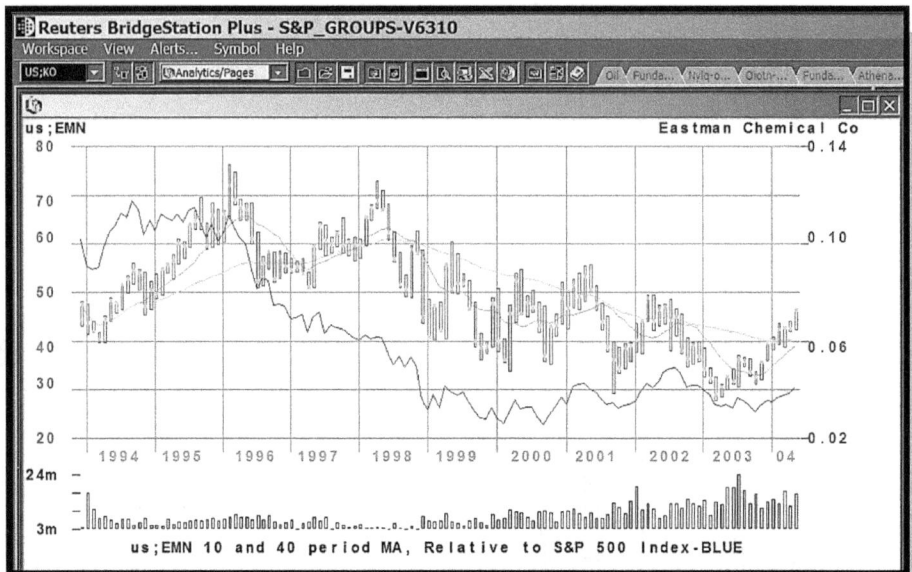

RSI Bear Market Oscillator Range*

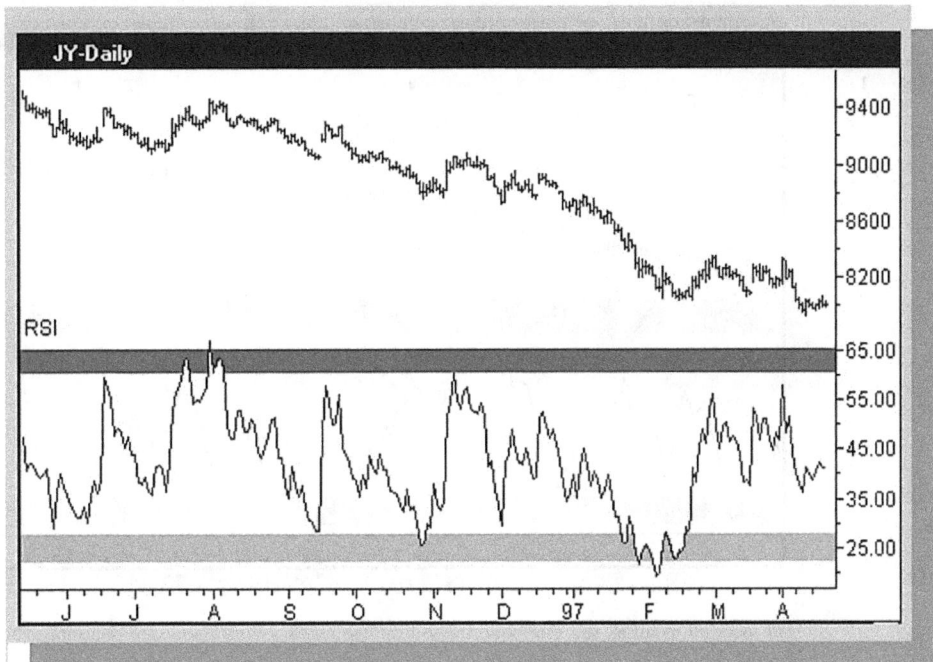

*For more information, see *Technical Analysis for the Trading Professional* by Constance Brown (New York: McGraw-Hill, 1999).

RSI Bull Market Oscillator Range*

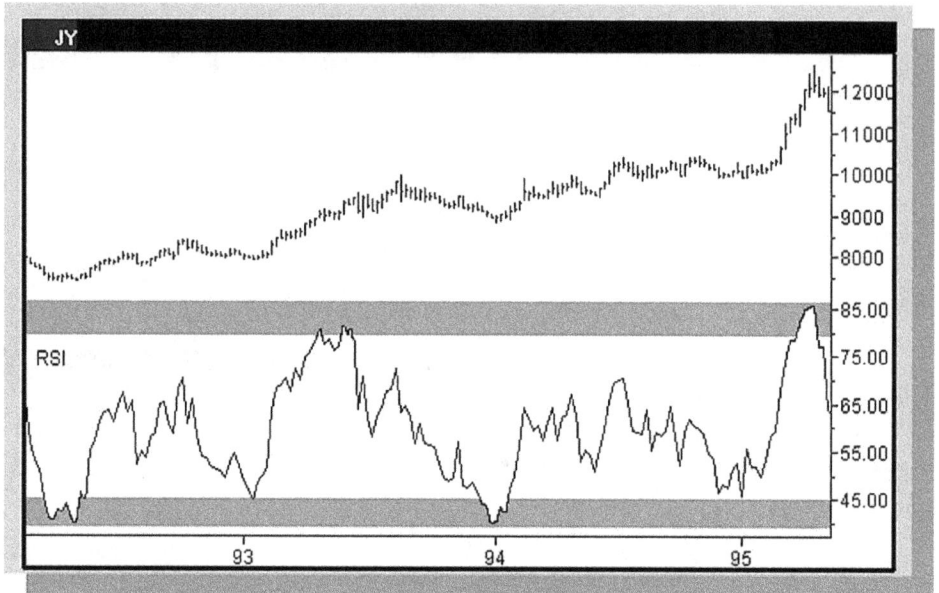

*For more information, see *Technical Analysis for the Trading Professional* by Constance Brown (New York: McGraw-Hill, 1999).

RSI Hidden Negative Reversal

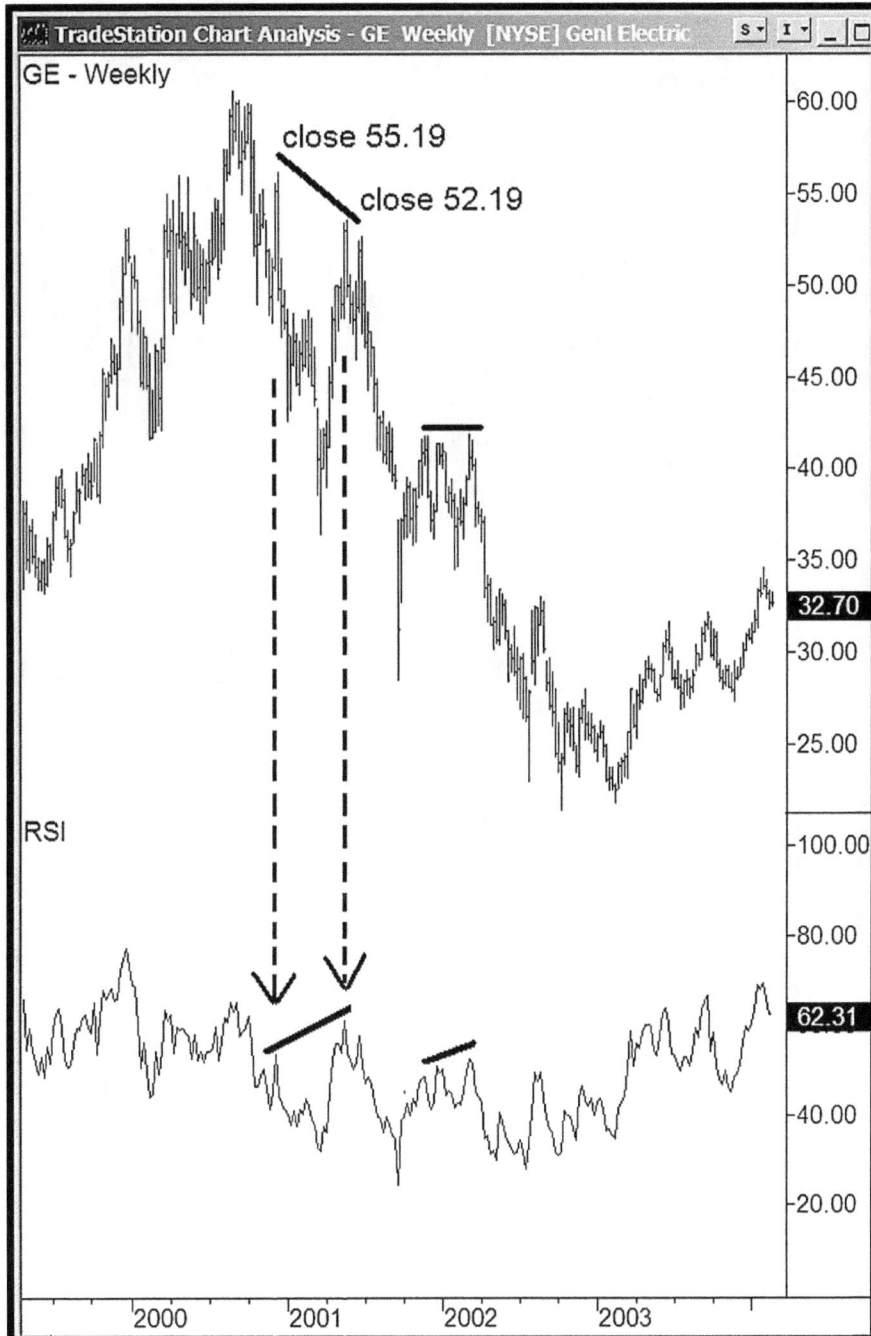

RSI Hidden Positive Reversal on Support

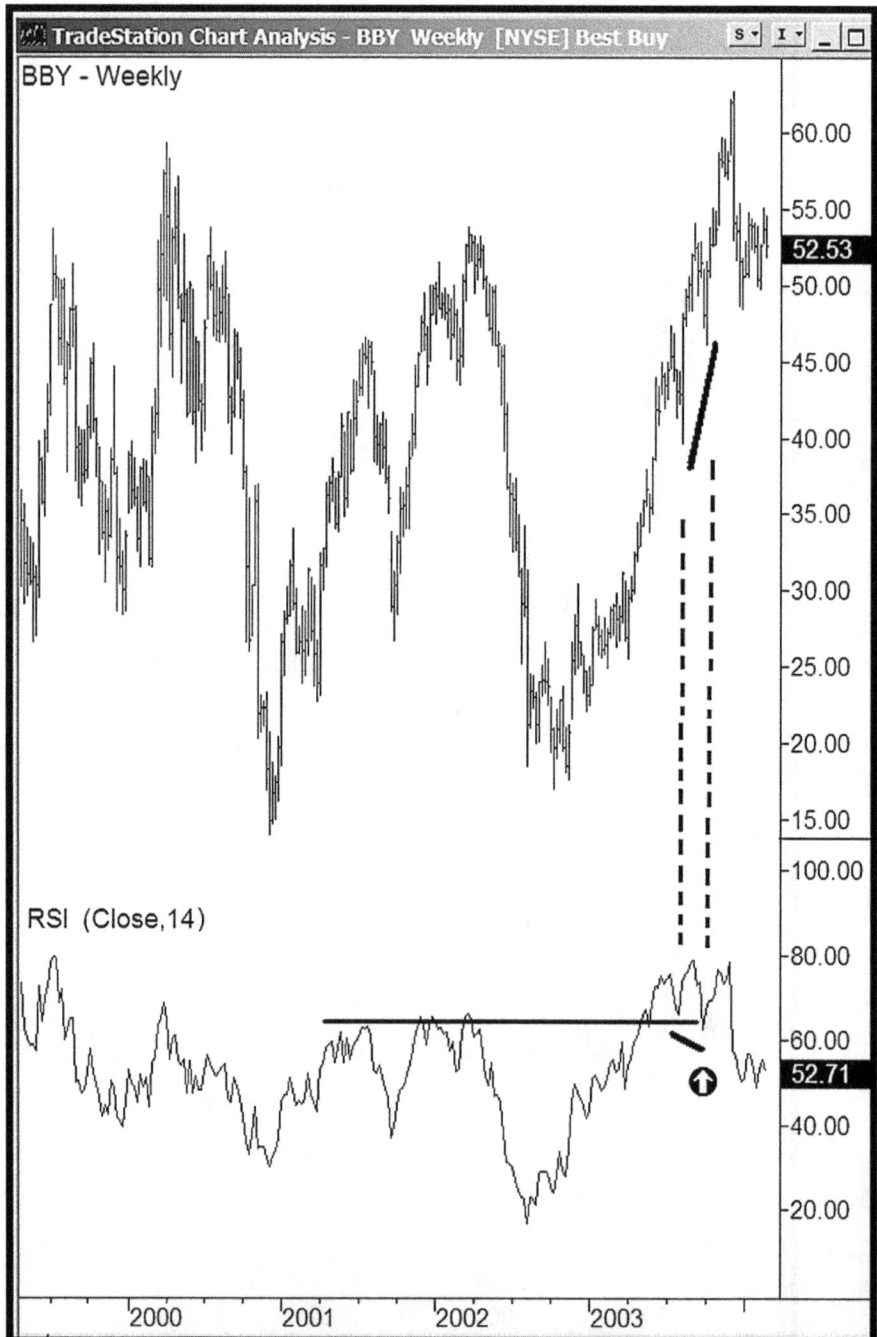

Seasonal Comparison Analysis

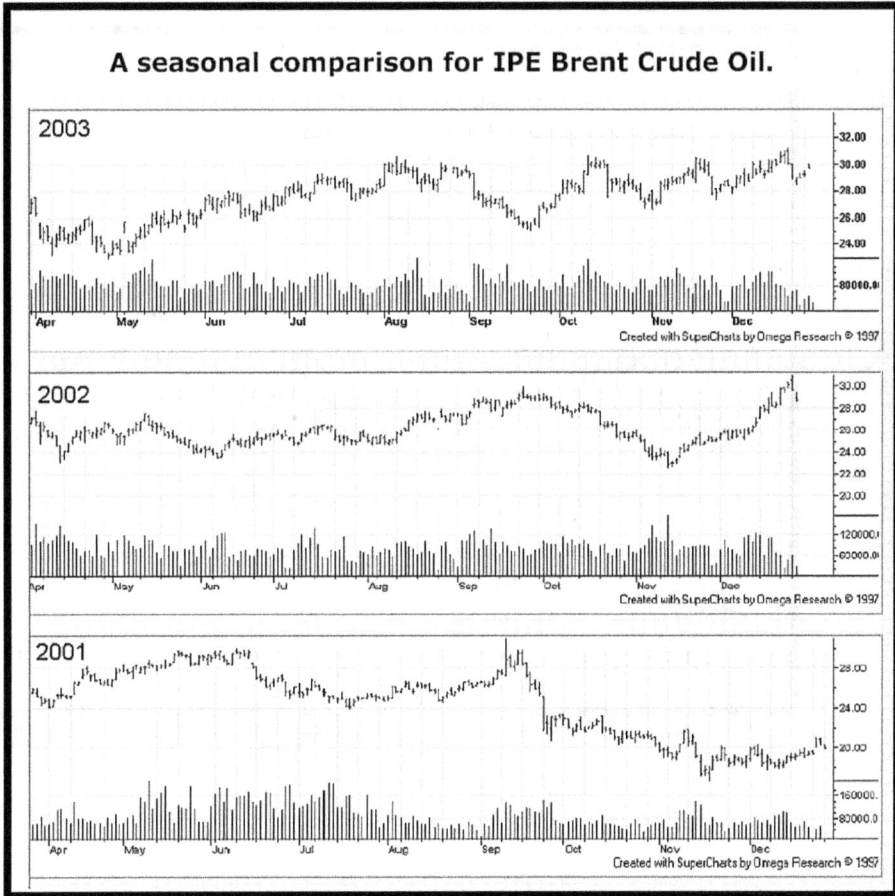

A seasonal comparison for IPE Brent Crude Oil.

Sentiment Analysis Commitment
of Traders (Commercials Versus Speculators)

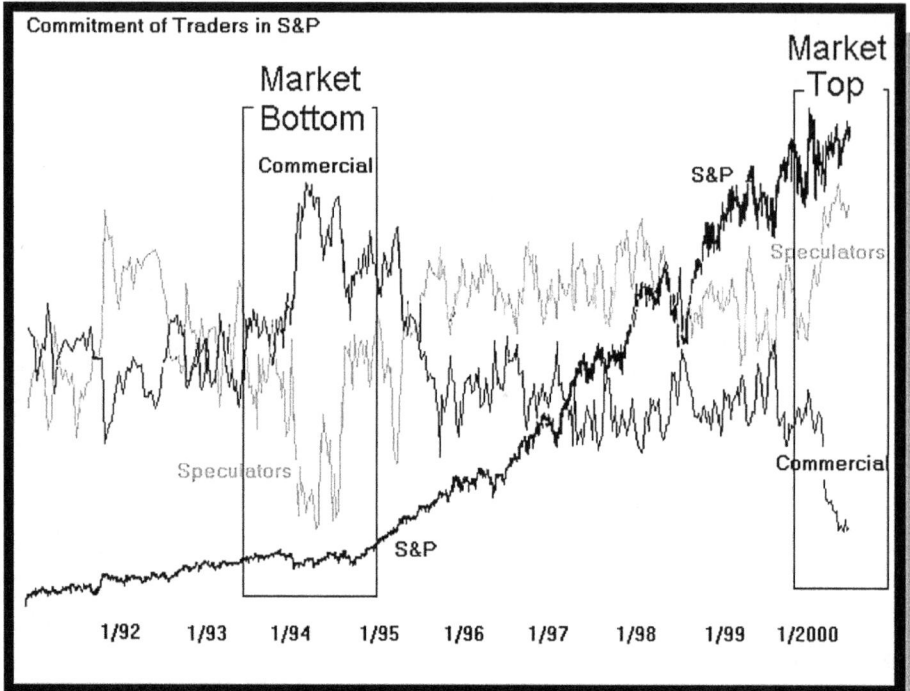

Commitment of Traders in S&P

SP500 Stock Sector Weightings within Index 1

```
2-BLOOMBERG                                                    _ □ ×
                                           N159 Index  GWGT

                    Index Group Weightings

  Ticker Search  [      ][GO]   Display    Edit   Output Results To   SPX Index
              As of 4/23/2004   [S&P 500 INDEX]   132 Groups
```

	Ticker	Name	% Weight in the Index	Index Divisor	Last Price
1)	S5PHAR	S&P 500 PHARM INDEX	8.210	2470.323	352.08
2)	S5IOIL	S&P 500 INTGR OIL&GS IDX	4.380	1923.886	241.21
3)	S5INDC	S&P 500 INDUS CONGL IDX	4.242	1303.018	344.88
4)	S5DBNK	S&P 500 DIV BANKS INDEX	4.133	1237.484	353.79
5)	S5SYSF	S&P 500 SYSTEMS SFTW IDX	4.011	860.512	493.81
6)	S5CMHW	S&P 500 COMPUTER HW IDX	3.229	987.223	346.48
7)	S5SECO	S&P 500 SEMICONDUCTORS	3.211	863.208	394.13
8)	S5CMEQ	S&P 500 COMMUNCTN EQUIP	3.113	2918.964	112.97
9)	S5ITEL	S&P 500 INTGR TELCM IDX	2.920	2838.446	108.98
10)	S5HYPC	S&P 500 HYPR & SUPRCNTRS	2.571	2596.312	104.90
11)	S5ODVF	S&P 500 OTHR DV FN SC IX	2.500	2115.230	125.20
12)	S5SOFD	S&P 500 SOFT DRINKS IDX	2.249	1030.303	231.27
13)	S5MLIN	S&P 500 MLTILN INS INDEX	2.103	496.173	449.09
14)	S5HCEP	S&P 500 HLTH CR EQIP IDX	2.103	420.631	529.61
15)	S5ELUT	S&P 500 ELEC UTIL INDEX	1.998	1499.835	141.10
16)	S5INBK	S&P 500 INVST BNK & BRKG	1.995	1652.171	127.95
17)	S5HOPR	S&P 500 HOUSEHLD PRD IDX	1.977	657.263	318.60
18)	S5RBNK	S&P 500 REGIONAL BANKS	1.925	1791.645	113.82

SP500 Stock Sector Weightings within Index 2

```
▓ 2-BLOOMBERG                                                    _ □ ×
                                                        N159 Index  GWGT
                      Index Group Weightings

 Ticker Search  [    ] GO    Display      Edit    Output Results To  SPX Index
```

	Ticker	Name	% Weight in the Index	Index Divisor	Last Price
19)	S5MOVI	S&P 500 MOVIES&ENTR IDX	1.867	1313.425	150.57
20)	S5AERO	S&P 500 AEROSP & DEF IDX	1.805	823.600	232.12
21)	S5THMF	S&P 500 THFTS & MRTGE IX	1.726	1711.978	106.79
22)	S5PROP	S&P 500 PROP&CASULT IDX	1.375	601.902	241.93
23)	S5CFIN	S&P 500 CONSUMER FINANCE	1.276	261.061	517.97
24)	S5HOMI	S&P 500 HOME IMP RTL IDX	1.228	337.448	305.63
25)	S5DPOS	S&P 500 DATA PRCS & OTS	1.199	687.138	104.86
26)	S5TOBA	S&P 500 TOBACCO INDEX	1.179	466.633	267.62
27)	S5PACK	S&P 500 PACKG FOODS IDX	1.171	535.827	231.50
28)	S5BIOT	S&P 500 BIOTECH INDEX	1.135	156.487	768.60
29)	S5LIFE	S&P 500 LIFE&HLTH IN IDX	1.050	536.795	207.28
30)	S5AIRF	S&P 500 AIR FT&LOG IDX	0.996	284.683	370.48
31)	S5BRDC	S&P 500 BDCST&CBL TV IDX	0.977	386.809	267.60
32)	S5DIVC	S&P 500 DIV CHEM INDEX	0.960	554.034	183.64
33)	S5MANH	S&P 500 MANG'D HLTH IDX	0.933	343.397	287.71
34)	S5INDM	S&P 500 INDUST MACHN IDX	0.855	299.377	302.41
35)	S5AMGT	S&P 500 ASST MNGMT & CST	0.850	702.060	128.20
36)	S5DCAP	S&P 500 DVRSFD CPTL MRKT	0.743	604.072	130.22

SP500 Stock Sectors Spreadsheet Template1

TradeStation Quotes - sectors

#	Symbol	Description	Last
1	@US.P	30 Year U.S. Treasury Bonds Co	113 26/32
2	DIA	Diamonds Trust,Series1	103.43
3	$INDU	Dow Jones Industrial Average I	10328.15
4	@GC.P(D)	Gold Continuous Contract Pit	422.00
5	QQQ	Nasdaq -100 Trust Ser 1	35.72
6	@ND.P	Nasdaq 100 Continuous Contrac	1439.50
7	@SP.P	S&P 500 Continuous Contract Pit	1121.60
8	SPY	S&P Dep Receipts	112.55
9	@DX.P(D)	U.S. Dollar Index Continuous Cor	88.74
10	S5ADVT ADVERTISING		
11	IPG	Interpublic Grp Cos	14.99
12	OMC	Omnicom Group	79.23
13	S5AERO AEROSP & DEFE		
14	BA	Boeing Co	40.15
15	GD	Genl Dynamics	87.26
16	GR	Goodrich Corp	28.11
17	HON	Honeywell Intl	33.67
18	LMT	Lockheed Martin	45.55
19	NOC	Northrop Grumman	97.15
20	RTN(HB)	Raytheon Co	31.00
21	COL	Rockwell Collins	31.38
22	UTX	United Technologies	85.08
23	S5AGRI AGRRCUL PDCTS		
24	ADM	Archer-Daniels-Midland	17.01
25	S5AIRF AIR FT&COUR		
26	FDX	Fedex Corp	74.02
27	R	Ryder System	37.77
28	UPS	United Parcel'B'	69.63
29	S5AIRL AIRLINES		
30	DAL	Delta Air Lines	7.82
31	LUV	Southwest Airlines	14.01
32	S5ALUM ALUMINUM		
33	AA	Alcoa Inc	34.80
34	S5APLS APPLICATION SOFTWARE		
35	ADSK	Autodesk, Inc	31.58
36	CTXS	Citrix Systems	22.19
37	CPWR	Compuware Corp	7.40
38	INTU	Intuit Inc	44.86
39	MERQ	Mercury Interactive	44.34
40	PMTC	Parametric Technology	4.52
41	PSFT	PeopleSoft Inc	18.44
42	SEBL	Siebel Systems	11.35

TradeStation Quotes - sectors

#	Symbol	Description	Last
47	S5APRE APRL RETAIL		
48	GPS	Gap Inc	21.57
49	LTD(HB)	Limited Brands	19.81
50	TJX	TJX Companies	24.27
51	S5AMGT ASST MNGMT & CST		
52	BK	Bank Of New York	31.98
53	FII	Federated Investors 'B'	31.64
54	BEN	Franklin Resources	56.00
55	JNS	Janus Capital Group	16.71
56	MEL	Mellon Financial	31.40
57	NTRS	Northern Trust	46.13
58	STT	State Street Corp	52.75
59	TROW	T.Rowe Price Group	53.83
60	S5AUTM AUTO MANUFACTURERS		
61	F	Ford Motor	13.54
62	GM	Genl Motors	47.24
63	S5AUTP AUTO PARTS & EQUIP		
64	DCN	Dana Corp	19.28
65	DPH	Delphi Corp	9.90
66	JCI	Johnson Controls	59.49
67	VC	Visteon Corp	9.40
68	S5BRDC BRDCAST & CABLE TV		
69	CCU	Clear Channel Commun	41.83
70	CMCSA	Comcast CI'A'	28.94
71	UVN	Univision Communic'A'	32.83
72	S5BIOT BIOTECH		
73	AMGN	Amgen Inc	59.17
75	CHIR	Chiron Corp	44.37
76	GENZ	Genzyme Corp	46.00
77	MEDI	MedImmune Inc	23.14
78	S5BREW BREWERS		
79	BUD	Anheuser-Busch Cos	51.10
80	RKY	Coors (Adolph)'B'	68.00
81	S5BUIL BUILDING PCT		
82	ASD	Amer Standard	110.98
83	MAS	Masco Corp	30.35
84	S5CASI CASINO & GAMING		
85	HET	Harrah's Entertainment	54.25
86	IGT	Intl Game Technology	44.33

SP500 Stock Sectors Spreadsheet Template2

TradeStation Quotes - sectors

TradeStation Quotes - sectors

#	Symbol	Description	Last
87	S5CMEQ	COMMUNICATION EQUIP	
88	ADCT	ADC Telecommunications	2.90
89	A	Agilent Technologies	31.43
90	ANDW	Andrew Corp	16.76
91	CIEN	Ciena Corp	4.96
92	CSCO	Cisco Systems	23.76
93	CMVT	Comverse Technology	17.81
94	GLW	Corning Inc	11.24
95	JDSU	JDS Uniphase Corp	4.17
96	LU	Lucent Technologies	4.09
97	MOT	Motorola, Inc	17.44
98	QCOM	Qualcomm Inc	65.27
99	SFA	Scientific-Atlanta	32.19
100	TLAB	Tellabs, Inc	8.73
101	V(HB)	Vivendi Univl SA ADS	25.87
102	S5CMSP	COMPUTER STG&PER	
103	EMC	EMC Corp	13.81
104	LXK	Lexmark Intl'A'	90.72
105	NTAP	Network Appliance	21.72
106	S5CMER	CONSUMER ELECTRIC	
107	BBY	Best Buy	48.63
108	CC	Circuit City Stores	10.95
109	RSH	Radioshack Corp	33.03
110	S5CMHW	COMPUTER HDWR	
111	AAPL	Apple Computer	27.75
112	DELL	Dell Inc	33.67
113	GTW	Gateway Inc	5.38
114	HPQ	Hewlett-Packard	23.02
115	IBM	Intl Bus. Machines	91.90
116	NCR	NCR Corp	43.18
117	SUNW	Sun Microsystems	4.22
118	S5CSTM	CONSTR MATRLS	
119	VMC	Vulcan Materials	46.54
120	S5CSTE	CONST & ENGIN	
121	FLR	Fluor Corp	39.05
122	MDR	McDermott Intl	8.76
123	S5CSTF	CONST & FARM MACH	
124	CAT	Caterpillar Inc	78.27
126	DE	Deere & Co	69.30
127	NAV	Navistar Intl	45.00
128	PCAR	Paccar Inc	55.95

#	Symbol	Description	Last
129	S5DPOS	DATA PROCESSING & OTS	
130	ADP	Automatic Data Proc	41.67
131	CSC	Computer Sciences	40.30
133	CVG	Convergys Corp	15.40
134	EDS	Electronic Data Systems	19.19
135	FDC	First Data	41.85
136	FISV	Fiserv Inc	35.67
137	PAYX	Paychex Inc	35.75
138	TSG	Sabre Holdings'A'	20.71
139	SDS	Sungard Data Systems	27.79
140	S5DEPT	DEPT STORES	
141	DDS	Dillard's Inc'A'	19.13
142	FD	Federated Dept Stores	53.93
143	KSS	Kohl's Corp	49.10
144	MAY	May Dept Stores	34.10
145	JWN	Nordstrom, Inc	39.51
146	JCP	Penney (J.C.)	34.87
147	S	Sears,Roebuck	42.65
148	S5DBNK	DIV BANKS	
149	BAC	Bank Of America	81.85
150	ONE	Bank One Corp	54.65
151	CMA	Comerica Inc	54.28
152	FBF	FleetBoston Financial	45.38
153	USB	U.S. Bancorp	27.74
154	WB	Wachovia Corp	46.56
155	WFC	Wells Fargo	56.92
156	S5DIVC	DIV CHEMICAL	
157	DOW	Dow Chemical	40.47
158	DD	Dupont(E.I.)Denemours	42.38
159	EMN	Eastman Chemical	42.72
160	EC	Engelhard Corp	29.90
161	HPC	Hercules, Inc	11.48
162	PPG	PPG Indus	57.66
163	S5DIVO	DIV COMM SERV	
164	APOL	Apollo Group'A'	85.04
165	HRB	Block (H&R)	51.08
166	CD	Cendant Corp	23.97
167	CTAS	Cintas Corp	43.43
168	DLX	Deluxe Corp	40.25
169	EFX	Equifax Inc	25.75
170	S5DIVM	DIV MTL&MIN	
171	FCX	FreePT McMoRan Copper&Gold'	39.28
172	PD	Phelps Dodge	81.64

SP500 Stock Sectors Spreadsheet Template3

TradeStation Quotes - sectors

	Symbol	Description	Last
176	S5DCAP DVRSFD CAPTL		
177	JPM	J.P. Morgan Chase & Co	42.03
178	S5ELCO ELEC COM & EQUIP		
179	APCC	Amer Power Conversion	22.36
180	CBE	Cooper Indus'A'	56.82
181	EMR	Emerson Electric	60.80
182	PWER	Power-One	11.08
183	ROK	Rockwell Automation	34.64
184	TNB	Thomas & Betts	21.83
185	S5ELEM ELEC EQP MFG		
186	A	Agilent Technologies	31.42
187	PKI	Perkinelmer Inc	20.88
188	SBL	Symbol Technologies	13.35
189	TEK	Tektronix Inc	31.93
190	TMO	Thermo Electron	27.95
191	WAT	Waters Corp	40.07
192	S5EMAN ELEC MANU		
193	JBL	Jabil Circuit	29.21
194	MOLX	Molex Inc	30.19
195	SANM	Sanmina-SCI	11.05
196	SLR	Solectron Corp	5.51
197	S5ELUT ELECRIC UTIL		
198	AYE	Allegheny Energy	13.58
199	AEP	Amer Electric Pwr	32.80
200	AEE	Ameren Corp	46.11
201	CNP	Centerpoint Energy	11.30
202	CIN	Cinergy Corp	40.93
203	CMS	CMS Energy	8.88
204	ED	Consolidated Edison	43.99
205	CEG	Constellation Energy Group	39.95
206	D	Dominion Resources	63.66
207	DTE	DTE Energy	40.93
208	EIX	Edison Intl	23.91
209	ETR	Entergy Corp	58.91
210	EXC	Exelon Corp	68.27
211	FE	FirstEnergy Corp	38.98
212	FPL	FPL Group	66.95
213	PCG	PG&E Corp	29.12
214	PNW	Pinnacle West Capital	38.72
215	PPL	PPL Corp	44.75
216	PGN	Progress Energy	47.03
217	PEG	Public Svc Enterprises	46.84
218	SO	Southern Co	30.37
219	TE(HB)	Teco Energy	14.30
220	TXU	TXU Corp	28.26

TradeStation Quotes - sectors

	Symbol	Description	Last
222	S5EMPL EMPL SERVS		
223	MNST	Monster Worldwide	24.82
224	RHI	Robert Half Intl	23.63
225	S5ENVR ENVIRONMENTAL SERV		
226	AW	Allied Waste Ind	13.01
227	WMI	Waste Management	29.59
228	S5FDRE FOOD RETAIL		
229	ABS	Albertson's, Inc	21.80
230	KR	Kroger Co	16.29
231	SWY	Safeway Inc	20.32
232	WIN(HB)	Winn-Dixie Stores	7.49
233	S5FOOT FOOTWARE		
234	NKE	Nike, Inc'B'	76.58
235	RBK	Reebok Intl	40.49
236	S5FRST FOREST PRODUCTS		
237	WY	Weyerhaeuser Co	65.11
238	S5GASU GAS UTIL		
239	KSE	Keyspan Corp	37.69
240	KMI	Kinder Morgan	62.49
241	GAS	Nicor Inc	34.85
242	NI	Nisource Inc	21.15
243	PGL	Peoples Energy	44.00
244	SRE	Sempra Energy	31.31
245	S5GENM GEN MERCH STORES		
246	BLI	Big Lots	14.46
247	DG	Dollar General	19.31
248	FDO	Family Dollar Stores	35.58
249	TGT	Target Corp	45.58
250	S5GOLD GOLD		
251	NEM	Newmont Mining	46.89
252	S5HCSV HEALTHCARE SERVICES		
253	RX	IMS Health	22.82
254	DGX	Quest Diagnostics	82.90
255	QTRN	Quintiles Transnational	0.00
256	S5HCDC HEALTHCARE DIST		
257	ABC	AmeriSourceBergen Corp	53.66
258	CAH	Cardinal Health	67.99
259	MCK	McKesson Corp	29.53

SP500 Stock Sectors Spreadsheet Template4

	Symbol	Description	Last		Symbol	Description	Last
260	S5HCEP	HEALTHCARE EQUIP		304	S5HOSP	HOUSEWARES & SPEC	
261	ABI	Applera Corp-Applied Biosys Gr	20.02	305	AM	Amer Greetings'A'	20.43
262	BCR	Bard (C.R.)	95.25	306	FO	Fortune Brands	76.75
263	BAX	Baxter Intl	30.62	307	NWL	Newell Rubbermaid	23.62
264	BDX	Becton, Dickinson	48.76	308	TUP	Tupperware Corp	18.85
265	BMET	Biomet, Inc	38.13	309	S5HYPC	HYPR & SUPRCNTRS	
266	BSX	Boston Scientific	42.66	310	COST	Costco Wholesale	37.85
267	GDT	Guidant Corp	63.16	311	WMT	Wal-Mart Stores	57.31
268	MDT	Medtronic, Inc	47.36	312	S5INDC	INDUSTRIAL CONGLOM	
269	STJ	St. Jude Medical	71.89	313	MMM	3M Co	87.18
270	SYK	Stryker Corp	88.00	314	GE	General Electric	30.06
271	ZMH	Zimmer Holdings	72.63	315	TXT	Textron, Inc	55.35
272	S5HCFA	HEALTHCARE FACIL		316	TYC	Tyco Intl	27.85
273	HCA	HCA Inc	39.99	317	S5INDG	INDUSTRIAL GASES	
274	HMA	Health Management Assoc	22.53	318	APD	Air Products & Chem	50.28
275	HCR	Manor Care	35.18	319	PX	PraxAir Inc	37.16
276	THC	Tenet Healthcare	10.75	320	S5INDM	INDUSTRIAL MACH	
277	S5HCSU	HEALTHCARE SUPP		321	CR	Crane Co	31.07
278	BOL	Bausch & Lomb	60.15	322	DHR	Danaher Corp	92.82
279	MIL	Millipore Corp	51.92	323	DOV	Dover Corp	40.23
280	S5HOMI	HOME IMPROV		324	ETN	Eaton Corp	59.54
281	HD	Home Depot	37.31	325	ITW	Illinois Tool Works	86.55
282	LOW	Lowe's Cos	56.17	326	IR	Ingersoll-Rand'A'	64.70
283	SHW	Sherwin-Williams	37.06	327	ITT	ITT Indus	79.97
284	S5HOME	HOMEBUILDING		328	PLL	Pall Corp	23.62
285	CTX	Centex Corp	53.92	329	PH	Parker-Hannifin	55.89
286	KBH	KB Home	79.20	330	S5INSS	INET SFT & SERV	
287	PHM	Pulte Homes	54.51	331	YHOO	Yahoo Inc	51.31
288	S5HOTL	HOTLELS		332	S5INSB	INSUR BROKER	
289	CCL	Carnival Corp	44.48	333	AOC	Aon Corp	26.15
290	HLT	Hilton Hotels	16.31	334	MMC	Marsh & Mclennan	45.15
291	MAR	Marriott Intl'A'	42.00	335	S5IOIL	INTG OIL & GAS	
292	HOT	Starwood Hotels&ResWorldwide	40.12	336	AHC	Amerada Hess	71.30
293	S5HOPR	HOUSEHOLD PRODUCTS		337	CVX	ChevronTexaco Corp	92.47
294	CLX	Clorox Co	48.74	338	COP	ConocoPhillips	71.91
295	CL	Colgate-Palmolive	55.69	339	XOM	Exxon Mobil	43.25
296	KMB	Kimberly-Clark	62.05	340	MRO	Marathon Oil	33.56
297	PG	Procter & Gamble	105.08	341	OXY	Occidental Petroleum	47.45
298	S5HOAP	HOUSEHOLD APPL					
299	BDK	Black & Decker Corp	57.05				
300	MYG	Maytag Corp	29.57				
301	SNA	Snap-On Inc	32.55				
302	SWK	Stanley Works	43.50				
303	WHR	Whirlpool Corp	67.94				

TradeStation Quotes - sectors

SP500 Stock Sectors Spreadsheet Template5

	TradeStation Quotes - sectors				TradeStation Quotes - sectors		
	Symbol	Description	Last		Symbol	Description	Last
342	S5ITEL INTGR TELECOMMUN			386	S5MUTI MULTI-UTILITY		
343	AT	Alltel Corp	49.73	387	AES	AES Corp	8.26
344	T	AT&T Corp	19.87	388	CPN(HB)	Calpine Corp	4.75
345	BLS	Bellsouth Corp	28.91	389	DUK	Duke Energy	22.39
346	CTL	CenturyTel Inc	27.28	390	DYN(HB)	Dynegy Inc	3.76
347	CZN	Citizens Communications	12.80	391	EP	El Paso Corp	7.13
348	Q	Qwest Communications Intl	4.36	392	MIR(HB)	Invalid Symbol	
349	SBC	SBC Communications	24.18	393	WMB	Williams Cos	9.57
350	FON	Sprint Corp(Fon Group)	18.12	394	S5OILE OIL & GAS EQU		
351	VZ	Verizon Communications	36.16	395	BHI	Baker Hughes Inc	36.00
352	S5INBK INVESTMT BANKS & BRKG			396	BJS	BJ Services	42.61
353	BSC	Bear Stearns Cos	88.76	397	HAL	Halliburton Co	30.13
354	GS	Goldman Sachs Group	103.55	398	SLB	Schlumberger Ltd	63.19
355	LEH	Lehman Br Holdings	83.17	399	S5OILD OIL & GAS DRILL		
356	MER	Merrill Lynch	59.57	400	NBR	Nabors Indus	45.34
357	MWD	Morgan Stanley	57.01	401	NE	Noble Corp	38.24
358	SCH	Schwab(Charles)Corp	11.46	402	RDC	Rowan Cos	21.32
359	S5LIFE LIFE & HLTH INSURANCE			403	RIG	TransOcean Inc	28.35
360	AFL	AFLAC Inc	40.58	404	S5OILP OIL&GAS EXPL		
361	JP	Jefferson-Pilot	54.75	405	APC	Anadarko Petroleum	51.22
362	JHF	John Hancock Fin'l Svcs	43.90	406	APA	Apache Corp	42.82
363	LNC	Lincoln Natl Corp	47.38	407	BR	Burlington Resources	62.71
364	MET	Metlife Inc	35.82	408	DVN	Devon Energy	57.09
365	PRU	Prudential Financial	44.88	409	EOG	Eog Resources	45.33
366	TMK	Torchmark Corp	53.74	410	KMG	Kerr-McGee	50.35
367	UNM	UNUMProvident Corp	14.51	411	UCL	Unocal Corp	36.82
368	S5MANH MANAGED HLTH			412	S5OILR OIL & GAS REFIN		
369	AET	Aetna Inc	89.03	413	ASH	Ashland Inc	46.37
370	ATH	Anthem Inc	89.77	414	SUN	Sunoco Inc	61.20
371	CI	Cigna Corp	57.91	415	S5ODVF OTHER DIV FINCL SERVICES		
372	HUM	Humana Inc	19.20	416	C	Citigroup Inc	51.72
373	UNH	UnitedHealth Group	63.16	417	PFG	Principal Financial Grp	35.61
374	WLP	Wellpoint Hlth Networks	112.96	418	S5PACK PACKG FOODS		
375	S5MLIN MULTI-LIFE INS			419	CPB	Campbell Soup	27.19
376	AIG	Amer Intl Group	71.50	420	CAG	Conagra Foods	26.81
377	HIG	Hartford Finl Svcs Gp	63.57	421	GIS	Genl Mills	46.47
378	LTR	Loews Corp	59.01	422	HNZ	Heinz (H.J.)	37.09
379	S5MOVI MOVIES & ENTR			423	HSY	Hershey Foods	82.74
380	AOL	Invalid Symbol		424	K	Kellogg Co	39.37
381	DIS	Disney (Walt) Co	25.09	425	MKC	Mccormick & Co	33.09
382	VIA.B	Viacom Inc'B'	39.17	426	SLE	Sara Lee Corp	21.68
383	S5METG METALS & GLASS CONTAINERS			427	WWY	Wrigley, (wm) Jr	58.75
384	BLL	Ball Corp	68.12				
385	PTV	Pactiv Corp	21.90				

SP500 Stock Sectors Spreadsheet Template6

	Symbol	Description	Last		Symbol	Description	Last
428	S5PAPA	PAPER PACKAGING		474	S5RAIL		
429	BMS	Bemis Co	25.94	475	BNI	Burlington Northn Santa Fe	30.96
430	SEE	Sealed Air	49.87	476	CSX	CSX Corp	29.73
431	TIN	Temple-Inland	63.22	477	NSC	Norfolk Southern	21.48
432	S5PAPR	PAPER PRODUCTS		478	UNP	Union Pacific	60.49
433	BCC	Boise Cascade	34.49	479	S5REIT	REAL ESTATE INV	
434	GP	Georgia-Pacific Corp	33.26	480	AIV	Apartment Investment & Mgmt'A'	30.30
435	IP	Intl Paper	42.32	481	EOP	Equity Office Properties Tr	28.89
436	MWV	MeadWestvaco Corp	27.95	482	EQR(HB)	Equity Residential	29.55
437	S5PERS	PERSONAL PRD		483	PCL	Plum Creek Timber	32.38
438	ACV	Alberto-culver	43.46	484	SPG	Simon Property Group	57.82
439	AVP	Avon Products	75.14	485	S5RBNK	REGIONAL BANKS	
440	G	Gillette Co	38.81	486	ASO	Amsouth Bancorp	23.62
441	S5PHAR	PHARMAC		487	BBT	BB&T Corp	35.30
442	ABT	Abbott Laboratories	40.65	488	CF	Charter One Finl	35.18
443	AGN	Allergan, Inc	83.35	489	FITB	Fifth Third Bancorp	54.91
444	BMY	Bristol-Myers SQUIBB	24.12	490	FTN	First Tenn Natl	47.29
445	FRX	Forest Labs	70.62	491	HBAN	Huntington Bancshares	21.81
446	JNJ	Johnson & Johnson	50.52	492	KEY	KeyCorp	30.18
447	KG	King Pharmaceuticals	16.61	493	MI	Marshall & Ilsley	37.99
448	LLY	Lilly (Eli)	65.86	494	NCC	Natl City Corp	35.42
449	MRK	Merck & Co	44.17	495	NFB	North Fork Bancorp	42.31
450	PFE	Pfizer, Inc	34.89	496	PNC	PNC Financial Services Group	55.88
451	SGP	Schering-Plough	16.25	497	RF	Regions Financial	36.32
452	WPI	Watson Pharmaceuticals	42.17	498	SOTR	Southtrust Corp	32.92
453	WYE	Wyeth	37.31	499	STI	SunTrust Banks	69.86
454	S5PROP	PROP & CASUALTY INS		500	SNV	Synovus Financial	24.06
455	ACE	ACE Limited	43.03	501	UPC	Union Planters	29.61
456	ALL	Allstate Corp	45.28	502	ZION	Zions Bancorp	57.02
457	ABK	Ambac Financial Group	73.57	503	S5REST	RESTAURANTS	
458	CB	Chubb Corp	68.86	504	DRI	Darden Restaurants	24.78
459	CINF	Cincinnati Financial	42.56	505	MCD	McDonald's Corp	28.55
460	MBI	MBIA Inc	62.61	506	SBUX	Starbucks Corp	37.88
461	PGR	Progressive Corp,Ohio	88.09	507	WEN	Wendy's Intl	41.17
462	SAFC	Safeco Corp	43.04	508	YUM	Yum Brands	38.36
463	SPC	St. Paul Cos	40.15	509	S5SEEQ	SEMICONDUCTOR EQUIP	
464	TAP.B	Travelers Prop & Casualty'B'	17.29	510	AMAT	Applied Materials	21.16
465	XL	XL Capital Ltd'A'	75.17	511	KLAC	KLA-Tencor Corp	50.53
466	S5PUBL	PUBL & PRINTING		512	NVLS	Novellus Systems	31.04
467	DJ	Dow Jones & Co	48.56	513	TER	Teradyne Inc	23.81
468	GCI	Gannett Co	88.52				
469	KRI	Knight Ridder Inc	73.53				
470	MHP	McGraw-Hill Companies	75.85				
471	MDP	Meredith Corp	49.93				
472	NYT	New York Times'A'	44.10				

SP500 Stock Sectors Spreadsheet Template7

	Symbol	Description	Last		Symbol	Description	Last
514	S5SECO	SEMICONDUCTORS		536	S5SPCH	SPECIALTY CHEM	
515	AMD	Advanced Micro Dev	15.55	537	ECL	Ecolab Inc	28.10
516	ALTR	Altera Corp	20.40	538	GLK	Great Lakes Chemical	24.11
517	ADI	Analog Devices	47.68	539	IFF	Intl Flavors/Fragr	34.71
518	AMCC	Applied Micro Circuits	5.82	540	ROH	Rohm & Haas	39.76
519	BRCM	Broadcom Corp'A'	39.78	541	SIAL	Sigma-Aldrich	55.29
520	INTC	Intel Corp	27.40	542	S5SPST	SPECIALTY STORES	
521	LLTC	Linear Technology Corp	36.42	543	AN	AutoNation Inc	16.88
522	LSI	LSI Logic	9.49	544	AZO	AutoZone Inc	85.41
523	MXIM	Maxim Integrated Prod	46.33	545	BBY	Best Buy	48.61
524	MU	Micron Technology	16.20	546	ODP	Office Depot	18.51
525	NSM	Natl Semiconductor	43.66	547	SPLS	Staples Inc	25.40
526	NVDA	Nvidia Corp	25.68	548	TIF	Tiffany & Co	38.72
527	PMCS	PMC-Sierra Inc	16.91	549	TOY	Toys R Us	16.86
528	QLGC	Qlogic Corp	42.20	550	S5STEL	STEEL	
529	TXN	Texas Instruments	28.79	551	ATI	Allegheny Technologies	11.70
530	XLNX	Xilinx Inc	37.67	552	NUE	Nucor Corp	62.24
531	S5SOFD	SOFT DRINKS		553	X	U.S. Steel Corporation	37.09
532	KO	Coca-Cola Co	49.86	554	WOR	Worthington Indus	19.04
533	CCE	Coca-Cola Enterprises	23.87	555	S5SYSF	SYSTEM SOFTWARE	
534	PBG	Pepsi Bottling Group	29.53	556	ADBE	Adobe Systems	39.80
535	PEP	Pepsico Inc	53.32	557	BMC	BMC Software	19.67
536	S5SPCH	SPECIALTY CHEM		558	CA	Computer Assoc Intl	26.97
537	ECL	Ecolab Inc	28.10	559	MSFT	Microsoft Corp	25.21
538	GLK	Great Lakes Chemical	24.11	560	NOVL	Novell Inc	11.58
539	IFF	Intl Flavors/Fragr	34.71	561	ORCL	Oracle Corp	12.03
540	ROH	Rohm & Haas	39.76	562	SYMC	Symantec Corp	46.89
541	SIAL	Sigma-Aldrich	55.31	564	S5THMF	THFTS & MRTGE	
542	S5SPST	SPECIALTY STORES		565	CFC	Countrywide Financial	94.72
543	AN	AutoNation Inc	16.88	566	FRE	Federal Home Loan	59.70
544	AZO	AutoZone Inc	85.40	567	FNM	Federal Natl Mtge	75.44
545	BBY	Best Buy	48.60	568	GDW	Golden West Finl	110.53
546	ODP	Office Depot	18.51	569	MTG	MGIC Investment	63.94
547	SPLS	Staples Inc	25.40	570	WM	Washington Mutual	42.92
548	TIF	Tiffany & Co	38.71	571	S5TIRE	TIRE & RUBBER	
549	TOY	Toys R Us	16.88	572	CTB	Cooper Tire & Rubber	19.85
550	S5STEL	STEEL		573	GT(HB)	Goodyear Tire & Rub	7.94
551	ATI	Allegheny Technologies	11.70	574	S5TOBA	TOBACCO	
552	NUE	Nucor Corp	62.24	575	MO	Altria Group	54.06
553	X	U.S. Steel Corporation	37.10	576	RJR	R.J. Reynolds Tobacco	59.46
554	WOR	Worthington Indus	19.04	577	UST	UST Inc	36.16
				578			

Statistical Linear Regression

Statistical Probability Calculations for a Price Range

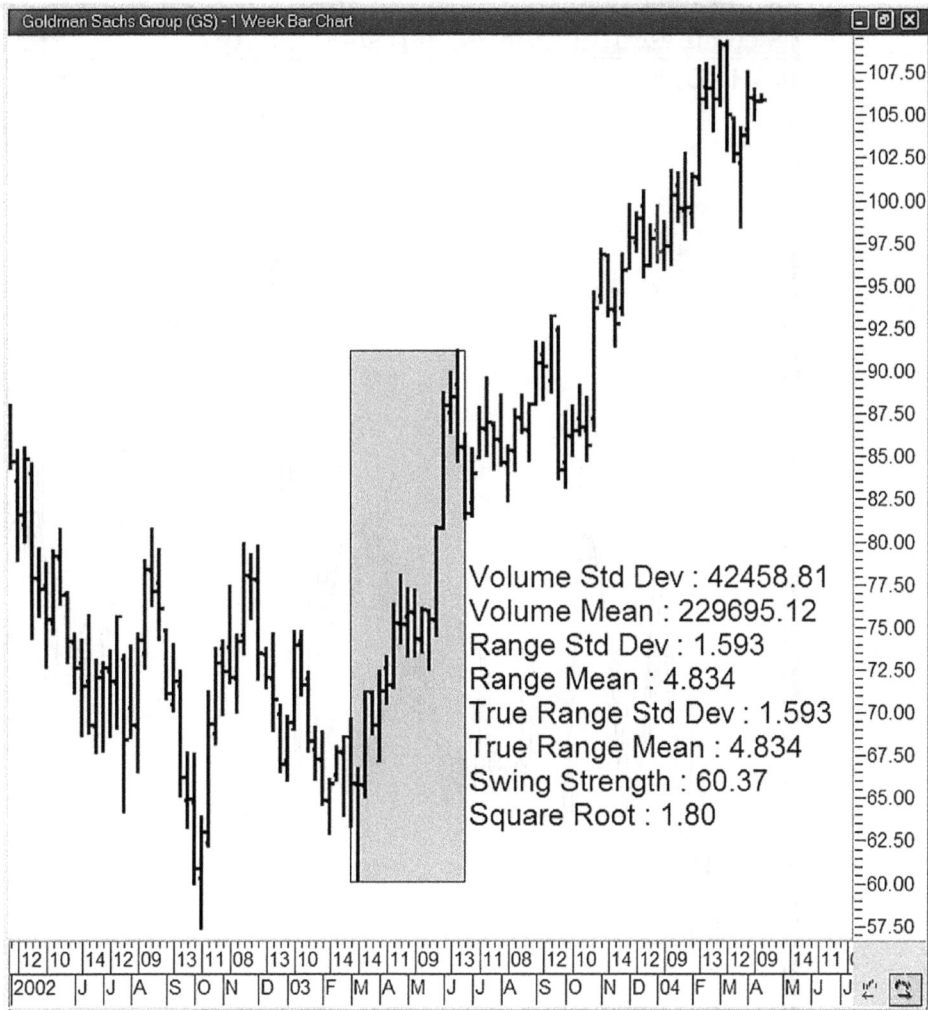

Goldman Sachs Group (GS) - 1 Week Bar Chart

Volume Std Dev : 42458.81
Volume Mean : 229695.12
Range Std Dev : 1.593
Range Mean : 4.834
True Range Std Dev : 1.593
True Range Mean : 4.834
Swing Strength : 60.37
Square Root : 1.80

Statistical Smoothed Linear Regression

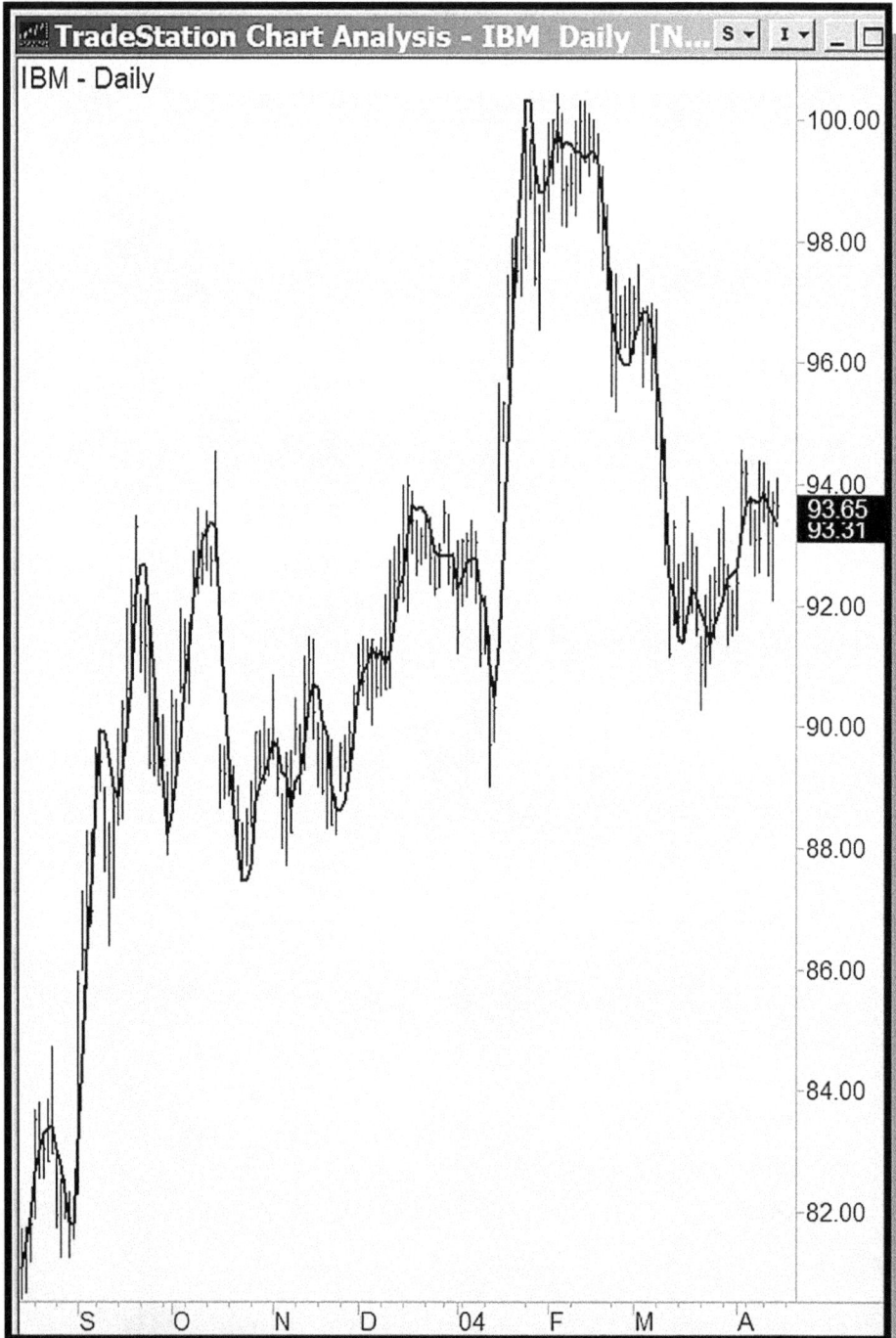

Statistical Standard Deviation Oscillator

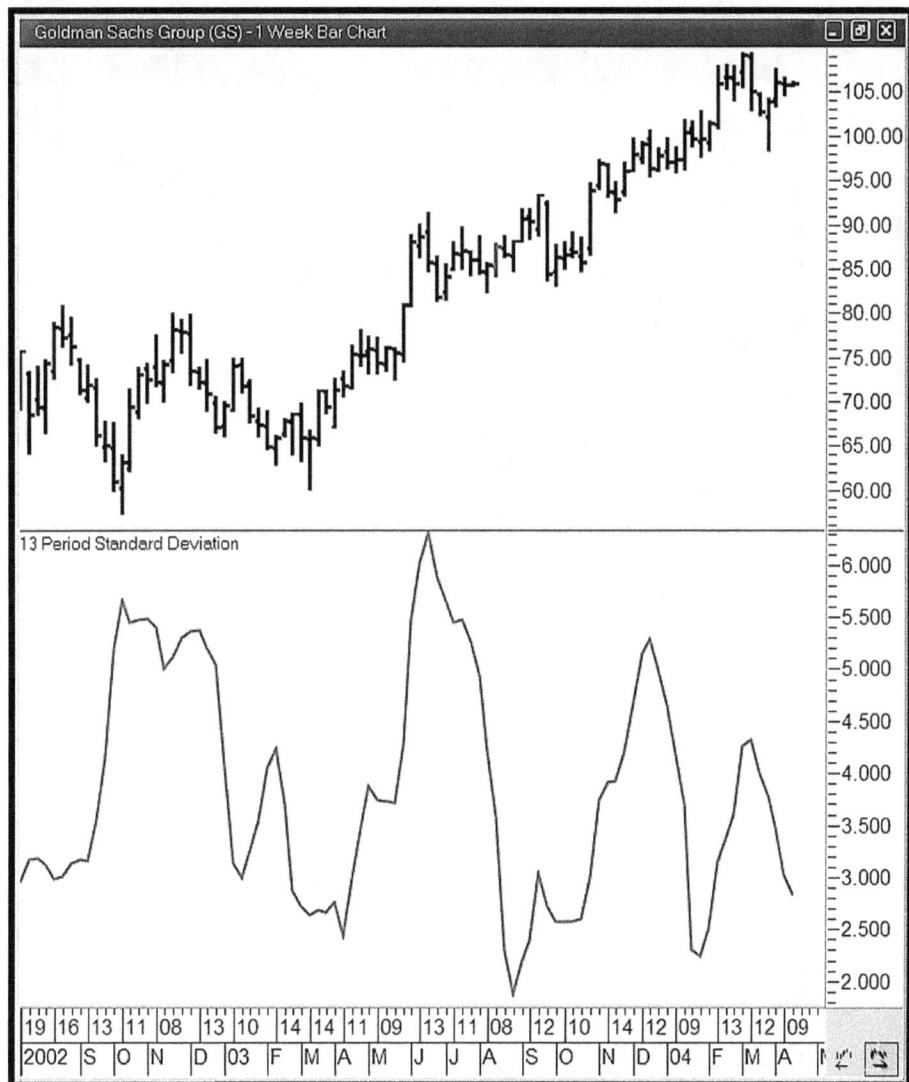

Goldman Sachs Group (GS) - 1 Week Bar Chart

13 Period Standard Deviation

Statistical Standard Deviation
Plotted as a Step Ladder Oscillator

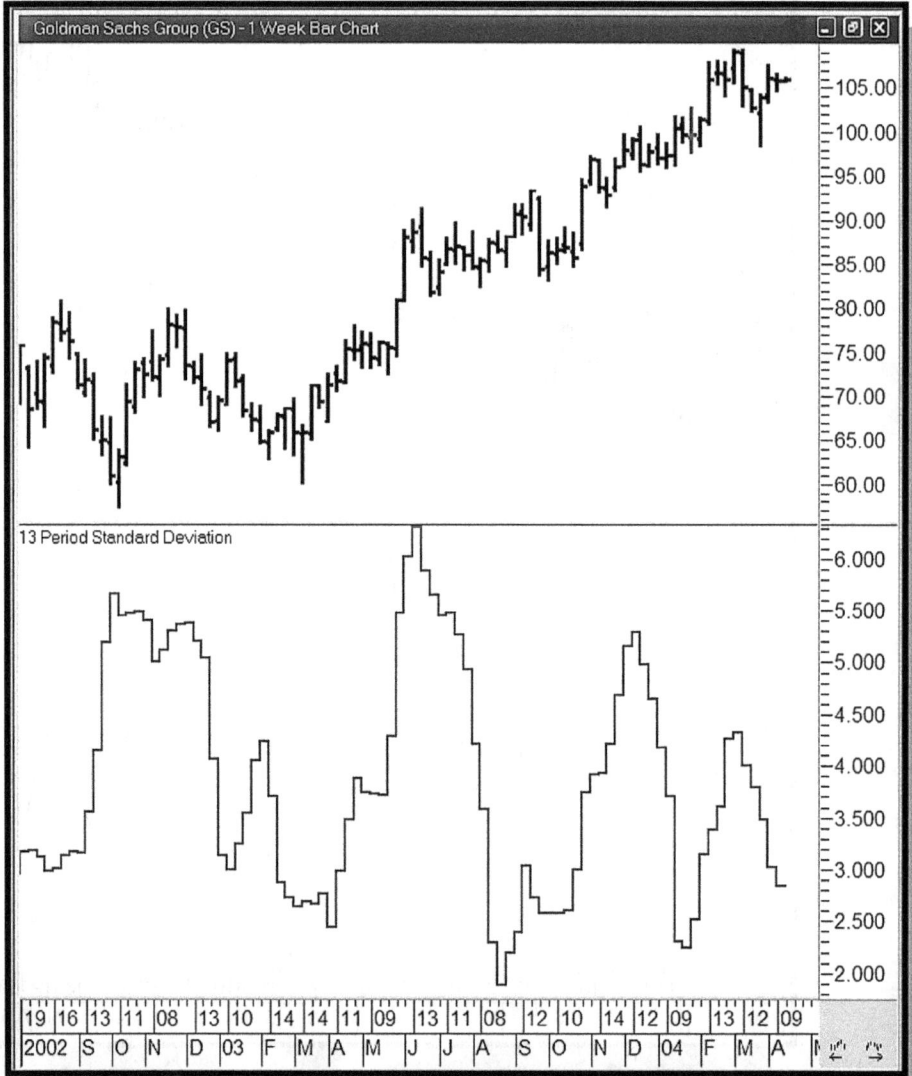

Statistical Synodic Square Curve

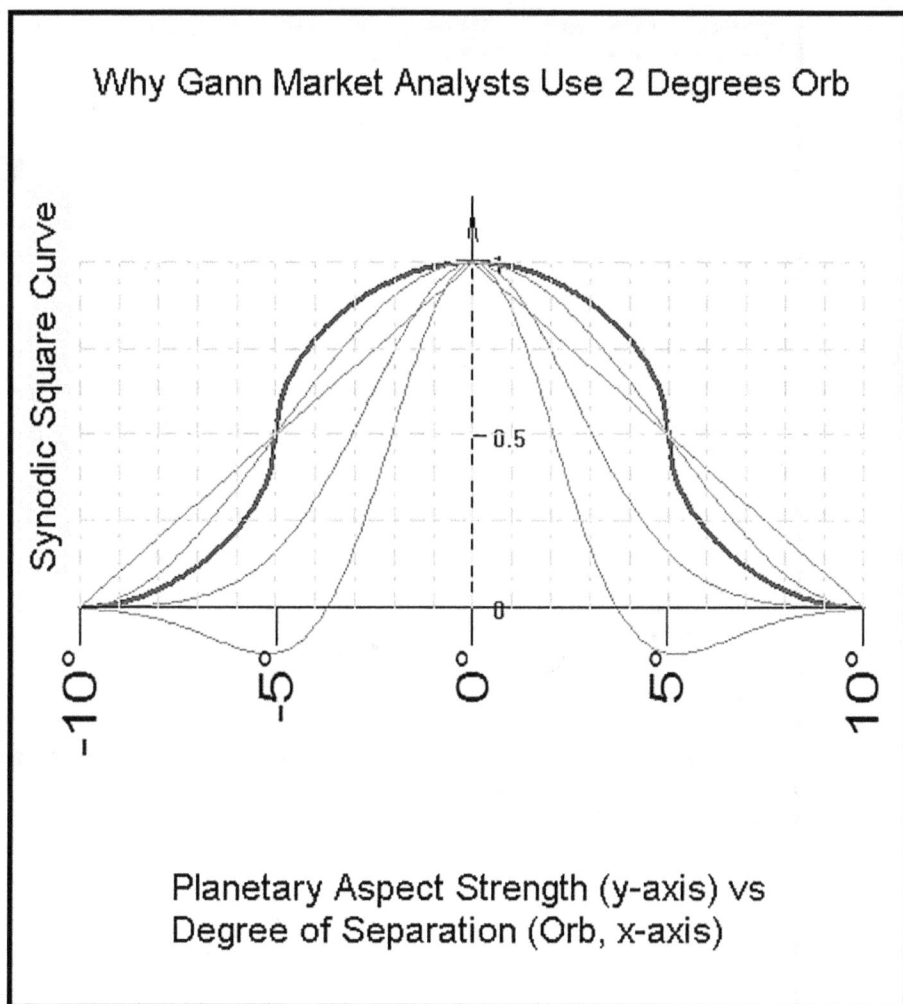

Why Gann Market Analysts Use 2 Degrees Orb

Planetary Aspect Strength (y-axis) vs
Degree of Separation (Orb, x-axis)

Stochastic Flutter

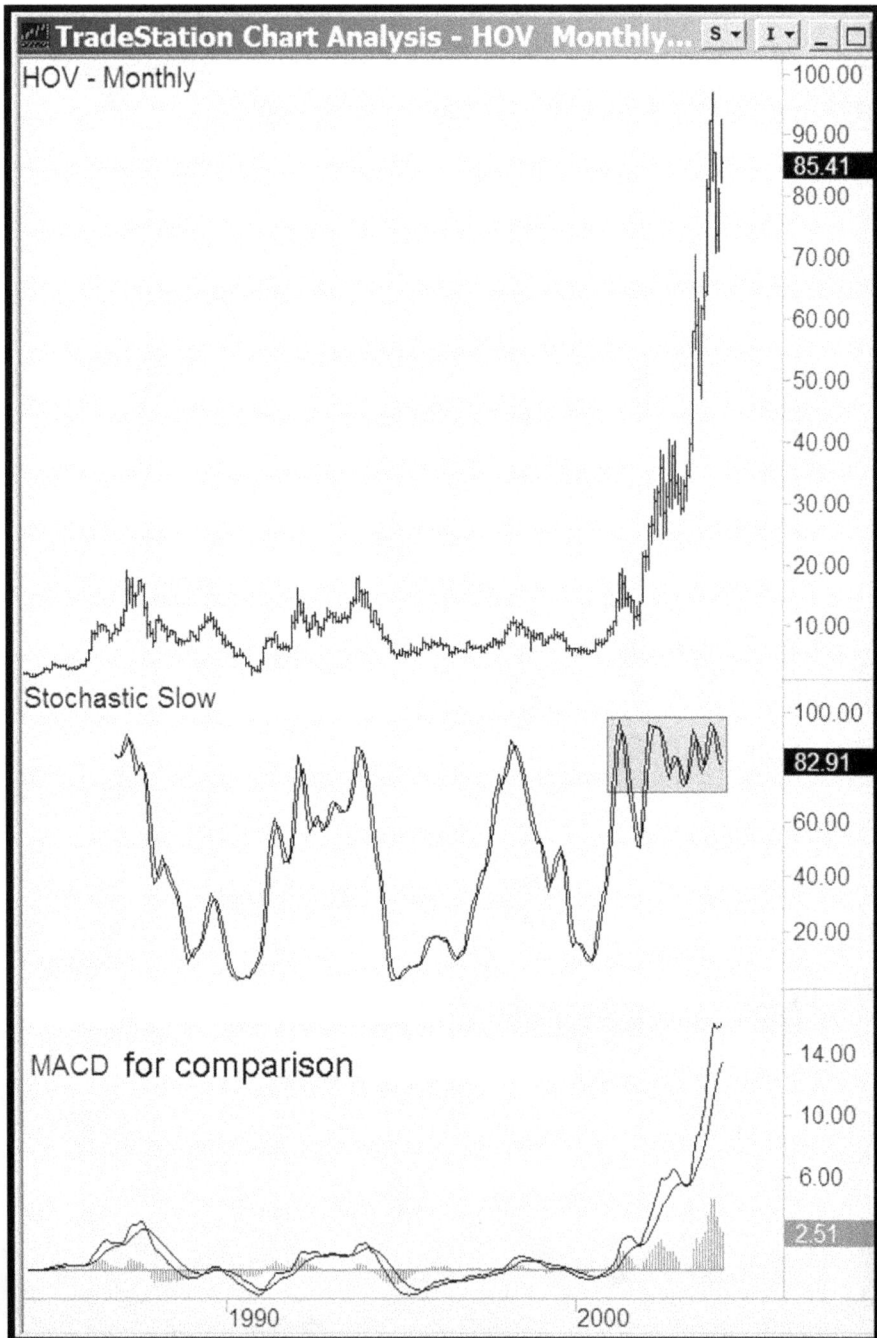

Stochastic Knee and Shoulder

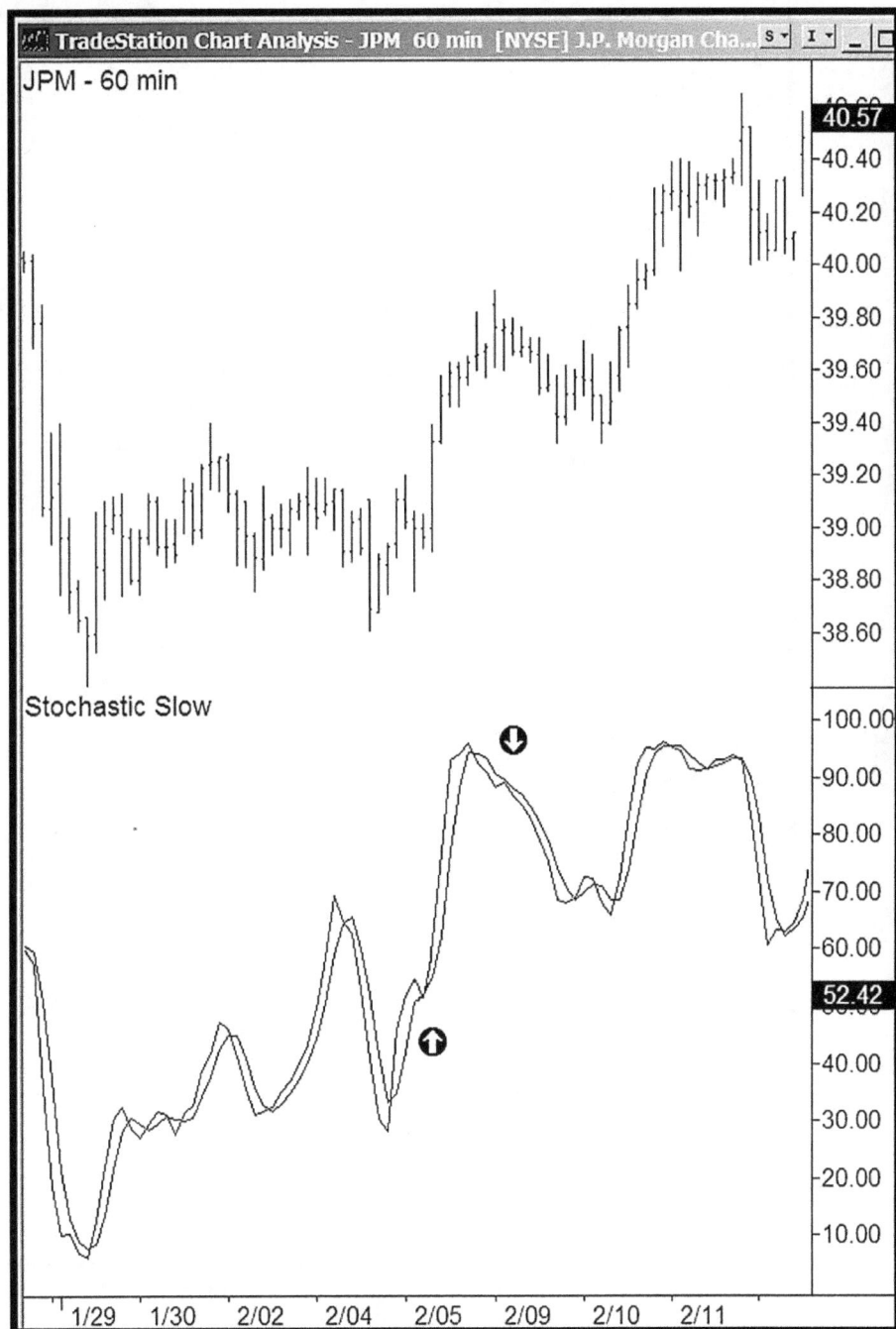

Stochastic Original George Lane Chart

Stochastic Period Setup

Support Becomes Resistance in Stochastics

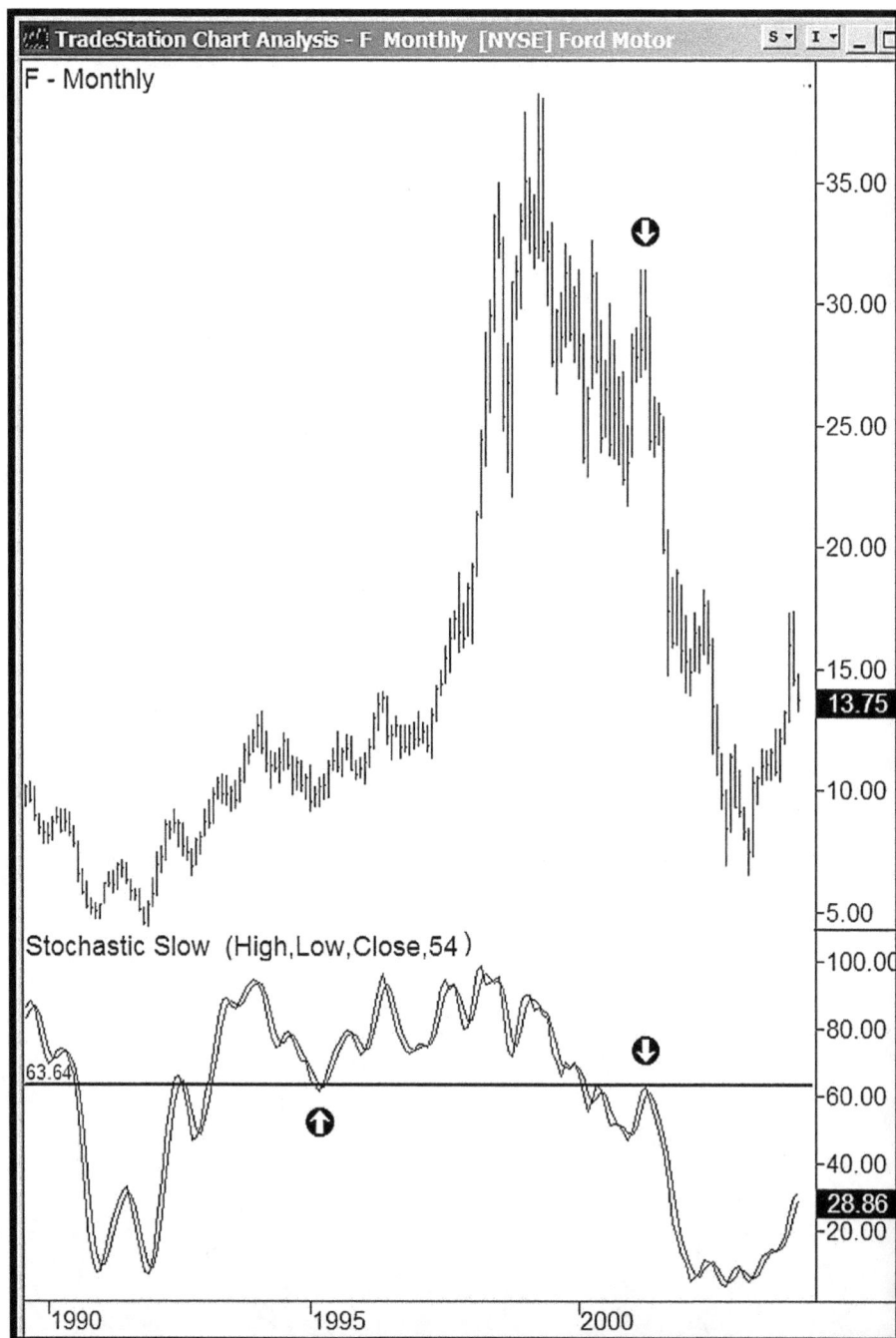

Support / Resistance: Arc Channel

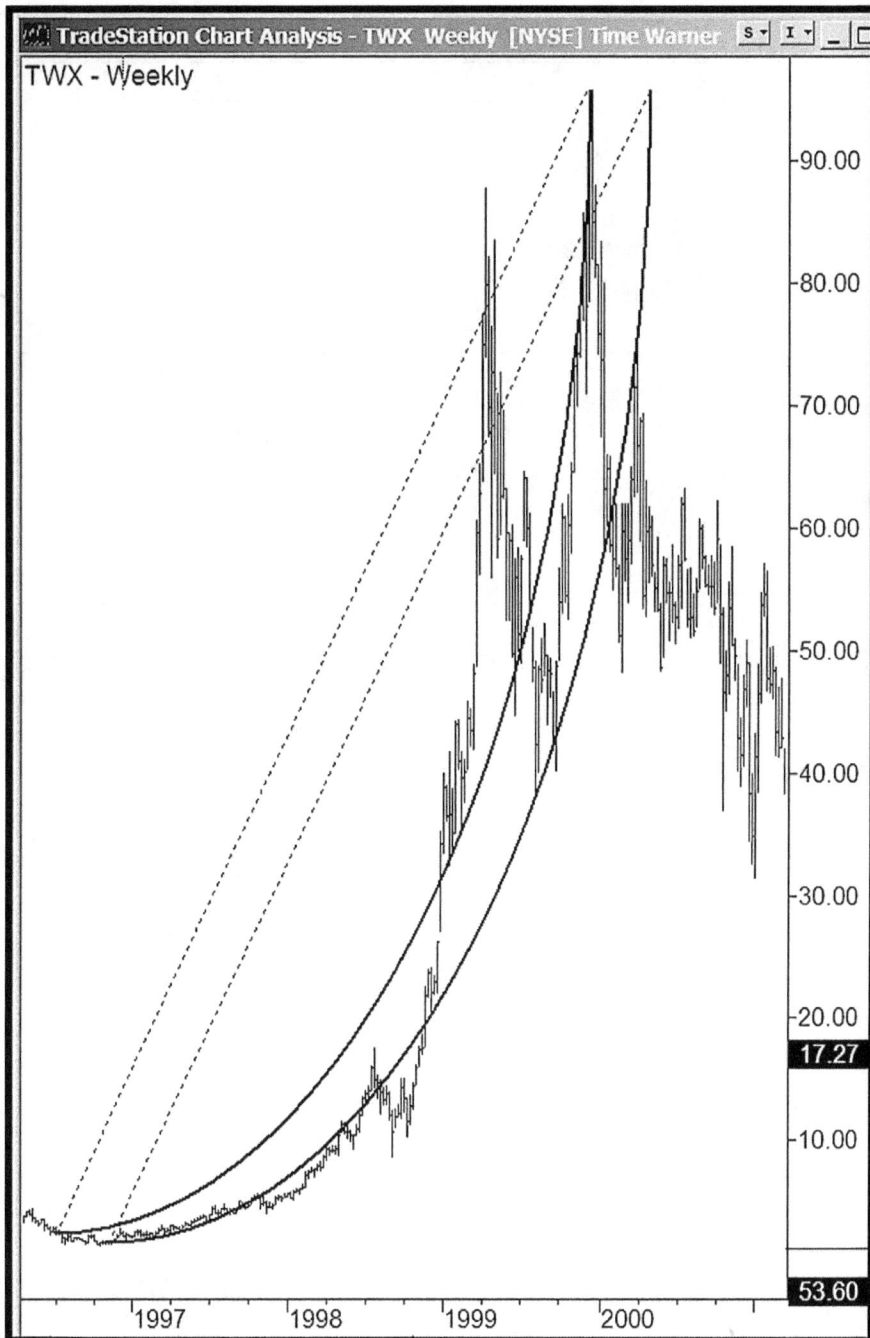

Support / Resistance by Subdividing a Range into Eights

Support / Resistance Defined by RSI

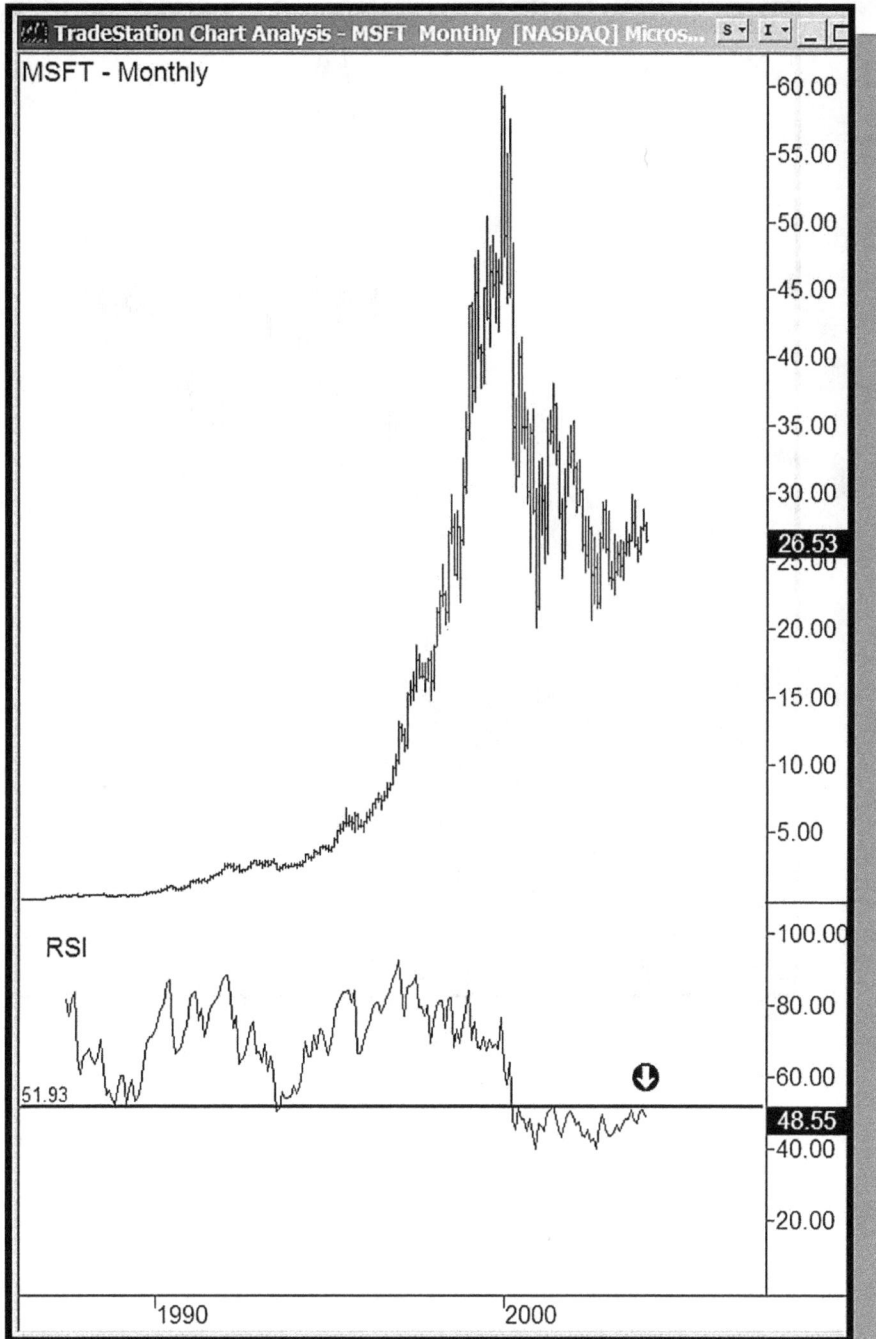

Support / Resistance: Gann Angles from Zero

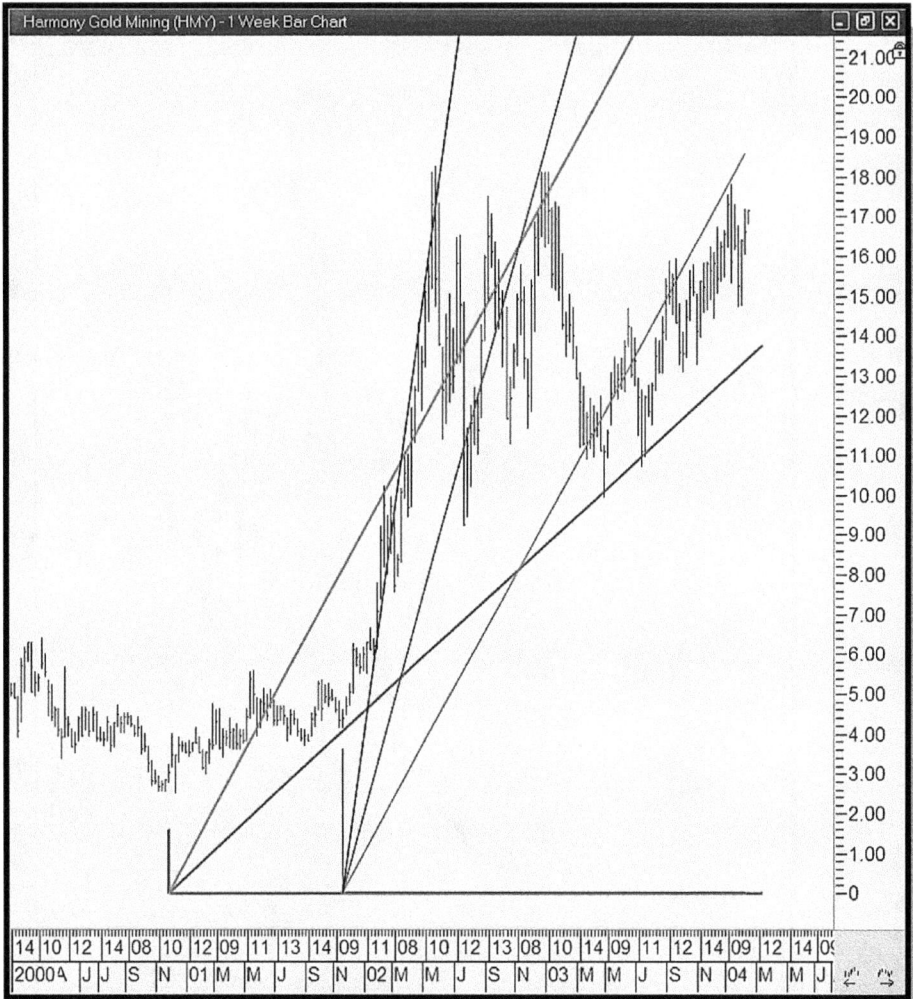

Harmony Gold Mining (HMY) - 1 Week Bar Chart

Support / Resistance: Gann Angles Projected from Zero

Harmony Gold Mining (HMY) - 1 Week Bar Chart

HMY - Weekly

Support / Resistance:
Gann Dynamic Harmonic Wheel Plotted on Prices

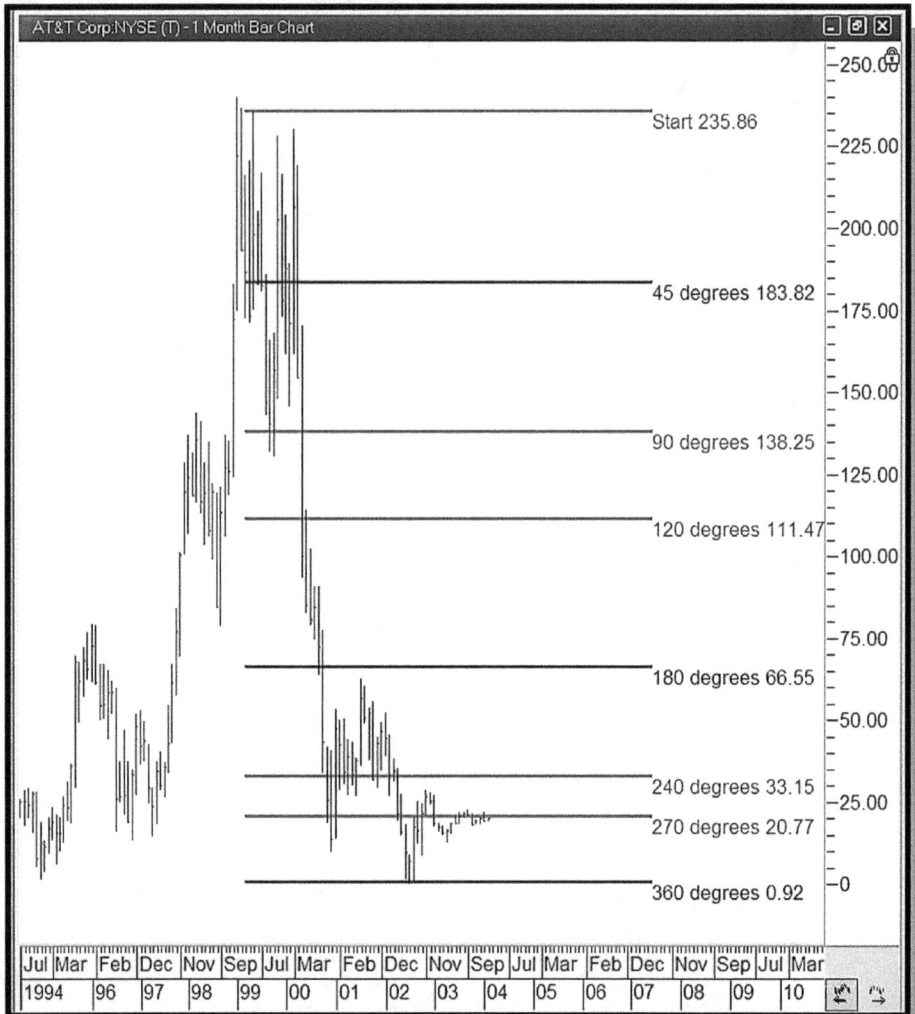

Support / Resistance: Gann Fan Angles

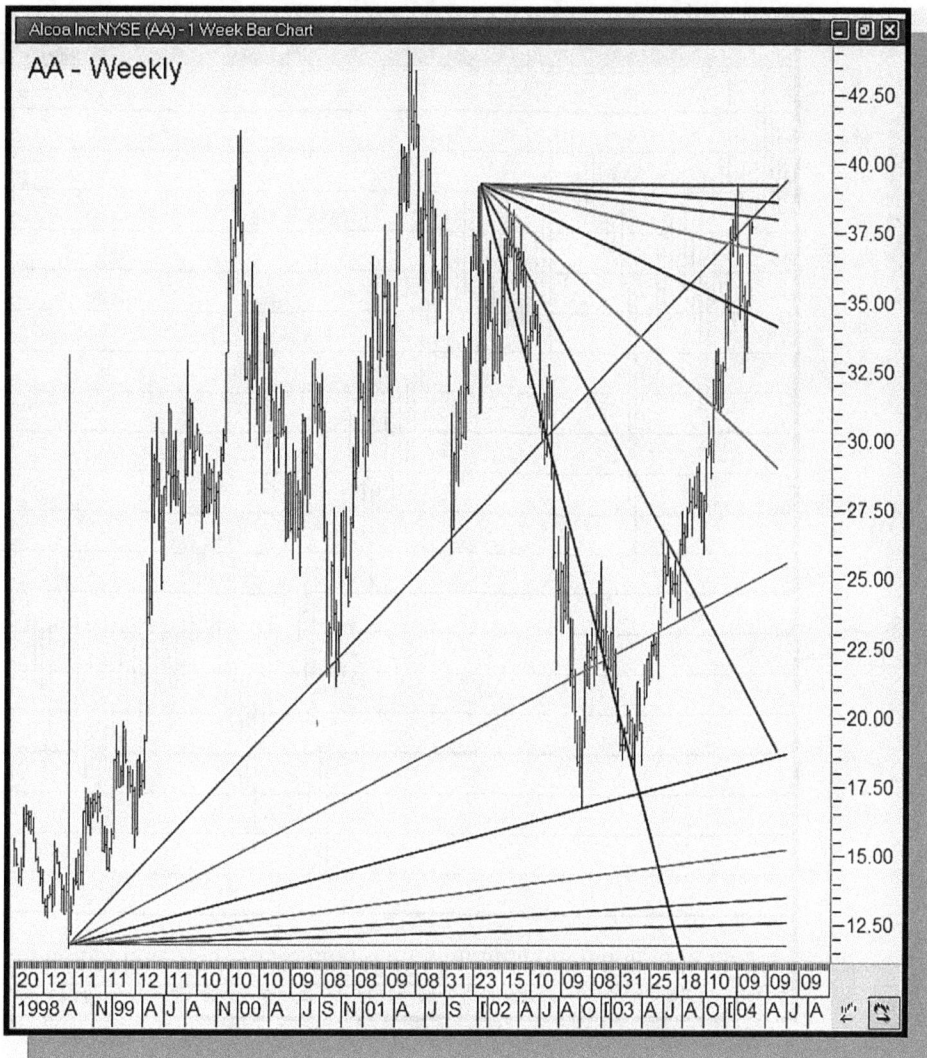

Alcoa Inc.NYSE (AA) - 1 Week Bar Chart

AA - Weekly

Support / Resistance: Gann Planetary Lines (Uranus 90-Degree Harmonics)

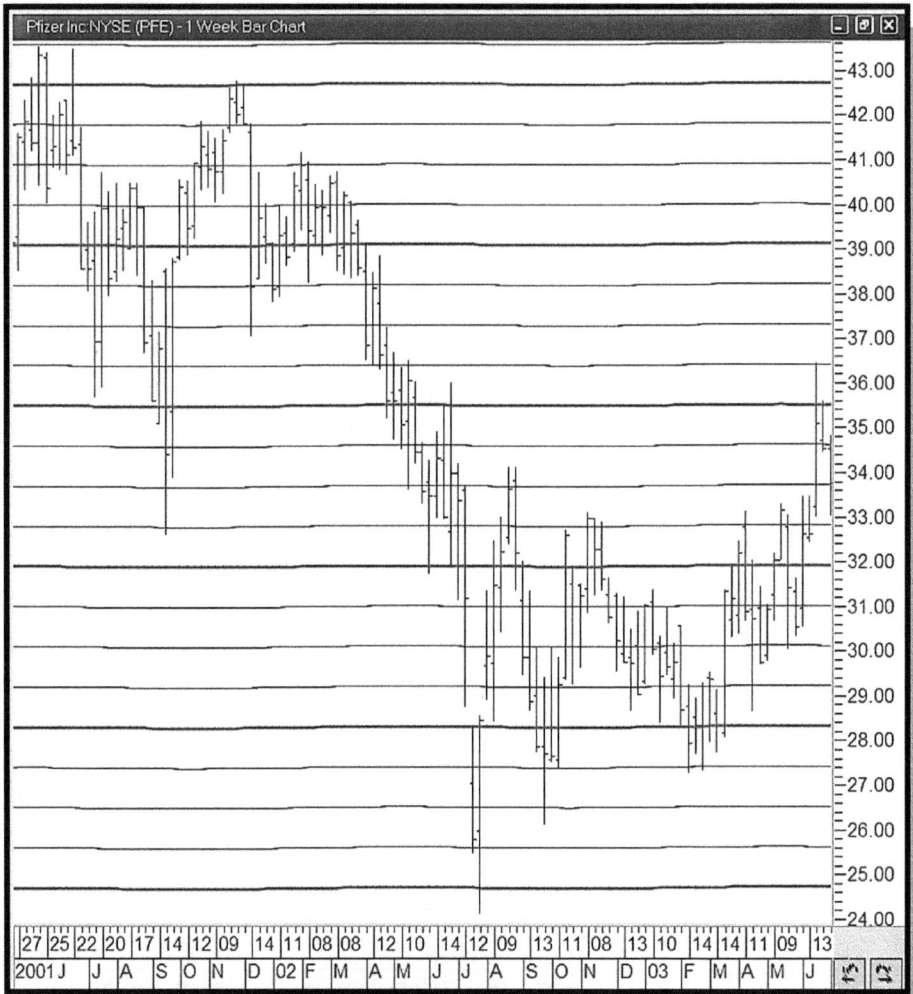

Support / Resistance: Gann Square of Nine, (Dynamic)

Support / Resistance: Gann Square of Nine, (Static from Zero)

Pfizer Inc.NYSE (PFE) - 1 Day Bar Chart

180 degrees 39.68

120 degrees 38.51

90 degrees 37.92

45 degrees 37.04

360 degrees 36.16

270 degrees 34.48

240 degrees 33.95

180 degrees 32.88

40.00
39.50
39.00
38.50
38.00
37.50
37.00
36.50
36.00
35.50
35.00
34.50
34.00
33.50
33.00
32.50

30 05 08 13 16 22 27 30 04 09 12 18 23 26 02 05 10 15 18 23 26 31 05 08 14 19

2003 04   Feb   Mar   Apr

Support / Resistance in a Downtrend

TradeStation Chart Analysis - GE Weekly [...

RESISTANCE

SUPPORT

60.00

55.00

50.00

45.00

40.00

35.00

30.10

25.00

2000   2001   2002

Support / Resistance in an Uptrend

Support / Resistance: Setting Arc in Parabolic Rally

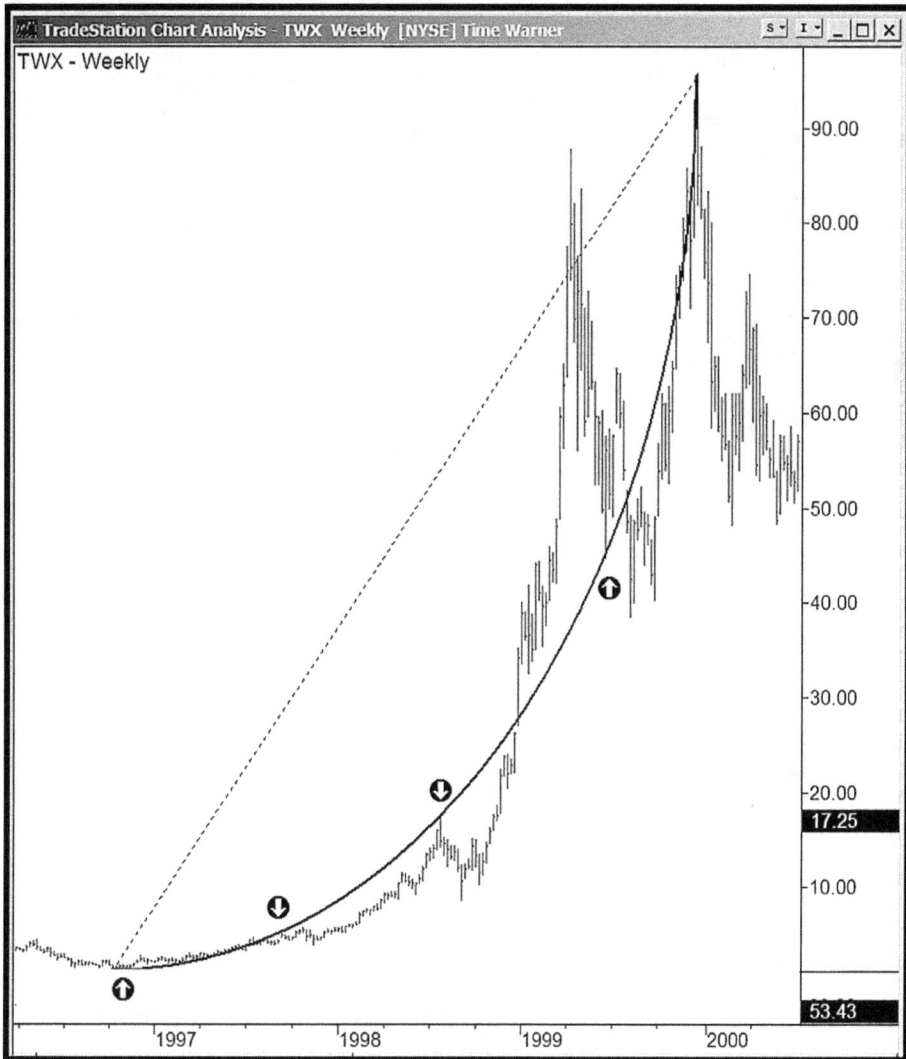

Support / Resistance: Time and Price

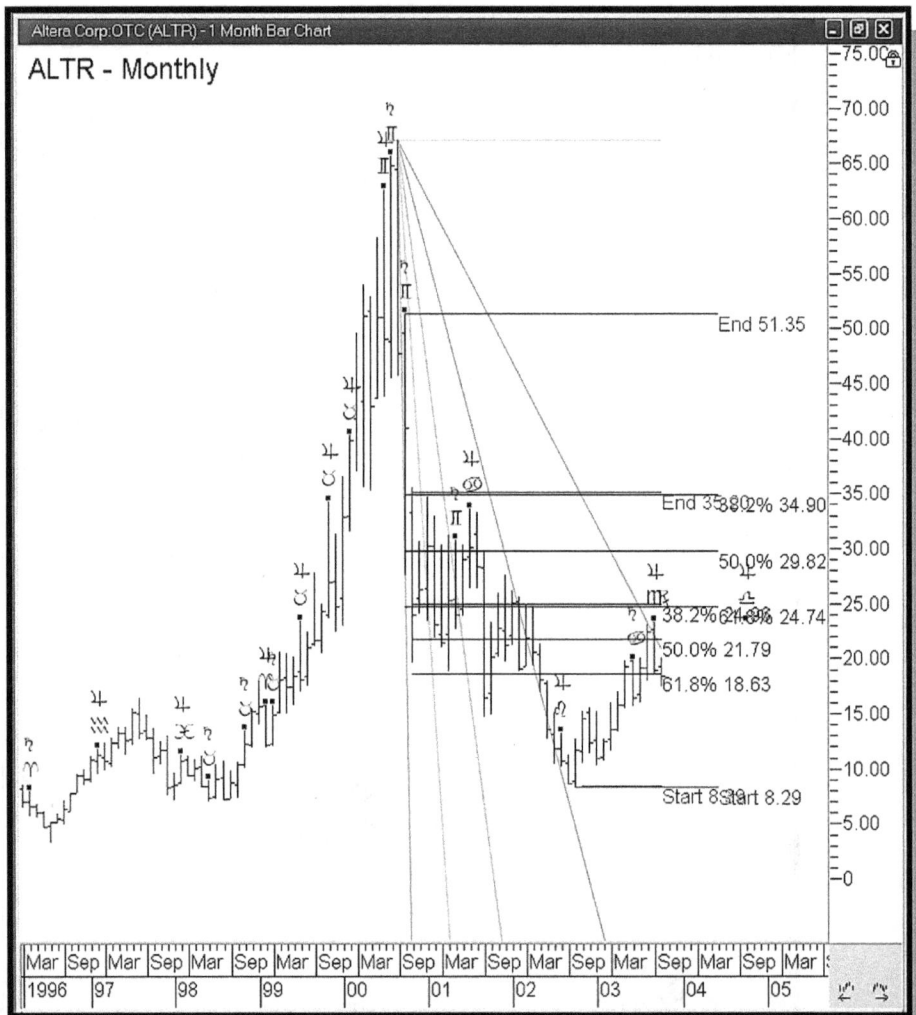

TED Spread

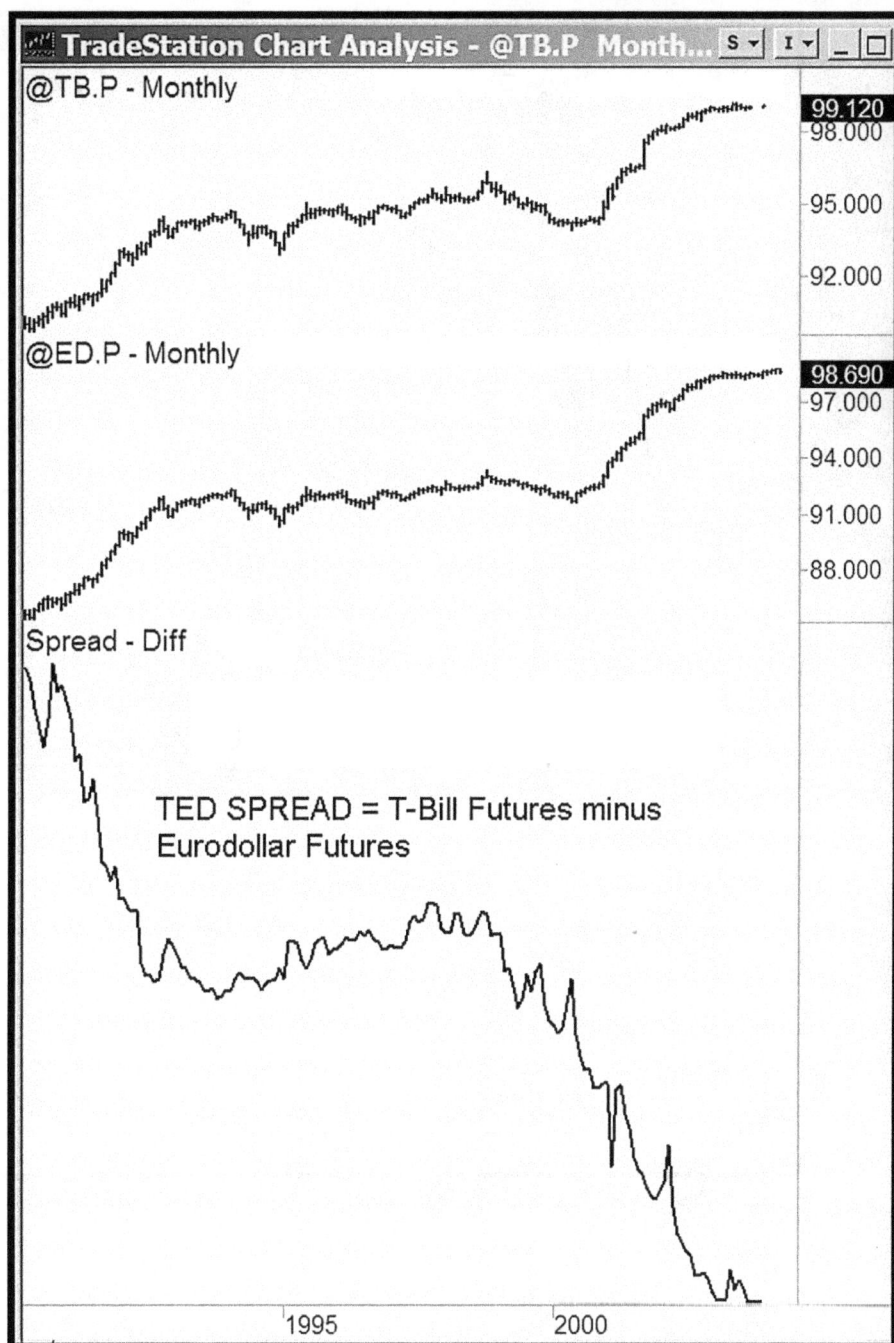

TradeStation Chart Analysis - @TB.P Month...

@TB.P - Monthly

99.120
98.000
95.000
92.000

@ED.P - Monthly

98.690
97.000
94.000
91.000
88.000

Spread - Diff

TED SPREAD = T-Bill Futures minus
Eurodollar Futures

1995   2000

Time and Price Gann Analysis Chart

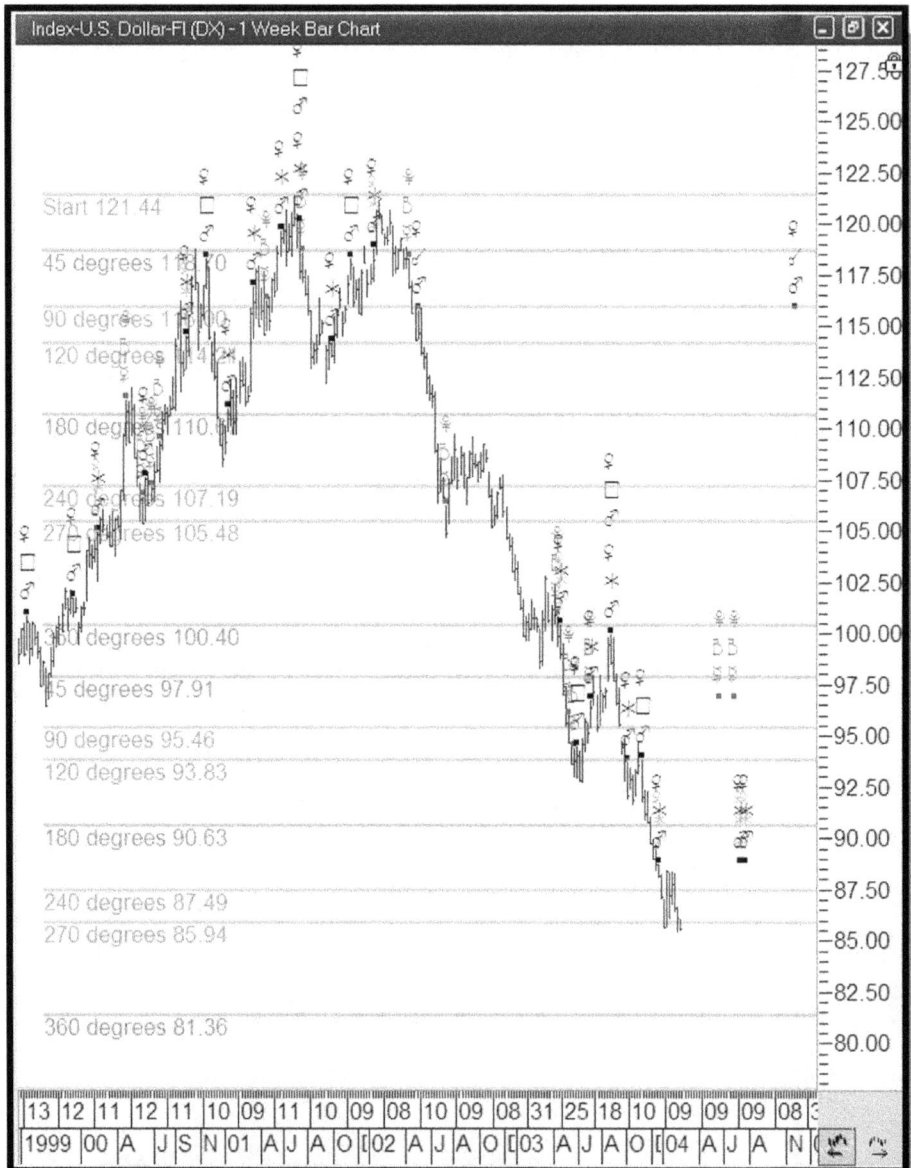

Time and Price Gann Calculator

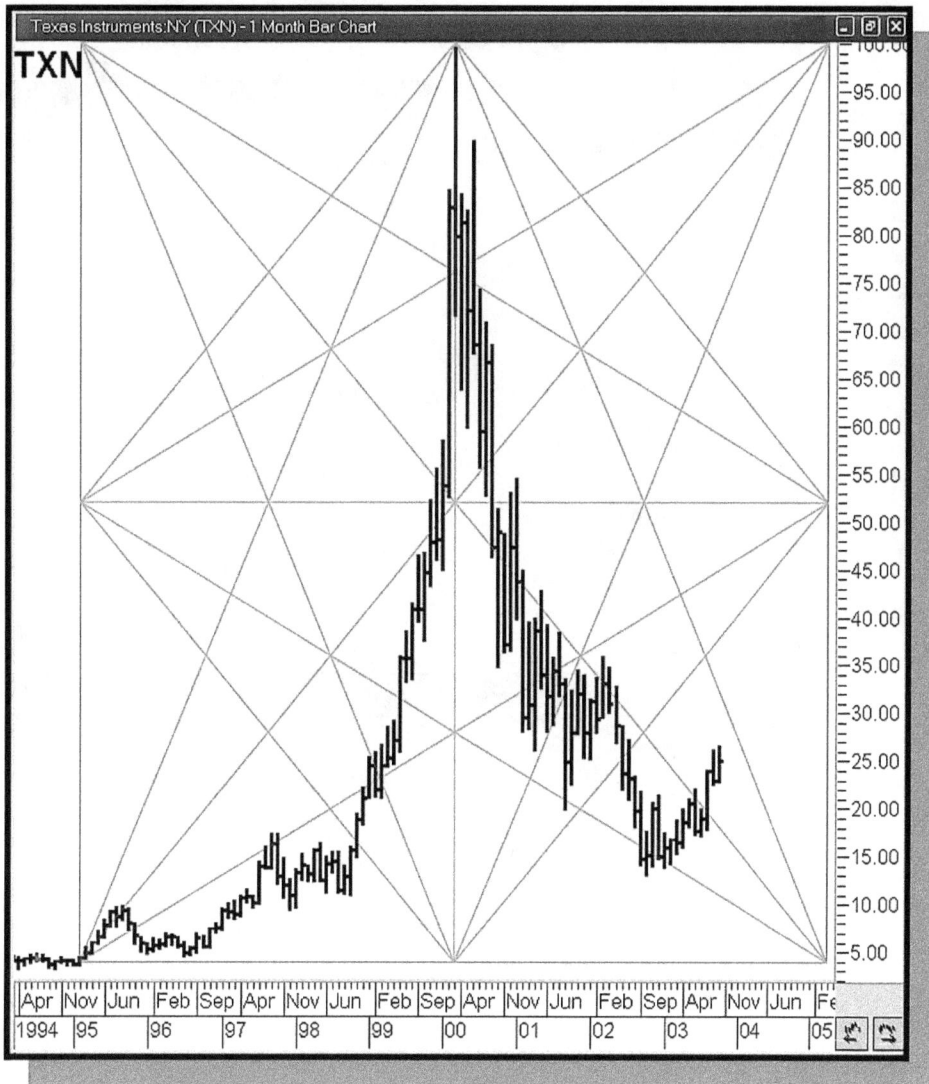

Texas Instruments:NY (TXN) - 1 Month Bar Chart

Time Pivot Calendar for Financial Global Markets

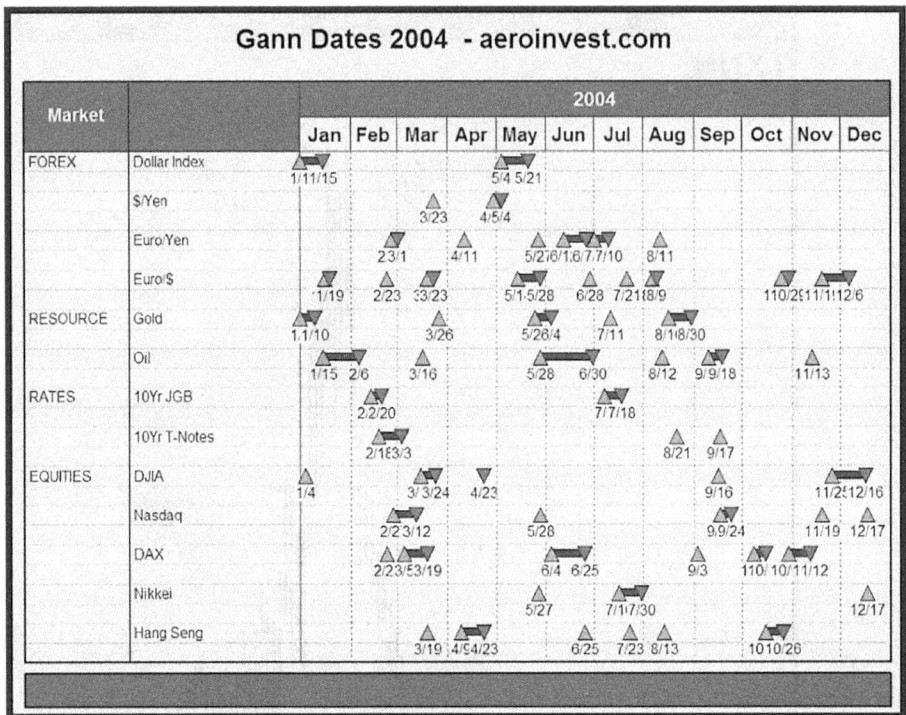

Gann Dates 2004 - aeroinvest.com

Market		Jan	Feb	Mar	Apr	May	Jun	Jul	Aug	Sep	Oct	Nov	Dec
FOREX	Dollar Index	1/11/15				5/4 5/21							
	$/Yen			3/23	4/5/4								
	Euro/Yen		2/3/1		4/11	5/27/6/1.6		7/7/10	8/11				
	Euro/$	1/19	2/23	3/3/23		5/1-5/28	6/28	7/21/8/9				11/2/11/11/12/6	
RESOURCE	Gold	1.1/10		3/26		5/26/4		7/11	8/18/30				
	Oil	1/15 2/6		3/16		5/28	6/30		8/12	9/9/18		11/13	
RATES	10Yr JGB		2/2/20					7/7/18					
	10Yr T-Notes		2/1 3/3						8/21	9/17			
EQUITIES	DJIA	1/4		3/3/24	4/23					9/16		11/2/12/16	
	Nasdaq		2/2 3/12			5/28				9/9/24		11/19	12/17
	DAX		2/23/3/19				6/4 6/25			9/3	10/10/11/12		
	Nikkei					5/27		7/1/7/30					12/17
	Hang Seng			3/19	4/5/4/23		6/25	7/23 8/13			10 10/26		

Trend and Countertrend Channels

Trendline: 45-Degree Rise with Square of Nine Grid

Semiconductors HOLDR (SMH) - 1 Week Bar Chart

Trendline: Acceleration

TradeStation Chart Analysis - HOV Weekly ...

HOV - Weekly

Volume   3646600.00

Trendline: Channel

Trendline: Internal

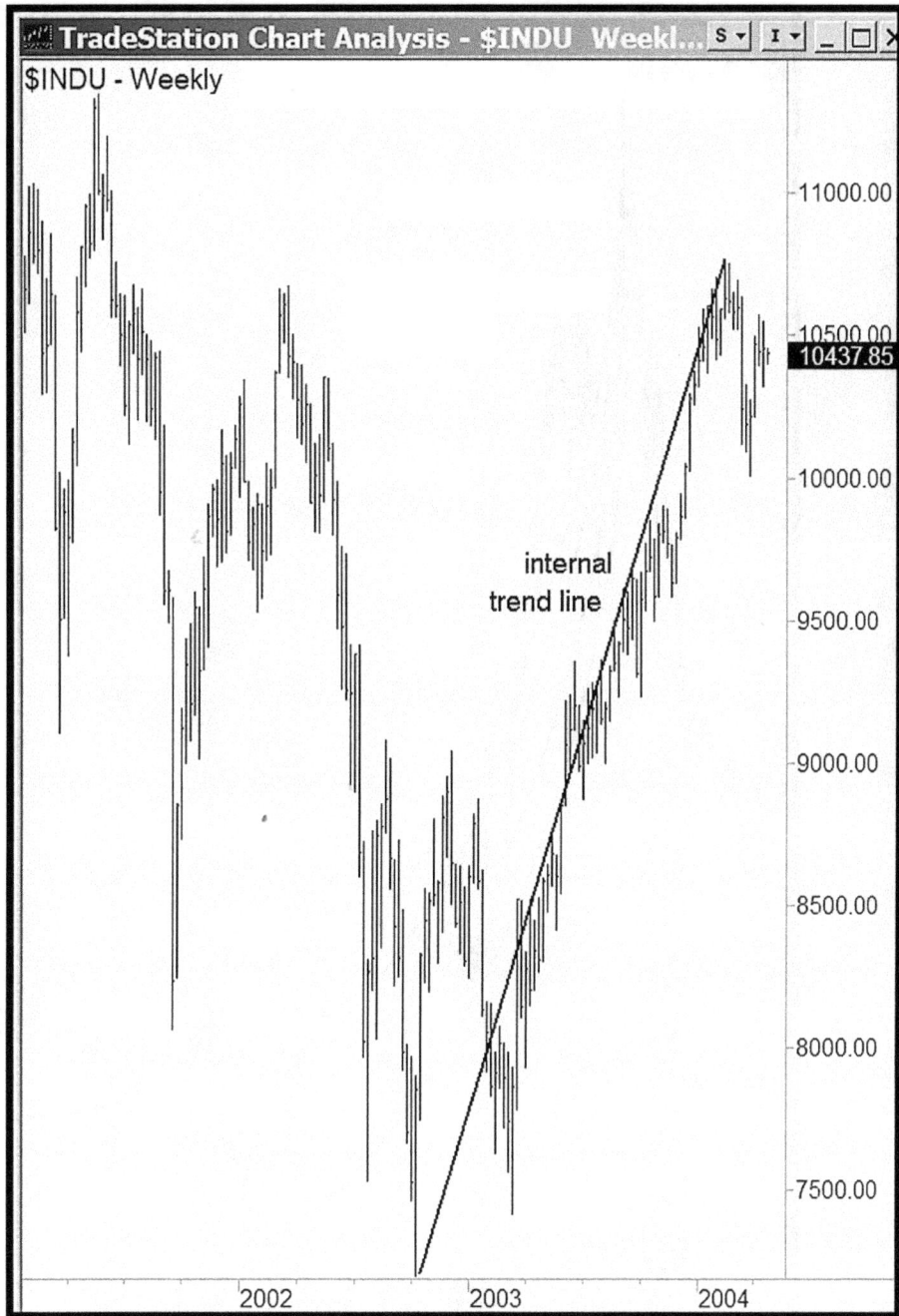

Trendlines: Arc Channel

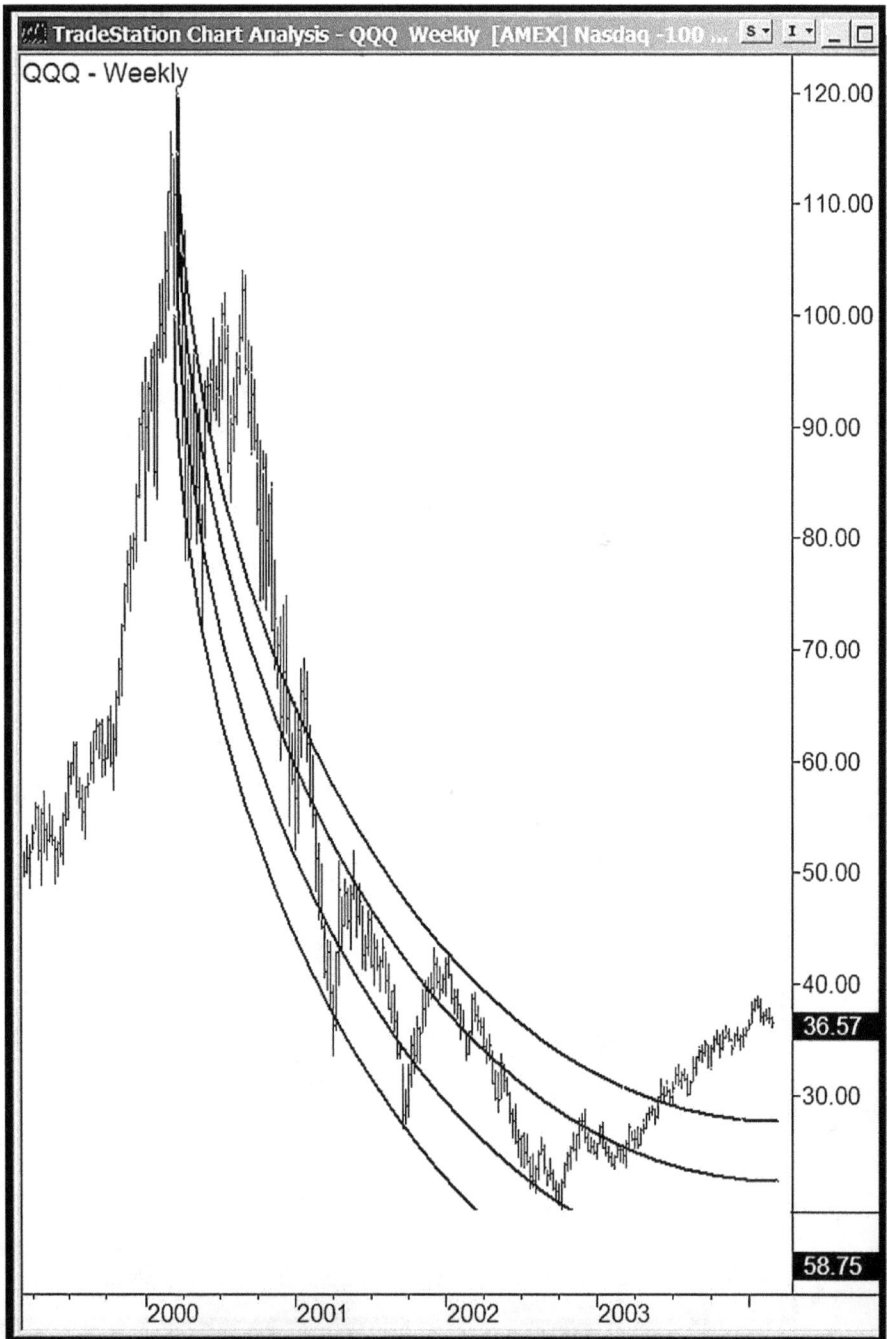

Trendlines Converging

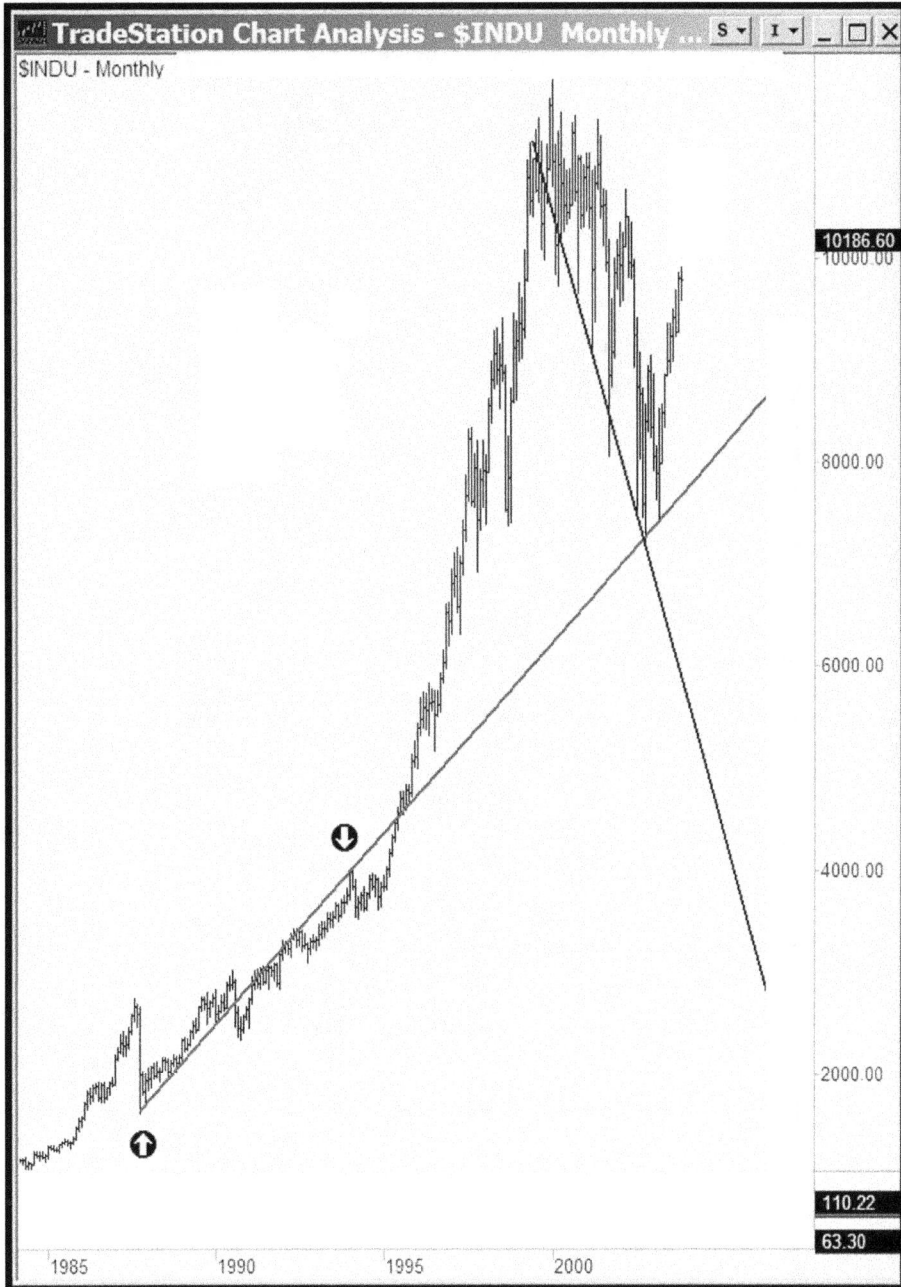

$INDU - Monthly

Trendlines Converging (Advanced)

Trendlines on Fundamental Data

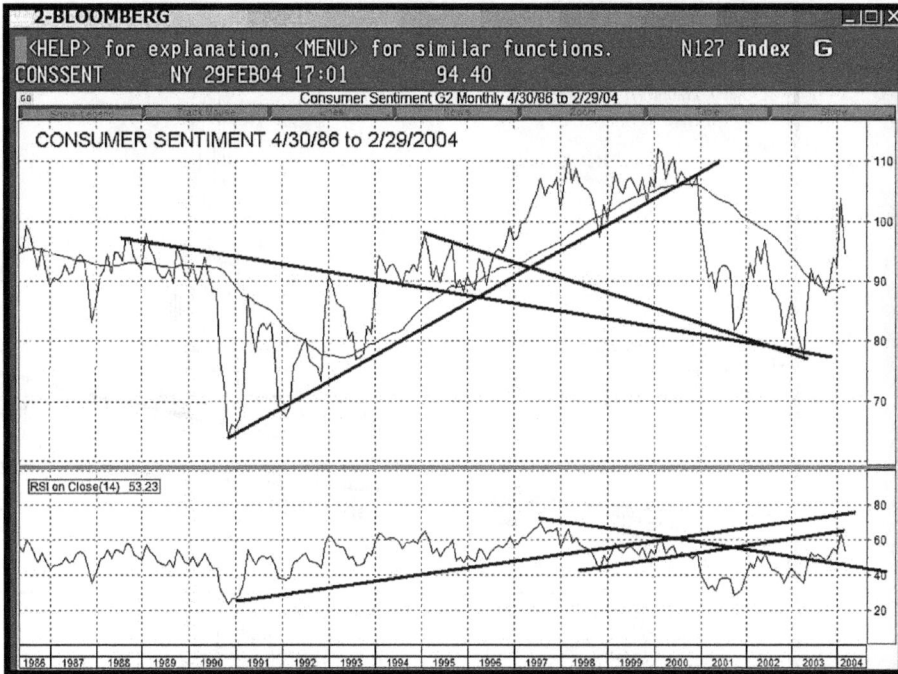

Trendlines on Indicators

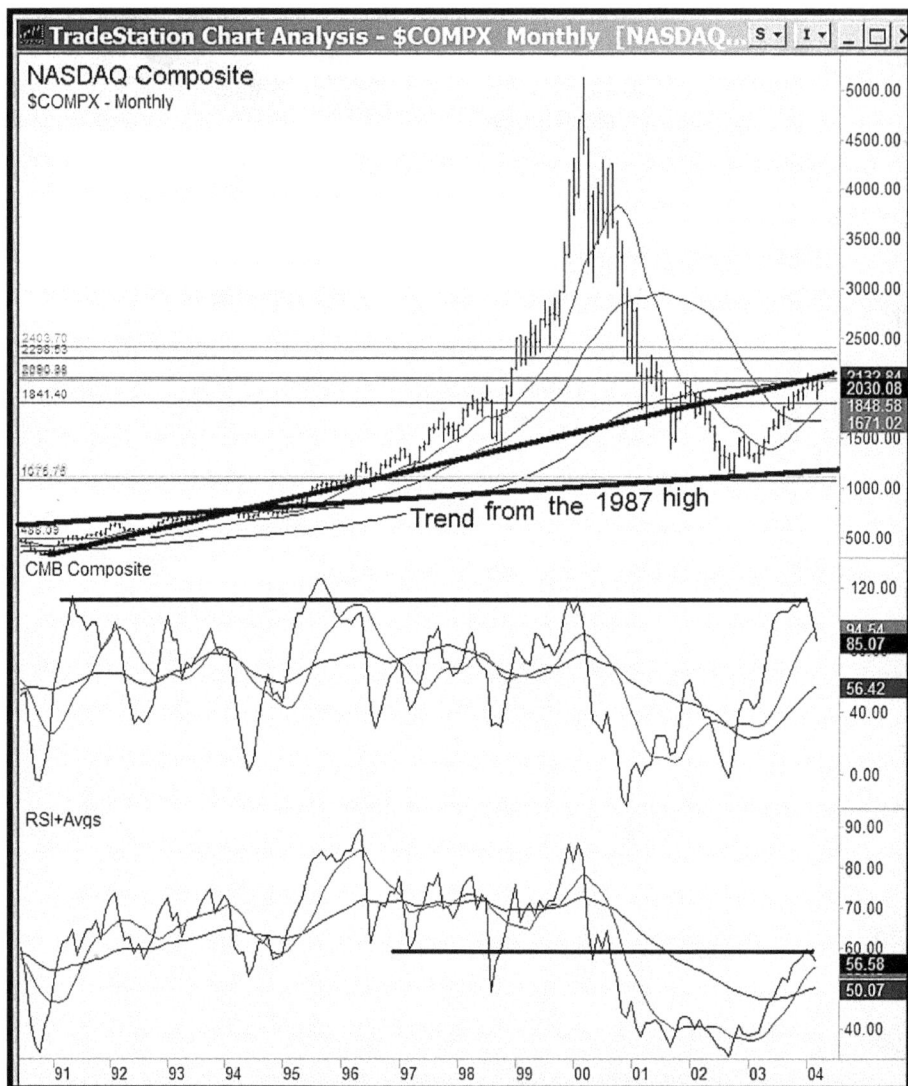

NASDAQ Composite
$COMPX - Monthly

Trend from the 1987 high

CMB Composite

RSI+Avgs

Trendlines: Parallel Channel Projected from Gaps

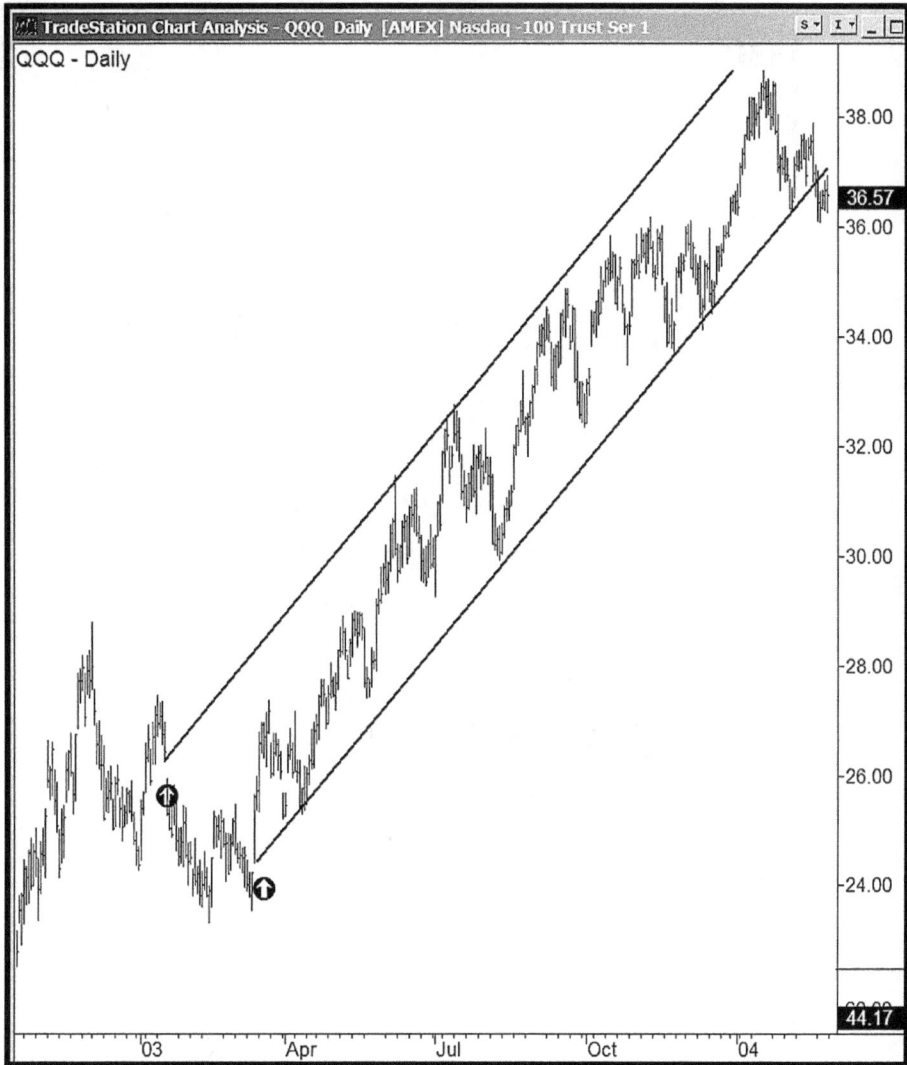

Trendlines: Parallel Projected from Gaps

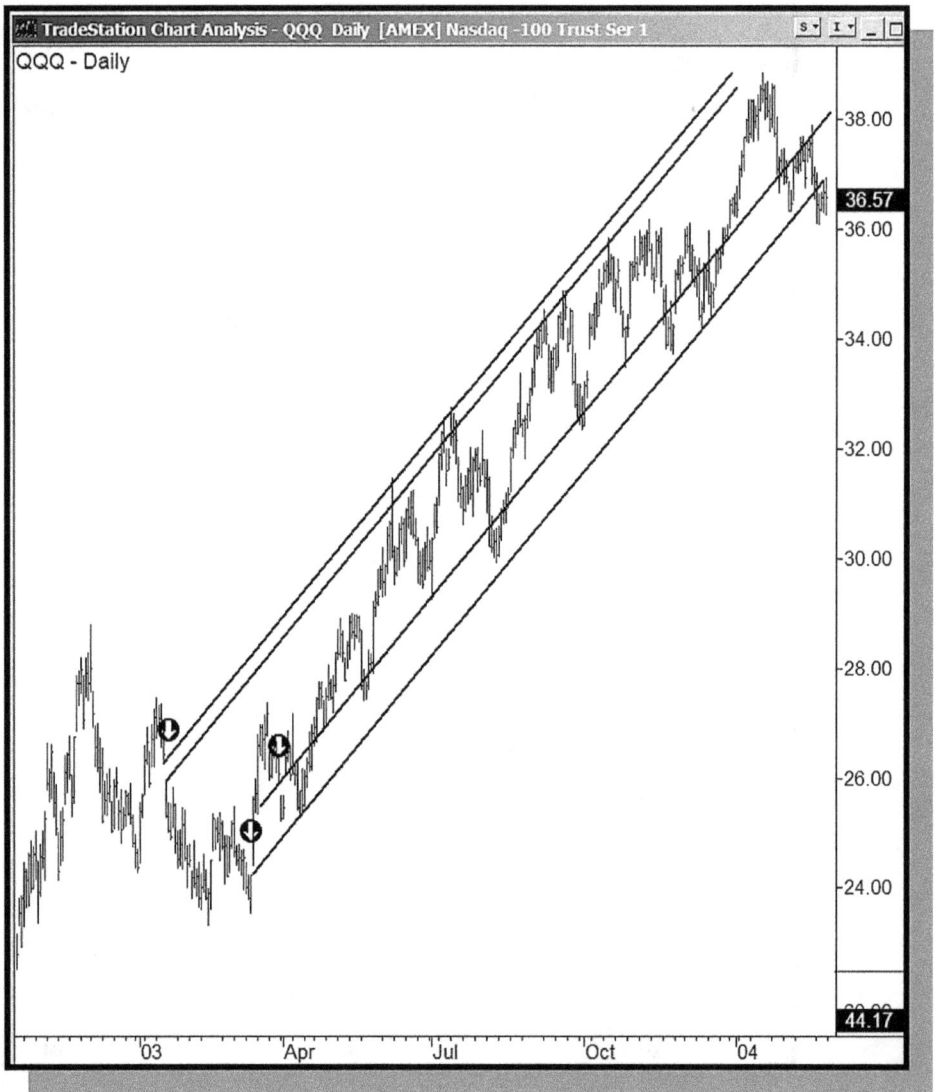

Trendlines: Parallel Set by Truncating Key Reversals Downtrend

TradeStation Chart Analysis - AMZN Weekly [NASDAQ] Amazon.cominc

AMZN - Weekly

Second

First
drawn

Trendlines: Parallel Set by Truncating Key Reversals Uptrend

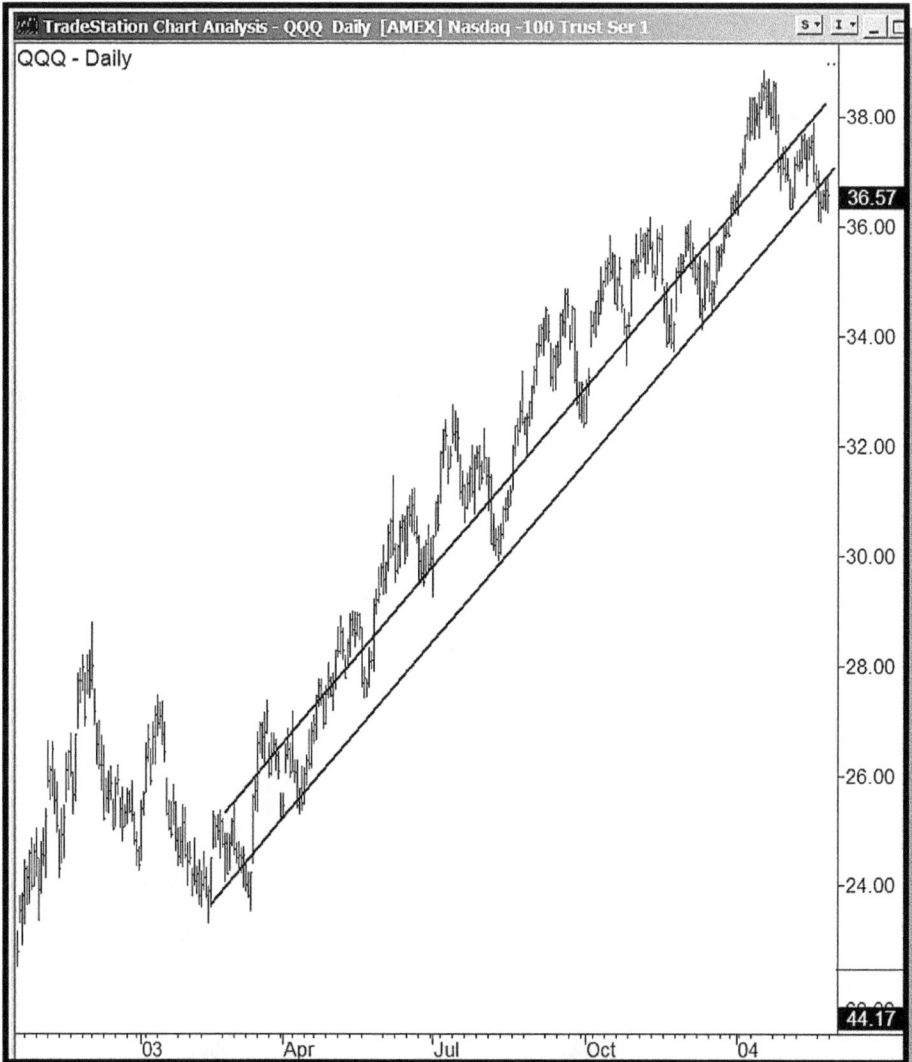

Trend Ranges within RSI*

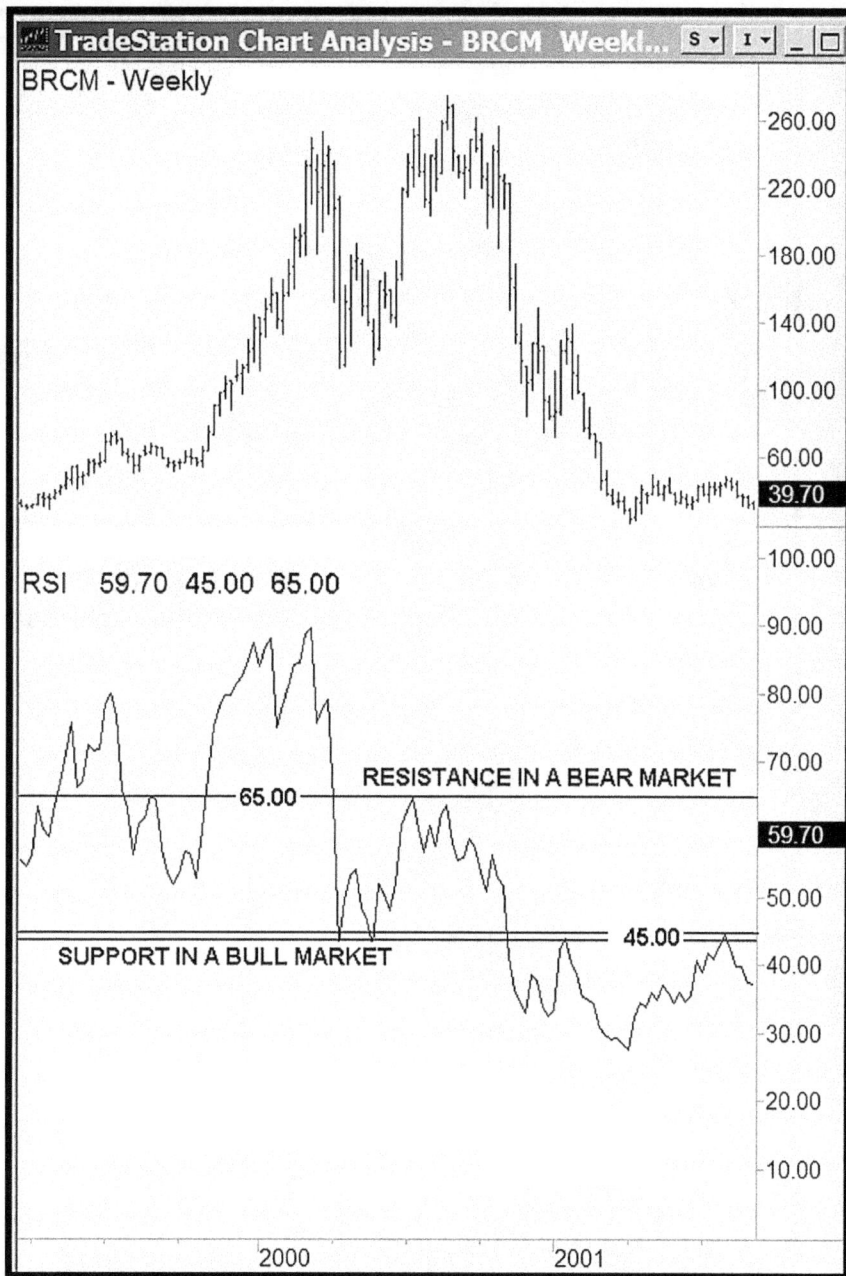

*For more information, please refer to *Technical Analysis for the Trading Professional* by Constance Brown (New York: McGraw-Hill), 1999.

Unconventional Displays: Histogram Comparison with MACD

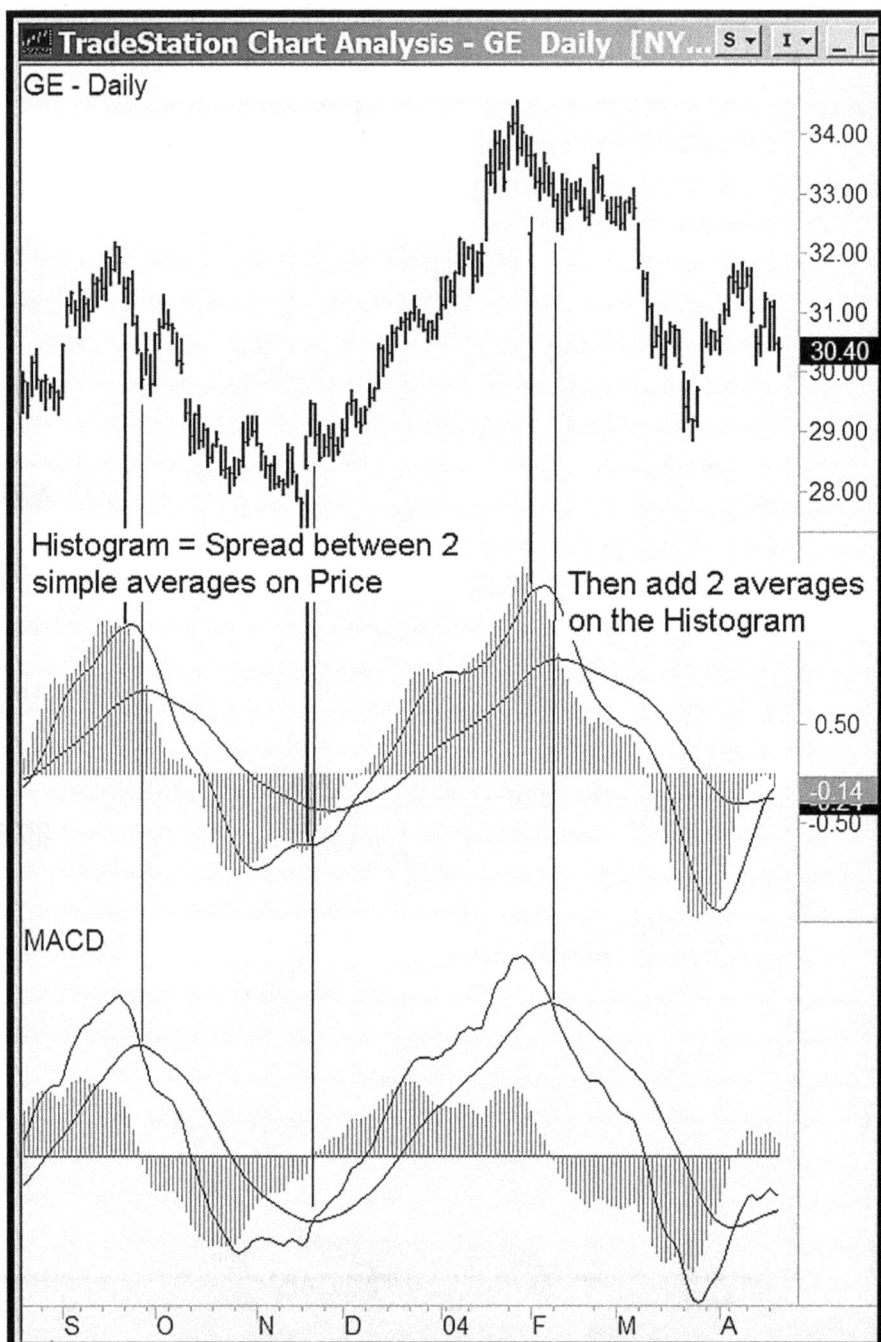

TradeStation Chart Analysis - GE Daily [NY...

GE - Daily

34.00
33.00
32.00
31.00
30.40
30.00
29.00
28.00

Histogram = Spread between 2
simple averages on Price

Then add 2 averages
on the Histogram

0.50
-0.14
-0.24
-0.50

MACD

S O N D 04 F M A

Unconventional Displays: Price Histogram with Smoothed RSI Histogram

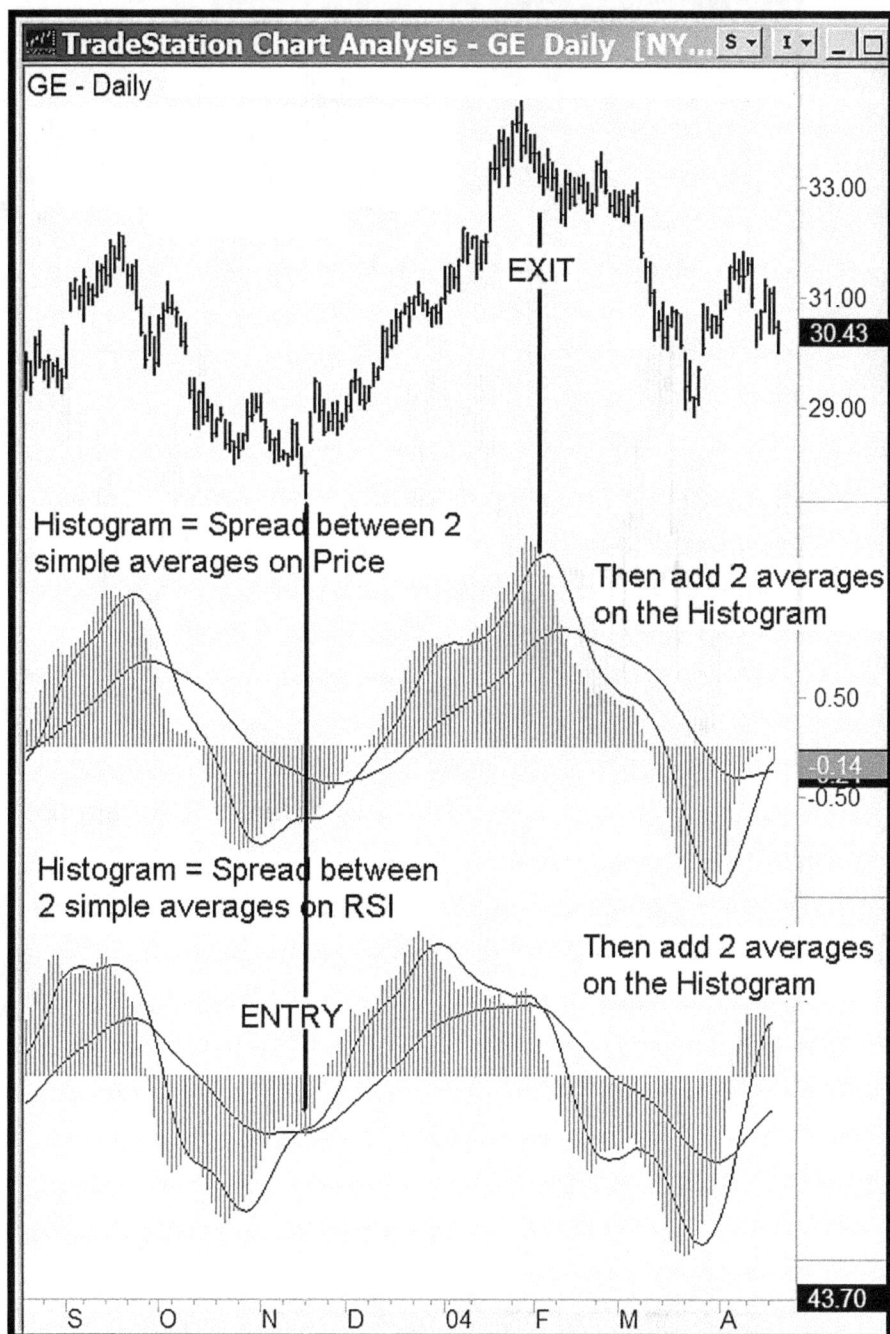

Unconventional Displays: RSI Multiple Periods

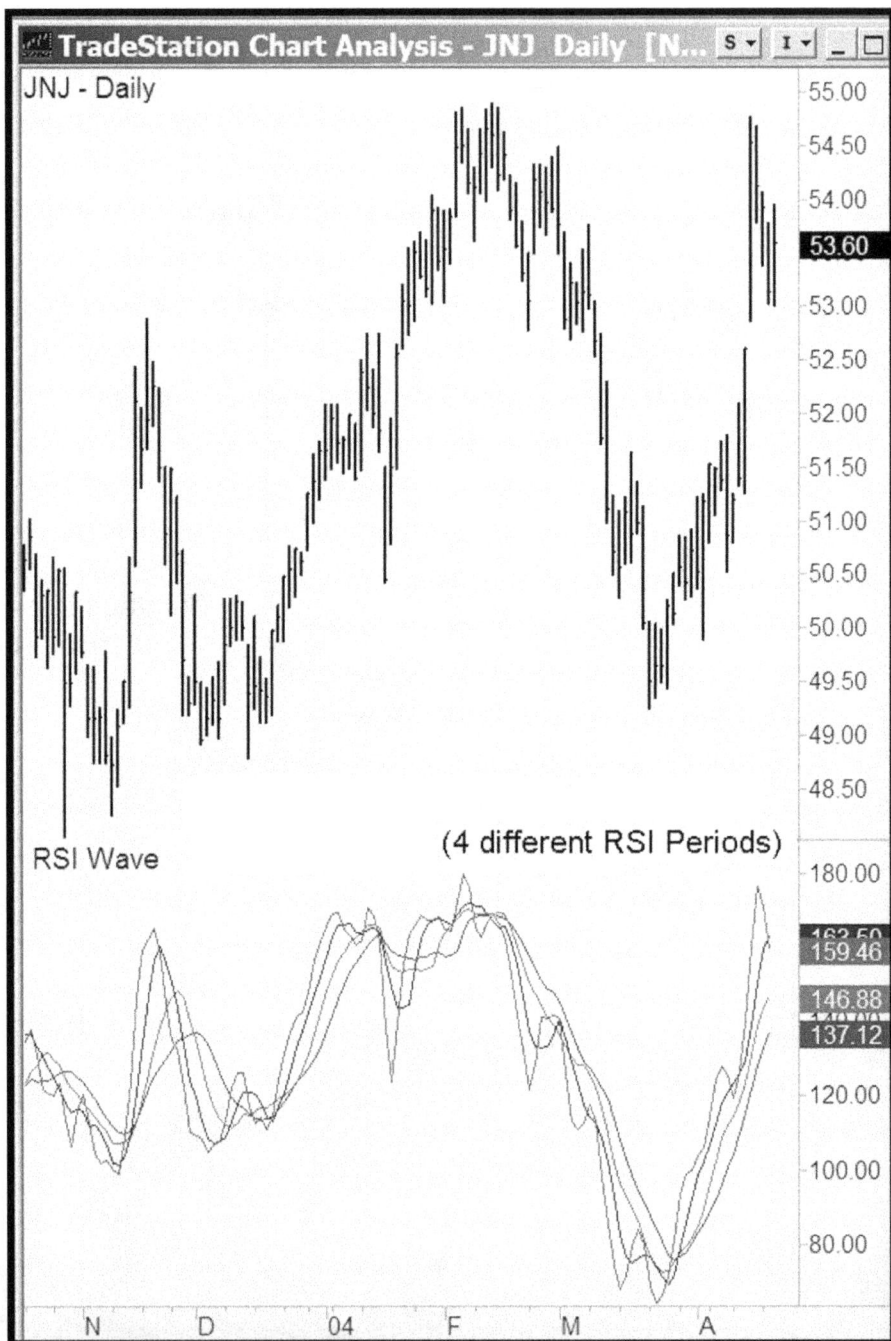

Unconventional Displays: RSI Overlay on Price

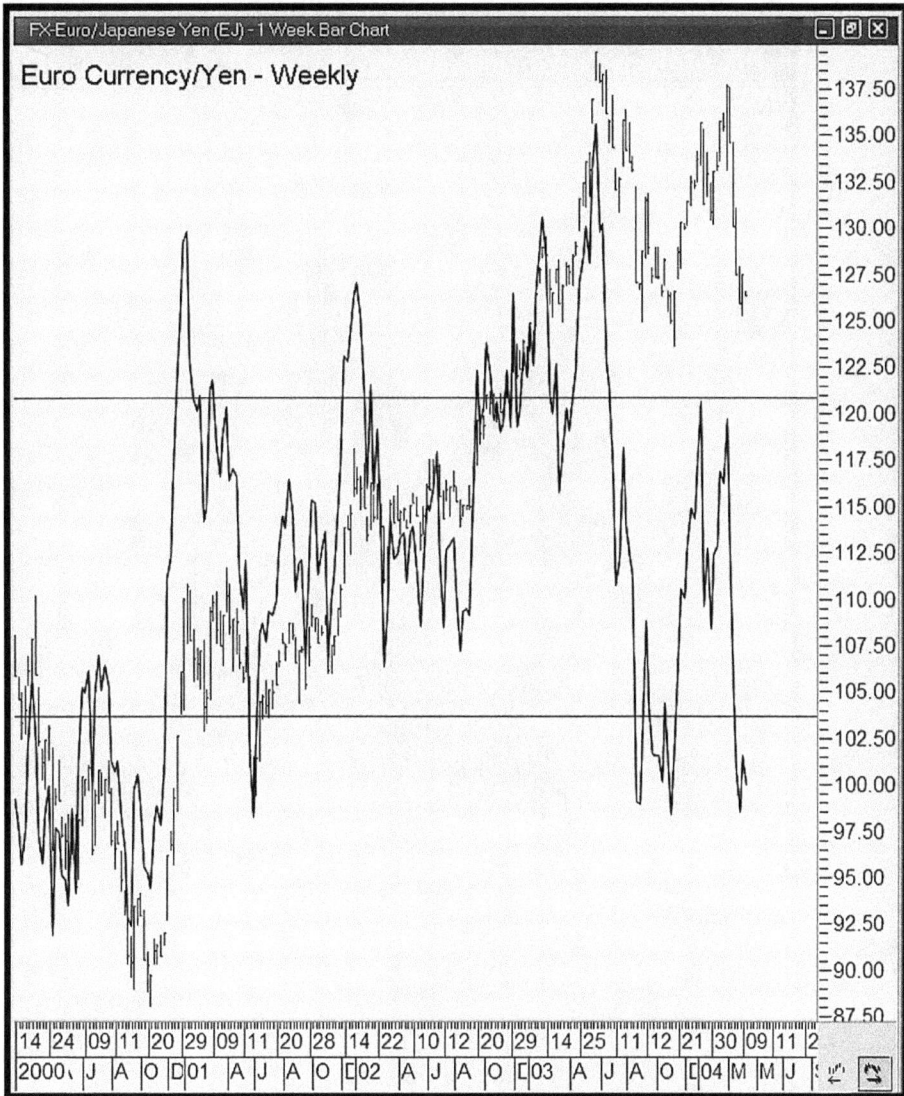

FX-Euro/Japanese Yen (EJ) - 1 Week Bar Chart

Euro Currency/Yen - Weekly

Unconventional Displays: Smoothed Regression Bands with RSI Delta Oscillator

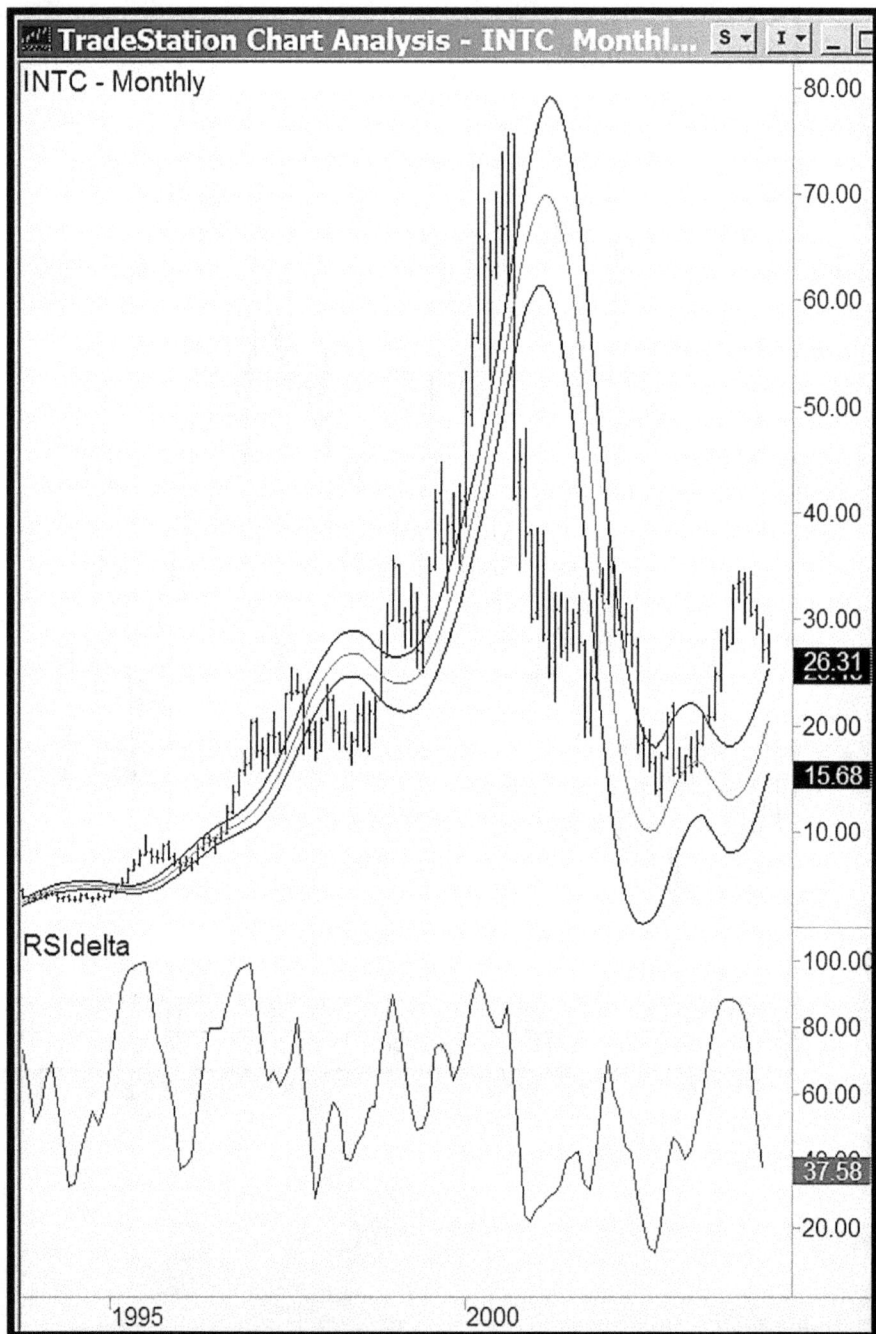

Unconventional Displays: Smoothed RSI and RSI with Averages

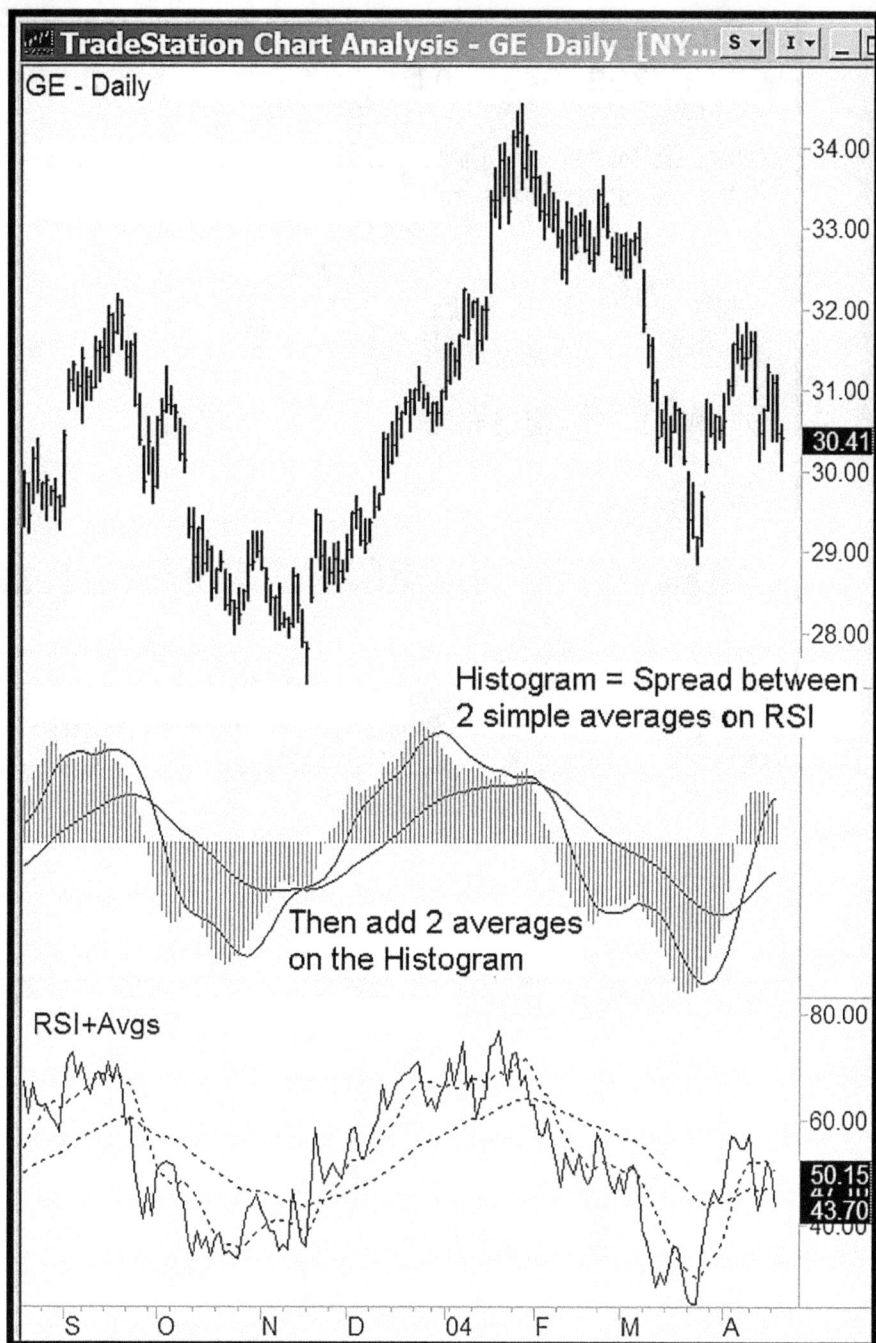

TradeStation Chart Analysis - GE Daily [NY... S ▾ I ▾ _ ▢

GE - Daily

Histogram = Spread between
2 simple averages on RSI

Then add 2 averages
on the Histogram

RSI+Avgs

Underlying Components of CRB Index

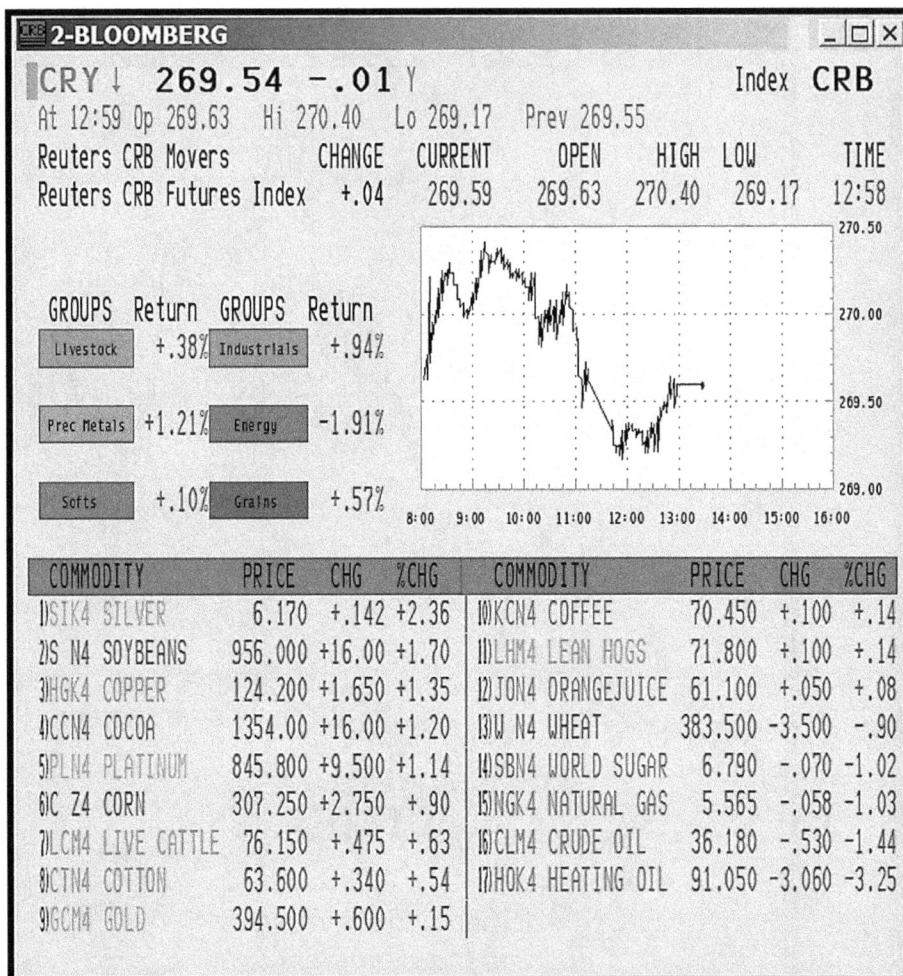

Volatility Bands: Bollinger

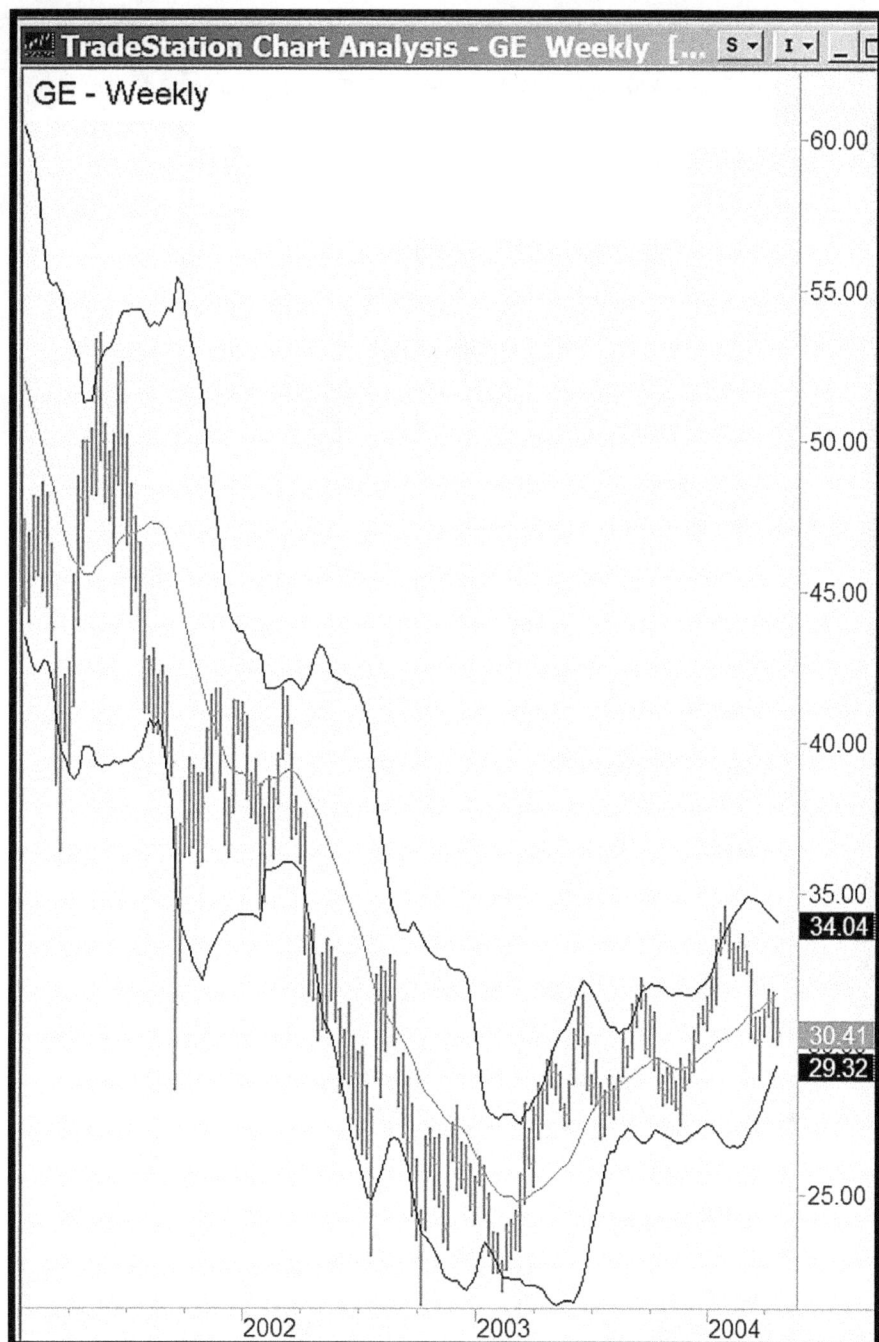

TradeStation Chart Analysis - GE Weekly [...

GE - Weekly

60.00

55.00

50.00

45.00

40.00

35.00
34.04

30.41
29.32

25.00

2002   2003   2004

Volatility Bands on RSI

Volatility Bands: Smoothed Regression and Error Percent Displacement

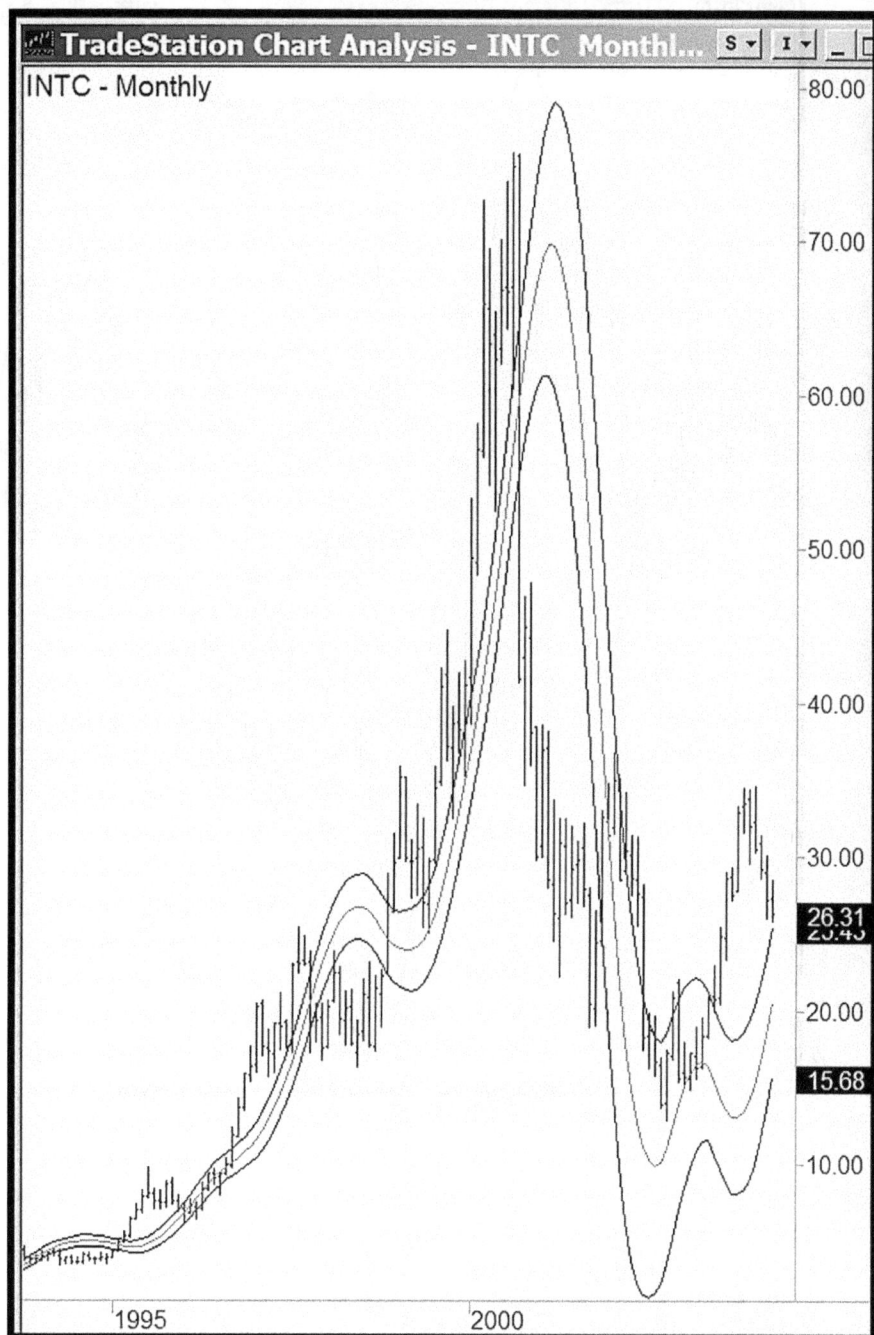

Volatility Bands: Smoothed Regression and Percent Deviation

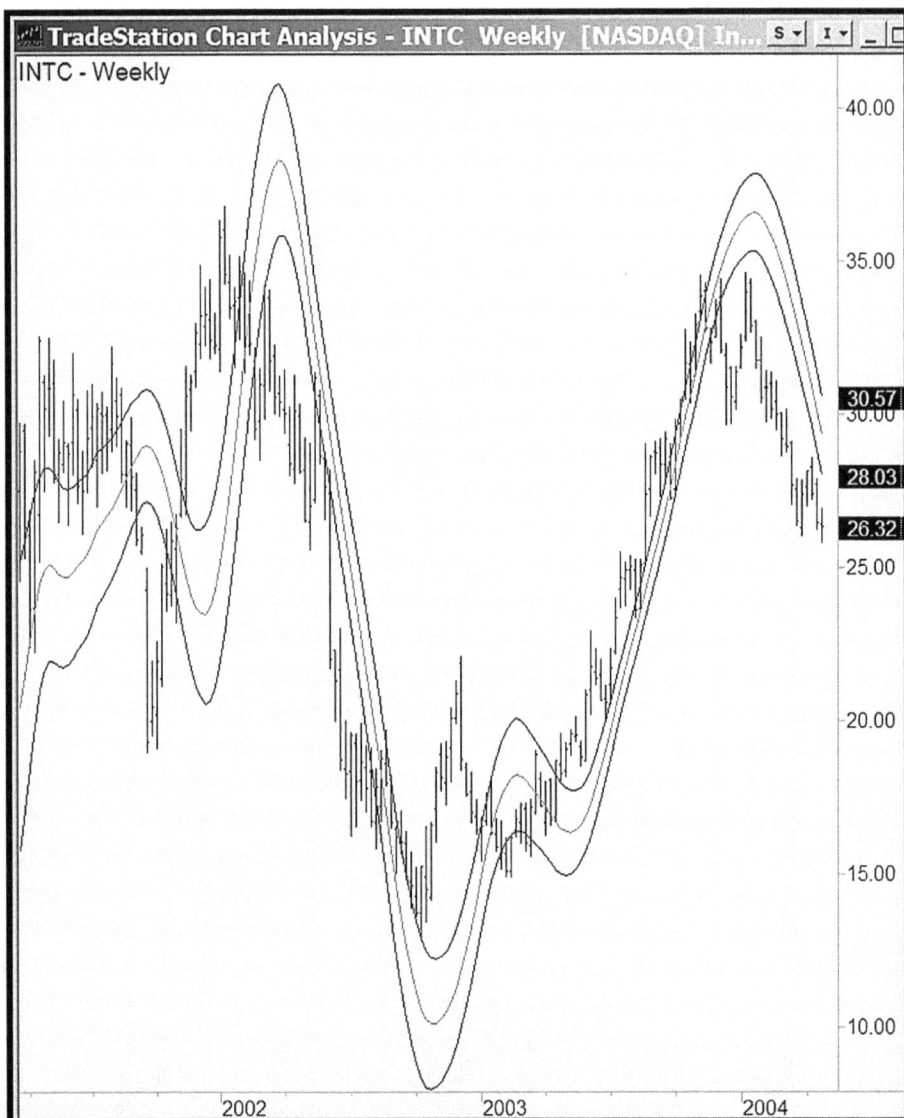

Volatility Bands: Starc

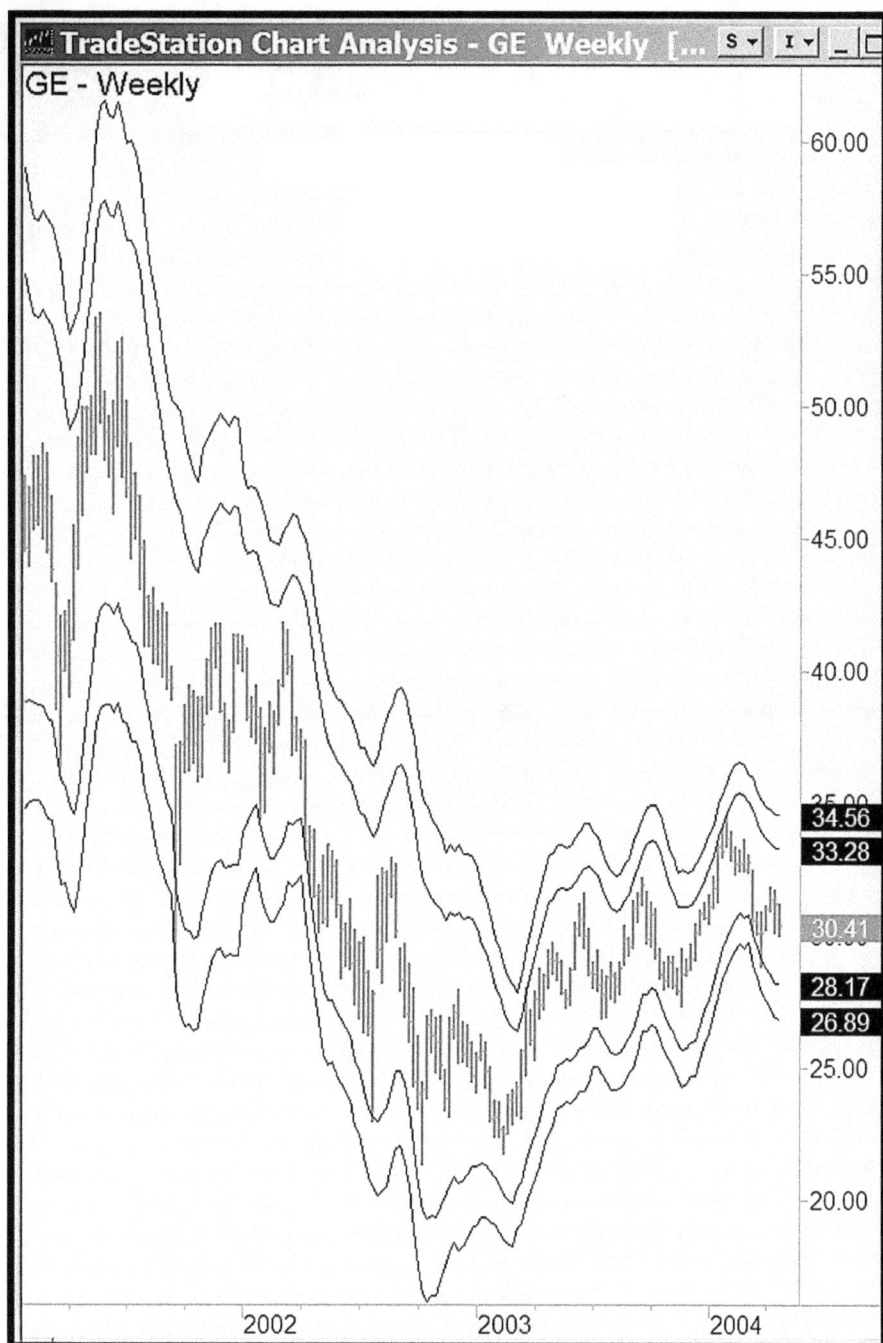

Volatility: Historical Price Volatility

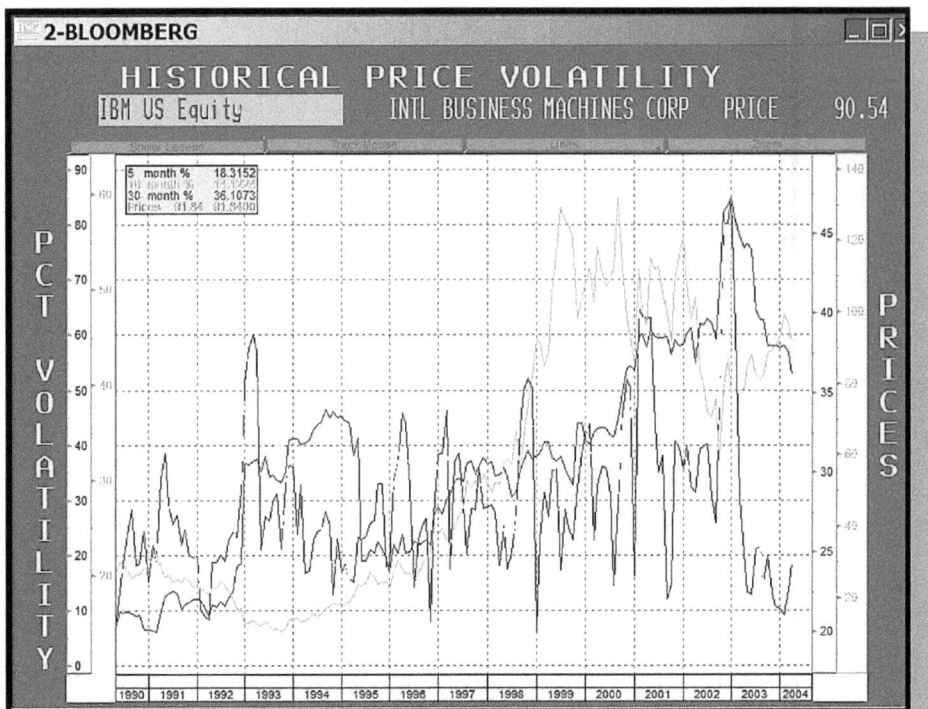

Volatility Index (VIX) and SP500 (Daily Comparison)

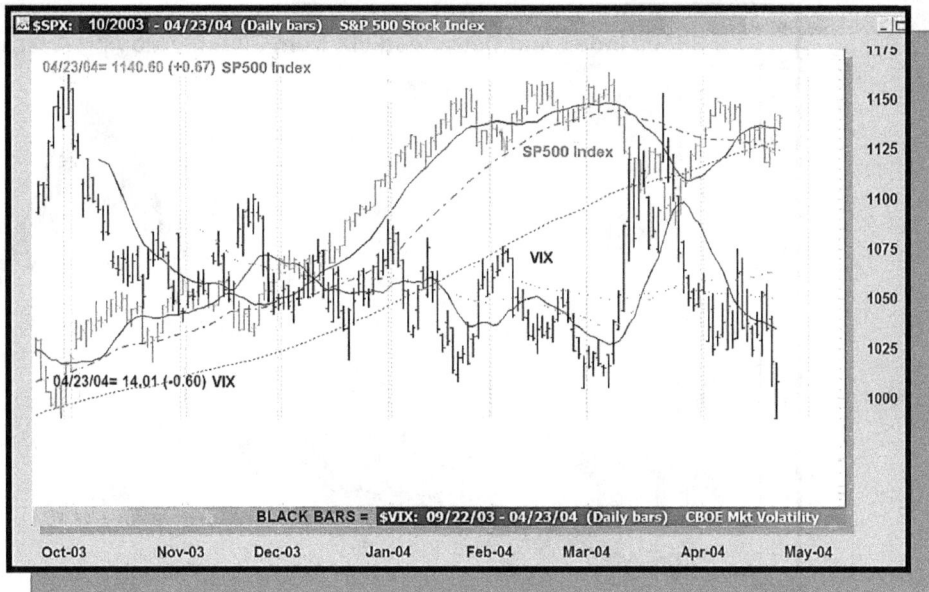

$SPX: 10/2003 - 04/23/04 (Daily bars) S&P 500 Stock Index

04/23/04= 1140.60 (+0.67) SP500 Index

SP500 Index

VIX

04/23/04= 14.01 (-0.60) VIX

BLACK BARS = $VIX: 09/22/03 - 04/23/04 (Daily bars) CBOE Mkt Volatility

Oct-03   Nov-03   Dec-03   Jan-04   Feb-04   Mar-04   Apr-04   May-04

Volatility Index (VIX) Detrended and SP500

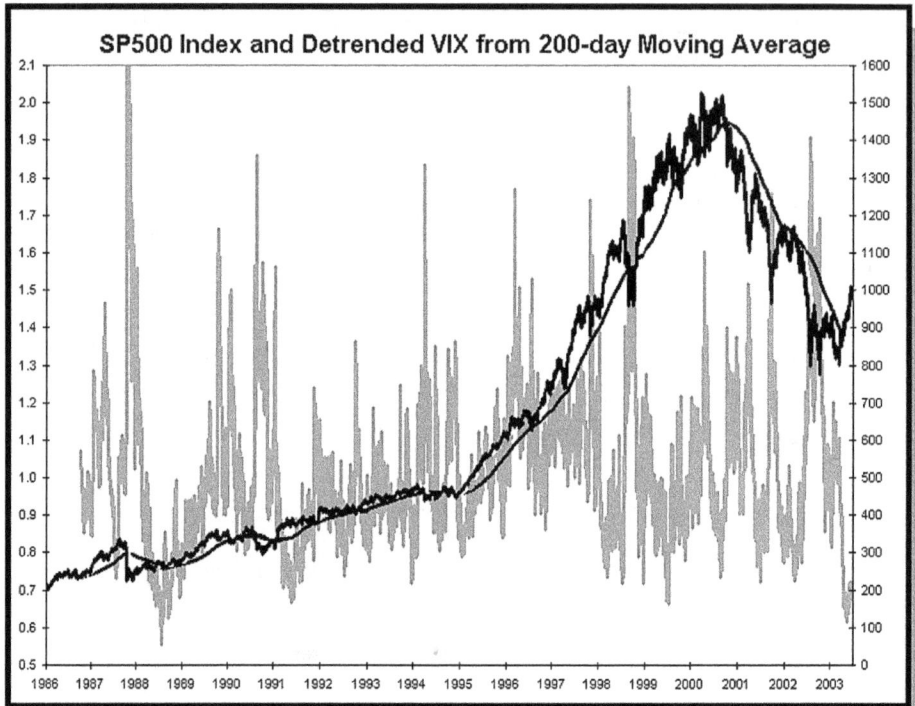

SP500 Index and Detrended VIX from 200-day Moving Average

Volatility Index (VIX) and SP500

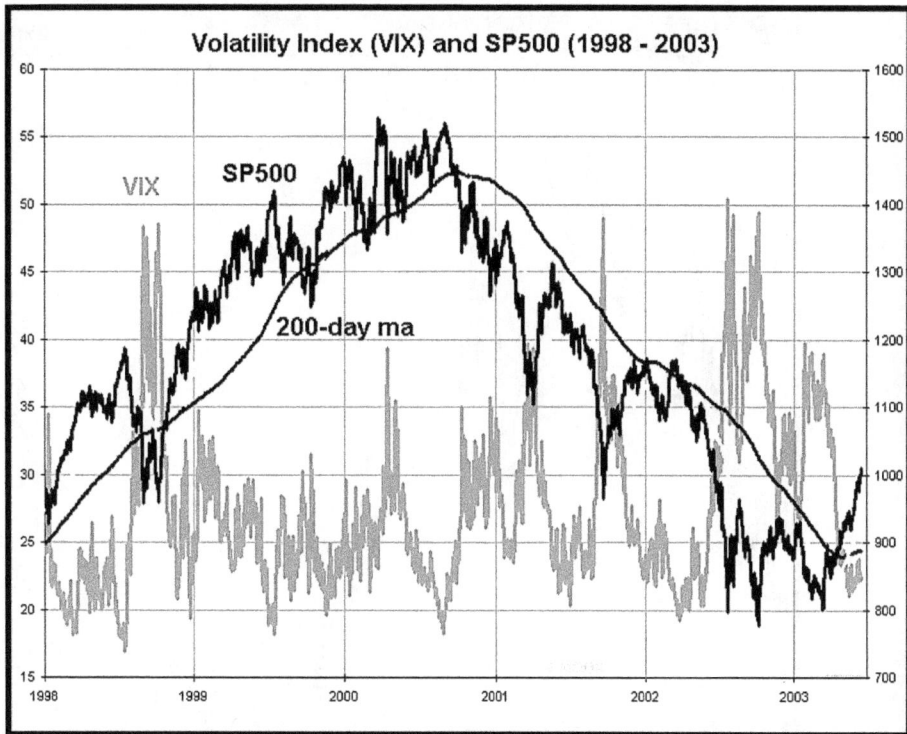

Volatility Index (VIX) and SP500 (1998 - 2003)

Volume Average with Directional Volume

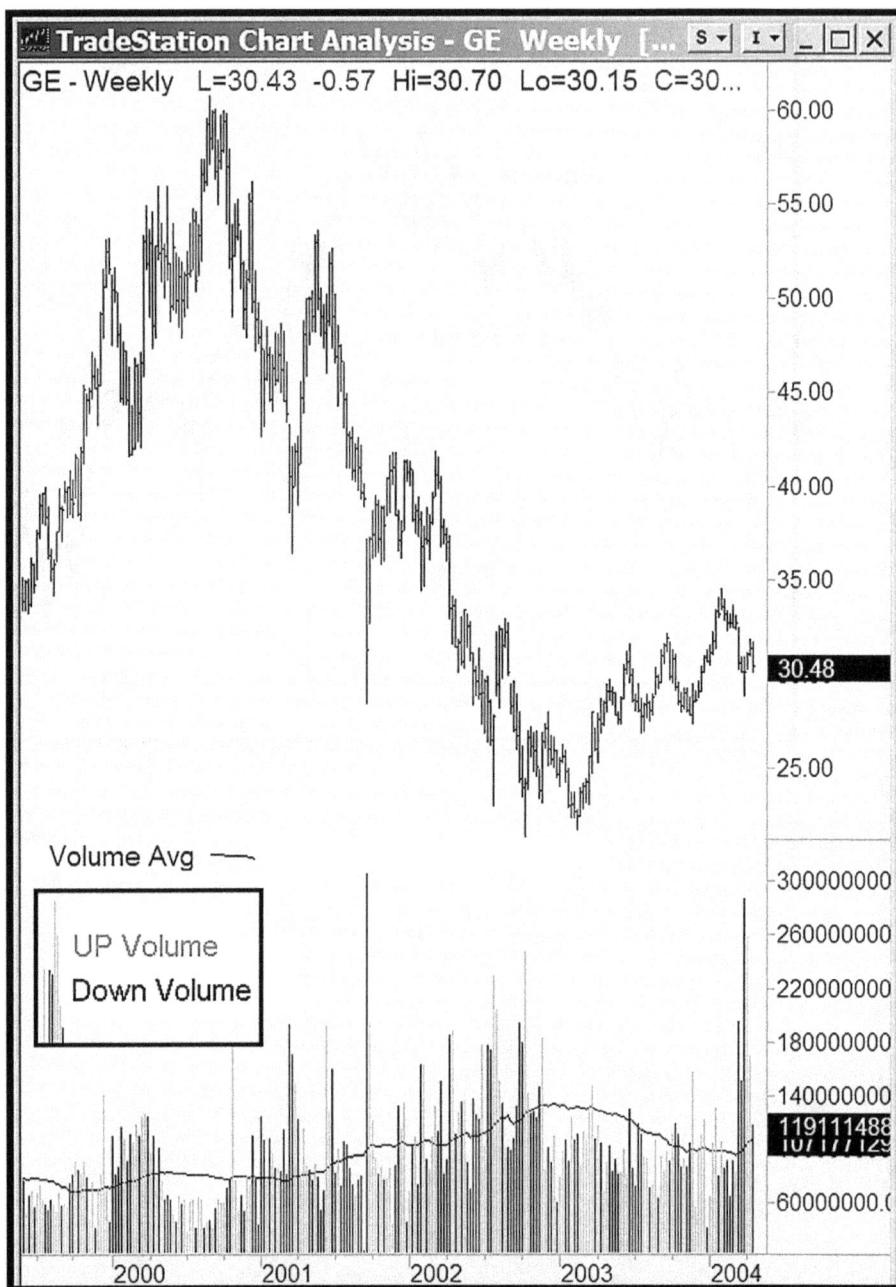

Volume Detrended

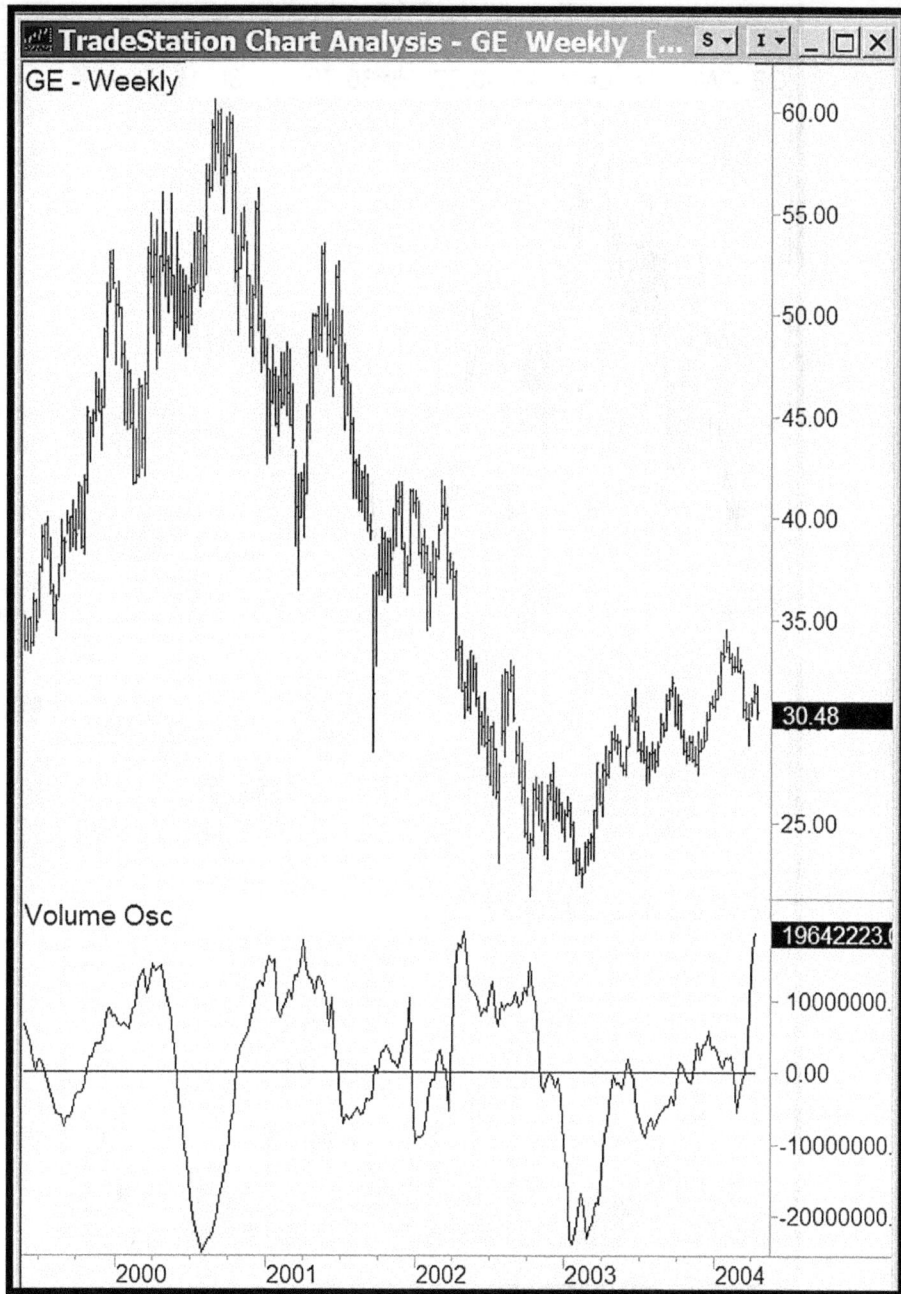

Volume: Double Bottom Confirmation on Lower Volume

Volume Increase with Trend Acceleration

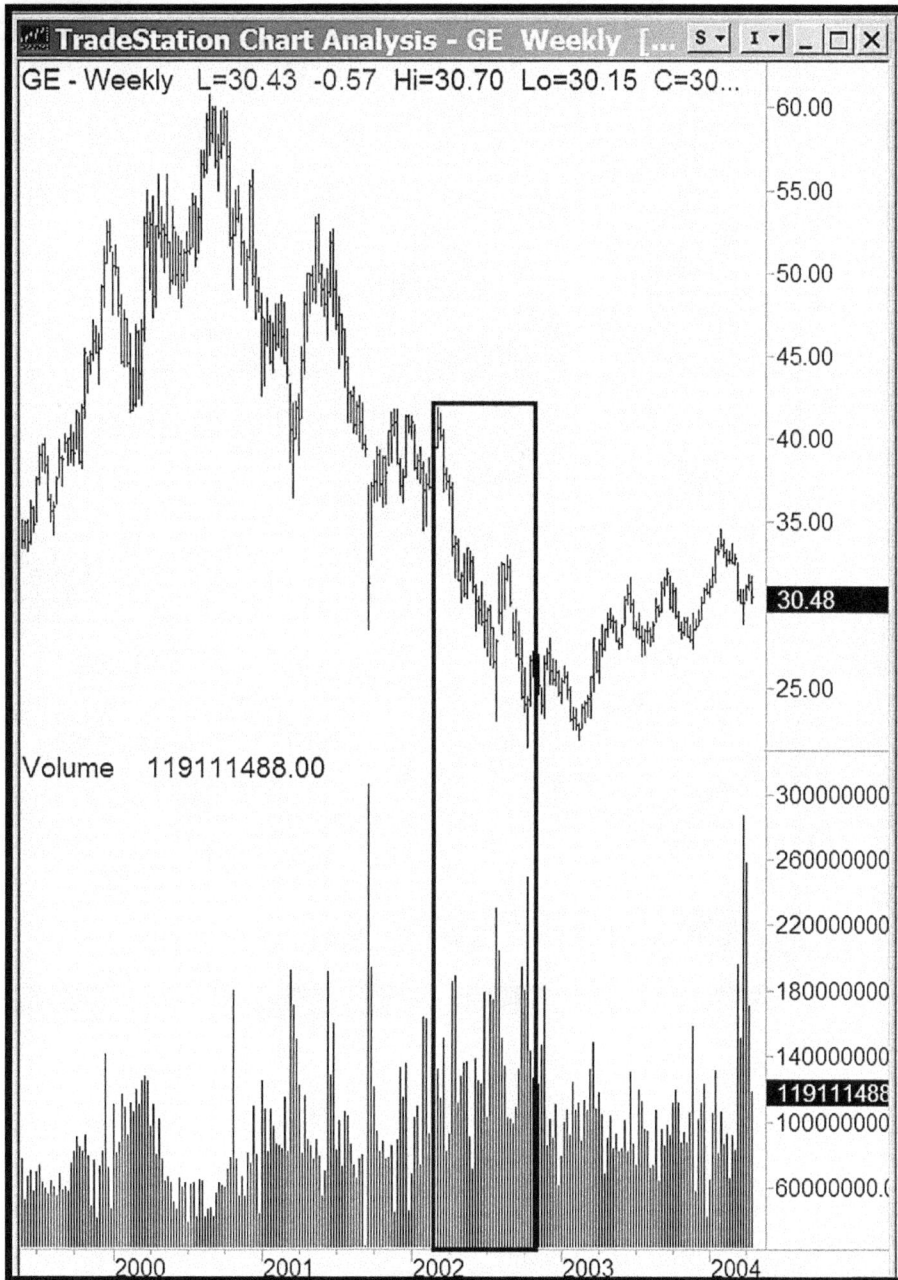

Volume Oscillator: On Balance Volume

Volume: Rate of Change

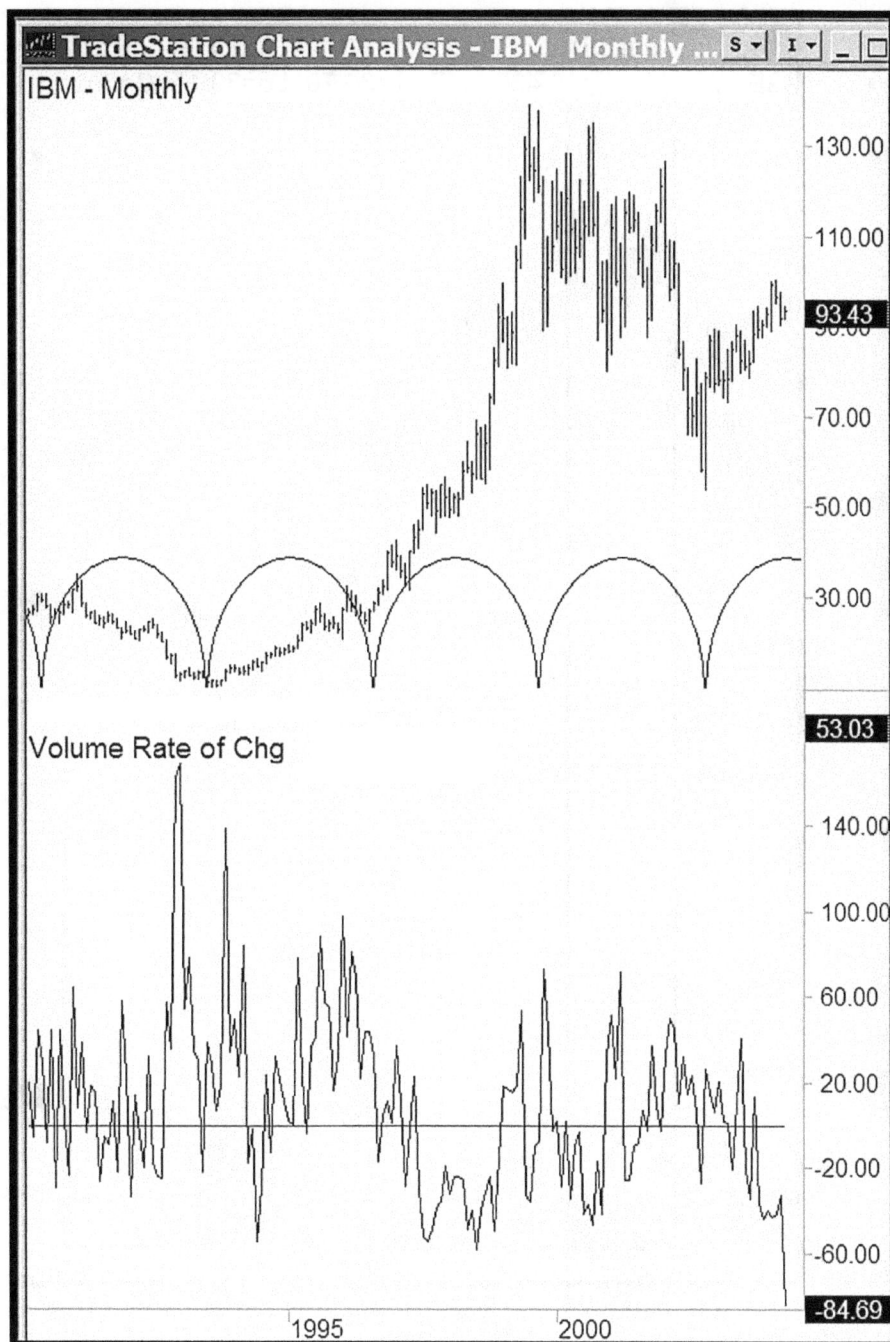

Volume: Warning Trend Waning

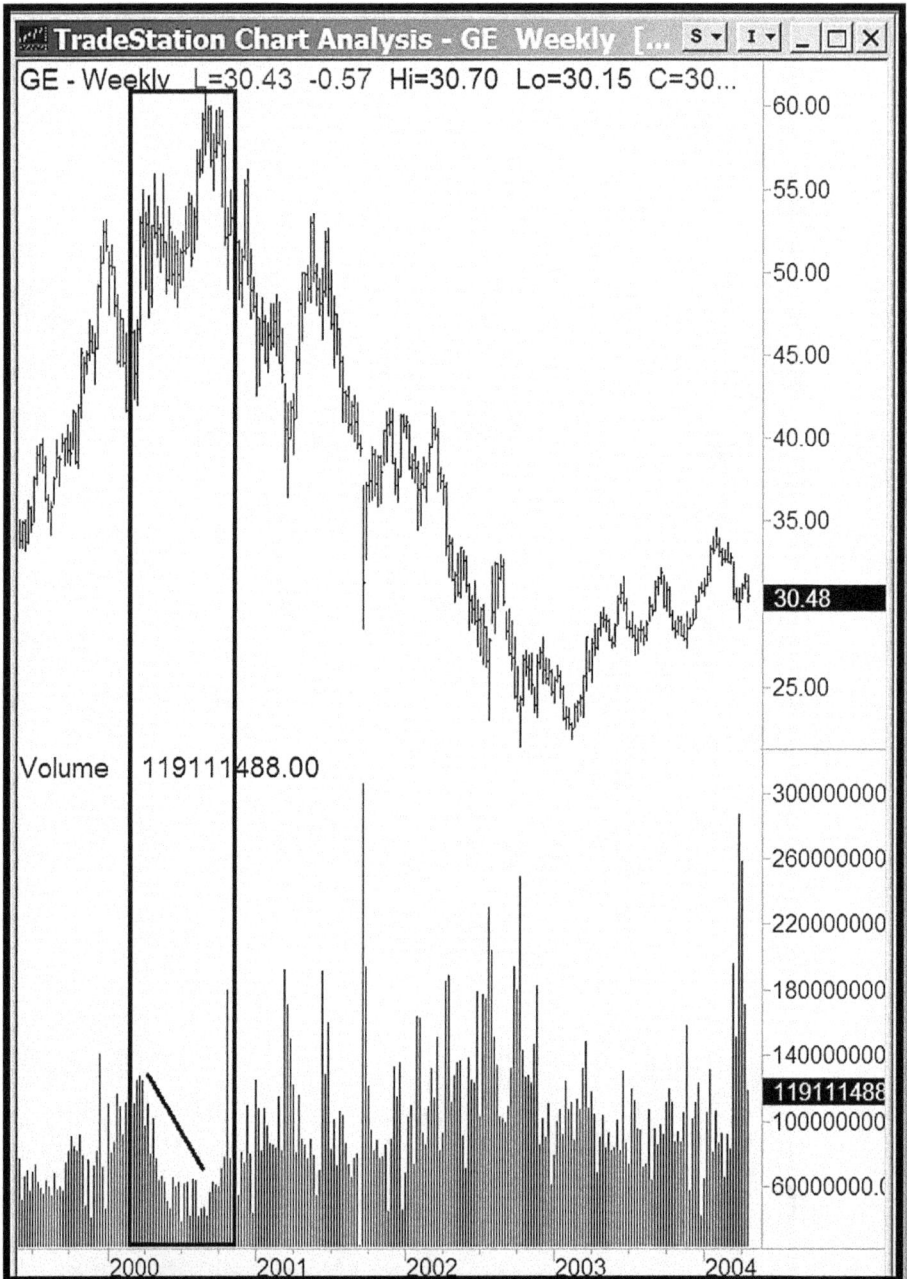

Yield Curve

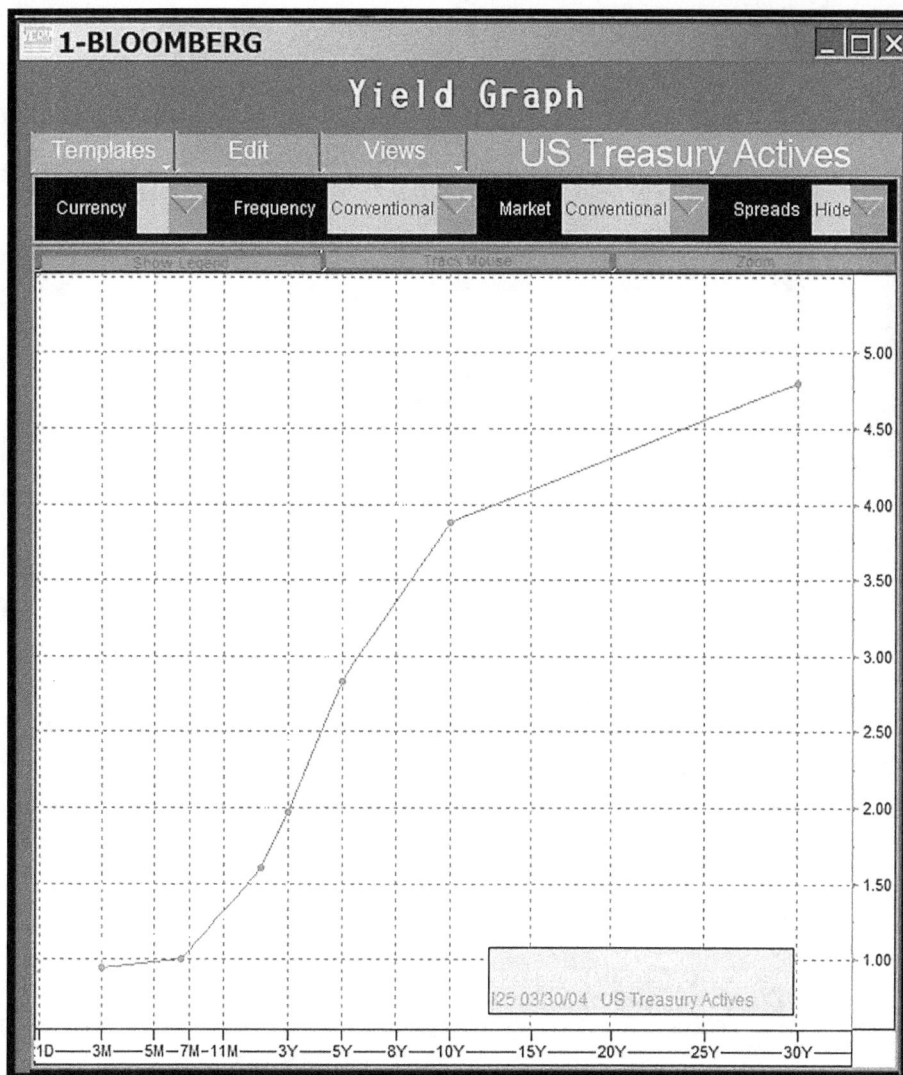

Yield Curve: Global Comparison

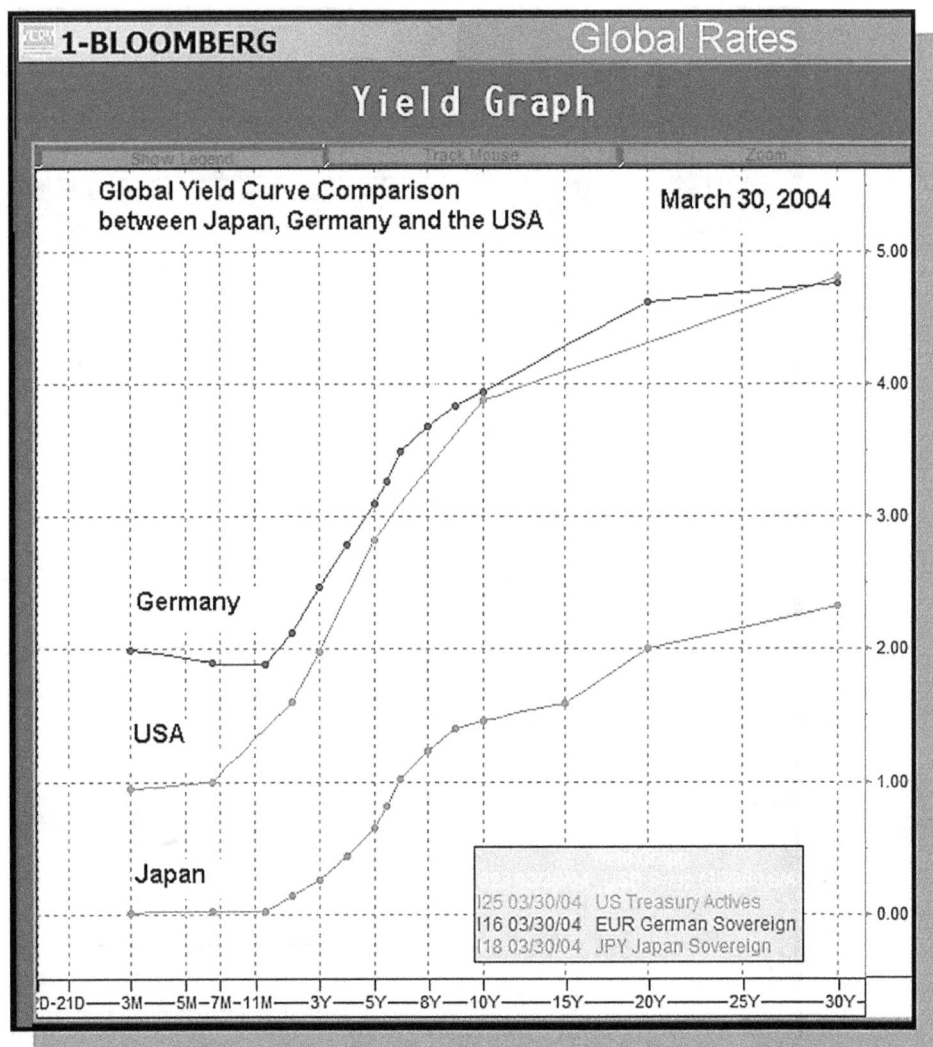

www.ingramcontent.com/pod-product-compliance
Lightning Source LLC
Chambersburg PA
CBHW061339210326
41598CB00035B/5822